AGE STUDIES

AGE STUDIES

A Sociological Examination of How We Age and Are Aged Through the Life Course

SUSAN PICKARD

Los Angeles | London | New Delhi
Singapore | Washington DC | Melbourne

Los Angeles | London | New Delhi
Singapore | Washington DC | Melbourne

SAGE Publications Ltd
1 Oliver's Yard
55 City Road
London EC1Y 1SP

SAGE Publications Inc.
2455 Teller Road
Thousand Oaks, California 91320

SAGE Publications India Pvt Ltd
B 1/I 1 Mohan Cooperative Industrial Area
Mathura Road
New Delhi 110 044

SAGE Publications Asia-Pacific Pte Ltd
3 Church Street
#10-04 Samsung Hub
Singapore 049483

Editor: Natalie Aguilera
Editorial assistant: Delayna Spencer
Production editor: Katherine Haw
Copyeditor: Bryan Campbell
Indexer: Charmian Parkin
Marketing manager: Sally Ransom
Cover design: Shaun Mercier
Typeset by: C&M Digitals (P) Ltd, Chennai, India
Printed in India at Replika Press Pvt Ltd

Library of Congress Control Number: 2016933341

British Library Cataloguing in Publication data

A catalogue record for this book is available from
the British Library

ISBN 978-1-4462-8736-1
ISBN 978-1-4462-8737-8 (pbk)

At SAGE we take sustainability seriously. Most of our products are printed in the UK using FSC papers and boards.
When we print overseas we ensure sustainable papers are used as measured by the PREPS grading system.
We undertake an annual audit to monitor our sustainability.

CONTENTS

ABOUT THE AUTHOR

 Susan Pickard is Reader in Sociology at the University of Liverpool and before this held posts at Salford, Birmingham and Manchester Universities. Her research has been published in a variety of journals including *Sociology, Ageing and Society*, *Sociology of Health and Illness*, *Social Science and Medicine* and *Biosocieties*, among others. *Age Studies* will be followed up by a monograph, *The Girl in Time*, to be published by Routledge.

ACKNOWLEDGEMENTS

Many people have helped in the gestation of this book over the years, ranging from sympathetic editors of journals, to colleagues at home and abroad, to scholars, living and dead, whom I have never met. However, I owe a particular debt of gratitude to the following people. Firstly, thanks to my colleagues at Liverpool for providing a wonderful atmosphere in which I was able to develop the research that went into this book and of whom Paul Jones was kind enough to read and comment on an earlier draft of the manuscript; also to the students who enrolled on my Age Studies module over the past three years and whose feedback helped enormously with the writing of these chapters. I also thank friends and colleagues outside of Liverpool, especially Toni Calasanti and Neal King, for providing me both with a warm and welcoming haven and writing space in their beautiful home at the foothills of the Appalachians, during my time at Virginia Tech in 2014, as well as with endless inspiration. Paul Higgs and Stephen Katz have also been very generous in their advice and encouragement during my work in this field. Thanks to the British Academy and to the Leverhulme Trust for providing research grants which made this work possible. At SAGE, I thank Delayna Spencer for invaluable editorial advice and a sensitive and sympathetic eye throughout the production of this book. I would also like to thank the anonymous reviewers who gave such brilliant and thoughtful feedback. At home, thanks to Reynard for his support and for his infectious can-do optimism which blew away the dark clouds of my own pessimism, and especially my mother, Isabel Martinez Pickard, whose talent lies in the art of ageing well, which is to say the art of living and to whom I dedicate this book.

1

AGE STUDIES: WHAT IS IT AND WHY DO WE NEED IT?

The Age System

To discover what we mean when discussing the age system we should consider the figure of the 'old Hag'[1] as depicted by Rodin.[2] The sense of horror and tragedy, of dread and pity we feel in her presence represents the distillation of the age system (which is also a sexist system) and as such defines it.

The old Hag appears in many forms but in each case she depicts the deep resistance towards old age that is located in our collective consciousness. A memorable section from towards the end of H. Rider Haggard's Victorian 'penny dreadful' *She* reads:

> I gazed at her arm. Where was its wonderful roundness and beauty? It was getting thin and angular. And her face – by Heaven! – *her face was growing old before my eyes*... she put her hand to her head and touched her hair – and oh, *horror of horrors!* – it all fell upon the floor... her skin changed colour, and in place of the perfect whiteness of its lustre it turned dirty brown and yellow, like a piece of withered parchment. ... Now the skin was puckered into a million wrinkles, and on the shapeless face was the stamp of unutterable age. I never saw anything like it; nobody ever saw anything like the frightful age that was graven on that fearful countenance. ... She, who but two minutes before had gazed upon us the loveliest, noblest, most splendid woman the world has ever seen, she lay still before us... hideous – ah, too hideous for words.

Thirdly, in a more contemporary version of the Hag (represented by the figure of Kate Moss, on the right), she is more ordinary and everyday than in our previous versions. Moreover, she is chronologically only middle-aged; the spectacular decline is shown by picturing her next to a much younger woman, Cara Delevingne (23 to Kate's 41) and meanwhile the traditional moral overtone is hidden within the 'neutral' language of a scientific discourse that identifies and analyses her facial faults and marks of age.

The article (Anon, 2015) which this photograph illustrates begins: 'It takes a brave – or foolish – woman to stand next to a rival almost half your age, especially when she's just taken your crown as the UK's highest paid supermodel... So how has Kate's face changed since she exploded into the British fashion world as a teenager in 1988 – before Cara was even born?' It then goes on to list these 'changes' (all negative) according to the following categories: (i) crow's feet and wrinkles; (ii) smoker's teeth; (iii) puffy cheeks; (iv) brittle hair; (v) thinning lips; (vi) greying skin, each problem employing the relevant expert opinion from dentists, dermatologists, 'hair scientists' and the like, the gleeful pleasure of the journalist barely suppressed beneath this.

In the photograph Kate Moss is positioned so that all these features are displayed to full effect: eyes crinkled up in a smile; shiny lips highlighting the loss of plumpness and pulled apart to reveal her imperfect teeth; cheeks puffed out to further accentuate the deep network of crinkles encircling her eyes. Meanwhile, her 'rival' (actually, her friend and someone whom she has mentored) stands next to her in the pose of a Renaissance painting's maiden, head lowered, large eyes raised, smile demure. Readers, especially those who remember Kate when she was herself the maiden figure, are surely unsettled by this transformation but the article seeks to reassure using scientific discourse to instruct us how Kate has committed a series of misdemeanours, indulging in excesses of alcohol, smoking, sunbathing, unseemly emotions. If Cara, and the readers, avoid these temptations, is the implicit message we too can avoid her fate: that of growing old.

Indeed, where Freud once suggested that sexuality lay at the heart of all our neuroses, and Erik Erikson later suggested that for the twentieth century our key problems, at a cultural and personal level, revolved around issues of identity, today it seems that our defining existential crisis is our fear of ageing and old age. Specifically, this concerns the repression of ageing and death (Brown, 1959). This fear, moreover, has real material consequences throughout the life course in terms of the organization of modern society, and indeed the above representations crown a system of stratification that ensures ongoing social inequality with an ideology that justifies it. The age system is a hierarchically constituted regime in which the role of particular ages and their relationship to each other underpin and legitimize an assortment of material and other inequalities. These work with other forms of inequality to produce a complex meshwork of social stratification (Calasanti and Slevin, 2001; 2006). Whilst non-adult stages are particularly disadvantaged, 'adulthood' is at once chronologically and symbolically constituted, meaning that some members of this category are more 'adult' than others. The most disadvantaged and devalued category of all, however, is that of old age. Age therefore serves as a 'master status' (Calasanti and Slevin, 2006: 5), its ideological power wielded through a 'master narrative of decline' (Gullette, 1997). Margaret Gullette has described how the plot of the narrative unfolds as follows: Youth is the best time of our life, associated with all things positive such as 'fun, energy, sexuality, intensity, hope' (1997: 5). As we approach mid-life we are taught to look for signs of decline signalled through events such as the 'Mirror Scene of Mid-life Ageing' or the 'Entrance into Mid-life Scene'. When we encounter these entry points – our shock at our lined face, reflected back at us from the mirror of a friend or lover's gaze, or photograph; surprise at the aged appearance of same-age peers; students who no longer recognize you as one of them but liken you to their parents; or, even worse, that moment when you realize you no longer relate to your students – we begin to lose our former confidence in our abilities, our self-esteem, our optimism, and thereafter we accelerate into 'declineoldage (single word) and death' (1997: 8).

Whilst decline ideology presents this stratification as a natural 'fact', it also presents as natural the concept that ageing accrues deficit and loss of a range of capitals. However, this is established through a range of meanings and imperatives that impact on all ages and stages in the life course. That is, just as one can only be a 'man' in a world that also contains women, one can only be young in a world in which other individuals are 'old' or indeed today 'middle-aged' (and the very meaning of youth is thus infused with such ideology). Age ideology, although superficially favouring 'the young', in fact has damaging consequences for everyone. So it makes 'youth' a space in which particular imperatives and modes of subjectification work, moulding the citizen in ways that are as dominated as they are dominant. For example, the fact that youth is commonly depicted in the West as the best time of our lives may mean that the very real problems and suffering experienced by the young are not taken seriously; or alternatively, structural obstacles may be misread as individual failure. Furthermore, the fear of ageing means that 'ageing' (which includes, but is more than the relational experience of, feeling 'old') is felt at ever-younger points in the life course (Gullette, 1997; 2004), the Hag trails her longer and longer shadow behind her through much of the life course and beyond a certain (increasingly earlier) age, today's birthdays are sources of melancholy or dread, especially for women. Many young women in my seminar groups speak of being 'traumatized' by turning 20, and, as well as the bruising I remember receiving from that age, I can recall traumas of earlier ages: the tingling anxiety of turning 13 and, before that, turning 11, which meant leaving primary school for high school and the hollow feeling in my stomach registering the first, but not the last, time when I felt the best of life was behind me already. Looking back, turning 30, 35 or even 40 were not the deeply significant events whose presence had brooded for some time on the horizon ahead with the dark weight of curtains about to come down. However, whilst they turned out in practice to be inconsequential in themselves, the dread I experienced in anticipation of such birthdays was very real, and, I see now, impacted deeply on my sense of self, of who I was and what I thought I could become, for much of my life.

Fear of ageing is one of the key vehicles through which society acts upon us from within and is thus an extremely powerful mode of social control. As well as proclaiming our value in terms of youthfulness, which overlaps with but is not absolutely the same as youth, it also encourages us to try to remain 'young'. Inevitably, this leads to an infantilization in which we remain not only youthful but immature, distracted by a thousand trivial decisions – what washing machine to buy, what TV station to watch – rather than taking responsibility for the kind of life we live: as Susan Neiman puts it, 'children make more compliant subjects (and consumers)' (2014: 186). At the same time, the mythologization of youth in itself induces compliance, as Neiman continues: 'by describing life as a downhill process, we prepare young people to expect – and demand – very little from it: especially where being young is not, actually, so wonderful' (2014: 17). It is thus extremely important in a political sense that we are alert to the age system and thus prepared to critique and challenge it.

In the following sections we shall prepare the grounds for this critique by exploring: (i) the psychic origins of the age system in the relationship with the Mother, including the contradictory desire for communion/separation and the splitting and projection of associated qualities onto separate genders and ages; (ii) its intellectual origins in a Cartesian worldview that echoes this process of separation and individuation with all its irresolvable fears and longings; (iii) its material aspect in a capitalist system in which age relations intersect with, and serve as vehicles for, a variety of other forms of inequality; (iv) its legitimation through intellectual thought and social theories in which sociology (albeit inadvertently) is also implicated. Although we start here with the micro level we could just as easily have reversed the order and started with the macro level, labelling this (i); the important point is that each level be considered not separate from, but rather involved in, a mutual and constitutive interplay with the rest. We will also (v) examine specific factors which mean that in late modernity the age system works in a particularly profound way to underpin an acute and growing social inequality.

Configuring the Hag

(i) The psychic beginnings in infancy

The beginnings of the age system are to be found in the dynamics of the first and primary social relationship, that is, in the psychic experience of the relationship with one's mother or mother-substitute in the very earliest days of infancy. This is discussed in some detail in the work of Dorothy Dinnerstein (1976), Jessica Benjamin (1990) and other object relations theorists. Indeed, the symbolic power of the Hag has its roots in the infant's struggle to individuate from an intensely close emotional and physical unity with the mother. Here, the psychic terrain is shaped by our social practices, both the expectations and interpretations that cultural narratives and practices bring to this relationship and the fact that institutional factors mean that responsibility for child-rearing falls mainly to women; the feelings of ambivalence and rejection towards the figure from which one must separate are then associated with the female body/self. Dinnerstein's (1976) classic account of how this 'shapes' the human condition remains just as persuasive, and relevant, today as it did when Dinnerstein wrote in the mid-70s (and indeed the social forms on which they are based – childcare responsibilities borne primarily by the mother, with little institutional support, among other things – remain all but unchanged since those times, in the UK and US at least). She argues:

> The child's bodily tie to the mother... is the vehicle through which the
> most fundamental feelings of a highly complex creature are formed and
> expressed... this tie is the prototype of the tie to life. The pain of it, and
> the fear of being cut off from it, are prototypes of the pain of life and the
> fear of death. (1976: 34)

Concurring with Norman Brown, she suggests that the socio-cultural denial of death –
including the horror of signs of ageing and senescence – results from our early
recognition of bodily vulnerability. Woman (or Mother standing for all female
bodies) is henceforth considered 'representative of the body principle in all of us that
must be repressed when we embark on any significant enterprise' (1976: 126). But
if the young mother reminds us of our intractable vulnerabilities, how much more
terrible to behold is the old mother, upon whose now-withered breasts we, who are
no-longer-children, once laid our heads?

   Simone de Beauvoir shared these sentiments, reflecting that 'from the day of his
birth man begins to die; this is the truth incarnated in the mother' (quoted in
Dinnerstein, 1976: 127). The Mother represents the state of immanence, the in-itself
which the Masculine subject needs to transcend.[3] The problem is that the paradoxes
which underlie an enduring form of existential anguish – the need for separation and
boundaries that shape our selfhood, the loneliness and alienation that threaten to
accompany this – rather than being integrated within the individual actor, are
instead projected onto this other individual, the Mother, who becomes simultaneously both the closest intimate and the quintessential Other. It turns woman,
Dinnerstein suggests, into a 'dirty goddess, a scapegoat-ideal, a quasi-human being'
(p. 155) well on her way to becoming a Hag, even as a young mother, embodying as
she does the 'mucky, humbling limitations of the flesh' (p. 133).

   According to Benjamin (1990) the problem lies in a subsequent conceptual mis-
identification both of the initial mother–infant attachment and of the subsequent
growing (self) awareness of the infant. The process is represented in developmental
psychology as a 'separation from oneness'. But this is an ideal of a golden past that we
project onto earliest infancy when in reality infants from the start engage in interpersonal connection with others. She suggests that the concept of separation as it stands

> contains the implicit assumption that we grow out of relationships rather
> than becoming more active and sovereign within them, that we start in a
> state of dual oneness and wind up in a state of singular oneness. (1990: 18)

This state of oneness – associated with mature adulthood – is underpinned by a
philosophy of individualism conjured memorably in the poem by Thom Gunn.[4]
Gunn depicts it as a state of extreme isolation, of alienation each from all, as if we
were all surrounded by a fog that separated us and obscured us from knowing anything beyond our own thoughts: 'No castle more cut off / By reason of its moat'.

We can indeed only guess at what others are perceiving and feeling, the poem suggests, and whether our reality is shared by others is ultimately unknowable:

> The street lamps, visible,
> Drop no light on the ground.
> But press beams painfully
> In a yard of fog around.
> I am condemned to be
> An individual

What begins as a misreading thus becomes a cultural ideology in which the psychic fear of being 'sucked in' or 'back' to what Freud and others portrayed as the oceanic wholeness of our pre-linguistic infancy in fact never completely abates but continues to threaten the 'disintegration' of our personhood, forever hovering 'at the border of the subject's identity, threatening apparent unities and stabilities with disruption and possible dissolution' (Grosz, 1990: 871). This is the definition of abjection: the 'abyss at the very borders of the subject's identity, a hole into which the subject may fall' (Grosz, 1990: 87). To offset this, rather than stressing autonomy and separation as developmental norms, as Piaget, Erikson, Kohlberg and others have done, Gilligan (1982), Benjamin (1990) and others concur with Dinnerstein in suggesting the importance of emphasizing a dual developmental thread which includes care and relationships as well as autonomy making it a 'dialectic of human development' (Gilligan, 1982: 174). In social terms, however, the effect of the cultural ideology produces an incomplete realization of individuation expressed through the gender binary itself (MacInnes, 1998), whereby dual but contradictory elements of this process – the requirement for independence and the capacity for relationality – are split apart instead of being integrated within the individual and rather associated with 'masculinity' and 'femininity'. This represents a 'defence against psychic insecurity' (MacInnes, 1998: 29).

Further examples of splitting are effected through the age system, where attributes that adults may find difficult to recognize in themselves – being symbolic of vulnerability or incompetence or of characteristics that do not comply with the value system determined by capitalism's framework – are projected onto children or old people, and which, though split off, remain powerful elements of their fantasy lives. This means that we not only organize childhood into a series of developmental stages defined with meticulous and ever-narrower precision but we also do the same at the other end of the life course, 'frailty' being increasingly scientifically portrayed in terms of discrete phases of 'undevelopment', or steps towards death.[5] This would suggest that, although suppressed in cultural narratives, and indeed socialization processes, the reintegration of ageing and death would certainly unsettle the psychic dread of the abject and of the Hag herself (Brown, 1959). It would also undermine the foundation of the age and gender systems.

(ii) Cartesianism and the individuation of modernity

Bordo (1986) vividly illustrates the connections between such psychic origins and their socio-cultural consequences through her depiction of Cartesian dualism as a process of separation and individuation from the female universe of the old medieval cosmos enabling the emergence of the disenchanted masculine universe of the modern era.

BOX 1.1

Cartesianism

Cartesianism, the philosophical system associated with René Descartes and particularly his Meditations, posits a fundamental 'dualism' whereby mind (*res cogitans*) and body/matter (*res extensa*) are of different and incommensurable substances. The first is a thinking substance, the second subject to the laws of matter and both requiring totally different forms of inquiry.

This involves interplay between cultural narratives and individual experience which is constantly repeated on an individual level as in Elias' (1978) account of how the years-long development of children replicates on a minute scale the centuries-long civilizing process undergone by nations. In an account of the 'dialectics of separation and individuation' which Bordo offers as a 'way of seeing the Cartesian era empathetically and impressionistically, through association and image' (p. 448) and drawing on psychological categories normally used to describe individual development, she highlights the links between scientific objectivism, the rejection of the body, and the establishment of the motif of the Hag as emblematic of all the forces of dissolution threatening patriarchal rationalist society.

She suggests that the process of separating from the Mother was enacted on a cosmic level during the Enlightenment period as it broke with the medieval regime.

BOX 1.2

Enlightenment thought

The Enlightenment, or more generally enlightenment thought, refers to a system of thought associated with science in particular. Associated with the work of Descartes and others in early modernity, it fostered rational, impersonal and universalizable methods, together with a commitment to universal laws and values.

The Universe was spoken of as a Mother in medieval times; medieval epistemology also contained 'feminine' qualities, such as 'sympathy' or connection in which subject and object were perceived to merge in the creation of meaning (Bordo, 1999; Foucault, 2002). Cartesianism represents a defensive mode of detachment, a reaction to the feeling of loss of unity with the world, which extends to emotions, values and external objects. Thus, objectivity can be read as a 'defiant gesture of independence from the female cosmos' (Bordo, 1986: 431) and a compensatory 'turning towards the paternal' in the form of transcendent values and law (Bordo, 1999: 62). Meanwhile, the pain of separating and remaining separate is now compensated for by the aim of controlling that being from which one has separated, which it terms 'female' and inferior. As a result the 'epistemic subject' is one who 'has become part of an objectified world over which we exercise mastery', resolving our lives into a sense of projects characterized by 'wanting and doing', 'making, producing and constructing' (Dunne, 1993: 366). The self, personhood, within this system, is then essentially male.

The world is kept at arm's length in this conceptualization wherein knowledge can only be truthful if it is obtained through detached, disinterested inquiry cleansed of value and sympathy and where even our most spontaneous, embodied gestures are based on an implicit theory of the world. Rationality, understood by Aristotle to include feeling and practical knowledge as well as detached logic, narrows and becomes gradually synonymous with instrumental rationality which is concerned with means–ends efficiency and encourages the subject to disengage from its messy and vulnerable existence (Taylor, 1992). Bordo goes on: 'The project that fell to empirical sciences and "rationalism" was to tame the female universe' (1986: 434). However, as with the abject body, this taming is always partial and unresolved: 'Like the infinite universe, which threatens to swallow the individual "like a speck", the female, with her strange rhythms, long acknowledged to have their chief affinities with the rhythms of the natural (now alien) world, becomes a reminder of how much lies outside the grasp of man' (1986: 454). Hence, it was the Enlightenment that also witnessed a rash of witch trials (most of whom were old women), part of an attempt to bring female knowledge of the healing arts in particular, under male control (Greer, 1991; Daly, 1991). This was all the more so as 'the meaning of life' – lost with the disenchantment of modernity – was transformed first into a collective sense of progress through history and, when that began to atrophy in the twentieth century, further transformed into the meaning of 'my life' – an utterly privatized individualized search (Moody, 1986). Today this meaning is shaped largely through consumerist lifestyles with the key determining value being that of choice itself.

Finally, with the Enlightenment came a 'civilizing process' which, as Elias has shown, applied an increasing subjugation of the body by the mind with increasing constraint of bodily gestures and reactions, leading to greater individualization, rationalization, privatization and autonomy (Shilling, 2012) and, conversely, horror and disgust towards their opposite.

BOX 1.3

The civilizing process

This refers to a system that spread from European courts down through the various layers of society during modernity. It constitutes a process of rationalization of bodies and behaviour, self-control and self-pacification, represented by elaborate systems of etiquette and manners.

The closed body extended control over the synapses and nerves, the urges and drives and orifices of bodies: everything from eating and defecation and copulation to expressions of anger and desire was subject to the sovereign control of the will. Unrealistic for the standard adult, it problematizes non-adult age in particular: childhood because, until children master these various forms of self-restraint, they are set apart from adults; and old people because continued control, or rather the presentation of an apparently controlled and controllable body, becomes harder to display in advanced age.

(iii) Capitalism and the work economy: a further separation from the Mother/Hag?

The Cartesian system is not just an intellectual approach but a 'practical metaphysics' (Bordo, 1999) and as such it informs all our systems and institutions, from our personal psychology, relationships of self to self and self to others, family dynamics, education, law and popular culture. Tracing its development through the nineteenth century, the processes of industrialization from the nineteenth century onwards added a material dimension to this separation first with the uprooting of traditional communities and the severance of ties formed by tradition and then with increasing rationalization, bureaucracy, alienation and the separation of individuals both from their work and from all other workers. Workers become 'appendage(s) of the machine' as Marx and Engels put it in the *Communist Manifesto* (2010: 30) and sell themselves 'piecemeal'.

BOX 1.4

Capitalism

According to Marx and Engels, this is a system comprising those who own the means of production (capitalists or the 'bourgeoisie') and those who own only their own labour (the proletariat). The relationship of the former with the latter is inherently exploitative and oppressive.

'Clock-time' became hegemonic time, rationalized and separated from the eternal time of medieval holy time. This valorized speed, future-projection and linearity, removing time from any sense of context, and attributing normative or 'standard' time to a range of activities for the purpose of regulating individuals. The nature of clock-time is closely implicated in age ideology: time measured by industrial machine-rhythms is finite, linear, measurable, characterized by speed and uniformity, and unlike other times is like capital itself in that, above all, it is not only scarce but can run out (Adam, 1990). The feeling of time running out generates an omnipresent anxiety in individuals and a desire to control or transcend time; the ageing mother's body then becomes additionally a symbol of the dreadful consequences of being overwhelmed, finally, by time. Similarly, within modernity, dependence, once considered a 'normal' aspect of life, and associated with wage labour and with men, women and all ages and stages, became problematized. Independence was considered the prerequisite of full citizenship, now signalled by one's involvement in paid work and denied to women, children and, after the establishment of retirement, old people (Fraser and Gordon, 1994). Moreover, 'dependence' gradually moved 'inwards' shifting from a social characteristic to what Fraser and Gordon call an 'individual personality register', in the sense of some psycho-social failure of individualization and stigmatized accordingly. Referring to the collapse of epistemological levels, the authors suggest that today:

> It still bears traces of the sexual division of labour that assigned men the role of breadwinners and women of caretakers and it is as if male breadwinners absorb into their personalities the independence associated with their economic role whilst female nurturers became saturated with the dependency of those for whom they care. (1994: 332)

Children and old people, similarly removed from the world of work, become most 'dependent' of all in this sense.

Systems of morality moved from a concern with the concrete and particular to the universal and abstract, as represented by Kantian reasoning which advocated that moral thought should proceed from the point of view of 'disinterested and disengaged moral actors' (Tronto, 1993: 9). Meanwhile, starting in the late nineteenth century and with increasing chronological definition up to the mid-years of the twentieth century, increasingly secularized states organized their subjects within a set of 'institutional boxes' comprising school, factory/workplace and workhouses/residential care homes and did so under the aegis of what Foucault calls 'pastoral' care, thus distinguishing it from disciplinary society. That is, directly owing to the disenchantment of society, 'it was no longer a question of leading people to their salvation in the next world, but rather ensuring it in this world' (Foucault, 1982: 215). Existential, if not transcendental, meaning, lost through disenchantment, is provided within this system by the ages and stages themselves, and, according to Foucault, salvation is synonymous, above all, with 'health'. In medicine, this was defined in narrower terms. Medicine, with the changes in epistemology related to the patho-anatomical techniques that emerged in the 1830s, was following an ever more reductionist Cartesian model, involving a clear separation of mind and body, patient and disease and the further subdivision of the machine-like body into systems and organs analysable in isolation both from each other, and from the lived context of the patient, proceeded apace. Health was reduced to normality in this model involving an ability to maintain one's functionality, so the body in old age becomes a constant reminder of the limits of physical self-control, and thus signifies precisely what bourgeois culture hoped to avoid: dependence, disease, failure and sin. This then, resulted in the 'ideological and psychological splitting apart of negative and positive aspects of growing old' (Cole, 1986: 121) suggesting that the good aspects were available to those with sufficient virtue (enterprise, conscientiousness, responsibility and so forth).

Late modern governmentality has overseen an intensification of this splitting with the 'good' citizen of all ages made in the mould of the enterprising self-regulated citizen, achieved through practices of 'freedom' and exercised through consumption. Both the organizational ethos of business and the norms of consumerism serve to further distance us from the Hag. Indeed, the difference between liberal and neoliberal regimes can be seen in an increasing distanciation of ageing and death from its place at the centre of life: no longer is economic behaviour about serving a Protestant God, as it was for the early capitalists, because God is now irrelevant since, as Wendy Brown puts it, the market has become *the* not *a* site for truth, including the truth of permanent youthful productivity and agency (Brown, 2015).

Organizational cultures project an image of immortality and focus on regeneration, valorizing the new, all strategies representing a denial of death, a process of feeding on the workers and disposing of them when they 'age' that Marx recognized as having a vampiric quality (Riach and Kelly, 2013). Consumerism similarly serves to effect a distance between our selves and any sense of our finitude. Noting that philosophers from Pascal to Kierkegaard have all acknowledged modern man's desire to 'constantly finish and to begin again from the beginning' (Bauman, 2001: 11), Bauman suggests that consumer culture shifts this impulse from an individual neurosis to a social and collective experience, which as well as ensuring social order and stability does so within the context of a culture that denies the Hag. That is, the cycle of buying and discarding and starting anew with a fresh purchase 'sublimates the wish to "constantly finish and begin again from the beginning" and forget about that end which is bound to finish it all' (2001: 11). Underpinned by a low rise in wages in comparison to the rising cost of living and an easy availability of credit, and in the twenty-first century, the introduction of 'austerity' measures in many Western countries, it signals a new phase of capitalism in the form of the debt economy. This has rendered the concept of independence ideological in the new sense of being linked to government retrenchment and increasing privatization (Eisenstein, 2005). Moreover, in late modernity the dualisms distinguishing active/passive, masculinity/femininity, young/old, producer/consumer, construction/essence, care/work and so on have been destabilized, often appearing together in new and complex combinations, but without replacing them, and indeed without shaking existing hierarchies. We can see elements of this in the new gender regime and in the 'new' old age, both of which mix elements of masculinity and femininity, youth and old age, depicted as gender-*neutral* and age*less*.

Medicine has continued to shape non-adult stages: the increasing association between old age and disease meaning that old age *is* bad old age, accompanied by a distinction between biological and chronological ageing, has led to the biologically youthful (those functioning as mid-life adults) distancing themselves from old age altogether. Similarly, the requirements on children to be enterprising and self-regulating has also led to many traditional aspects of childhood being viewed negatively, even seen as a disease and treated with drugs, for example, for attention deficit hyperactivity disorder (ADHD) (Wedge, 2015).

(iv) Social, cultural and symbolic approaches towards the Hag

It is within this expanded context that we can fully understand the symbolic location of the Hag. She comes to represent the loss and dissolution of a whole range of attributes and self-understandings that are repressed in the need for mastery of self, world and time. In the autonomous individual she remains the shadow, presenting the return of the repressed as an omnipresent threat. But worse, perhaps, and paradoxically, she also represents in her age and fragility the threat of the loss of the possibility of union, of the mythical wholeness which, according to the cultural myth of infant separation, we had to forsake in order to become persons. It is the sort of loss that we in the West might associate with growing up and which persists in a lifelong nostalgia, like that of an exile who can never return home. For women, the fear of the Hag may be commingled with the fear of turning into one's own mother (in the sense of a socially marginal, devalued subject). For men, whilst earlier in the life course it may represent fear of their hidden vulnerabilities, as they enter old age this transforms into the fear that they too are becoming feminized through both the physiological and social consequences of ageing in an ageist society.

Some of our most profound cultural attitudes towards age are crystallized in the vampire narrative, a vivid example of which is provided in the opening to *New Moon*, the second book of the 'Twilight' saga by Stephenie Meyer (and movie of the same name). The scene takes the form of a dream recounted by the main character, Bella, on the eve of her birthday. Bella's boyfriend, Edward, is a vampire, frozen at an eternally young seventeen, whilst Bella is about to turn eighteen, eliciting a whole array of anxieties. In the dream, Bella finds herself in a sunlit meadow together with her dead grandmother (and Edward arrives a little later).[6]

First, Bella notes her grandmother's appearance, the extreme agedness of the beloved face:

> Gran hadn't changed much; her face looked just the same as I remembered it. The skin was soft and withered, bent into a thousand tiny creases that clung gently to the bone underneath. Like a dried apricot, but with a puff of thick white hair standing out in a cloud around it.

The fact that her grandmother has been dead these past six years seems to confirm the recognition, within the dream itself, that she is dreaming. But strangely, every movement or gesture of Bella's is at the same time made by her grandmother. 'Our mouths – hers a wizened pucker – spread into the same surprised half-smile at just the same time.' Finally the recognition dawns upon Bella that the old woman before her is not, in fact, her Grandma Marie but her own self, many years in the future, reflected back at her in an enormous gilt mirror:

> With a dizzying jolt, my dream abruptly became a nightmare.
>
> There was no Gran.
>
> That was *me*. Me in a mirror. Me – ancient, creased, and withered.
>
> Edward stood beside me, casting no reflection, excruciatingly lovely and forever seventeen.
>
> He pressed his icy, perfect lips against my wasted cheek.
>
> 'Happy birthday,' he whispered.

Although the old woman is portrayed tenderly, at least when Bella mistakes her for her grandmother, what turns the dream into a nightmare is the distance the image opens up, both between the lovers and between what Bella is now and what she will one day be, a fact that sets up a split at the core of her being. (The last lines of the excerpt from H. Rider Haggard express the same sentiment: 'And yet, think of this… it was the *same* woman!') But if Bella cannot accept ageing at some level she cannot accept life at all, not even her youth, which some maintain is the best bit, because ultimately it means nothing without the 'old' against which backcloth it is always already contrasted. Simone de Beauvoir captured this paradox with the lines: 'If we do not know what we are going to be, we cannot know what we are: let us recognize ourselves in this old man or in that old woman' (1996: 5). Of course, this being a fantasy novel, Bella chooses a fantastic way out of this conundrum, opting for a non-human life in which she can live forever young. So far this is not an option open to the rest of us.

Both our institutions and our intellectual theories bolster each other in terms of normalizing and embedding the age system in our everyday practices. Psychological theories of development, biomedical approaches to health and normality and sociological theories of gender and identity are all infused with age-ideological assumptions including: the normality of stability over change; the taken-for-granted arc of growth–stasis–decline; and the centrality of the youthful perspective in theory-building.

We can also perceive the age system in symbolic terms, by means of a dimensional grid relating to the four key domains, namely the body, identity, place and social class which, in every society, in all eras, according to Peter Stallybrass and Allon White, are 'all constructed within interrelating and dependent hierarchies of high and low' (1986: 2). Within this system, the extremes are particularly important, for it is here that our struggles for order and sense are put to the test, our unresolved paradoxes illuminated and the interplay of rules and transgressions located. If we then consider where the lowest points in all four domains intersect we will find the poor, old, frail woman. This explains the power of the Hag to disgust where Menninghaus' description links the sensation of disgust to this process of 'social othering'. She notes: 'Everything seems at risk in the experience of disgust. It is a state of alarm and emergency, an acute crisis of self-preservation in the face of an unassimilable otherness' (2003: 1). The Hag is the symbol, nested within modernity, of the aspects of life from which our intellectual and social system has painstakingly worked to distance us; but this is at the same time constituted by our hierarchies and does not exist outside them.

Within this framework, 'resistance' takes the form of 'transgression' but Mary Douglas' (1966) work suggests that it is not straightforward rule-breaking or reversal of the existing norms – the low pole replacing the high – that is perceived as most threatening but rather ambiguity and disorder: the presence of hybridization of categories (Jenks, 2005). Examples might include: the 'woman' who is no longer fertile; the child who is precocious either in talent or in perpetrating 'adult' deeds (sex, murder); the old person who enjoys dependency. This threatens, Douglas suggests, our sense of order and sense-making but simultaneously highlights the underlying order that nevertheless exists (social constructions of women's 'telos' (still) lying in reproduction; children as asexual, etc.). For that reason, it has the potential to be both radical and conservative. Foucault puts the pessimistic view: 'Transgression contains nothing negative, but affirms limited being' (1977a: 35) whilst Stallybrass and White remain more sanguine about its potential suggesting that, despite its undoubted absorption in the established order 'it *may often act as catalyst* and *site of actual and symbolic struggle*' (1986: 14; original emphasis). Where ambiguity plays a particularly prominent role in the system it is strongly associated with pollution beliefs. According to Douglas, pollution beliefs do the job of mediating the friction between tensions within the system, for example between political and legal changes and socio-cultural continuity. Thus, the idea that the Hag is dangerous and can have power over us – such as in the witch figure – also suggests that our new norms of anti-ageism and age fluidity co-exist with older attitudes towards age.

This symbolic grid enables us also to discern that it is in the particular ambiguity of mid-life, a state of being that is neither young nor old, in which many are experiencing the onset of ill health, redundancy and financial constraints, where others are at their peak powers, and in which individuals oscillate between positive and negative views of their capability, that the most potent threat to the age system resides (Gullette, 1997). This explains the increasing problematization of mid-life that is a feature of social discourse. Seeing through age ideology at this stage renders individuals potentially ungovernable and the system potentially unworkable.

Meanwhile age ideology underpins an increasing social inequality as we discuss next.

(v) Social inequality: degrees of distance from the Hag

The antithesis of the Hag, representing the culturally valorized pole, modernity's aspiration, is vividly captured in a scene within the 2011 sci-fi movie *In Time* (directed by Andrew Niccol), in which grandmother, mother and daughter appear at a party side by side, all indistinguishable from the other, all three not a day beyond twenty-five physiologically speaking, within a regime wherein money buys time (see http://www.examiner.com/slideshow/in-time-movie-stills).

Indeed *In Time* suggests an alternative possibility to the progress-followed-by-decline arc that characterizes age ideology. In this film, set in a dystopian future and depicting a super capitalist state with extremes of wealth and poverty, people stop ageing physically on their twenty-fifth birthdays: thereafter they must 'buy' time (measured in minutes or hours) through their labour (regularly downgraded so that their wages buys them less of it). At the other end of the scale the rich accrue capital as vast amounts of time (measured in hundreds and even millions of years) amassed in the cavernous vaults of time banks. Money, in this film, *is* time. This is a society that has banished the Hag, or at least repressed her (death comes to the youthful but only to the youthful poor) so in many ways, then, it represents the apogee of the Cartesian dream.

This can be seen as an exaggerated metaphor for today's society and for the increasingly symbolic nature of adulthood therein. The top 1 per cent of the population in the UK (comprising a large proportion of the 'adults') receive upwards of 15 per cent of all income (risen from an average of around 7 per cent in the 1970s), just behind the US where the percentage is above 20 per cent. Today this group owns over a third of all marketable assets (excluding housing) whilst the bottom half (the 'children' symbolically) share 1 per cent of the nation's total wealth (Dorling, 2014; Roberts, 2011); in the US the top CEOs make 331 times the salary of average workers in a gap which has grown by 1000 per cent since 1950 (Dill, 2014, 2013). Professionals are part of the better-paid 99 per cent, rather than constituting part of the elevated group, suggesting in addition their loss of socio-political influence, as compared with the bankers, financiers and corporate chief executives who make up the 1 per cent.[7] In a situation of such growing inequality, where health disparities and mortality rates are also class-related throughout the life stages, the rich (mostly financiers) can project all their fears and vulnerabilities onto the poor, from whom they are increasingly removed, insulating themselves from the fear of ageing and death. Through their consumer power they are able to use all the latest medical and other interventions to stay 'youthful' – visible ageing itself becomes the sign of the abject – and ultimately, they hope to defy death itself in a logical extension of the capitalist mastery of *res extensa*. The extreme (high) position of our symbolic grid is represented by companies like the Alcor Life Extension Foundation which offers cryonics at a very high price and also assists with the legal preservation of one's assets for the time when one is revived, a time when 'ageing itself will be a treatable, reversible condition as medicine attains full control of the human body at the molecular level' (see www.alcor.org/). More moderate examples are represented by the numerous biotech Silicon Valley companies serving the interests of the very rich both as potential consumers of life extension technologies, and as beneficiaries of profits in what is becoming a highly lucrative business opportunity. In parallel, the disempowered are increasingly infantilized, their incomes akin to 'pocket money' to the rich, with resultantly decreased control and autonomy in work and life.

One of the main objections to the argument that age and ageing is increasingly important is the suggestion that age norms are more relaxed than they ever have been and that the distinction between all ages is lessening. But here *In Time* again provides some clues as to the broader meaning and purpose of this apparent age equality. *In Time* has only one valid age category – that of mature biological youthfulness, associated with the prime of life – and what lies to either side is childhood and death (but not old age in this instance). Inequality is centred around the ability to maintain a greater or lesser degree of rational adult personhood, through either enterprising activities by the elite or donkey work necessary for material survival by the poor, each involving varying degrees of time-capital. Mega-capitalists, like Marx's vampires, draw their supplies of time from the youthful labour of their workers. That is, this age stage is a symbolic category only loosely attached to chronology. In late modernity also, to an important extent, ages and stages have become symbolic categories detached from chronology and synonymous with individualized qualities, from irrationality, to responsibility to dependency and invested with more or less value, material rewards, and social power.

I will argue in this book that in late modernity the fluidity of age norms ('agelessness') is one factor, alongside a rhetorical commitment to gender equality, that has served as a 'solvent' (Eisenstein, 2005), albeit unwittingly, to release groups formerly 'protected' from the market into first, the labour economy, and, thereafter with the rise of neoliberalism, the ensuing market society (Sandel, 2012). The blurring of clear age categories co-exists with symbolic forms of adulthood that may not coincide with 'chronological' adulthood. This symbolic 'age patriarchy' holds power, shaping material conditions and cultural norms. Age, gender and class together underpin a cultural and material infantilization of those who have not acquired sufficient capital to be full adults. Age norm fluidity encourages a valued idea of the 'self', transcending age groups as agentic, autonomous and self-determining, through enterprising skills and consumer-based lifestyles. Age ideology serves powerfully to naturalize these changes, and to obscure the deepening structural inequalities that cross-hatch society. Moreover, of all body-based characteristics that have been employed to justify inequality – such as gender and race – age alone remains a 'fact' in both the popular and much of the intellectual imagination, and thus is all the more powerful for that.

Age studies, age ideology and social theory: the scope of this book

As a sociological text, this book positions itself within a disciplinary tradition whose central concepts, such as class and identity, are somewhat atemporal in their focus and do not incorporate change over the life course, except as crisis or discontinuity. Indeed, the founding fathers of sociology all assumed a Cartesian perspective, privileging rational (prime-of-life male) action and treating women as pre-social. The normative viewpoint from which society was viewed and theories elaborated was that associated with prime of life/mid-life. 'Age' remains mostly the interest of subfields, comprising childhood, youth studies and social gerontology and is otherwise introduced as an add-on to mainstream sociology's key theories. Despite the insights that arose from feminism, race and disability studies, the opportunity either to build a more temporal or longitudinal element into mainstream theorizing, or to test the applicability and complexity of mainstream theories across the fluctuations of the life course, has not been seized, leading to acquiescence in the age-ideological assumptions of scientific and lay views.

This book will begin to address this issue first by suggesting two methodological approaches in the form of delineating parallels with: (i) the class system; and (ii) the gender regime, demonstrating how (a) the age system is a socially constructed vehicle for inequality, in parallel to the former two systems, but also (b) how age works with class and gender to naturalize social inequality. It will then seek to explore a range of lived experience, including identity and embodiment, gender and sexuality, together with the analytic concepts employed to understand them, examining in each case: (i) how age serves to introduce socially constructed hierarchies in these fields; and (ii) how sociological theories, perhaps with modification, can serve as tools to identify and challenge this process, including the age ideological foundations of our social world as set out in the preceding pages.

In this aim, this book positions itself within the remit of age studies which Gullette defines as 'the interdisciplinary movement that wants to disrupt the current age system in theory and practice' (1997: 18). In attempting to denaturalize age ideology and critique age relations, this book is informed by three methodological assumptions and one ontological conviction, or belief about the nature of being; in addition it has a critical aim and a particular standpoint, all of which I will detail next.

The first methodological assumption contends that both the possibilities and constraints contained within each stage of the life course cannot be understood without examining the intersections with class and gender in particular. Thus, none of the stereotypical attributes of the life stages are attributable to age in itself: not the opportunities of youth (for some), nor the disappointments or transformations of mid-life (for others), nor the comfortable leisured lifestyle in young-old age, nor the constraints and challenges, social, material and physical in old-old age (for such are the stereotypes attributable to each stage of the life course) are attributable to *age itself*.

The second methodological assumption moves away from a strong constructionism in holding that the material attributes of the body that change and fluctuate through the life course, without our conscious involvement, are as much a part of our embodied ontology as is the self-invention that postmodernity celebrates. However, the meanings of these bodily states have their source in society, in particular in the hierarchical structures that separate ages from each other as well as stratifying them internally, all cross-cut by the axis that places youth to the positive side and old age to the negative. The 'realness' of age extends to the concrete experience associated with our existence as beings-in-time, and our positioning at stages of the life course, but both the meaning and the embodied experience of age(s) is entirely variable according to the wider cultural scripts and social practices. Notions of a 'universal' or timeless experience of age and ageing themselves require critical scrutiny rather than serving as a starting assumption.

The third methodological assumption derives from feminist standpoint theory, which argues that all knowledge is 'situated knowledge' (Harding, 2004). The 'legitimate' or intellectual tradition, they note, from science and medicine through to the canons of English literature, is patriarchal, infused with the perspective of bourgeois men and positions women as Other, a normative position that carries the label of 'objectivity'. What is notable is the extent to which both this tradition *and* feminist epistemology contain a normative age perspective: that of the prime-of-life adult. From this understanding comes the importance of foregrounding one's own perspective, and not presenting it as 'disinterested', including when discussing the topic of age.

For this latter reason I feel it is important to declare at the outset something of my own perspective. This book is written from the standpoint of a woman, now in mid-life, who has been fascinated by age, ageing and old age since I was three or four years old. This was the time in my life when I spent every weekend from Friday night to Sunday afternoon at my grandmother's house so that my parents could watch their little (failing) shop without having me as an additional worry. Despite the age gap of some 75 years, it was the similarities between Nana and I that struck me most forcefully, not just the dispositions and shared family history, but also the knowledge that we occupied a different place in society to the grown-ups (Nana was not a 'grown-up', I understood, but an 'old lady') and that, through and beyond that, the existential similarities of childhood and old age brought us together. For example, we shared a similar phenomenological experience of time and space, valued the garden, playtime and mealtimes more than the grown-ups seemed to. Yet, in other ways, my approach to my grandmother abounded in contradictions and paradox. She was physically robust, digging her garden and determinedly walking half a mile up a steep hill to the nearest shop, always in her best cream coat and hat, but my parents thought of her as weak and fragile and I learned to hold both 'truths' simultaneously in my head. The intimation of hidden fragility may have lain beneath my obsessive anxiety that she was going to die, and probably soon, maybe even today. I shared her bed during these weekend sojourns and I would always awaken what seemed like hours before her and lie there watching the ponderous rise and fall of the big mound of her body beneath the eiderdown, listening to her laboured breathing, terrified that it would stop.

One evening some fifteen years later I found myself sharing these experiences with fellow undergraduates at a writing group to which I belonged. The story I had brought along to read recounted a weekend I had spent with my grandmother all those years ago and I remember feeling really flattered when it received particularly rapturous praise from two young men. 'I felt, when you were reading it,' said the tall, blond one called Henry, in nostalgic tones, 'that you could have been talking about *my* grandmother.' At Oxford many boys had gone to Harrow or Eton and Henry was among them. This group of gilded, godly youth seldom if ever talked to us plebs except, with awkward politeness, if we happened to be partnered up with them at tutorials, or in muted heterotopias like this College club. Uncommonly flattered as I was in this context, his remark also filled me with some confusion, however; I thought back to my grandmother's cold and draughty rented house and tried to imagine Henry in such surroundings, seated at his grandmother's knee; could it be possible? Pulling myself out of my reverie, I thanked him, but just as I was doing so, I noticed something hard and crystalline about his gaze, and I felt myself frozen in it, fixed and tiny. At once I knew that the two paces between us encompassed a vast distance; although I did not then have the sociological theories to explain all this it was clear that this both was and was not the same old age we were talking about. Thus from these beginnings, and other such defining moments, I have nursed a lifelong interest in age in general and old age in particular, in its phenomenology and politics, in the nature of the relationship between generations, in the intersections between poverty and privilege and the co-presence of general truths and unique details that mean that old age, perhaps above all other ages, both unites and separates us.

This leads directly to the **critical part of this project** (in the sense coined by Horkheimer, aiming at changing, rather than simply understanding, society) which moves beyond analysis to posing two specific questions:

(i)   How do we imbue ages and stages with roles and meaning outside those associated with current hierarchies, dualisms and polarities? And

(ii) How do we re-envision the meaning of old age and thereby undermine age ideology's grip on our cultural imagination? Specifically, how do we challenge the view of ageing-as-deficit, and replace it with a more balanced and positive (but not age-denying) sense and significance that impacts on our embodied ontology throughout life more generally?

In short, the book asks, not only: can we see things differently? But also: how can sociological theories, rendered sensitive to age and change, contribute to seeing and doing otherwise? This question acquires urgency in the context of increasing longevity throughout the developed world. The latest World Health Organization figures (2015) suggest a life expectancy of 87 and 80 for Japanese women and men respectively at birth, in what is the longest-living advanced urban country (behind Monaco); the figures for the UK are 83 and 79 respectively. In Japan, 26 per cent of the population is aged 65 and over, making it a hyper-aged society; UK and US figures are at 17 per cent and 14 per cent respectively (Coulmas, 2007). Meanwhile, the oldest old is the fastest-growing section of the older population throughout the developed world (Higgs and Gilleard, 2015).

Finally, the **underpinning ontological conviction** follows this critical aim, and it is that regimes that foster freedom can be distinguished from those which do not; that different regimes do not simply involve different clusters of knowledge/power but that some of the latter are more conducive to human growth/wellbeing/self-expression, for majority and minority groups, than others. It is for this reason that this book positions itself within the Enlightenment tradition, whilst recognizing both the myopias and excesses particularly in the application of its principles at the hands of the philosophers and scientists that followed Descartes. For the latter reasons, it employs both hermeneutics and genealogy which are often seen as contradictory or clashing methodologies. Whilst the first is, of course, central to the Enlightenment tradition, and used by both Marx and Freud among others in pursuit of 'the truth', the latter, associated with Foucault and other deconstructionists, sees only more combinations of power and knowledge with no essential foundation of truth lying at the bottom. However, employed together they correct each other's blind spots, as Ferguson suggests: 'genealogy keeps interpretation honest, and interpretation gives genealogy direction' (1993: 30) in terms of its political aims. That is, whilst a search for foundations may be misplaced, still this does not rule out the possibility of flourishing and emancipation. Regardless of whether we are aware of it personally, the age regime is one of those things that limits flourishing and challenging it is thus an emancipatory aim.

In addition, in working within the Enlightenment tradition, I wish to highlight two contradictory strands which Charles Taylor (1985) describes in terms of: (i) the aim of objectivity; a Cartesian throwing-back of the individual thinker on his/her own responsibility which 'requires him to build an order of thought for himself' (1985: 182). But 'he' must do so impersonally in a way that underpins scientific knowledge and general 'truths'; (ii) the Romantic emphasis on the particularity and originality of the individual, the authenticity that constitutes standpoint. I will draw on both approaches in this book. So the idea, for example, originating with Descartes, to stop living blindly through experiences – to disengage from them, to treat them as objects – engenders a radical reflexivity, depriving the experience of its power. Such an approach is necessary to see how the age system operates independently of us and works through our assumptions including our age identities. On the other hand, the search for an authentic age identity that then follows involves throwing ourselves fully into the experience, 'being "all there", being more attentively "in" our experience' (Taylor, 1985: 163), so we come to distinguish our true lived experience from the hegemonic discourses associated with ages and stages. The ultimate paradox, however, is that the Enlightenment tradition that has worked for hundreds of years to distance us from the Hag is also the system that can help us return to her.

Organization of the book: a guide for readers

The chapters of the book build on each other and all address the questions listed in this introduction. They can also be read in blocks, organized around particular themes, as described below.

Chapters 2 and 3 consider how a focus on class and gender respectively, illuminates the age regime in so far as they present parallel systems of hierarchical stratification and also work with and through age. We note that class, gender and age intersect in terms of the role they play in underpinning the current capitalist regime and indeed we demonstrate that the rhetoric of gender equality and age fluidity, no less than social mobility and meritocracy, are key to the governing project of late modernity. Chapters 4 and 5 critically examine the life course as a concept and practice, and the way ages and stages within them, and the age identities associated with each stage, are framed according to the developmental ideology of growth–stasis–decline. These chapters pose such questions as: What is the relationship between the fluidity of age norms, individualization and modes of inequality? How are intellectual disciplines themselves implicated in the naturalizing of inequality and how can we use their resources instead to view age and ageing through the life course in ways alternative to the dominant paradigms? Chapters 6, 7 and 8 return to the theme of the intersection of the age and gender regimes and examine: (i) norms of embodiment; and (ii) modes of sexuality, both of which establish hierarchies of masculinity over femininity at key ages as well as youth over age. New gender norms, involving complex new hybrids within these hierarchies may also; (iii) give rise to disorders or problematizations for women in particular, associated with clashing configurations and irreconcilable paradoxes. Chapters 9 and 10 explore representations of different age groups in a variety of media, from advertising to literature to policy rhetoric, noting that the defining perspective is always that of the dominant adult group and that one of the key conceptual vehicles for representing age groups and age relations – namely the concept of generations – emphasizes conflict as well as obscuring issues of class and gender. Chapter 11 explores ways of constructing authentic age identities (outside normative stereotypes) in individual biographical narratives using a combination of theoretical reflection and practical examples. Chapter 12 returns to the critical questions posed at the start of the book and suggests that it is the adult stage above all that, linchpin of the age system as it is, requires careful rethinking, particularly the role of work and the meaning of maturity.

A final note is that, in all of the above, in exploring the intersections between age and other inequalities, the book focuses particularly on gender and class, and again, for reasons of space, can only acknowledge, but not consistently include, the importance of other sources of inequality such as race, disability, sexuality and other characteristics. Indeed, and secondly, whilst not reducible to them, many of the disadvantages often attributed to race among other things can be explained with reference to class and socio-economic disadvantage and it is on these that I will focus.[8] In addition, women are discussed more than men, and femininity more than masculinity because the former are qualitatively more disadvantaged and disadvantageous in both the age and gender regimes. This will, however, generate insights of relevance more broadly: the 'feminization' of society works with two other closely related currents in society, namely infantilization and the generalization of tropes formerly associated with ageing subjects, in ways that are disempowering to all.

BOX 1.5

The Hag

The figure of the Hag is being employed in this book to symbolize the constitutive limit of the age system as it exists in the West. She epitomizes our view of ageing as decline and loss of self and our horror at the loss of choice and control that finds its ultimate expression in death. To the question that haunts us as we move through the life course, 'How can I change whilst remaining myself?' she seems to offer the terrifying answer: 'You cannot'.

CHAPTER SUMMARY

- This chapter sets out the terrain the book will cover. It begins with a discussion of the age system, its origins and embedding in layers of our social, material and intellectual world and identifies some methodological tools for the book's inquiry.

- It then poses an analytic and critical task to be addressed over the course of the book.

- The analytic task will be to examine, over a range of themes central to both lived experience and sociological theorizing: (i) how age serves to introduce hierarchies in all these fields; and (ii) how sociological theories can best serve as tools in identifying and critiquing the age system.

- The critical task asks: (i) how do we imbue ages and stages with roles and meaning outside those associated with current hierarchies, dualisms and polarities? and (ii) how can we re-envision the meaning of old age and thereby undermine age ideology's grip on our cultural imagination?

Further questions

1. How adequately has social theory approached the subject of age and ageing?

2. To what extent can we understand social attitudes towards old age as aspects of 'age ideology'?

3. How do views on age reflect approaches to freedom?

Talking point

The figure of the 'witch' has been consistently used in history to problematize certain older women who have characteristics that are described as 'unnatural'. In its sixteenth-century version, Charles Taylor suggests that the witch-burning craze allowed the expression of tensions resulting from the switch from a living to a dead cosmos. Throughout their long history, the witch trials predominantly targeted poor older women who were married but had no children – a theme that continues in today's culture, albeit in Disneyfied form, for example, in Roald Dahl's *The Witches* who detest children and seek to kill them all. Today, female political leaders or their professional wives such as Margaret Thatcher, Cherie Blair and Hillary Clinton have all been called witches: the term refers to different 'unnatural' qualities than in the above examples, but refuses to die. Consider some of its links with: (i) women's social roles; and (ii) the psychic dimension we have discussed in this chapter.

Key texts

The following texts provide a useful overview of the major themes covered in this book, including **age relations**, **age ideology** and some of the key challenges to the latter: Calasanti, T.M. and Slevin, K.F. (eds) *Age Matters: realigning feminist thinking*, London: Routledge; Dinnerstein, D. (1976) *The Mermaid and the Minotaur: sexual arrangements and human malaise*, New York: Harper & Row; Gullette, M.M. (1997) *Declining to Decline*, Charlottesville: University of Virginia Press; Gullette, M.M. (2004) *Aged by Culture*, Chicago: University of Chicago Press; Mintz, S. (2015) *The Prime of Life: a history of modern adulthood*, Cambridge, MA: the Belknap Press of Harvard University Press; Neiman, S. (2014) *Why Grow Up?* Harmondsworth: Penguin; Pilcher, R. (1995) *Age and Generation in Modern Britain*, Oxford: Oxford University Press; Woodward, K. (1991) *Ageing and its discontents: Freud and other fictions*, Bloomington: University of Indiana Press.

Notes

1. 'She who was once the beautiful helmet-maker's wife'.

2. I will be using the term 'Hag' rather than 'crone' in this chapter and through-out the book to refer to the old-woman figure. This is because I wish to stress thereby the connection between the old woman and women at earlier points of the life course. In this sense, the etymological meanings that include a female demon; an evil or frightening spirit; a nightmare; and an ugly or evil-looking woman and/or one who is intractable (Daly, 1991: 15) are all intensified in the figure of the old woman rather than appearing there anew.

3. I give these names a capital letter to emphasize the Mother/Feminine and the Masculine as principles or cognitive styles, equating to nurturance/passivity and activity, with their embodiment in actual men and women being a cultural not biological fact, as Susan Bordo (1986) also stresses.

4. From 'The Human Condition' originally published in Gunn, T. (1957) *The Sense of Movement*, London: Faber and Faber.

5. Penelope Leach identifies seven stages for the under-fives; similarly, versions of a frailty scale name seven major gradations (from very fit to severely frail) (see Leach, 1977, quoted in Hockey and James, 1993: 86; also Rockwood et al., 2005).

6. From Meyer, S. (2006) *New Moon*, New York: Little, Brown, pp. 3–6.

7. The US and the UK are the quintessential neoliberal states, a fact that is reflected in the degree of socio-economic equality, they are second and fourth in terms of wealth inequality worldwide; lower inequality is found in other European coun-tries such as Sweden, where 1 per cent take 7 per cent of the GDP. Nevertheless, the trend throughout Europe is towards increasing inequality.

8. For example, Sean F. Reardon's work at Stanford indicates that the 'class gap' is now twice that of the 'race gap' see: https://cepa.stanford.edu/sites/default/files/reardon%20whither%20opportunity%20-%20chapter%205.pdf

2

CLASS STRATIFICATION AND AGE

Background

Analysis of the structures, processes and consequences of the stratification of society by social class has been critical to the disciplinary focus of sociology since its inception. Early approaches held that the concept of class could also be used to explain other dimensions of inequality, including gender and age (Bradley, 1996). Today, an understanding of the unique aspects of these various forms of social inequality, as well as their intersection with each other, are considered equally necessary. Alongside this, is recognition of the social changes that have undermined the traditional class approaches suggesting that, whilst class relations continue to be of great importance in explaining social stratification, a new approach to class analysis may be necessary to capture these new forms and expressions of social inequality. By the latter I refer to cultural class theories within a context of individualization. What has not been recognized, however, to anywhere near the degree it merits, is the role that age as a system plays in underpinning the social class structure as it appears today. Indeed in this chapter I make three key assumptions:

(i) class works through age;

(ii) age naturalizes and obscures the inequalities instated through class (and gender and other modes of stratification);

(iii) class stratification can serve as a model through which we understand age as a mode of social stratification.

These three elements allow both systems to be more effectively identified and critiqued. This is important because class is increasingly being seen as impossible to challenge; likewise, the rising inequalities in the Western world are presented as something akin to an act of God.[1] Unravelling their careful constructions, including as they work in and through age, will indicate that this is certainly not the case.

AIMS OF THE CHAPTER

- We examine classical and contemporary approaches to the analysis of class, with the critical addition of looking at how they map onto age.

- We consider, using empirical examples:

  (i) How class is reproduced through age and stage.

  (ii) How the class structure illuminates the age system and vice versa.

  (iii) How age, gender and class intersect to produce complex forms of inequality throughout the life course.

Classical theories of class

Marxist and **neo-Marxist** approaches concentrate their analytic energies on two main classes (the bourgeoisie and proletariat) linked together through exploitation and struggle, based on relations of production. Class is an objective situation, whether individuals recognize it or not, but in recognizing it they thus move from classes-in-themselves to classes-for-themselves. Ideology is one of the key ways through which the dominance of the ruling class, and the exploitation of the labouring class, is legitimated. Whilst Marx and Engels refer to it in terms of a 'superstructure' of ideas and beliefs, Althusser ties ideology to material structures including law, religion, education and the family and also gives attention to how we as individuals are interpellated or induced to recognize ourselves in various social roles and identities.

By contrast, **Weber** emphasizes status groups which may or may not overlap with classes; the main difference is that, whilst 'classes are stratified according to the production and acquisition of goods... status groups are stratified according to the principles of their *consumption* of goods as represented by special styles of life' (Weber, 1978: 937; original emphasis). This approach focuses on stratification within, as well as between, classes, as well as charting the social mobility that may take place within this context.

Functionalist approaches, meanwhile, adopt the premise, as Bradley summarizes, that 'if social institutions exist they must have a useful function' (1996: 61). Durkheim lays emphasis on class divisions as fulfilling functions for society, rather than causing oppression and negative division, for example, encouraging healthy competition between those who hold the necessary skills for a job and reinforcing the idea of meritocracy based on skills and ability. Whilst the heyday of functionalism lay between the 1940s and 1960s, for sociology, its explanatory value, certainly in broader society, has not disappeared. Indeed it is currently enjoying a resurgence of popularity in British politics associated with discussion around 'IQ' as a factor determining social mobility (e.g. Cummings, 2013; Johnson, 2013) as well as the social impact of global competition. For example, as the mayor of London declared, in relating that harsh social and economic contexts sort the men from the boys: 'I am afraid that a violent economic centrifuge is operating on human beings who are already very far from equal in raw ability, if not spiritual worth' (Johnson, 2013). It also has salience in health inequality discourse in the notion that poorer people have less ability or knowledge around self-care or have inferior physical capital which results in, not from, their 'natural' class positioning.

Despite their differences, Durkheim, Weber and Marx all concur in emphasizing the economic basis of class and these theories gave rise to several different forms of class concept and measurement all based upon the assumption that occupation and income are central to the workings of class, a belief similarly underlying government policies directed at redressing inequalities in education and so on. As we will see below, from the 1990s onwards different approaches to conceptualizing and measuring class have become increasingly salient and this has been accompanied by a shift to the rhetoric of a 'classless society'. We turn to this next.

Class in late modernity

Traditional methods for identifying and analysing class are no longer sufficient for the new social and economic conditions that emerged in the latter decades of the twentieth century. These conditions include a feminization of class (McRobbie, 2004; Morgan, 2004): that is, women's new place in the work economy is underlined by a new significance given to women in defining class itself. In a similar vein, class has been statically conceived, congealing around adult occupational forms, which today requires a broader view that sees an ongoing potential for class differentiation in later, including post-retirement, life (Formosa and Higgs, 2013). Meanwhile, the work of authors included in the collection edited by Toni Calasanti and Kathleen Slevin (2006) demonstrates that none of these categories make sense unless they are considered as intersecting with other key ascribed identities.

Before going on to discuss other ways of approaching inequalities, including but not restricted to class, let us first spend some more time examining the nature of the socio-economic changes that underpin them.

Late modernity: how inequalities work through ages and stages

Late modernity (also called by the names of 'high', 'advanced' or 'second' modernity) has seen the introduction of a large number of changes to the economy (and to the class system associated with it). Firstly, there have been radical changes to the industrial base: we have become post-industrial in the UK and in most other Western countries (as has Japan and other advanced eastern capitalist nations) with a shift from a production-based economy based on a large manufacturing base to a service-based society of 'consumers'. With half the manufacturing jobs that existed in the 1970s having disappeared, this has sometimes been described as a 'second industrial revolution' (Roberts, 2011). In terms of relations between capital and labour, where Marx identified a 'double freedom' involving (i) the cutting of feudal and traditional ties, together with (ii) the freedom to sell one's labour, this second revolution involves another double freedom, (a) bringing into the market groups formerly sheltered from it, such as women and older people, whilst also (b) releasing workers from all values except those associated with the market (Brown, 2015). In class terms there has been a 'polarization of social inequality (in the form of an elite and a precariat)' (Savage et al., 2013: 246) resulting in a return to earlier levels of class stratification, that is, before the 1918–78 period when the UK, among other countries, enjoyed the greatest equality it has ever experienced socio-economically (Dorling, 2014).

Whilst the traditional working class has shrunk, the middle class has both swollen in numbers, drawing from the working class for its service sector jobs, and become increasingly 'ordinary' in material terms in the process (Dorling, 2014; Roberts, 2011). Along with this has come a post-Fordist system of working practices characterized by, above all, 'flexibility', meaning the end of jobs for life and the advent of enduring uncertainty but with it an ongoing opportunity/obligation to change jobs and careers, and a greater involvement of women in the workplace. Indeed the workplace has become 'feminized' in the dual sense of it being characterized by a preponderance of office-based work, and by work involving a large (and often part-time) contingent of female workers (and increasingly young, old and immigrant labour of both genders). However, a decline in the growth of the middle class, having reached its limits through absorption of many of the working class, and the resultant stagnation of social mobility, have seen (i) a loss of 'real work' for all classes and (ii) relatedly, the creation of 'shadow work' that eats into our so-called 'free time' (see Ehrenreich, 2015). The former (i) stems both from technological advances and from increased bureaucratization. With respect to (ii) individuals are increasingly burdened with 'unpaid, unseen' jobs, from maintaining and servicing internet connections to helping one's child succeed at school. Meanwhile, the upper classes have reinvented themselves in the form of transnational finance capitalists, a sector with immense wealth that, far from being feminized, is 80 per cent male in both the UK and USA (Dorling, 2014) (and many of the women in that category have acquired their wealth from men, through divorce and inheritance).

Late modernity is also characterized by a set of cultural practices and social norms which have been described in various ways that highlight either their oppressive nature (as in neoliberalism, the work of Nikolas Rose and liquid modernity, the different but equally cautionary interpretation of Zygmunt Bauman), or the mixed dangers and opportunities (Beck and Beck-Gernsheim, 2002; Beck, 1992), or the more optimistic account represented by the 'reflexive modernization' theory of Anthony Giddens (1991) in which we are set free from the constraints of tradition in a way existentialists could only dream of (and which include older age groups and women, in many ways, for the first time) including in terms of securing our own class position. All these theorists are referring, with different emphases, to the end of overt government intervention in the lives of its citizens and the shift to a more indirect governance of consumers by self-regulation and expert guidance. The ideal-typical citizen in this setting is epitomized by the responsible, autonomous, self-initiating, self-surveilling actor whose needs and skills are perfectly aligned with those of policy. Whilst Rose (1999) and others highlight the disciplinary practices that mould individuals at their core, meaning that government is something effected through the subjectivities of governed individuals, the more optimistic emphasize, to varying degrees, the creativity and agency inherent in the withering-away of the iron hand of tradition. All theorists agree (though Giddens gives it less emphasis than the others) that social problems and persisting social structural constraints are in such a way turned into individual problems or, using the terms of C. Wright Mills (1959), that the link between private troubles and public issues is lost or submerged. Foucault's work on governmentality (1982) particularly captures the shift within modernity regarding the interplay between structure and agency and the gradual shift towards using agency and subjectivities (conscious and affective/unconscious/irrational elements) for regulating populations within an individualized society. Foucault's approach also permits the additional insight that the loosening of class identities has taken place within a neoliberal discourse in which capitalism has been able to assert itself as the 'saviour' at the 'end of history', replacing Marx's heroic proletariat in that role, for its part in introducing technological progress, material abundance and an underpinning social stability (Seabrook, 2013). Most of all, there is no longer any credible and popular alternative to this system, for, along with the demise of the industrial working-class political base, the system 'disseminates the model of the market to all domains and activities – even where money is not at issue – and configures human beings exhaustively as market actors, always, only and everywhere as *homo oeconomicus*' (Brown, 2015: 31).

These various changes, as noted, suggest the need for a different analytical framework for identifying 'class' and we will consider next (acknowledging their interconnectedness): (i) the cultural class approach; and (ii) individualization theory, and in each case the role of age therein.

Firstly, Bourdieu's **cultural class theory** moves away from an occupation-based class system and provides a cultural approach to class, emphasizing the role of lifestyles in cultural, social and material reproduction (and power) and as such builds upon Weber's model of status groups and stratification according to taste and lifestyle. The 'social space' in Bourdieu's model is captured through a complex mix of economic and cultural capital which constructs classes relationally through a 'system of differences' in which finely graded capitals are positioned. Because of this, and because of the increasing equality of the 99 per cent squashed below the elite in the UK and US, distinctions are sharply and finely drawn: 'the closer together class fractions are, the sharper is likely to be the boundary between them in terms of its symbolization' (Jenkins, 2002: 143). Although a standard criticism hinges upon the determinism inherent in this depiction, more recent approaches (Savage et al., 2005) develop the agentic dimension of Bourdieu's model. The focus here is not on economic determinants centred upon the nature of occupation, the traditional focus of class analysis, but on a 'more "micro" interest in how the effects of class are produced through individual actions drawing variously on "assets"' (2005: 32). This sees the relationship between class and economics unfolding through layers of cultural and social fabric, with the symbolic both constitutive of, and shaped by, class position. This approach is particularly useful for understanding the nature of stratification over the life course, emphasizing as it does, the way that capital – including economic, social, physical and cultural forms – has the potential to accumulate in specific fields and be converted into resources within a context of temporality. Further useful elements include the concept of relationality which gives prominence not to the groupings but to ambiguity, boundaries and boundary-setting *between* groupings and also highlights the importance of subjective assessments of one's positioning. Here, 'taste' (*goût*) and 'disgust' (*dégoût*), related etymologically, play a complementary role in boundary-setting, and indeed these responses, and the social marking they constitute, become even more important in the absence of imposed social hierarchies – of role and position – characteristic of modernity.

Secondly, another prominent contemporary theory that explains class relationships within a new relationship between structure and agency is that of the **theory of individualization.** Beck and Beck-Gernsheim (2002) suggest that individualization involves a different class formation – not post-*class* but post-*traditional* classes – in which age plays a role almost as salient as that of class in previous times, at least in terms of processes of collective identification. Late-modern society, according to this thesis, is composed of atomistic individuals so separated from each other in their need to balance risk and opportunity (in what they call a 'tightrope biography' (2002: 5)) that they cannot make common cause nor perceive that there is a 'standardized collective character' to such individualized experience (p. 31). This includes the introduction of age as a divisive factor instead of class. Such a discourse becomes easier to accept where sharp discontinuities in employment have also introduced ruptures between generations, particularly evident in the working class where formerly both identities and skill/workplace knowledge were passed down (Roberts, 2011) (and in the space left behind 'generational war' as a mode has been inserted, among other things, as we see in Chapter 10). Chronological age is a factor associated with reduced life opportunities for some but not for others. In the former case, this is attributed to a variety of causes, including the physical ageing that accompanies hard labour or poor lifestyle as well as societal ageism. But time also enables the already privileged to accumulate further advantages, so that whilst for people in the lower socio-demographic brackets (especially women and members of minority races and ethnicities) average earnings tail off before mid-life, those in the top 1 per cent of the population tend to be in their mid-fifties and above (Dorling, 2014) with middle-aged men occupying top positions in public sector leadership as well as banking and politics.

Class, gender and age

One approach developed within feminism that has considered the relationship between class and gender is that of dual systems theory. This is a 'synthesis of Marxist and radical feminist theory' (Walby, 1990: 5) which sees both capitalism and patriarchy as shaping the contemporary gender regime, with some analysts seeing these as distinct and others as intertwined and thus inseparable. Walby's contribution to this debate has been to suggest that the major change historically has been the shift from a private to a public form of patriarchy, wherein women's entry into the workforce leads to new and complex forms of oppression that seductively masquerade as liberation. The theory of intersectionality, meanwhile, adds to this by seeing multiple systems of inequality impinging upon an individual. One approach is to explore the degree to which intersectionality can be explained by reference to one key system of oppression, usually that of class, whereby for example, gendered, aged and racialized practices are relational aspects of the capitalist mode of production (Moore, 2009). In the case of age, however, as we will see, it is important to recognize its unique properties alongside its interaction with other systems of oppression (Calasanti and Slevin, 2006).

Empirically, considering gender and class firstly, we can see that they intersect in multiple, complex ways. Bradley (1996) points out that classes are both divided by gender, for example in the notion of distinctive men's work and women's work, but also 'gendered'. By this she suggests that 'gender is integral to processes of class formation, action and identification' (1996: 74) and sexuality is also part of this. An example of the latter is how working-class women's reproductive role and domestic duties were crucial to capitalism's ability to exploit the industrial proletariat, through women giving emotional support to their husbands, providing a home for them and producing a new generation of workers to replicate the process. Bev Skeggs (1997), Steph Lawler (2000) and others also point out that gender styles differ for each class and, in being associated with different roles and expectations, ideologies of masculinity and femininity also contribute to the gendering of class. One way in which class divisions are maintained in contemporary times is through the gendering of available occupations, with care-giving seen as 'women's work' for example, as well as the filling of part-time and insecure positions preponderantly with women (Skeggs, 1997). However, notable class differences are identifiable in this, namely a 'gender convergence' (among middle-class professionals) simultaneous with a class divergence (between middle and working classes). In this process, middle-class women have served as 'standard bearers' for a particular model of citizenship reproduced through education and other forms of cultural distinction (McRobbie, 2004: 101). Nevertheless, men overall remain at the top of the social structure (in terms of heading up private companies, political office and state bureaucracies) and women remain at the bottom (over-represented in the marginal, flexible employment associated with the service industries) (Morgan, 2004; Roberts, 2011).

As far as the lived experience of the intersection of gender, class and age is concerned, whilst men and women both experience ageism at work, more women than men experience ageism with regard to appearance and sexuality and women are also more likely to experience discrimination on account of being either too young or too old (Duncan and Loretto, 2004). The trajectory for women proceeds 'from being considered a "flighty young piece", or "hearing wedding bells", or "raising a family and not really committed to her work" to "it's that age – the change"' (Itzin and Phillipson, 1995: 85, quoted in Duncan and Loretto, 2004: 102).

Although profoundly structured, then, one can certainly see how the dizzying effects of these various positions can contribute to the appearance not just of individualization but also of personal responsibility for success and failure.

In this section, looking at how class maps onto age, we consider three themes – (i) How is class reproduced through age and stage? (ii) What does an examination of the class structure tell us about the age regime? (iii) How does age-based inequality work with other unique dimensions in society in the 'intersectionality' approach?

(i) How is class reproduced through age and stage?

Poverty in childhood is one of the key ways class makes itself felt early in the life course. The rising inequality in the UK is reflected in the fact that childhood poverty is severe in relation to the rest of Europe (Ridge, 2002); but at the same time Ridge points out that the individualized nature of society means that 'children's lives are diverse and their risks and experiences of poverty will differ' (2002: 25). However, one key way in which poverty in childhood is discussed is in relation to 'generational justice' and the questions that tend to be asked are not how does inequality affect children in comparison to one another, but: 'Are children "richer" or "poorer" than other age groups?' (James and James, 2012: 93–4). Moreover, where poverty in childhood has been addressed in policy, historically, a consistent motivation for this has been the need both for global competitiveness of the nation and for preventing class conflict. It has also been a way through which governments can intervene in, and regulate, the lives of adults through 'improving' parents: Prime Minister Tony Blair, for example, professed that a key aim was to make parents better citizens by means of education, literacy, parenting classes and nutritional advice, all within an enterprise model (Ridge, 2002).

The category 'children' conceals vast degrees of internal heterogeneity and inequality. Ridge describes how children in poor households very quickly 'learn to be
poor'. Deprivation in terms of pocket money means that children fail to learn socio-
economic competency and develop their capacities as economic actors as well as
participate socially, keeping up friendships and interests. Whilst many children
attempt to ameliorate this by undertaking paid work, there is a class differential in
patterns of employment with working-class children taking on more work and for
longer hours. This in turn sets up tensions between the demands of school and paid
work and cuts into time for social interaction. Today, within the UK, estimates of the
level of employment among young people aged 13–17 suggest that 43 per cent have
some sort of paid employment and most of these children are thought to be working
illegally. Children undertake a range of jobs and those in low-income families sup-
plement the household income with their earnings (Ridge, 2002).

Moving to youth, and seeing education as a key vehicle for class reproduction,
we can identify a complex interplay of class and gender differences. There is no
doubt that there has been a remarkable transformation in terms of girls' success at
school and university since the 1980s, when they began to overtake boys. By 1996
in the UK, girls outperformed boys at ages 7, 11 and 14 in National Curriculum
assessments; by 2001, 56.5 per cent of girls were achieving grades A*–C in five or
more subjects at GCSE level compared with only 45.7 per cent of boys, and the
current gap of around 10 points in achievement is now long-standing (Department
for Education and Skills, 2007). This is mirrored in higher education, where girls'
share of undergraduate places at university first rose above 50 per cent in 1996
(Dyhouse, 2014).[2] However, an emphasis today on gender and particularly on the
greater achievement of girls, obscures the overwhelming effect of class difference
where in fact, 'in the UK social class, rather than gender, is the primary predictor
of achievement' (Francis, 2010: 23). Using entitlement for free school meals
(FSMs) as an, albeit blunt, dividing line between classes, Francis notes that nearly
double the proportion of girls and boys not claiming FSMs achieve five or more
GCSE grades A*–C and that white working-class British girls receiving FSMs are
outperformed by middle-class white boys by 19 per cent. Sixteen-year-olds who are
'not in employment education or training' (NEETs) are concentrated in deprived
areas and the fact that a disproportionately higher number of middle-class children
are categorized as of 'high' ability as compared to working-class children in the
first place, indicates the very construction of 'ability' in middle-class terms
(Walkerdine and Lucey, 1989). Certainly, however, girls' success is of great symbolic importance within the late modern capitalist formation in signalling the new
requirements of the 'docile and productive' worker. Ringrose comments: 'Girls'
new found "equality" and power becomes a meritocratic formula, a signifier, a
"metaphor" for the hard work needed to attain educational and career success'
(Ringrose, 2007: 485).

In terms of higher education, for those 35 per cent of young people who move
directly from secondary education into university (45 per cent attend by age 30),

the result of this expansion of higher education is that qualifications at all levels have been devalued in terms of the opportunities opened up in the labour market. This means that A-levels are now expected where not long ago GCSEs were sufficient. The chances of securing a good job, moreover, are related to the university at which one studied: there are high-, middle-, and low-ranked universities suggesting that 'whenever social class differences are suppressed at one level of education, they consistently and immediately pop up elsewhere' (Roberts, 2009: 360). Roberts also points out that middle-class parents help their children succeed in numerous informal and formal ways, such as helping them get into good schools, paying for additional private tutors, supporting them financially so they are not required to work whilst studying, and securing them internships through their own contacts which then – inevitably – lead to the good jobs that are presented as being won on 'merit'. No doubt merit also features; but such rhetoric disguises the very real structural advantages that allow individual merit to shine through in the first place. As a corollary of this, by contrast, Roberts (2009) also rightly argues that working-class behaviour should not be judged as deficient here, as it is through the hegemonic middle-class perspective, for example, the notion of 'poverty of aspiration', but rather seen as reasonable in the context of the limited nature of working-class opportunities. This means that working-class families judge that the investment they will need to secure a middle-class job will not pay sufficient dividends and instead use their cultural and social capital to attain manual jobs, apprenticeships and the like, bypassing higher education (Roberts, 2009).

Turning next to mid-life, we find mid-life professionals doing best (in terms of conditions, prospects and remuneration including future pensions) in the current employment conditions, with young people and older late-career workers doing worst (Roberts, 2011). But at the same time a focus on age again obscures the significant heterogeneity within each category. So whilst the 'winners' in globalization (and this applies across Europe and the US) might be the men in mid-career, these latter are professional men, qualified, experienced and middle class, whilst by comparison, mid-life 'male employees with low human capital resources... prove to be exceptionally vulnerable in globalized labour markets' (Buchholz et al., 2009: 60). Mid-life women also experience marginalization, as well as employment in insecure work, but again the class difference is most strident; for example, in the UK, middle-class skilled professional mothers of children under the age of five are 30 times more likely to work full-time than working-class mothers who mostly work part-time (Roberts, 2009) (for further contextual details about differing European countries, see Buchholz et al., 2009).[3]

Retirement, meanwhile, has always been used as a device for regulating the labour supply in the interests of the employers. In the 1950s post-war-reconstruction period in the UK, pressure was placed on older workers to delay leaving work. By the 1980s early retirement was the vogue because of youth unemployment. By the early 1990s declining birth rates and increased life expectancy led governments to try to reverse these trends. However, despite anti-age discrimination legislation, such as banning age-based obligatory retirement (first in 2006 and extended in 2011), other forms of informal discrimination persist (Duncan and Loretto, 2004). Moreover, ageism is a highly flexible concept and whilst young workers also report experiences of discrimination (Loretto et al., 2000), workers are configured as 'old' at vastly different points in the life course depending on both the needs of the employment and the classed nature of the work. In general women are perceived to be 'older' than men at any given age in a way that negatively impacts their employment prospects (Itzin and Phillipson, 1995). Today, not only is early retirement no longer the norm but also it is projected that retirement age will rise to 69 by the 2040s (Prime, 2014). Moreover, to leave the workforce 'prematurely', in mid-life for example, is often both the result of, and underpins further, disadvantage. A cautious estimate is that nearly one million people aged 50–64, particularly those aged 55–59, are involuntarily jobless, 'pushed out of their previous job through a combination of redundancy, ill health or early retirement' (Prime, 2014: 7). Whilst most early exits are involuntary due to illness or care-giving duties to others, coupled with lack of support from employers (such as failing to allow more flexibility) and a more structural tendency for employers to discriminate in redundancy decisions against older workers (Phillipson, 2013), these have a hugely detrimental effect on post-retirement income. Leaving the workforce at 55 rather than 65 could result in a private pension that is 37 per cent smaller according to research by the Department of Work and Pensions (Prime, 2014). With or without early exit, approaching retirement is a highly stratified experience and consists of a 'two nations in retirement' polarity (Vickerstaff, 2010) in which professionals have choice over whether to remain in (well-paid) work while the disadvantaged often have no choice: either because their jobs are no longer available to them or because of poor health.

Health inequalities are associated with class inequality which increases with age, producing an accumulation of (dis)advantage over the life course, this directly impacts not just on the greater degree of impairment for poorer people but on life expectancy, which between those in London's rich and poor wards is now nearly 25 years. Inequality in life expectancy has increased in the rest of the UK – by 41 per cent for men and 73 per cent for women in the past twenty years (Pickett and Wilkinson, 2014) – a finding echoed in the US (Dorling, 2014). In the UK the lower the life expectancy, the fewer years people can expect to live free of disability: so whilst men in the least-deprived areas can expect nearly 70 years of healthy life expectancy, those in the most-deprived can expect only 55 (for women it is 71 and 57 respectively (Norton and West, 2014)).

Meanwhile, pensioner poverty reflects occupational activity earlier in the life course. Access to a private (non-state) pension is significantly skewed towards the higher socio-economic groups; in the UK, 75 per cent of managers and professionals are members of such schemes, compared with 33 per cent of those in routine and semi-routine occupations (Phillipson, 2013). Some 20 per cent of all UK employees now believe that they will never be able to afford to retire (Dorling, 2014).

(ii) How does the class structure illuminate the age system and vice versa?

By remembering the highly manipulated divisions associated with class we will be better placed to deconstruct age categories and identify the constructed nature of their so-called 'natural' character. We will also see more clearly that in turn, and teleologically, age 'naturalizes' the class system, suggesting the inevitability of people's position at various points occupationally and in terms of income and status; and confirms the inevitability of the age system in so doing. The following two quotes, by Bourdieu and Foucault respectively, draw attention in general terms to this close parallel. They indicate that age divisions are both socially produced (in the way class is produced), and fundamental to the process of ordering and governing a late modern economy.

> Classification by age (but also by sex, and of course, class...) always means imposing limits and producing an *order* to which each person must keep, keeping himself [*sic*] in his place. (Bourdieu, 1993: 94; original emphasis)

> These divisions – whether our own or those contemporary with the discourse under examination – are always themselves reflexive categories, principles of classification, normative rules, institutionalized types; they, in turn, are facts of discourse that deserve to be analysed beside others; of course they also have complex relations with each other, but they are not intrinsic, autochthonous, and universally recognisable characteristics. (Foucault, 2002: 22)

The Marxist-inspired (political economy) approach mostly associated with critical social gerontology (e.g. Phillipson (1982), Townsend (1981) and Walker (1980) in the UK; Estes (1979) in the US) highlights the creation of inequality both within and via age groups. The idea of older workers being surplus to labour requirements was crucial to the development of pensions both in the UK and US; retirement provided for industrial capitalism a means of challenging security of tenure or jobs for life, a step in the movement from gemeinschaft to gesellschaft (Fennell et al., 1988) and introduced cheaper labour in the form of young people (and older people increasingly encouraged to work beyond retirement age in low-paid work). Whilst it also introduced particular hardships for working-class retirees, such policy was justified by rhetoric emphasizing the 'burden of age' which was able to foster public support for low pensions. Should 'retirement' still appear something 'natural' to readers today brought up to take it for granted, it may be useful to compare this with the structured dependency of childhood as created through the introduction of mass education and the removal of children from the workforce in the nineteenth century. In a very short period of time, this process changed working-class children's identity from 'worker' to 'schoolchild' and thereby created the image of 'childhood' as we know it today, although at the time, especially for working-class parents who relied on the income from their children, it was education that seemed unnatural in childhood, not work.

'Structured dependency' also brings about division between and within age groups. In late modernity, structured dependency is perhaps most starkly notable for the younger age groups consisting of the extension of both the school-leaving age and of the numbers involved in higher education for young people, the raising of the age at which they can obtain welfare benefits in their own right, and the difficulty in achieving stable employment and financial independence. We have noted in the previous section how both young and older people often occupy marginal roles in the work economy. However, despite their shared or parallel experiences, antagonisms between age groups are also established directly through the work economy. So, leading on from the point we have already made about the emphasis on the educational and work success of younger women today, Walby notes:

> There are new divides opening up between younger and older women, as younger educated women are more likely to be in employment, more likely to get better jobs and careers, while older women who built their lives around quite different expectations of a woman's life… face an older life in poverty. (1999: 5)

Next, looking at the discourse of 'choice', which is a key element of the individualization thesis and the connected cultural class approach, we can see that individuals at all stages of the life course are being encouraged to make sense of their life chances through choice. For youth, Roberts (2009) shows that from the 1950s onwards, 'choice' has been a way for young people to understand the transitions they are facing; but the evidence suggests that opportunities remain structured and, crucially, that choice does not significantly impact on outcomes today even in conditions of individualization where more choices are seemingly available (Roberts, 2009). Transitions into the workplace are more complex and uncertain than they used to be and at 16, 18 and 21 young people's destinations more uncertain. Certainly they are obliged to make choices in a way that is unprecedented. But, Roberts concludes: 'there is not a shred of evidence indicating that the overall role of choice in explaining outcomes has expanded' (2009: 365).

Choices are also required at mid-life but many of these relate to maintaining an active lifestyle and staying 'young' literally and metaphorically. That is, to be seen as an enterprising worker is to be youthful in terms of appearance, disposition and skills, and the nature of enterprise does not welcome any qualitative shift in these qualities later in life. Research suggests that, despite the prohibition of age discrimination in employment since 2006, older workers still face obstacles to both gaining a job and progressing in the workplace (Vickerstaff, 2010). Moreover, the old image of capitalists as vampiric retains continued significance in the context of the prevailing 'youthful' norms according to Riach and Kelly (2013) who note that in the field of labour 'the individual must be able to regenerate themselves in order to stay "relevant"' (p. 10). They go on:

> The image that is synonymous with an older worker may embody what
> organizations are continually trying to avoid: the old, worn-out, out-of-
> date, unfit parts of an organization that need to be replaced or hidden in
> some way. (p. 8)

Noting the encouragement of therapeutic breaks such as sabbaticals to make burn-
out and its redress the responsibility of individual employees, they conclude:

> The problem lies... in the denial of mortality that persists through these
> organizational strategies, brands and policies. As workers are increas-
> ingly encouraged to buy into a vampiric organizational discourse of
> regeneration, the possibility for any acknowledgement of the ageing and
> mortal body is negated or denied. Instead, workers can either be useful
> (and so youthful) vampiric accomplices, or old, depleted and potentially
> disposable mortal resources. (p. 10)

This approach, whilst crystallized at mid-life, impacts on all ages, shortening the
working life of employees at both ends and admitting for no real qualitative distinction in terms of experience where qualities such as 'maturity, security and experience'
are valued little if at all and where the accent instead is on 'flexibility, adaptability
and energy', associated with the younger worker (Riach and Kelly, 2013: 12). The
emphasis is on an ageless productivity that has lost all notion of age-related expectations in terms of stage or career trajectory, as was once embodied in the older
apprenticeship model as well as public sector age-related salary scales.

  Turning to old age, Chris Gilleard and Paul Higgs (2000) and Formosa and Higgs
(2013), among others, argue that in late modernity for the first time the later period
of life, post (first) retirement, is likely to be just as constitutive of class position as
the work-oriented adult stretch that precedes it. This occurs largely through cultural,
rather than structural, processes, centred on consumerism. Gilleard and Higgs
(2000) see in late modernity a much more self-determined and agentic period of later
life associated with a new socio-material context devoid of the previous material
need and involving the ending of institutionalized retirement. This underpins the
'division' of old age into a more aspirational third age and the residue that is the
fourth age, with self-determination, not determinism, underpinning both in terms
of self-care, lifestyle choices or their failures. Higgs and Gilleard (2005) emphasize
that there is no straightforward translation from occupation or lifestyle situation
earlier in the life course and position in old age because of the centrality of such
choice and because, relatedly, there are advantages and also risks involved in the
de-institutionalization of old age (Higgs and Gilleard, 2006). (That is: both governments and employers have withdrawn from taking 'responsibility' for older people
after retirement with occupational and other private pensions necessary as individuals take responsibility for their own wellbeing). In the US this risk element has been

particularly developed, even for high-income employees, with the introduction in 1978 of the so-called 401(k) pension plans which, in common with the general trend for employers to shift from a direct benefit (DB) to direct contribution (DC) scheme, transfers responsibility and risk for retirement income to employees. Best results require a complex knowledge of financial markets and investment approaches and illustrate the need for financial literacy that is beyond the reach of many, if not most, employees. Indeed, individualization of risk certainly has an effect on people's fortunes after retirement. Research found that people entered the low-income threshold (as defined by Age UK's research of less than £293 per week for a couple, or less than £197 for a single person before housing costs, on 2010–11 figures) for the first time on retirement for one or more of the following reasons: never having made pension savings other than the state pension; stopping work; having worked in an intermediate occupation such as a skilled trade, administration or sales; becoming single (Norton and West, 2014).

In addition to this new personal risk, in practice, certain key choices may be more structured than they appear and the overwhelming evidence suggests that attitudes towards retirement and experience after retirement, including not only income but also health status and leisure, are all highly structured by class and to a lesser extent gender. Vickerstaff and Cox's (2005) research suggests that the 'individualized' retirement trajectories that are in evidence today do not imply greater individual choice for many people but rather relate to contingent factors: not only the resources the individual has built up during their working lives, but also wider conditions in the economy together with the employer's very particular, local policies. They are, then, really 'risk' trajectories. This, they suggest, has parallels with young people's transition to independence: they no longer make 'cohort related "mass transitions" into work at given ages' (2005: 80) but the outcomes remain as structured by class origins as ever. The same is true for transitions into retirement and Guillemard (1997) suggests that, more generally, these experiences relate to 'the decline of age-based criteria as markers of the life course' (1997: 454; quoted in Vickerstaff and Cox, 2005). Ultimately, the benefits of 'de-institutionalization' of the life course, including retirement, were enjoyed by the middle-class respondents in their study and for the others 'the form that structured individualization took... was less to increase the majority of people's range of alternatives and choices over when and how to retire and more to enlarge the range of risks they had to cope with' (2005: 92). We might go further to suggest that here the third and fourth ages function like two separate classes, whose delineation from each other is the result of ongoing boundary work (Skeggs, 2004). It is here that the visceral attitudes towards the norms of the fourth age – disgust, fear and loathing among them – echo the middle-class approach to the working class, especially where the divisions are in some cases particularly finely drawn and relational (Skeggs, 2004). That is, the third age only exists in relation to the fourth; similarly the fourth age, though in some aspects similar to the earlier institutional old age, or real old age, is an entirely different experience in a society wherein it is the minority, as opposed to the majority, experience. The same is true, of course, of poverty in a society of abundance like today's (Seabrook, 2013); the result is exclusion, reduced personhood and partial citizenship, as well as shame and (self) loathing.

Juxtaposing age and class can help to remind us that both systems serve the purpose of keeping the Hag at a distance from those with power and status. In many ways the current neoliberal regime has more in common with the first industrial revolution than with the mid-century 'welfare' or 'social' regime, and according to Campbell (2013), the smokestacks and the bonus respectively sum up these regimes, the purpose of both being to 'broadcast hierarchies and the *necessity* of inequality' (2013: 9; original emphasis) with an ideology of 'natural talent' and 'superior abilities' to justify it (Johnson, 2013) enabling this new upper class to project human vulnerabilities onto the poor and old.

(iii) How do age, gender and class intersect to produce complex forms of inequality throughout the life course?

This theme emphasizes the importance of age in shaping, as well as being shaped by, multiple other inequalities, especially gender and class. It focuses upon a system of 'age relations' (Calasanti and Slevin, 2001) with three key dimensions centred more upon inequality than difference. These comprise the way that: (i) age serves a social organizing principle; (ii) different age groups gain identities and power in relation to one another; and (iii) age relations intersect with other power relations. Together these aspects of age relations have consequences for life chances across the life course. It enables us to understand 'how all of our positions and experiences rest on power relations based on age' (Calasanti and Slevin, 2006: 5).

This framework particularly illuminates how the gender regime works through age and class. In education, as noted, there is a gender differential whereby over all classes and ethnicities, girls outperform boys by nearly 10 per cent (Francis, 2010) at all stages of National Curriculum assessments, GCSEs and A-levels. Girls have indeed become hypervisible in both policy and lay discourses for 'outperforming' boys in terms of exam results leading to a new conceptualization of their place in society, a 'revolution' almost as great as that which led to the construction of the category of youth in the first place. Although, as we already discussed, such a perception conceals a great deal of class stratification, nevertheless this has enabled the construction of the 'Girl' as a shorthand term for conscientious self-mobilization and social mobility. McRobbie sees such young women as being positioned, through such discourses, as 'ideal subjects of female success, exemplars of the new competitive meritocracy' (2013: 718) and their skills are also ones that are valued in the labour market for what she calls 'willingness, motivation and aptitude' (2013: 728).

BOX 2.1

The Girl

Social theorists have recognized young women – often referred to as the Girl – in education and the earlier years of their working lives as 'standard bearers' for the new economy through their achievements, consumption (including personal grooming) and work ethic. They thus both stand for, and enable the shift from, one form of work economy to another.

But this valorization of the Girl can only be truly understood in the context of the shift in employment from the production of the industrial mode to a flexibilized service sector where what had traditionally been 'women's styles' of employment is extended to other groups and welcomed by employers seeking to transfer risk. This also gives older women workers, configured as the 'flexible female', an advantage over older, male workers insofar as they are more useful for 'poorer working conditions, lower rates of pay and lower status jobs' (Moore, 2009: 658). They are also considered more docile – reliable, punctual and so on – than younger women.

But this is directly linked to class and gender inequality over the whole life course. Approximately six million women are part-time workers and they earn £5.15 less an hour than full-time men whilst two in five part-time women earn less than the living wage (TUC, 2014). Meanwhile, and directly shaping the latter gender pay gap, women spend three times longer on domestic duties than men and for those with children, not only does women's input far exceed men's but also women working both part- and full-time in the UK and the US spend longer on childcare than did women during the 1950s (Campbell, 2013). Whilst gender differences in domestic and care duties increase over the life course, it is in retirement that the full cost of gender-unequal practices is evident: in the UK 13 per cent of women qualify for the full basic state pension compared with 92 per cent of men, reflecting life course differences, and exacerbating the feminization of poverty (Thane, 2006); similarly, in the US, women are likely to be twice as poor as men (Estes, 2001). We have already noted the importance of class-based health inequalities but gender is another vehicle of inequality, with health worse for old women as compared with old men within each social class (Arber and Cooper, 2000). The continuance of, and indeed dependence on, this gender differential in the socio-economic system has led to various ways of characterizing it, such as 'neopatriarchal neoliberalism' (Campbell, 2013) and 'a historically specific androcentric form of state-organized capitalist society' (Fraser, 2009: 104) though in fact neither takes account of the key role that age plays in this system.

As far as men are concerned, and again fundamentally linked to the shift in employment norms and the loss of most traditional working-class jobs in industry, the hegemonic masculinity associated with working-class status in youth in particular works to exacerbate class inequalities underpinning working-class boys' (white and black especially) educational underperformance. However, middle-class men in high-status City finance are able to use hegemonic norms to enhance their capital at work up to mid or late middle age. In a study of City traders in the upper age bracket for this profession (40s and 50s), lifestyle was used to demonstrate continued fitness for purpose in terms of the male hegemonic values espoused by the working environment. Rather than a decrement in value with time, the body 'battle hardened' through disciplined and punishing fitness regimes underlines the traders' possessions of an 'accumulative body display[ing] embodied capital, accrued over time, as people move through fields of exchange' (Riach and Cutcher, 2014: 775). Indeed, these workers continued to embody 'the hypermasculinized ideal of the City' through fitness regimes that portrayed professional qualities – vigour, tenacity, resolve, strength – all clearly producing what the authors call a body 'built to last' (p. 783). Of course, this approach also has a time limit, and although all traders were planning to retire by age 55, this decision was influenced by the knowledge that this was also the upper age limit for their age-defying strategies to be effective.

Conclusion

This chapter has demonstrated that the age system functions fundamentally like a class system, dividing people and groups and introducing inequalities that work with class inequalities in very particular ways through the life course. For this reason, analysis of the age system illuminates the working of the class system and vice versa. Indeed, age enables class-based inequalities to work materially, and ubiquitously, whilst all but obscured beneath the ideology of age differences. In youth, 'choice' is structured and outcomes of choice reveal not individual failings but often invisible structural barriers to success (invisible to individuals themselves). In mid-life and beyond, inequalities of health, wealth, housing and status that accumulate through, and are productive of, multiple disadvantages over many years are often blamed on age alone. In particular, Gullette suggests that mid-life is an 'ideological crux' of the age system, which she defines as a nodal point, when 'subjects must obey or the system fails' (1997: 12). Although this works differently for men and women, with different ideologies applying to both, ultimately class introduces greater inequality than sex.

In a poignant discussion of the myth of the individualized society, Roberts observes that people, including members of the now 'excluded class' of the working class, blame themselves and hope only that their children or grandchildren will benefit from the increased opportunities on offer – higher education, cheap loans, and the bright promise of meritocracy; young people similarly aspire to join the system, rather than overturn it, as once they dreamed (Deresiewicz, 2014). Class politics has been replaced by attempts to join the middle class, which has absorbed what would have been working-class leaders, whilst the Labour Party has remodelled itself as the 'party of aspiration' in a discourse of consumerism, identity politics and individual talent and hard work. Women's full-scale involvement in the labour economy has resulted in a rhetoric celebrating the full attainment of gender equality thereby under-mining feminism's older political aims, including change to the mode of capitalism and its reliance on women's unpaid domestic labour. In these conditions, 'politics' Roberts reflects ruefully, 'has nothing more to offer' (2011: 232) the working class; politics, indeed, is nothing other than the market. But the class system works through the age system and by deconstructing the latter the hope is that we may contribute towards pricking the mythology that is a necessary part of the former.

CHAPTER SUMMARY

- In this chapter we explored the parallels between class and age as systems of stratification.

- We can 'see' age differently if we see it as having structural, material and cultural aspects linked to inequality.

- We looked at various theoretical approaches to class-based stratification and explored how well they illuminated age stratification.

- We looked at how different ages are drawn into the class system and inequalities imprinted with the stamp of age.

- We also looked at how the age and gender regimes intersect with class in ways that intricately and persuasively naturalize both age and class ideology.

Further questions

1. What role do the main theories of class give to age and ageing?

2. How useful is it to think of age grading as akin to the class structure?

3. How do the binary discourses of deserving/undeserving poor and good/bad ageing through history serve to justify inequality?

Talking point

Lawler (2005) draws attention to the symbolic realm in demonstrating how the working class is 'othered' in the dominant class-ideological representa-tions by means of a number of techniques including: (i) their association with their bodies; (ii) their depiction in terms of 'lack' (in both material resources and taste); (iii) images associating them with decline (they were once 'noble'

salt-of-the-earth who have degenerated into foul-mouthed chavs; (iv) their feminization, applying especially to unemployed working-class men, as well as
retired older men; (v) their association with feelings of horror and disgust. Can
you trace a similar process in terms of boundary-setting with older people?

—— **Key texts** ——

The major class approaches and their link with age are captured in some of the
following. On **class generally** see Roberts, K. (2011) *Class in Contemporary Britain*
(second edition), Basingstoke: Palgrave Macmillan; on **individualization and risk** see
Beck, U. and Beck-Gernsheim, E. (2002) *Individualization: institutionalized individualism and its social and political consequences*, London: Sage; on **cultural class**
see Bourdieu, P. (1984) *Distinction*, London: Routledge, Kegan and Paul; on **the
link between class and gender** see Walby, S. (1990) *Theorizing Patriarchy*, Oxford:
Blackwell; on **class, age, gender and race**, see Bradley, H. (1996) *Fragmented Identities:
changing patterns of inequality*, Cambridge: Polity; Calasanti, T.M. and Slevin, K.F.
(eds) (2006) *Age Matters: realigning feminist thinking*, London: Routledge; on
class in childhood see Hendrick, H. (2003) *Child Welfare: historical dimensions,
contemporary debates*, Bristol: Policy Press; Ridge, T. (2002) *Childhood Poverty
and Social Exclusion: from a child's perspective*, Bristol: Policy Press; for **class in
youth** see Furlong, A. and Cartmel, F. (1997) *Young People and Social Change*,
Milton Keynes: Open University Press; for **class in later life** see Phillipson, C. (1982)
Capitalism and the Construction of Old Age, London: Macmillan; Minkler, M.
and Estes, C.L. (eds) (1998) *Critical Gerontology: perspectives from political and
moral economy*, New York: Baywood; Formosa, M. and Higgs, P. (2013) *Social
Class in Later Life: power, identity and lifestyle*, Bristol: Policy Press. Although we
are not going into detail about **race** in this book, the following books are recommended for those who wish to read further: Anthias, F. and Yuval-Davis, N. (1993)
Racialized Boundaries, London: Routledge; Blakemore, K. and Boneham, M.C.
(1994) *Age, Race and Ethnicity*, Milton Keynes: Open University Press; Mac an
Ghaill, M. (1988) *Young, Gifted and Black*, Milton Keynes: Open University Press.

Further resources

The Trades Union Congress (https://www.tuc.org.uk/) has plentiful up-to-date information
on age equality and gender equality issues in employment.

The International Labour Organization (http://www.ilo.org/global/publications/lang--en/
index.htm) has research reports on a range of issues regarding employment, including how
they affect a range of age groups globally.

The Joseph Rowntree Foundation (http://www.jrf.org.uk/) is a site dedicated to research on issues of poverty and social inequality.

The impact of inequality on health is the subject of a blog from the Faculty of Public Health available at http://betterhealthforall.org/about-fph/

Notes

1. Indeed, Seabrook (2013) suggests that the glamour that surrounds the new super-rich is semi-mystical in nature, calling into question the secular nature of western society; the old religious virtues – poverty, frugality and so on – have similarly transformed into signs of failure. See also Norman Brown's Freudian view of this.

2. This experience is also found in the US among other countries.

3. Despite local differences, across European and other Western countries such as the US and Canada, mid-life professional men enjoy stable careers but young people, old people and women in mid-life have had to endure sometimes quite radical changes.

3
GENDER STUDIES AS A PARADIGM FOR AGE STUDIES

Background: the old body as outside culture

In the last chapter we suggested that the first step towards challenging the age system is to see it as a socially constructed system of stratification, with ideological and material aspects and with parallels to, and interconnections with, social class. Indeed, we suggested that age ideology is able to naturalize other forms of social stratification through positing age as something natural and inevitable. However, because there is likely to be considerable resistance (both at an individual and social level) to seeing age as *other* than natural, biologically determined and therefore incontestable, in this chapter I will suggest the use of some further analytic tools sufficiently powerful to meet this challenge. These will be drawn from feminist epistemology which has successfully deconstructed the assumptions of the gender order and whose tools, applied to the ageing body, are thus likely to prove equally adroit in terms of the age order.

The important connection between patriarchy and ageism seems to have been repeatedly recognized by key feminists, especially as they themselves moved through the life course. Simone de Beauvoir, Betty Friedan, Germaine Greer, Eva Figes and latterly Lynn Segal, among others, all turned their attention to later life, seeing many similarities between the experience of being female and being old. Indeed, this chapter will demonstrate how and why feminist-theoretical approaches can provide a paradigm which age studies may usefully employ in combating age ideology. In this chapter we focus particularly on the old body – including the oldest old – not because there is something exceptional about it, but because as a signifier it seems so unassailably to indicate the limits of discursivity, and to present us with the bald facts of materiality that close in on us all, eventually signifying the limits of discourse itself. If we can challenge the 'natural' quality of the oldest old bodies, logic suggests, then we can do so for all bodies, no matter what their age.

AIMS OF THE CHAPTER

- We focus on two key concepts associated with feminist epistemology and after explaining how they were originally used to 'deconstruct' the female body we consider how they can be applied to the older body similarly.

- These concepts are:

    (i)   The distinction between sex and gender, a seemingly basic but absolutely crucial manoeuvre in peeling back the patina of ideology to see how it transformed 'a physical fact... into a category of thought' (Delphy, 1984, quoted in Howson, 2005: 57).

    (ii) The 'body as situation': as developed by Simone de Beauvoir, this concept asserts the intrinsically social nature of the biological body. In *The Second Sex* Beauvoir presents a detailed existential account of the experience of female embodiment in all its different aspects within patriarchal society which further enriches the sex/gender binary analytically by demonstrating that both categories are inseparable in lived reality.

- We turn next to the use of particular tools in analysing how femininity is performed in embodied terms. These are the concepts of

    (i)   'womanliness as masquerade'; and

    (ii) the 'male gaze' and we consider how both can be applied, in a parallel fashion, to understanding the way the older body is similarly enfolded in ideological wrappings which claim to depict its essential nature.

- We then discuss the arguments for not just deconstructing gender but also moving beyond it altogether.

- Finally, we explore how the gender regime and the age regime are linked structurally and what lessons we may take from this.

Concepts and methods from the feminist toolbox

Concept 1: Sex/gender distinction

The distinction between sex and gender detaches biological and physiological differences associated with women and men from the social roles accorded them and also from the subjectivities and psychologies associated with social roles. Pioneering feminist scholarship (Oakley, 1972), building on early work on sex roles by Stoller (1968) and others, distinguished between *sex*, referring to the pre-social raw material, the natural, physiological 'given', and *gender*, signifying the normative roles per-formed by bearers of particular sex characteristics. This distinction then made possible a critique of the sexual division of labour, and more broadly, instated through these roles. Subsequent historical evidence further demonstrated how this strict body-based binary classification emerged during a distinctive phase in moder-nity, in which the new practices of pathology and anatomy, interlinked with broader social changes, underpinned the practice of highlighting *difference* between bodies (Laqueur, 1990). In this, the male body was taken as a standard from which the female body deviated: a move of particular utility for patriarchy at a time when women's legal, political and social rights were being circumscribed. A long period followed in which biology continued to be used in arguments regarding women's 'natural' (that is, inferior) position in society (see Showalter, 1997; Lock, 1993; Martin, 1987).

Judith Butler (1993, 1990) influentially attacked the 'material realities' of biology from a more critical angle, through extending understanding of the nuanced interplay between sex and gender. She explained this interplay in terms of the 'sedimentation of gender norms' that 'produces the peculiar phenomenon of a "natural sex"... which, in reified form, appears as the natural configuration of bodies into sexes exist-ing in a binary relation to one another' (1990: 191). This identity, she argued, is not stable but must be constituted and reconstituted 'through stylized repetition of acts' (1990: 191). In other words, sex is as constructed as gender. As historical research had done for the original sex/gender delineation, feminist research in biology has subsequently supplied empirical evidence to this aspect of Butler's thesis, suggesting that 'mattering' of the body through performativity has 'real' consequences biologi-cally with social context key to, for example, the development of the brain's structure leading to subsequent gendered differences in cognition not present in very young children (Fausto-Sterling, 2003).

Applying the sex/gender distinction to the older body

Let us look next at how awareness of the separate concepts of role and physiology help us to unwrap the layers and levels of meaning contained within the experience and perceptions of old age today. In particular, we will consider how attitudes towards the physiology of the older body have provided justifications for a limited social role.

Cumming and Henry (1961), who were the first to construct a theory around the social role of old age, emphasized a mutual 'natural' disengagement on the part of older people and society, based on the inevitable decline associated with old age and serving to ensure the 'proper' functionality of society (see Lynott and Lynott, 1996). Later theoretical developments, such as the political economy approach, in criticiz-ing society's approach to old people in terms of its constructing old age in a state of dependency (through compulsory retirement and low state pensions) then blam-ing the old for this, nevertheless inadvertently emphasized in their critiques the 'weaknesses, vulnerabilities and frailties' of older people (Gilleard and Higgs, 2000: 14). This, at least implicit, assumption of feebleness and physical weakness remains the default position among sociologists (with the exception of critical gerontologists). Biological capital is assumed to be incontestably depleted in old age as in the following statement by Wainwright and Turner: 'Our stock of physical capital is transient: it grows and then declines with age' (2006: 242) (although their own study shows that this is almost entirely relational to the field, where ballet dancers may feel themselves ageing in their twenties and be considered 'too old' before they reach the age of thirty). The biomedical body is also the body that appears in medical sociology's discussions of health in old age. So, for example, Bury and Wadsworth state that many health problems are strongly associated with biological age and of these 'the very old emerged as the most affected by disability' (Bury and Wadsworth, 2003: 116). Health problems, they note, are removed from society and culture, constituting as much a feature of the 'biological clock' as are growth spurts earlier on. What is striking is that, where in earlier phases of the life course they describe 'the dynamic character of the developmental processes at work' (p. 112) identifying social context as key, for example, to prenatal development, they at least partially withdraw this possibility from older bodies, reverting to a view of them as succumbing to 'nature'.

However, it is more interesting to take these manifestations, and expectations, of decline as the object of scrutiny in itself: that is, to explore whether, to paraphrase Judith Butler's work on gender, a 'sedimentation of age norms produces the peculiar phenomenon of a naturally aged body or a "real old person"'; and whether 'this is a sedimentation that over time has produced a set of corporeal styles which, in reified form, appear as the natural configuration of bodies into age' (see Butler 1990: 191). After all, this is what Connell has to say about the role of internalization and fantasy in confirming masculinity's greater power at the physiological level:

> The social definition of men as holders of power is translated not only into mental body-images and fantasies but into muscle tensions, postures, the feel and texture of the body. This is one of the main ways in which the power of men becomes 'naturalized', i.e. seen as part of the order of nature. (Connell, 1987: 85)

The parallel in older people's marginalization from social power and the frail 'nature' of their bodies seems self-evident. Likewise, Bourdieu sees women's subordinate social position mirrored in a physical demeanour indicative of a performed inferiority. Drawing on his early ethnographic fieldwork amongst the Kabyle he observed:

> Female submissiveness seems to find a natural translation in bending, stooping, lowering oneself, 'submitting' – curved and supple postures and the associated docility being seen as appropriate to women. (2001: 27)

The striking resonance between this image and the stereotypical posture associated with kyphosis in old age should at least give us pause before we accept it as 'natural', attributable to osteoporosis, or muscle wastage, but not to embodied social inferiority, nor, for that matter, to subtle resistance to productive norms – presenting oneself strategically as enfeebled – in a way that mirrors symbolic representations of old age (Hockey and James, 1993). Whilst certainly 'real' bodies yield to 'real' time-related changes, attributing these changes one-dimensionally to biological factors is to acquiesce in an individualization and privatization of lifelong social insults as well as the particular hierarchies that infuse both representations of old age and social relationships, which is the essence of biopower. In addition, the feminization of older men's bodies signals not just a series of observable physical or hormonal changes but also a social marginalization that works through the highlighting of difference (Laqueur, 1990). Moreover, the notion that, for example, slowing gait is a *deleterious* change may not be such a doxic assumption, to use a Bourdieusian term, in other cultures which do not possess our modernist intent to control the environment and master both ourselves and the world in pursuit of competitive achievement (Yalom, 1980).

The distinction between *chronological* and *biological* age, increasingly made in biogerontology and geriatric medicine, and underpinning the distinction between the third and fourth ages, offers an opportunity to distinguish the materiality of the body and its meaning in a way that parallels the sex/gender distinction. However, care is needed here as this separation has its origin in biological and biomedical discourses and as such involves the equation of youth with health in a way that naturalizes age ideology. We can see this more clearly if we trace this distinction to its nineteenth-century origins and the birth of patho-anatomical techniques, which enabled physicians to identify the physiological characteristics of older bodies that separated them from younger people. These characteristics designated old bodies physiologically as a 'normal abnormal' which rendered them vulnerable and requiring expert scrutiny (Katz, 1996). More recent medical approaches have stressed: (i) a continuity of physiological norms across the life course, thereby transforming the 'normal abnormal' into the 'pathological' for those older people who deviate from them and cannot remain *biologically* 'young' (Rowe and Kahn, 1987); (ii) their theoretical treatability (and indeed preventability) combined with appropriate self-care and lifestyle choices designed to preserve mid-life norms. Bodies which exhibit physiological continuity with the norms of middle-aged bodies belong to a 'third age'; they are chronologically old but physiologically youthful. *Real* old age, meanwhile, is the unhealthy fourth age, cut adrift from youthful norms, dependent and 'at risk' and constituting the core patient group of geriatricians. We can also see the binary alternatively, in the third age representing the 'masculine' ideal comprising a body amenable to the autonomous, rational will, where health and ageing are a 'choice'. The fourth age, by contrast, like a garden gone to seed, is returned to Mother Nature; like Durkheim's women, it is pre- (or perhaps post-) social.

The concept of the 'body as a situation' offers an alternative and equally helpful approach to this, centred upon the phenomenological experience of the lived body. We turn to this next.

Concept 2: Simone de Beauvoir: 'the body is a situation'

The 'body as situation', derived from the work of Simone de Beauvoir, is a model for explaining how the 'reality' of the body is experienced entirely within the terms of one's culture and society. It is particularly helpful in allowing us to work with elements of both structure and agency (Moi, 1995). This is because there is no 'bottom layer' of corporeal reality upon which social mores are added, as the two-levelled concept of sex–gender implies, but the two are inextricably fused. That is, in Beauvoir's approach the body: (i) is always already a social body; and (ii) is demonstrated to be such in the most intimate and personal, as well as the most public and formal, of all its experiences.

In powerful passages throughout Beauvoir's *The Second Sex* and *The Coming of Age* the body-as-situation concept perfectly captures the experience of: (i) being a woman in an unabashedly sexist society (*The Second Sex* was written in 1949); and (b) being an older woman in a sexist and ageist society (*The Coming of Age* was written in 1970). Let us consider the former text first (which also, briefly, discusses the older woman). *The Second Sex* offers a tutorial on the effects of the ideology of femininity at its most powerfully hegemonic on a woman's experience of embodiment. Primarily, the effect of such ideology means that it is all but impossible to be both a 'woman' and a 'person' (in the sense of self-actualizing adult citizen) leading to a woman's 'profound' alienation from her body and in particular from those 'feminine' functions of her body as experienced during procreation, birth or motherhood. Thus, youth is marked by the experience of 'strange and bothersome breasts', painful menstruation, 'headaches, over-fatigue, abdominal pains' (1997: 353) associated with the menstrual cycle. During pregnancy the woman is 'ensnared by nature... an incubator... who has become life's passive instrument' (p. 512–13); 'she becomes in part another than herself'. Finally, in old age she is 'suddenly deprived of her femininity... the fertility which, in the view of society and in her own, provides the justification of her existence and her opportunity for happiness' (p. 587). Whilst this analysis serves as an important corrective to the hegemonic notion that youth is good, and that all things about 'being young' are positive, Beauvoir demonstrates that there are mixed fortunes for the old woman. On the one hand, she is restored to herself following menopause, when 'she is herself, she and her body are one' (1997: 63); on the other, this comes at a high price: the woman's death as a woman, that is, the death of her femininity and sexuality. It is, then, precisely the moment she stops struggling against this social death and accepts it that she becomes 'complete' – not alienated – that is 'an old woman', where reconciliation of body-self requires acceptance of her new (diminished) status. Thus, our subjectivities, embodied self-identities and experience of our bodies are shaped and moulded by our experience of being a 'woman' or an 'old woman' within the context of such ideology.

We experience ourselves, and others relate to us, in the mode that society constitutes us such that there is no doubt about the reality of such attributes: they are social facts.

The analytically empowering notion of body-as-situation lies in two aspects represented by the combination of facticity and freedom in existential theory. 'Facticity' comprises a woman's tangible physicality – her periods, her breasts, her skin colour and muscle strength, together with social context, including an enframing patriarchy and age ideology. However, regardless of facticity, an individual always has ontological freedom, although the sphere of this freedom may be compromised. Thus Beauvoir certainly feels that women's reproductive role imparts to her particular phenomenological obstacles but at the same time she asserts: 'I deny that [the biological facts] establish for her a fixed and inevitable destiny. They are insufficient for setting up a hierarchy of the sexes; they fail to explain why woman is the Other; they do not condemn her to remain in this subordinate role for ever' (Beauvoir, 1997: 65). For an explanation of this we must turn to history: women's central role in reproduction over long centuries without either reliable contraception or alternatives to breastfeeding led men into making social arrangements that gave them more developed public roles, accompanied by an ideology that emphasized its naturalness (MacInnes, 1998). This is what Bourdieu means when he talks about the need to search for the 'incessant labour of reproduction' of the structures of male dominance. The division of labour established through woman's reproductive biology links further to the concepts of immanence and transcendence. In Beauvoir, immanence refers to the object-like thing-in-itself, the inertness of materiality, as well as bad faith and unconscious existence. Transcendence, by contrast, signifies the 'for itself', the state of fully self-aware human existence and freedom associated with 'subjectivity, autonomy and creativity' (Young, 2005: 31). This sets up a problem for the female subject, more so than for the male, specifically in the form of a tension between freedom and its lack. But social facts can be replaced by other social facts. Thus, Beauvoir notes that whilst women's bodies will always be subject to certain embodied physiological events, they need not experience them negatively or as restrictive of freedom. The woman will continue to bleed, have pregnancies, and so on. But a physiological event is first and foremost a *social* event. Social discourses and practices determine whether a woman's physiological events will work to restrict her opportunities to be a person or not; freely available contraception, abortion, cheap and good childcare facilities, codes of equal parenting and so on will all make a difference to this.

Clearly, the same holds true for older bodies. Ageing-as-decline is a social fact; in existential terms, a facticity. But our ontological freedom means that we have some power to shift this, in ways however tiny and restricted (and Beauvoir certainly indicates that class serves to constrain freedom with as much force as gender), quite apart from anti-ageing medicine. We can, for example, develop a different age consciousness and see our ageing embodiment and our older selves differently as well as put these ideas into general circulation to inform others. This can, for example, involve challenging the use of metaphors such as decline, degeneration, feeble, enervated and weak, employed both in lay or clinical discourses, to describe the ageing body.

However, in Beauvoir's opinion, for age to be a stage of life not thus characterized by diminution of power (individual and social), in a way currently enjoyed only by the elite, would require a greater social transformation than that facilitating gender equality. Rather than a shift of gender relations *within* capitalism, she suggests it requires an end to capitalist society altogether. Because of the 'using up' of human beings within the system, like any other tool or commodity, the system does not permit a decent old age for its labouring classes, by definition. However I would suggest that both such optimism (for gender) on the one hand and such pessimism (for age) on the other fail to convince; gender equality cannot be accomplished in isolation as it is part of an overarching structure in which the denigration of the body in general, and of the woman's body and the old body in particular, are inter-linked. We will return to this in the last section.

Firstly, however, I pick out two very specific tools from the feminist toolbox that are consistent with the theoretical frameworks discussed so far. The first one illuminates the performance of femininity through the feminine 'masquerade' and the second explores how this performance is perceived by the gaze of others (with both being fundamentally linked).

Method 1: From the feminine masquerade to youthfulness as masquerade

> We know that gender is a performance because we can see it feigned so well. About age as a performance, we need to start the arguments. (Gullette, 2004: 159)

In the paper by psychoanalyst Joan Riviere originally published in 1929, the feminine masquerade is a gender performance akin to wearing a 'masque' that is intended to distract patriarchal society from the fact that certain professional and other self-actualizing women are subverting traditional gender expectations and becoming more 'masculine', in the sense of moving into masculine terrain. This may serve to reassure both the woman herself that despite her achievements/capacity/intelligence she remains 'feminine' enough to attract the admiration of men, and to reassure men that she presents no 'threat'. The concept of masquerade is not unlike the Goffmanesque focus on performance, wherein the display of expected feminine norms is a key requirement in successful impression management for an adult female. But Riviere, like Judith Butler, goes further in suggesting that there is no 'true' femininity buried beneath the masquerade; that femininity *consists* in such a masquerade (and is thus something that all women, not just the self-consciously masculine, intellectual woman, perform, although perhaps less consciously or reflexively).

Kathleen Woodward has applied this notion to the idea that ageing – specifically the display of youthfulness-in-old-age – is also a performance in the manner of a masquerade. Woodward suggests that it is both a way of concealing and a way of telling the truth, sometimes one, sometimes the other, sometimes a play between both: the 'radical contingency' Butler (1993: 157) refers to in arguing against essences or bodily foundations. (Indeed, we will talk later in this book about how age is performed and where this performance is ironic or subversive, as in 'age as drag'.) McRobbie (2013) identifies a further kind of masquerade as central to the post-feminist regime. The latter has been defined in various ways, including as a new stage in gender equality as well as gender backlash and perhaps most helpfully as the presence of new and old inequalities and possibilities intertwined in a confounding knot. One of the keenest analyses of post-feminism is offered by Rosalind Gill (2007a) who identifies a distinctive 'sensibility', comprising such diverse strands as: (i) self-surveillance and monitoring; (ii) self-discipline; (iii) an emphasis on choice; and (iv) the return of traditional modes of femininity in terms of self-presentation, style, the importance given to domesticity and motherhood, often justified philosophically in terms of a gender essentialism (Catherine Hakim is one proponent of the latter); and (v) an increased importance given to the body and self-presentation. This sensibility is infused with an aggressively jocular irony, mocking in advance objections to the 'raunch culture' as Levy (2005) has termed the brand of old-fashioned sexism currently back in vogue, which in its current manifestation is presented as women being in the driving seat, 'choosing' to be objectified (as self-expression/career move/their own pleasure) and the critic herself the problem, for being humourless/frigid/too old to understand. However, although the post-feminist masquerade is both knowing and ironic about the idea of femininity, a woman employing the masquerade may find that, instead of giving her distance from her femininity, it ensnares and entangles her more deeply in its ideology. In the 'post-feminist masquerade' the woman adopts traditionally feminine modes of behaviour but with a playfully detached style. McRobbie comments:

> This signals that the hyper-femininity of the masquerade which would seemingly re-locate women back inside the terms of traditional gender hierarchies, by having her wear spindly stilettos and 'pencil' skirts does not in fact mean entrapment since it is now a matter of choice rather than obligation. The woman in masquerade is making a point that this is a freely chosen look. (2013: 723)

So far, so good. And yet, if we look more closely, 'the theatricality of the masquerade [is] once again [a] means of emphasizing... female vulnerability, fragility, uncertainty and the little girl's "desire to be desired"' (2013: 725). Thus, before we realize what is going on we find,

> it operates with a double movement, its voluntaristic structure works to conceal that patriarchy is still in place, while the requirements of the fashion and beauty system ensure that women are still fearful subjects, driven by the need for 'complete perfection'. (Riviere, 1929: 42; in McRobbie, 2013: 726)

That it is a sophisticated weapon of the patriarchy (whether or not women choose it voluntarily) is clear in its highly normative dimensions. So, for example, strong social sanctions operate against the older woman who dares assume the feminine masquerade without obvious irony and self-deprecation: Madonna is a very obvious case in point. She causes offence by presenting a hyper-feminine sexualized appearance despite being middle-aged. Indeed, the visceral public reaction she often elicits – embarrassment and disgust – is a clear sign that she has transgressed the boundary between youth and age which is both hegemonic yet shaky in terms of the melding of boundaries that hints at the clearly constructed aspects of the distinction. Although Microsoft's face analysis tool 'How Old Do I Look?' identified the 56-year-old Madonna as 27 (Hunt, 2015) her well-known chronological age is more important to the youthful male gaze savagely upholding this distinction, and with it, this hegemony.

Method 2: From the male gaze to the age gaze

Since a key paper by Laura Mulvey (1975) deconstructed the screen gaze of cinema and identified the perspective that we are encouraged to collude with whilst watching a movie, as in life, as the 'male gaze', we have been aware that what we consider our spontaneous aesthetic or other assessments or judgements are nothing of the kind. They are indeed deeply ideological, hierarchically structured and view women from the male, objectifying perspective. Woman on screen, she notes, is the 'bearer of meaning, not maker of meaning' as she is in the gaze in life; the audience, regardless of their actual gender, assume the point of view of the male character as they gaze upon the female character. The viewer's power is dependent on her *lack* of power; his centrality and agency is dependent on her holding a passive role in the mise-en-scène of life itself. This is a male gaze that extends beyond cinematic contexts to all social situations, having its origin in social representations of women and the ideology of femininity stemming from the eighteenth and nineteenth centuries, in which women 'were cast as the inscrutable Other, as agents of the incapacities that beset us all' (Poovey, 1984: 5). Berger's (1972) analysis of this has become justifiably well known, in its pithy and lucid phenomenological description, and is still highly relevant. See Box 3.1 below for a summary.

BOX 3.1

John Berger on the male gaze

The social presence of a woman is different in kind from that of a man. A man's presence suggests what he is capable of doing to you or for you.... By contrast, a woman's presence expresses her own attitude to herself, and defines what can and cannot be done to her... To be born a woman has been to be born, within an allotted and confined space, into the keeping of men. The social presence of women has developed as a result of their ingenuity in living under such tutelage within such a limited space. But this has been at the cost of a woman's self being split in two. A woman must continually watch herself. She is almost continually accompanied by her own image of herself... And so she comes to consider the surveyor and the surveyed within her as the two constituent yet always distinct elements of her identity as a woman. (Berger, 1972: 46)

Woodward (2006) builds on this concept to show that, no matter our own age, we view older people though a youthful gaze. Just as female spectators at a movie theatre assume the male gaze, so 'in general we cast ourselves as younger in relation to the old person we see on the screen or in a photograph' something she labels 'the youthful structure of the look' (2006: 164). The ageist look, moreover, precedes even the male gaze: the person is old first, male or female second. Indeed, the youthful gaze construes embodiment in old age not only as functionally problematic but also as aesthetically offensive. In her ethnography of older people receiving bathing care, Julia Twigg's homecare-workers 'couldn't stop staring' at older people's 'weird' bodies; on their part older people felt themselves to be 'ugly lumps' (2000: 155) compared to the 'young and beautiful' care assistants. This has consequences beyond that of surface appearance: in matters of bodily performativity, function and health, viewing older bodies 'through the eyes of the youthful structure of the look' (Woodward, 2006: 167) normatively determines the distinction between 'positive' and 'negative' changes. This, then, explains the need for masquerade, being a performance staged for the real or imagined gaze of a spectator at the prime of life.

As we will see in subsequent chapters, the combined male and age gaze – the hegemonic gaze – is internalized by women throughout the life course, serving to objectify their own bodies and judge their appearance and sexuality through the male/youthful gaze within, giving them a double disadvantage. This suggests the contortions that women have to undergo to be judged properly feminine/youthful. (Hybrid gender patterns make this even more complex, as we see later in the chapter.) By contrast, whether masculinity is defined in opposition to femininity, or vice versa, ultimately its key strength lies in the fact that the 'self' behind both gazes is masculine and its default position is therefore as subject not object, as owner of the gaze, not primarily its target.

From deconstructing gender to the end of gender

Recognition that gender is a social construction or performance has led to suggestions that only an end to gender altogether as a classificatory practice in institutions, practices, everyday assumptions and, eventually, the psyche itself, can end gendered inequality. Judith Lorber is particularly associated with this approach; we consider next her arguments both concerning its significance as an aim together with how it might take place. Firstly, she suggests that degendering is potentially valuable because the idea that gender divisions are 'natural', whilst never entirely fading into oblivion, has in fact acquired renewed scientific legitimacy involving genetic, hormonal and other physiological explanations and provides 'the very structure of women's inequality' (2000: 82). A second consequence is not, however, the end of sexual difference but rather the end of a particular hierarchical organization of sexual difference. Gendered characteristics are misrecognized as attributes of differently sexed bodies, and serve as fetishes, whilst not in any case corresponding to empirical reality (MacInnes, 1998). Furthermore if we, as individuals, wish to lay claim to the full range of characteristics that relate to nurturance, relationality, affect as well as those characteristics associated with the rational world, we need to degenderize them. This will liberate the true heterogeneity of individual (non-gender-specific) differences, which are in any case arrayed along a continuum, not split by a dividing line, and which are cross-cut by other ascribed and personal characteristics that add complexity in a way that the binary does not admit. What forms of femininity and masculinity will arise thereafter is an open question.

However, in more immediate and pragmatic terms there are some dangers, and these directly relate to the historical fact that gender equality and the needs of global capitalism have become aligned. The market's gender blindness, which is perhaps a more accurate description of its approach than gender equality, means that women's other, private roles in the home and family are overlooked, leading to equality in the public domain co-existing with social inequality, and hampering women's performance in both spheres (Eisenstein, 2005). The end of gender as an ideal should, then, be tempered by the considerations of the situated body as a lived reality within a particular social context. This will involve different but equally complex challenges for women across the life course.

Turning now to the parallel, but different, case of age, the end of age hierarchy were it possible would certainly not imply *agelessness*. Andrews (1999) suggests that this latter is a form of false consciousness, an acquiescence in an ageist culture that denies any value to experience, saying, as with Lord Henry Wotton to Dorian Gray, 'youth is the only thing worth having'. Certainly, as Beauvoir, Friedan and others have pointed out, to reject association with a 'spoiled identity' – to deny one is 'old' in the terms society sees being old – may be a necessary, if provisional, form of resistance for many. Indeed, if we apply these insights to the ethnographic data gathered by Kaufman (1986) and Thompson et al. (1991) in which older participants all claimed to be 'young' or 'ageless' we can see that what the respondents are laying claim to is a self that does not diminish with old age. So for example, Thompson et al. state:

> Few if any of our interviewees actually fit the stereotypes of old people as being passive, inactive, helpless, dependent, rigid in their thoughts or behaviour, old-fashioned or unproductive. Instead, their lives are characterized by variety, vitality, diversity, activity, energy, interest: by 'youthfulness' in attitude, outlook, and activity (including paid employment), regardless of their age. (1991: 121)

Let us now examine some of the other social and material obstacles that are held to obstruct the advent of a truly egalitarian gender regime, and consider their relevance to the age regime.

Linking of the gender regime and the age regime

One of the insights that has hopefully emerged from the preceding pages is that gender and age are linked epistemologically, phenomenologically and politically. Friedan notes that, just as the 'feminine mystique' had women in the grip of a gender ideology when she was writing in the 1950s and 1960s, so the 'age mystique' is comparable to describe older people's experience. Having said this, however, the age regime is more obdurate, she maintains: somehow denser and more paralysing, because it is threatening at some profound level (what we have noted as the fear of the Hag) 'emanating not an aura of desirability but a miasma of dread' (1993: 8–9). Similarly Beauvoir, in *The Second Sex*, talks with optimism about the future possibilities for gender equality but observes, bitterly, that to change the age system, which is a lifelong process of exploitation and oppression, to make it possible that 'in his last years a man might still be a man' [*sic*] (p. 542) requires not 'higher pensions, decent housing and organized leisure' (p. 542) but radical systemic change to the capitalist mode of production.

But is this the case? Is the age regime so much more intransigent than the gender regime? Returning to our earlier question, could it be that Beauvoir was: (i) overly pessimistic with regard to the former; and/or (ii) overly negative with the latter; or (iii) are these in some ways the wrong questions and should we be looking at something that links both regimes at the structural level? To answer this, let us first examine the characteristics of the current gender order. Research has identified a complex co-existence of old and new norms and expectations around femininity and masculinity within a neoliberal social order underpinned by individualism. This leads to certain tensions and paradoxes that run like a rift through women's subjectivity and lived experience such as increased levels of autonomy and expectations of self-realization co-existing with traditional expectations regarding what constitutes 'proper' or conventional femininity (Budgeon, 2014), especially consistent with heterosexual desirability. A cultural assumption of gender equality, backed by a host of equality legislation, co-exists with ongoing gender inequality with respect to childcare, domestic responsibilities and overall earnings in the workplace, which means that individualization is incomplete for women (Beck-Gernsheim, 2002). However, in the context of a more general emphasis on choice, gender inequality is also individualized, posited as the result of individual failings or the facts of interpersonal dynamics within the workplace for example (Connell, 2000).

Tallying up the pluses and minuses suggests the following. In both the UK and the US, on the positive side: (i) women are exceeding men in terms of educational achievements in secondary and higher education; (ii) the proportion of women in the labour market has increased (just under 50 per cent in UK and over 50 per cent in the US); (iii) the pay gap between men and women has narrowed, albeit unevenly over the life course. On the negative side: (i) women experience both 'glass ceilings' and 'sticky floors'; (ii) 'women's work' in cleaning, cooking and caring is both under-valued and far exceeds men's contribution; (iii) the gender pay gap which has closed for young women is re-established after her twenties and/or with motherhood, increasing with each child, both in relation to men and in relation to women without children; (iv) there is a persistence and perhaps increase in cultural gender (in)equal-ity operating through norms of femininity and sexuality (Gill, 2007a) that apply throughout the life course.

The above discussion also indicates the profound degree to which the age and gender regimes intertwine both symbolically and materially. Specifically, there is an emphasis on youthful modes of femininity in what Whelehan has termed the 'girling of popular culture' (2013: 78) with an onus on empowerment through one's youth-ful body or sexuality. We will return to this later. But first, carrying out a parallel tally, if we assess how the changes since the late 1970s have impacted on old age in particular, we can identify, on the plus side: (i) the end of compulsory retirement; (ii) introduction of anti-ageist legislation; (iii) the end of a totalizing identity in terms of 'old age' now being differentiated through the third and fourth ages; (iv) the loos-ening of constraints in terms of dress codes and norms surrounding involvement in a wide range of events including travel, leisure and education. On the negative side, (i) the gender pay gap increases for a woman in her forties and fifties and by the time she reaches retirement it is substantial. As well as the previously noted disparity in state pensions, single men received on average £85 per week from occupational pen-sions whilst women receive only 68 per cent of this, at £58 (Foster, 2013); (ii) the positive third-age identity is sustained by the creation of a fourth-age identity, which serves as the repository for all the fears and revulsion we have of ageing and old age (Higgs and Gilleard, 2015); (iii) representations of older people in the media are often negative, either depicting them as burdens in terms of health and social care needs, or relatedly, suggesting they possess more than their fair share of money/property/welfare (Harris, 2015); (iv) for older women in particular, the loosening of age-norms in terms of dress codes has brought the body into sharper focus, rendering its presentation a site of additional ongoing surveillance and regulation, where dress-ing age inappropriately involves social opprobrium or the loss of cultural capital.

We have already noted how rhetoric emphasizing agelessness and gender equality or neutrality has served as a solvent in freeing up traditional loyalties and practices, preventing the full involvement of women and old people in the labour force. We have also noted how the manifold shifts which the capitalist system underwent was made possible by the full-scale incorporation of women into it, enabling the shift to a service-based home workforce within a globalized economy. This further served both patriarchy and individual men through the ending of the family wage which enabled men's 'flight from commitment' (Ehrenreich, 1983) leading to the growth in single-parent households, mostly headed by women. We can already say then, that Beauvoir was indeed correct in her particular idea about the achievability of gender equality, at least where the aims of liberal feminists (such as herself) were to provide women with the means of personal autonomy through employment, or obtaining a 'piece of the pie' (Eisenstein, 2005: 495). Older people – at least those within the productive third age – have also helped themselves to a hearty chunk; but what Beauvoir and other feminists did not anticipate was how such changes enabled the spread of poor working conditions and low wages making the fourth age more inevitable for poor old women in particular (as we see in Chapter 8). Feminism aided capitalism in other ways, moreover, including lending it 'feeling currents', involving a new 'spirit' that includes contradictory elements of hedonism, productivity, assertiveness, autonomy, docility and 'youthfulness'; the latter are also features associated with an ageless society and flexible life stages, and all of which are to be incorporated into feminine (and masculine) personalities, in order to be considered 'successful' in different ways, at all ages.

Indeed, the successful 'Girl', as a material and symbolic trope, crystallizes both the age and gender regimes, and we look at her features in more detail next.

The Girl, femininity and age

We have encountered the Girl several times in our discussion so far and noted how she is interpellated as educationally successful, personally and socially self-actualizing and the ideal-typical neoliberal worker. She possesses many traditionally masculine attributes, whilst remaining firmly heterosexual, fertile, 'feminine' and above all young. But in the central place she occupies in the current gender order the Girl simultaneously opens up and closes down practices of gender equality throughout the life course. In the current gender regime we find plural and hybrid femininities and masculinities, associated with the change in educational and employment conditions, as well as the new mentalities – emotional literacy, entrepreneurialism – associated with the requirements of late modern capitalism. However, successful femininity is composed of features that, whilst including some aspects traditionally associated with masculinity, do not ultimately challenge the gender regime, as it is configured to be reassuringly feminine and thus complementary to hegemonic masculine dominance.

This configuration also brings age into centre stage (Budgeon, 2014; McRobbie, 2009; Negra, 2009). Indeed, age anxiety is a key regulatory device for women today and women are implicated in very specific ways in the time economy of post-feminism (Negra, 2009). This lies not just in the fact that 'post-feminism seems to be fundamentally uncomfortable with female adulthood itself, casting all women as girls to some extent' (p. 14) but also in the way it employs the time pressures involved in juggling multiple roles to suggest ways in which professional women in particular are deficient in terms of their femininity. This inability to manage time, including the competing timescapes in which she is involved, is one pressure resulting in 'retreatism' to pre-feminist modes of subjectification (cooking, full-time motherhood, retro-femininity and so on). Moreover, the Girl's success is strictly time-limited; as we noted earlier, although overall girls outperform boys at school and the full-time gender pay gap has closed for younger women it widens for women in their 40s and 50s and in addition, occupations and professions in which women succeed are associated with a fall in status and value (Walkerdine et al., 2001). In addition, the Girl's sexual and aesthetic capital is predicated on youthfulness.

Thus, age works as a conservative force in the gender regime, ensuring that any 'power' the Girl might access has a built-in obsolescence, leaving hegemonies basically untouched. Similarly, the gains that older people have made in terms of employment and societal norms depend on their remaining youthful. By contrast, men's power and social value increases with age (up to a certain threshold) in terms of employment, sexuality and aesthetics, among others. Moreover, continuing the parallel with the gender regime: whilst we have seen how the gender regime has become more complex, relational and nuanced, yet still supportive of hegemonic masculinity, we can see that an equally complex pattern applies to the age regime; in the next chapter we will look in more detail at how the blurring of boundaries between the different ages and stages has enabled the insertion of a new age patriarchy. The latter involves the dominance of the self-regulating entrepreneurial self which appears to transcend specific age categories to some extent whilst increasing the emphasis on remaining youthful which, by definition, is the main characteristic of an already male productive, entrepreneurial self.

To sum up, a focus on age reveals many ongoing inequalities in the gender regime, not least between women of different ages, that disadvantage women in relation to men. This suggests that we cannot see the gender regime in separation from age and indeed, that the deeper structures linking the age and gender regimes are intimately connected to the capitalist formation today. Beauvoir's critique in *The Coming of Age*, that system change was required to enable an old age dignified by the qualities of full personhood, 'that a man might still be a man' [*sic*] (1996: 542) as she put it, should thus be extended to the earlier part of the life course too. Certainly, Beauvoir would not have found the fact that women have joined men in the (increasingly oppressive) workforce sufficient to foster the possibilities of self-actualization and liberation to which she was committed.

Conclusion

In this chapter the object of critique has been the concept of the ageing body as 'natural', succumbing to forces of biology characterized by negative attributes such as deficit and decline. Challenging this view requires the use of powerful conceptual tools such as those found in feminist epistemology as they have proved particularly trenchant in a similar undertaking with gender. I suggested that, as with social class, the age and gender regimes are not only constructions of similar nature, but also mutually implicated in such a way that not only can analysis of one help illuminate the other, but true gender equality cannot be attained without age equality. In this respect, I also noted the importance of the Girl in crystallizing the nature of the gender and age regime. We will return to this figure in subsequent chapters, looking through her as through the lens of a kaleidoscope in which shifting patterns and formations coalesce around our themes. Finally, we have already suggested the limits of liberal feminism; parallels can be made with anti-ageist discourses which have denied that old age is any different to mid-life.

What can feminist approaches bring in terms of suggesting future possibilities? Drawing on the work of Kathy Ferguson (1993), we can ask: what kind of person or selfhood, in a liberated and non-patriarchal world, does feminism hope and aim for (throughout the life course)? Taking our starting position to be the Hegelian 'male-ordered subjectivity', the quintessential Enlightenment self that both privileges masculinity as selfhood itself and characterizes it in terms of independence/isolation, conflict/dominance, Ferguson notes that whilst liberal feminism, such as that of Beauvoir, posits a female version of the Hegelian self, radical feminism sees a different essential female self and 'linguistic feminism' sees gender differences as constituted by language . None of these versions are adequate in isolation but all are useful, she thinks, if one uses them 'ironically'; that is, with some distance, fostering 'mobile subjectivities' which will enable 'living with the tensions and incompatibilities that result from such a strategy' (1993: 182). In other words, we can be committed to seeking out greater equality and freedom, whilst being alert to the 'cunning' of history, or the new nexuses of power/knowledge that mix new freedoms with new oppressions, dancing between subjectivities to avoid their snares. This has clear pointers in terms of deciding the nature of the age identities we would wish to claim in the context of a reconfigured age system – a point to which we will return throughout the book.

CHAPTER SUMMARY

- In a similar way to the previous chapter's focus on class as a parallel stratification system, we took gender studies as a model for illuminating the age system.

- Key approaches that have been utilized to help 'denaturalize' both femininity and masculinity were then applied in the same way to denaturalizing the characteristics of age and ageing.

- These include the sex/gender distinction; the situated body; the female masquerade; the male gaze, all of which were then applied to the ageing body-self.

- Finally we suggested that the age and gender regimes are fundamentally linked and that the freedoms and constraints of one illuminate those present in the other.

Further questions

1. How helpful is feminism in helping us to understand and deconstruct age ideology?

2. What are the similarities and differences between the male gaze and the youthful gaze?

3. To what extent can we make parallels between the social construction of gender and of age? Are there limits to this connection?

Talking point

Julia Twigg has explored the extent to which older people use clothes and fashion to defy age-related norms more broadly. Pointing out that clothes are ideological: they 'naturalize hierarchies of power and status' (2013: 8), she asks, 'How far are they able to use clothing to resist, reinterpret or redefine dominant messages about age?' (2007: 286). Certainly, a stroll around the floor of Topshop reveals all ages from pre-teens to women in their seventies and older perusing the rails, sometimes in the role of helping a younger family member, but often alone and clearly shopping for themselves. Diana Athill sums up this sense of freedom and self-expression that characterizes such an experience. She notes: 'I have a freedom of choice undreamt of by my grandmothers' and says that, along with cosmetics, this is a way of making 'age look, and therefore feel less old' (2008: 14). However, Twigg found that age norms in dress style still apply, though less clearly: at one extreme older people are required to signal competence in terms of continued social personhood in a clean, neat, pressed presentation (jeopardized by stains, creases, holes and other signs in a way far less forgiving for women than for men); more generally, displays of sexuality are stigmatized (indicated for women particularly in the length of skirts and necklines) signified in a general 'toning down', which again affects women far more than men. This indicates clothing and style as a means of maintaining gender inequality in and through old age. Indeed, Twigg suggests that where once clothes were used to differentiate social class (in addition to gender) the overwhelming distinction effected through clothes is now, above all others, *that of age*; Twigg observes, 'it is this that underlies the sense that ultra-fashionable styles look "odd" or "unsuitable" or "ridiculous" or "sad" on older people' (2013: 31).

What might this suggest about the intertwining of the age and gender regimes?

—— **Key texts** ————————————————————————

The key works cited here are firstly by Simone de Beauvoir and Betty Friedan: Beauvoir, S. de (1997) [1949] *The Second Sex*, London: Vintage; Beauvoir, S. de (1996) [1970] *The Coming of Age*, New York: Norton; Friedan, B. (1963) *The Feminine Mystique*, New York: Norton; Friedan, B. (1993) *The Fountain of Age*, New York: Vintage. Important **commentaries on Beauvoir's philosophy** can be found in Moi, T. (1995) *What is a Woman? And other Essays*, Oxford: Oxford University Press. For **contemporary overviews of the gender regime(s)** in younger and older age see Segal, L. (2007) *Slow Motion: changing masculinities, changing men* (third edition), London: Palgrave Macmillan; Segal, L. (2013) *Out of Time: the pleasures and perils of ageing*, London: Verso. For the **post-feminist gender regime** see McRobbie, A. (2009) *The Aftermath of Feminism: gender, culture and social change*, London: Sage.

Further resources

The Everyday Sexism site (http://everydaysexism.com/) is a resource for sharing stories of sexism in everyday contexts that are often normalized as part of 'that's just life'.

There is a similar site for ageist experiences (http://everydayageism.blogspot.co.uk/) run by EURAGE, a cross-European research project based at the University of Kent.

4

CONSTRUCTING AND DECONSTRUCTING AGES AND STAGES OF THE LIFE COURSE

Background: ordering by age

In this chapter we will be viewing the life course as one of the most powerful vehicles of an age system that is key to the governing, ordering and meaning-making processes of society today. This order asserts the hegemonic dominance of productive and youthful (prime of life, not literally 'young') adulthood, establishing an age patriarchy which socially and economically subordinates the other categories of the life course. 'Adulthood' is synonymous with power.

Taking up the argument from Chapter 3, we argue that in parallel with the complex range of freedoms and constraints that comprise post-feminism, we can view the age system as similarly opening up and closing down possibilities (for all ages) in a range of dimensions. The key framework through which it works is that of the life course. The modern life course is built upon the tripartite structure of education, work/domestic roles and retirement, and of the three it is work that takes centre stage (Kohli, 2007) and provides life with much of its meaning. However, since the latter part of the twentieth century we can observe several key shifts to its construction:

(i) The ending of rigid age norms and distinctions co-exists with a strengthening age patriarchy, whereby all ages are being held to the standards and ideals of what we might call 'symbolic adulthood'.

(ii) Work remains of key importance and indeed this has now extended to include women and people formerly in post-retirement categories.

(iii) There is a corresponding infantilization associated with the fluidity and incompletion of each life stage.

(iv) There is a heightened emphasis on remaining youthful, where youth is synonymous with the productive, entrepreneurial self as well as 'fun, energy, sexuality, intensity, hope' (Gullette, 1997: 5).

(v) However, and finally, an emphasis on the fluidity of age norms obscures the ongoing presence of classed and other structured hierarchies.

AIMS OF THE CHAPTER

- The chapter will examine the 'construction' of the modern life course, taking a genealogical view.

- It will then look at the construction, within this framework, of the individual ages and stages, from childhood to old age.

- For both of the above we will examine how the concept of 'development', taken from biology and psychology, imparts a certain meaning to the overall life course as well as to the individual stages.

- We will also look at the relaxation of specific age norms and the blurring of boundaries between age groups which seems to contradict our suggestion of age patriarchy.

- Finally, we consider alternative approaches to conceptualizing the life course that may help unfix these ideological meanings and substitute more helpful alternatives.

Genealogy of the life course

Let us begin by considering how the contemporary life course came to assume the form it has. In medieval times, the life course was divided into many stages or sequences, of which three, four, six and seven were common, with the schema of four ages (linked to the physiological theory associated with the humours and the seasons/elements) being most influential during this whole period. As Burrow (1988) has pointed out, these stages, however numbered, all integrated individual lives (the microcosm) into the natural order (the macrocosm). In the physiological theory of the four ages (*pueritia, adolescentia, iuventus* and *senectus*) particular seasons were associated with particular ages. Importantly, death was not closely linked to old age; before 1850 nearly 60 per cent of all deaths occurred among people 15 years or younger; another 20 per cent of deaths took place among those aged between 15 and 45 (Mintz, 2015). Further distinctions of meaning were connected to social class with old age far more valued in nobles than serfs (Thane, 2000).

The onset of modernity disembedded individuals from this divine and natural order, including from traditional forms and roles in communities and families, which were replaced by new social mechanisms productive of order and of which the life course was key among them. As already noted in Chapter 1, this order worked partly through the use of the concept of time, and it did so by introducing the notion of 'lifetime' as a key structural feature linked to a set of chronological age stages (Kohli, 2007). In the UK, the Act for the Registration of Births, Deaths and Marriages (1836) was the first step that led to official classification by age.

As noted, the modern life course was built upon the tripartite structure of education, work/domestic roles and retirement, reflecting the switch from an emphasis on an aristocratic and religious ethic to a bourgeois ethic in which ordinary life itself constituted a calling (Taylor, 1985). Work did not just take centre stage but provided life with much of its meaning. However, what we think of as the standard template of the life course, complete with male breadwinner role, female housewife and nuclear family, bordered by schooling on the one hand and retirement on the other, despite its 'archetypal' aura in the collective consciousness, is in fact characteristic of a very brief interlude in our history. Associated with a particular model (Fordist) of economic production, it mostly applied to the middle class from the 1930s, taking till as long as the 1970s before it filtered down through all classes whereupon, almost immediately thereafter, it began to fragment (Hunt, 2001). This encompassed the era of the 'normal' American family identified by Parsons (1991) as comprising a monogamous couple at its core which provided the stability necessary for the successful socialization of children (Lee, 2001). In first modernity, formal age regulation occurred both through institutional thresholds for education and retirement age but also through informal 'norms' in the form of a 'prescriptive timetable' that acted as 'prods and breaks upon behaviour' (Neugarten, 1965: 711). Despite the very concise period of its ascendancy, the enduring grip the idea of this family type retains on the social imaginary is evident not just in the realm of nostalgia or fantasies about gender and age roles but also in government policy where there is a lag between age-graded social policy and the more diverse reality. So, for example, policy retains assumptions relating to the institutionalized life course including clear entry to the workforce and withdrawal from it after a lifetime in employment which may no longer reflect lived experience. Finally, whilst in today's society there is flexibility surrounding timetables, nevertheless: (i) individual choices remain heavily structured by class and gender patterns; and (ii) they are shaped by an internalized sense of success or failure (Radl, 2012).

In the next section we will consider the impact of the shift from the medieval wheel of life to the modern life course on the ages and age relations within the latter.

Medieval to modern: replacing wheels with staircases

The replacement of the 'wheel of life' by the 'life course' reconstituted the social imaginary not just with respect to the whole life course but also with regards to one's position with it at any given age. The complex framework of the former is found in the de Lisle Psalter (Figure 4.1 on page 88), a celebrated fourteenth-century image of the wheel of life, wherein we find depicted symbolically the fact that 'each age is equidistant from God, who stresses their subordinate but equal status' (Dove, 1986: 15). Whilst not removing classed aspects altogether this spiritual dimension did give an alternative meaning to the ages unconnected to worldly success. Furthermore, all ages are equal; none make sense without being seen as rooted in an entire life cycle. In addition, the concept of spiritual ages did enable old age to be valued in a way that contrasts with modern associations. So, we find the idea that one was likely to be more spiritually developed as one aged. As Tom Cole (1992) notes, 'the concept of spiritual ages allowed for the paradoxical unity of physical decline and spiritual ascent' (1992: 6). It was possible to be a wise child ('"*puer senex*" grave and wise beyond his years' (Dove, 1986: 36)) as well as a youthful old person ('*senex fortis*'), such states deriving their meaning from spiritual advancement, whereby one transcended one's bodily age to attain a more advanced spiritual age. It was agedness of the soul that was the measure (Burrow, 1988).

But with the emergence of the 'life course' framework, the ages of life became the 'stages of life', associated with the civilizing process that moved from externally imposed discipline to internalized processes of self-control. In addition, a new iconographic representation of the life course as a staircase had emerged by the sixteenth century, rising and falling in a pyramid shape with all its connotations of progress followed by decline. Other imagery representing the life course that appeared through modernity include variously: life as a pilgrimage or journey; as a game; as a series of stages linked to Darwinian evolution, economic growth or developmental psychology (Mintz, 2015). All of these, however, are built upon a staircase pattern giving particular emphasis to childhood and youth. For example, of Erikson and Erikson's (1997) eight stages of psychosocial development, six are concerned with the period from infancy to youth positioned on the ascent and only two concerned with adulthood and old age, the latter two being accorded developmental tasks that are rooted in concerns about both younger generations and one's personal past. Over this period, time was constituted as a limited commodity not unlike money and one of the ideas associated with the Reformation was that it could run out before one attained salvation (Cole, 1992). This was accompanied by a shift from the notion of 'contemplation' as the highest pursuit to an emphasis placed on activity, which again fitted with the centrality of ordinary life. Later, but not until the twentieth century and especially with the fourth stage of the epidemiological transition[1] (Olshansky and Ault, 1986), we have a complementary shift culturally and philosophically from a central importance given to mortality, to an emphasis on 'natality' (in the words of Hannah Arendt) in line with the privileging of youth over old age (Neiman, 2014).

The life course then instated a paradigm switch in the relationship between age and youth and their respective values vis-à-vis each other. The shift can also be illustrated with reference to the change in representations of the body in which *homo clausus* as established through the civilizing process was depicted as a separate self-contained individual, the links in the chain to others all sundered, generation from generation, individual from individual, minds from bodies and nature from culture. Bakhtin observes of the life course:

> All that happens within it acquires one single meaning; death is only death, it never coincides with birth; old age is torn away from youth; blows merely hurt, without assisting in an act of birth. All actions and events are interpreted on the level of a single individual life. They are enclosed within the limits of the same body, limits that are the absolute beginning and end and can never meet. (1984: 322–3)

It appears very much, superficially at least, that in today's risk society, the life course, as a regular and regulated mechanism, has broken down and its standardized and institutionalized character lost. Certainly, many changes have taken place and, although there is the same tripartite division, the direction of movement through the life course is not unilinear and nor are the three stages cleanly demarcated from each other in individual lives and associated strictly with particular time periods. On the other hand, work remains the definitive role, and one that extends its logic – both practically and in dispositional terms – into childhood and old age and which has furthermore also claimed women, giving to their lives the tripartite structure that most did not have in Fordist times (Kohli, 2007), and corresponding to the 'masculinization' of female biographies (Esping-Anderson, 2005). At the same time, developmental logic continues to underpin the life course but its application is more individualized with full realization of developmental potential as an individual 'achievement' rather than a societal given. This, as we have suggested, indicates a further stage of individualization in neoliberalism, this time releasing people from their age classes to a large degree and focusing on their individual properties more carefully, in a new articulation of biopower. It is the mixture of new freedoms and new constraints with older sediments that is most notable here and which will be illuminated in greater detail if we now turn our attention to how individual stages are constructed within this framework, beginning with childhood.

The social construction of childhood

Aries' (1962) still-influential, if somewhat flawed, thesis demonstrates that childhood as we know it today with its range of social and psychological meanings did not exist in earlier times. That is, it was not conceived as a life stage separate from, and incomplete in relation to, adulthood (and youth). It is the institution of education above all that underpinned the construction of childhood as a distinct life stage, firstly for upper-class boys and only later spreading out to encompass children of other classes (and genders) with the Forster Education Act of 1870 extending education to all (and compulsion introduced in 1880). Education worked hand in hand with the newly developed science of psychology to identify the attributes of child-hood. We will examine both in turn.

The role of education

With modernity, schooling became a vital link in the process of governing and the instating of order, stability and productivity as individual attributes, a key part of the liberal, and later neoliberal, approach to governing. Socially exclusive schools in the sixteenth century instilled discipline and were part of the civilizing process for aristocratic families, regarded as having the purpose of

> breaking the natural ferocity of human nature, to moderate the passions and to impress the principles of religion and morality and give habits of obedience and subordination to paternal as well as political authority. (Cunningham, 2006: 85)

For upper-class girls, education was mostly 'education for marriage'. Poor boys received little by way of education and did not stay at school past seven or eight years of age when they were required to contribute to the family economy. In other words, from the start, 'time' as a resource differentiated children by gender and class, with boys having more 'time' as children (that is, at school) and upper-class boys having a childhood, in crude terms, a couple of centuries before poor boys.

In the nineteenth century, mass education appeared to be the 'solution' to two problems of government: crime and pauperism (that is, the kind of poverty that required poor relief) (Walkerdine, 2005). This was in line with a shift in governance from a coercive form to a liberal one working to shape subjectivity; education was a tool for making the masses 'rational'. At the same time, childhood became identified as a site of investment for the future, a feature deemed necessary following both the extension of voting entitlements to working-class urban men from 1867 as well as the competitive needs of international capitalism. Education for the masses was, in this context, about producing particular kinds of citizens in a well-ordered, efficient and competitive nation state. The establishment of education for the working class, how-ever, did more than contain the threat of this class; it introduced a huge transformation into the subjectivity of children, rendering the child a being that was 'dependent' and embedded within the framework of the family (and thence the state). Both child-workers and the urchins, or 'street arabs', were considered 'precocious' with knowledge acquired through experience and taught by community and family and thus dangerous (Hendrick, 1990). Recreating their subjectivities in the trope of 'school pupil' in accordance with middle-class norms and values would, it was hoped, turn them into 'children' again (in the sense of being dependent, powerless and malleable by experts).

Weber's theory of authority has been utilized as a concept through which to inter-pret the dominance adults wield over children's lives as a form of 'age patriarchy' (Hood-Williams, 1990) see Box 4.1 overleaf for a definition of this term.

BOX 4.1

Age patriarchy

Weber identified three types of authority: rational-legal (based on law and bureaucracy); traditional (based on custom and practice); charismatic (based on personality/leadership). Age patriarchy combines elements of all three types of authority with father-child the ideal-typical model.

This involves not only economic dependence but also control by adults over children's space, time and bodies and imposes upon children a specific kind of dependency characterized by 'obedience': 'Children are clearly not supposed to be the centres of their own determination' (Hood-Williams, 1990: 110). Today, age patriarchy retains a classed dimension whereby socially excluded children and their families are particularly targeted by a raft of measures with the intention that

> *their* children have to be *made* children again, for they are often 'unnatural' in their manner, as in, for example, their inability to conform in school, their semi-criminal activities, their presence on the streets when all 'normal' children are indoors and in bed, and in their general precociousness. (Hendrick, 2003: 238; original emphasis)

Age patriarchy, as manifest through educational surveillance and other regulatory measures, has indeed increased in contemporary times. For example, in the case of UK children, the early years foundation stage assesses children's development and school-readiness at age five, involving the rational qualities of counting, letters and picture recognition after which the children take a reading test at age six (end of first year of compulsory schooling). The national curriculum demands testing children at school and occurs at ages seven and eleven for Key Stages One and Two; the last years in high school are marked by national exams in the form of GCSEs, AS- and A-levels. All of these test the pupil's successful transformation into a rational and civil subject. But this has led to concern from parents and others about so-called 'exam factories' (Anon, 2014) that turn schooling into a prolonged period of testing, rather than encouraging learning for its own sake, and leading to enormous anxiety among children. In addition, compulsory schooling has extended ever further in both age directions, with the raising of the school (or equivalent training) leaving age from summer 2015 to the age of 18 (it was age 10 in 1870, 15 from 1944 and 16 from 1972) paralleled by a growing emphasis on pre-school education and nursery schools (Prout, 2005). Meanwhile, leisure activity is increasingly regulated with after-school clubs and an emphasis on 'productive' leisure time, be it music, sport or other activities. Other examples of age patriarchy include the use of 'behaviour contracts' which stress parental involvement, a greater emphasis on homework and action against truancy. All these measures are calculated to produce an ideal-typical relationship between adults and children of 'dependence, socialization, punishment, obedience, responsibility, duty' (Hendrick, 2003: 242). This, Prout (2005) further suggests, represents a 'refocusing of modernity's drive to control the future through children' (2005: 33) in line with a clear vision of 'standard' adulthood on the model of the reflexive, entrepreneurial self (as we see later in the chapter). 'Excellence in schools' (Department for Education and Employment, 1997) for example states: 'Our children are our future as a civilized society and a prosperous nation' (quoted in Hendrick, 2003) which, no less than in the nineteenth century, sees children as a form of capital and schooling as a key vehicle for regulating and governing the population. Indeed, we are witnessing a rationalization of education, remembering Weber's warning that this is what happens when instrumental reason – means–end efficacy – displaces all other forms of action, such as that informed by values. Where education was once about equipping children to live as reasoning and reasonable citizens of a liberal polity, its focus today is on measuring skills required for the labour economy. As we have noted in previous chapters, and will discuss further in Chapter 5 in particular, today the 'subject of value' within school and the ideal subject of the neopatriarchal regime are that of the Girl; her characteristics reflects such rationalization.

The role of developmental psychology

From the start of the twentieth century, education has worked closely with the science of psychology. Psychology was originally embedded within an evolutionary approach that maintained that a child growing up proceeds through all the stages that human society experienced since 'savage' times, known as the theory of recapitulation (Cunningham, 1991). In this paradigm, children exhibit an 'impoverished beginning' (Slee and Shute, 2003: 67) and move along a universal path in which stages of cognitive reasoning utterly transform the child's consciousness via a series of disconnected leaps and steps rather than a continuum, thus depicting an ontological rupture between childhood and adulthood. The work of Piaget (1927) constitutes the archetyal example of such theories (Walkerdine, 2005). Piaget identified four key developmental stages involving closely defined time scales. The first is the *sensorimotor* stage (birth to two years) where intelligence is located in motor actions; the next, the *preoperational* stage extends from two to seven years, and this is linked to intuitive reasoning; *concrete operational* logic predominates in the stage from seven to eleven; and finally, *formal operations* develop from age twelve and over (Stainton Rogers, 2003). Kohlberg's influential theory of children's moral development further extends the concept of rationality with the sixth and final stage representing a fully rational style of disengaged moral reasoning 'orientated towards individual autonomy, impartial judgement, and behaving in an objectively fair and rational way' (Sugarman, 2001: 90).

Despite the contemporary abandonment of the explicitly evolutionary aim of psychology, the model of psychological development retains a telos centred on the development of a productive, rational individual; progress and evolution remain powerful ways through which to interpret these stages (Burman, 2007) and the focus individualizes the differences associated with structural inequalities. Dorling (2014) suggests that a key term here is the concept of 'potential' which he calls the 'give-away word that implies the inevitability of large disparities in ability, and consequently in income' (2014: 44) later in life, but which obscures the fact that such 'potential' is as much social as individual. Attempts to move beyond this include see-ing childhood not (just) by reference to the adult states that remain to be achieved but rather in terms of a uniqueness meaning that 'at the level of behaviour, values, symbols, games, beliefs and oral traditions there may be a dimension exclusive to the child' (Hardman, 2001: 504). The line between accepting this and subscribing to an essentialized view of childhood is of course a fine one but acquaintance with the historical construction of childhood can certainly help one stay on the right side of it. So it might be more helpful to approach sociological accounts concerning the 'disappearance' of childhood within the terms of Bourdieu's idea of social power. For example, Postman (1984) suggests that the accessibility of information as far as children are concerned especially through the TV (and increasingly other electronic media) has melted the boundary between adulthood and childhood, formerly estab-lished through the age-graded skill of reading. Clothing, food and activities that are increasingly common to both children and adults further corroborate this fact. Against this, we can find evidence to suggest that the boundary has been constructed ever more powerfully, with clear markers including the raising of the school leaving age as well as increased surveillance during schooling. In addition, the introduction of children's rights, for example, in the form of the UN Convention of the Rights of the Child, is justified by their being defined as dependent and vulnerable. Moreover, this constructedness has been made in relation to an adulthood that is also changing and insecure, meaning vulnerability and dependence on the one hand can no longer be compared with stability and autonomy on the other. However, this is Postman's (linked) point in that he perceives the 'end' of childhood to be embedded in the social disempowerment of *all* citizens (not an essentialist view of childhood, after all, tak-ing thereby a structural view of age stages, to which we return later in the chapter). Age patriarchy, indeed, is not confined to children.

One of the consequences of this continued, and strengthening, distinction between childhood and adulthood, is that continuities and similarities between children's and adult's lives are overlooked and downplayed. So, for example, the 'work' that chil-dren do, whether at school or in the many part-time jobs they combine with schoolwork, including care-giving to adults or siblings, although increasingly oner-ous, somehow does not count as 'real work', because children do not work, by definition. Moreover, children also contribute towards adult success (Leonard, 1990). Directly, this includes running family businesses, helping mother's paid domestic work and, indirectly, raising their parents' social status, in terms of social and cultural capital: hence those ubiquitous children's photographs proudly dis-played upon the office desk. Most of all, Leonard suggests, in a disenchanted world:

the 'work' required of most children today, however, is… that of giving meaning to adults' lives…. Children are objectified as 'the reason' a father goes out to work and struggles to earn a living. Children prove their mother's femininity. Children provide a sense of immortality… (1990: 46)

Construction of the category of youth: the best time of one's life?

Youth is another category that was constructed slowly over the Middle Ages and differentiated from both childhood and adulthood over this period although in many ways it has always been, and remains, harder to define in terms of its boundaries on either side. In pre-industrial society, the onset of youth as a stage came with children leaving their families to go as servants or apprentices and thus as a period of life was characterized by some detachment from family of origin. Only after 1900 did the conceptualization of youth as 'teenagers' emerge (Pilcher, 1995) with their particular saliency emerging after World War Two when they increased as a proportion of the population and also started to earn the sort of wages that made them a distinctive consumer group with their own 'youth culture' (Pilcher, 1995). Where children are seen as what they will become, youth occupies a somewhat ambiguous position between what they no longer are (that is, children) and what they nearly are (adults) and for that reason many researchers working in the youth studies field suggest youth be seen not as a life stage but as a *transition* (Pilcher, 1995). This emphasizes the fact that youth draws its meaning from comparison with, and differences from, adulthood (and thus obscures the fact that adulthood also draws its meaning from what it is not, including youth).

In late modernity, youth's boundaries with childhood and adulthood are increasingly blurred (Furlong, 2013; Jones, 2009; Furlong and Cartmel, 1997), again paralleling the experience of childhood, as we noted above. These are largely due to social changes, especially protracted and complex transitions from dependence to independence across a range of dimensions: work, home, life, finances and so on. Developmental psychology also plays an important role in shaping the contours and meaning of youth with theories 'naturalizing' this liminal period through such concepts as the 'mind of the moratorium' or a period of 'structured irresponsibility', rather than seeing it as a social creation related to the attainment of social powers (and affecting personality and mentality accordingly). This is encapsulated in the recent theory of 'emerging adulthood' (Arnett, 2000) that depicts a new psychological 'truth' generated by late modernity, which is presented as something both related to the structure of the brain, but also as arising with and through social circumstances. These latter comprise: (i) the change from an industrial to an information-based economy and the increase in the need for post-secondary education, so transitions to career, marriage and parenthood take place later than ever before; (ii) opportunities for women to enter the workplace; and (iii) sexual freedom (leading to marrying ages) – all of which delay 'adulthood' proper (bound up as they are with those roles). The key developmental task involves a shift in the focus of the individual, from dependence on family to creation of new responsibilities, home, commitments and families. But although emerging adulthood is socially contextualized, insofar as it is a feature of late modernity, it is also presented as possessing strong biological elements in the form of 'physiological and neural development unique to the age period' (Tanner and Arnett, 2009: 41). This includes brain plasticity up to the age of 25 involving a 'sensitive period' in which the brain's neural pathways are malleable followed by a 'fixing' of the brain in particular ways. This indicates a continuing evolutionary approach, linking the development of individuals and societies in some overall architecture (without recognizing the primacy of the social, however, as would for example the 'situated body'). The authors stress that these are 'global changes' although the West has experienced them first. Two questions about the meaning of such changes immediately present themselves. Firstly: do such indeterminate boundaries with adulthood make it harder or easier to acquire adult privileges and powers? And secondly, who gains and who loses through such changes among young people today?

With regard to the first question, differences between the experience of youth today and that of their parents include the fact that in the parents' generation there were 'normative timetables' regarding the timing and sequencing of key transitions that no longer exist in the same way and in addition there were gendered transitions with women leaving home to get married rather than to live alone (Jones, 2009). Today, young people spend longer in education, are likely to enter employment much later than their parents' generation and are likely to exhibit passage in and out of these states. Evidence suggests that the fuzziness of these boundaries has made possession of adult privilege far harder to attain. This indeterminacy also increases ontological insecurity (Giddens, 1991) in which, for girls, this may be all the greater, due to the break in continuity between their mothers' and their own generation and because elements of the new and old co-exist alongside each other in their lives (Beck and Beck-Gernsheim, 2000).

Turning to the second question, as noted in Chapter 2, what appears at first glance to constitute increased opportunities for all seems rather less the case in practice. The transformation of higher education from an elite to a mass experience belies its continuing highly stratified character, with important divisions between elite and low-status institutions as well as between particular courses within institutions (Roberts, 2011). The consequence of qualification inflation, whereby employers are able to seek graduates for positions that could once be accessed by a high-school diploma, has not been an increase in highly desirable jobs; rather it has fuelled a process of professionalization, whereby a range of careers once associated with sub-degree forms of training now require or prefer those trained to degree level. The low pay and insecure nature of 'graduate jobs' also results in young people's prolonged semi-dependence on parents and a graduated entry to employment (Furlong, 2013). Other ways in which youth transitions exhibit a strongly classed characteristic centre on their duration. Jones (2009) highlights 'slow-track' transitions, associated with the longer educational and post-university training periods of middle-class youth and the 'fast-track' patterns of working-class individuals (although in their case, longer-term interdependence in terms of family formation is, arguably, more strongly marked), suggesting that still 'youth is a luxury to which the poor have no access' (p. 112) – a fact which has a long history. Indeed, the fast-track forms are often not manifestations of an 'agency' that is an expression of reflexive choice but more often shaped by the need to escape untenable situations in terms of family life or poverty at home (Jones, 2009). Whilst working-class youth may arrive at adulthood more swiftly, the spaces of adulthood they occupy – in terms of employment opportunities, health and housing – are, as we saw in Chapter 2, invariably less desirable.

But here it is important to give some more thought to the position of girls and particularly to considering what role and meaning the trope of the 'successful Girl' possesses for the category of youth. The Girl achieves success through her own conscientiousness and volition, decontextualized from any class or other social situation, which underpins the rhetoric of individual responsibility for success and failure. The problem lies in the gap between the discourse of meritocracy, in which all governments since that of John Major have insisted the UK is a 'classless society', and the real constraints that remain in place, albeit obscured by the conditions of individualization. This appearance, belied by reality, is what Furlong and Cartmel call the 'epistemological fallacy' and suggest it is most acute for the youth of today who blame themselves for failures they would once have attributed to the class society. Neiman sees the root of this problem in the shift to natality in modernity, whereby, she suggests, 'every birth may hold the promise of a completely new beginning, but every experience reveals, soon enough, that we are born into webs of relations that constrain as they sustain us' (Neiman, 2014: 98). We can then ask whether this valorizing of the Girl has shifted the developmental model somewhat from that of the default male actor. Burman (2005) suggests that the answer to this is, partly, yes. Clearly, feminine development – where it also mixes traditional elements of agency and rationality associated with masculinity – is emblematic of success. The fact that masculine development also requires feminized tropes in a new civility underpins the frequent diagnosis in boys of ADHD, which serves to mark the previously normal high-spirited young male as dysfunctional in developmental terms within this regime. But on the one hand, subsequent research applying Kohlberg's (revised) methodology found no difference between girls and boys in moral reasoning (Tronto, 1993) and it is likely that the advent of a gender-neutral national curriculum in the UK generates in both middle-class boys and girls the same kind of moral dispositions associated as it is with preparation for the public domain. On the other hand, Burman also suggests a new temporalization of development, in a twist on the Freudian concept of the primacy of childhood: an ongoing return of the adult self to the past, through a focus on the inner child, which can now be blamed for current problems, rather than looking for their source in structural factors. This encourages individuals to engage in a loop within themselves, both backward and forward looking, with a self increasingly individualized both socially and psychically. The ideal-typical example of this, Burman suggests, is represented in the character of *Amélie*, the heroine of the eponymous movie, who seeks to intervene in the lives of strangers in order to right the harms done to them in childhood and clear the obstacles to present-day self-fulfilment.

Constructing adulthood: normalization and problematization

The 'taken-for-granted' character of adulthood is evidenced in the fact that whilst there are sociologies of childhood, youth and old age, there is no 'sociology of adulthood' (Pilcher, 1995). But this in itself is, of course, ideological, disguising the labour which goes into constructing this life stage: the fact, for example, that its stability and completion are, particularly today perhaps, 'fictional' (Walkerdine, 2005). Part of what shaped adulthood as a distinct life stage were the processes of exclusion we have already discussed with children and old people being removed from work roles. Moreover, one of the reasons for the invisibility of adulthood as a stage is because its history is effectively the history of private life, specifically work, marriage and family life/parenting (Mintz, 2015). Of these, if education is the defining characteristic of childhood, then work is the defining attribute of adulthood, underpinning the long lead into it from youth as well as the distinction with older ages. In addition, it is the 'norm' from which other stages deviate, the benchmark against which all other life stages are measured, as 'stable, complete, self-possessed and self-controlling… capable of independent thought and action' (Lee, 2001: 5) and above all, rational.

The genealogy of such an ideal self can be traced back to Plato (Taylor, 1985) with important twists and modifications evident over time. For Plato, rationality (which alone enables freedom) is self-mastery and control of emotions and impulses by the detached individual capable of objectifying the world as well as his own body (the ideal self is male of course) and his emotions. But, as Taylor explains (1985) for Plato, reason was intrinsically connected to a vision of a meaningful cosmos and this was not the case for Descartes and his successors. Similarly, the Aristotelian 'science of man' attributed to 'man' a telos or essential nature and 'ethics' served as a guiding framework through which to realize that nature (MacIntyre, 2007). For Descartes and the modern scientific worldview that followed, reason as the foundation of competent personhood was stripped of transcendent meaning and reason mutated into a technique or ordering of logical processes of thought. The meaning of rationality today is largely defined in procedural terms, comprising instrumental means–ends consistency and specifically associated with the mature adult: Piaget's stages of childhood development check for and measure advances towards this state, judged by ability to order and classify the world, separating self and others, using conceptual thought and increasing degrees of abstraction. Appropriate dispositions to achieving those ends include enterprise and responsibility, with correct exercise of 'choice' at every life stage framing age-appropriate 'success'. Incorrect choices are those not just made by the young or the senile but also exhibited by the feckless working class, indicating that in today's individualized context 'whilst adulthood enjoys "ideological dominance" some adults are clearly more "grown up" than others' (Pilcher, 1995: 96). This further suggests the symbolic nature of adulthood which, whilst overlapping, is not exactly synonymous with the chronological category. (That higher-class adults are more 'adultlike' than their lower-class age peers is not, of course, a new idea and it underlies the linkage of dependence historically to wage labour, indicative in working-class appellations of 'lad', 'boy', 'son' (Cunningham, 2006). Other parallels include the fact that pre- and early modern proletarian dress paralleled the development of children's dress, their association with practical as opposed to abstract thought and so on (see Firestone, 1970).)

One way of understanding this ambiguity between symbolic and chronological adulthood is through further exploring the genealogy of dependency. Historically, this involved a shift from a pre-industrial emphasis on the poor (men and women) as dependent because of their need to sell their labour, through to industrial times that constructed women, children, old people and the poor as dependent (because they were *not* able or self-sufficiently able to sell their labour). In late modernity many women claimed independence (through work especially) whilst 'a more stigmatized but still feminized sense of dependency attaches to groups considered deviant and superfluous' (Fraser and Gordon, 1994: 311) such as the unemployed and fourth age. An increasing distinction between chronological and symbolic adulthood strongly suggests the advent of an individualized (rather than individually directed) life course dependent on individual accumulation of skills and capital.

In addition, whilst classed differences remain salient, a newer and more general problematization has impacted all mid-life adults. A crisis discourse co-exists with the 'prime of life' ideal, a dual construction that has older foundations in the psychological theorizing associated with Jung, who saw mid-life as an opportunity for greater self-understanding but one precipitated by an agonizing loss of everyday meaning (and which indeed we can trace back to Dante). In contemporary times, mid-life is split into two 'poles' or binaries, one 'good' and one 'bad' (just like all other ages) (Strenger and Ruttenberg, 2008). In late modernity, this sense of crisis arises in particular from the individualization processes that mean adulthood is no longer the time of stable certainties it used to be but partakes in the risk and fluctuations of all other phases of life. So the centrality of work remains but is characterized by a split between the overworked and underworked; women are employed in unsatisfactory part-time work; bankruptcy is common; and symptoms of stress and anxiety have reached chronic proportions (Mintz, 2015). In many instances the 'good' and 'bad' poles operate together within the same discourse and this in itself may be meaningful: 'we should notice the extent to which the muddle in itself constitutes a "message"' involving middle-aged subjects in 'emotional and cognitive oscillations' (Gullette, 1998: 7–8). On the one hand, one is at the height of one's powers; on the other 'these same feelings of decline and self-doubt undermine the

critical potential inherent in that long rich time of life when we possess both knowledge of the workings of the world and maximum power to make change' (Gullette,
1997: 2). This underlines how, like emerging adulthood, an individualized discourse
separates adults from each other in their common stress, anxiety and uncertainty,
where success and failure are rendered individual attributes, regardless of gender,
class and other constraints that underpin such outcomes and experiences.

From 'old' age to the 'third' and 'fourth' ages: the changing construction of later life

All the ages we have looked at so far are historically contingent; old age is no different. For much of the twentieth century old age traditionally began at the age of
retirement or senior citizenship at 65 or 60. However, Roebuck (1979) concludes
from her historical investigation that 'there is no physiological basis for a sound
clear-cut definition of old age' (p. 416) and moreover, that the entry point indicating
old age has been highly variable throughout history and within different societies.
No definition of old age existed in the UK, throughout the period of the Poor Laws
which enabled each application to be treated on its own merit; age only became
salient when an aged person had sunk into deep poverty through inability to make
a living (including through begging) (Thane, 2000). Indeed, the Royal Commission
on the Aged Poor concluded in 1895: 'neither by statute nor order is any limit of age
fixed at which a man or woman is to be regarded as no longer able-bodied' (quoted
in Roebuck, 1979: 419). Only when the introduction of national old age pensions
began to be discussed did the question arise in government and policy circles of what
the age threshold would be for receipt. Precedents for pensions, both in the friendly
societies which existed at the time to support workers in different occupations, and
in other European countries, indicated enormous variability depending on the rig-
ours of the industry: miners, puddlers, dock labourers and other such workers,
obviously suffered from reduced capacity to meet the demands of such work in
comparison to, say, an administrator or teacher and retired at correspondingly different ages; or in different terminology 'got old' at different times. Policy-makers'
concerns centred on managing the working-age population and specifically with
reducing unemployment. However, when institutional retirement was established
discourses such as disengagement theory (Cumming and Henry, 1961) justified it as
natural and inevitable, positing a joint social and personality-centred withdrawal
from the world and a decrease in roles but these did not take into account the perspectives of older people themselves.

Today, the ending of mandatory retirement was accomplished in 2011 in the UK.
However, people still prefer to retire at a standard age (state pension age) (Kohli,
2007) and decisions to leave work before State Pension Age (SPA) (which importantly
are *rising* throughout western Europe and North America) are connected with classed
and gendered norms (Radl, 2012). Exhortations by the government encouraging

people to retire later are framed entirely within the rationale of averting the shortfall in pension funds in an age of government retrenchment. This shift also ties in with deeper changes in society, particularly the introduction of a distinction between the third and fourth ages. The third age is a term introduced into the discourse surrounding age by Peter Laslett (1991), who wished to acknowledge a more positive experience of ageing made possible by a change in demographics, economics, health and dispositions. The four ages are summarized by Laslett as follows:

> First comes an era of dependence, socialization, immaturity and education; second an age of independence, maturity and responsibility, of earning and saving; third an era of personal fulfilment; and fourth, an era of final dependence, decrepitude and death. (Laslett, 1991: 4)

Demographically, the third age requires that at least 10 per cent of the national population be aged 65 and over; this phenomenon Laslett (1991) sees first emerging in the UK in the 1950s and then establishing itself 'as a settled feature' in the 1980s in the UK and earlier in other European countries (such as Italy and Scandinavia). This suggests that the third and fourth ages are aspects of an individualized society. The third age also requires 'comfortable living standards' for a critical mass of persons of that age (which he suggests should be 10 per cent of the total population of the over-65s). Indeed, in its representation, the third age is not old age at all, in the traditional sense: it is agentic and productive, though not necessarily involving paid work; it is youthful and healthy, an identity constructed through consumerism (Gilleard, 1996) and involves the broadening of the hegemony of adulthood to the latter years, including in physiological ideals of the body.

The geriatric syndrome or diagnosis of 'frailty' is the most direct marker of enforced exit from the third age into the dreaded fourth age, although as we shall see in Chapter 8, despite an immense and ongoing effort by many geriatricians to define and redefine its aspects, it remains imprecise, characterized rather by normative views about what it is to be a 'standard adult' and involving a structured dependency or marginalization. The fourth age is also given shape and meaning by lifespan developmental psychology where it is characterized by loss in two components of intellectual functioning: the 'mechanics' (reasoning, spatial orientation, perceptual speed) and the 'pragmatics' of cognition, associated with cultural practices and acquired knowledge (Baltes et al., 1999). It presents a mirror image to the Piagetian emphasis on a child's developing rationality (Baltes and Carstensen, 1996; Baltes and Smith, 2003) an un-development on the downward curve, involving a 'crumbling' of qualities like 'mastery' and 'autonomy' and 'cognitive potential' (Baltes and Smith, 2003) that define standard adulthood psychologically. The result of all this structural erosion is that 'the self is at its limits of functioning in the fourth age' (2003: 125). This is no more or less than the staircase of life folding in upon itself and slowly collapsing. The requirement for 'cultural input' into 'biology' increases, at the same time that it becomes less effective as the 'role' of biology becomes stronger.

Despite personality approaches within life-course psychology (from Jung to Neugarten, Guttman and Tornstam) that highlight the growth and deepening of certain aspects of adult personality in later life, this 'measuring' approach directly underpins delineation of the 'stages' – third from fourth – and means that the development that occurs into the fourth age is lost from view where 'decline' and 'growth' are seen as antonyms and where qualitative changes are swept aside in the quantitative perspective, perhaps because our fear of the Hag closes down our imaginative empathy. Moreover, this decline is foretold in the very terms and values selected at the outset, those of autonomy, mastery and separation, against which the fourth age is seen to be wanting. As such it says more about the ideals of adulthood than about 'old age' per se. Hazan suggests that old age alone seems to suggest an essence of the Other: 'the "old savage" who was exiled from anthropology has become a popular, albeit abominable "savage old" in contemporary culture' (2009: 65).

In practice, most societies have treated the category of old age in one of two ways, sometimes alternating between both (Phillipson, 2013). These comprise: (i) treating old age as a unique category, distinct from others, with its own needs, role and meaning; (ii) approaching it as continuous with the rest of the life course. Both possess advantages and disadvantages. In the first case, this includes the marginalization and 'othering' of old age, associated with structured dependency, even as pensions were extended to all. In the second, the failure to see old age in terms other than decline, with success consisting in prolongation of mid-life norms, results in the advantage for some of achievement of a third age identity and for others, bestows the disadvantage of the fourth age. What would seem the best option is the combining of elements of both approaches – recognition of some unique aspects as well as continuities, together with a valuing of the former (unlikely, within the context of the third/fourth-age framework, however).

Relaxation of age norms and the blurring of boundaries between ages

The discussion of age patriarchy in the previous sections seems to contradict suggestions that the increasingly blurred boundaries between age categories is accompanied by a relaxation of age norms (Levin, 2013), so that there is less and less differentiation in terms of role, work, general activities, appearance, lifestyle and leisure. In fact, as we will see, such blurring and relaxation is a key aspect of age patriarchy. Firstly, let us recap the key changes that have occurred in the configuration of ages and stages as follows: (i) the erosion of childhood as a chronological category with clear boundaries; (ii) the prolongation of youth; (iii) the uncertainty of adulthood; and (iv) the pushed-back boundaries of old age. Let us look at these in a little more detail. With regard to childhood, there are indications of its boundaries – as they existed for much of the twentieth century at least – being eroded, both through access to forms of adult knowledge at younger ages (Postman, 1984) as manifest in sexual activity, beauty norms, eating disorders and violence, as well as the earlier introduction of self-surveillance as represented by educational practices appearing ever earlier in life. Some examples taken from the US include: as many as 18 per cent of girls under 12 years of age wear eyeliner, mascara and lipstick regularly; half of 3–6-year-old girls worry about being fat; 80 per cent of all 12-year-olds have dieted (Levin, 2013), whilst marketing directs many of its products – including sexualized clothing – to children. Next, youth (ii) has become prolonged, associated with the state of 'emerging adulthood' and delayed passage through some of the key 'transitions' associated with adulthood, such as full-time employment, establishment of separate households, marriage and children. Much of this relates to the increasing number of young people pursuing higher education, and the new conditions of employment, which means that many young people take far longer than their parents did to establish independent households. There is a more unstable/fragmented adulthood (iii), characterized by returns to education for retraining purposes (either to acquire new skills for one's existing career or to embark on a different career(s)), periods between work, and the demise of both jobs and marriages for life. Finally, late adulthood/old age (iv) is characterized by varied trajectories of retirement, including retiring early, remaining in one's career past traditional retirement age, ending full-time work and taking a variety of part-time jobs, retiring and embarking on education/a new career, or a mixture of the above, blurring the boundary with the 'second' age.

But why should the question of the existence or loss of childhood (or the loss of a 'real old age' for that matter) be an important one? And what is its connection to age patriarchy? Postman describes how adulthood has for much of the century leading to the 1970s been about understanding mysteries – sex, violence, tragedy – formerly hidden from children but now no longer so, since they have access to electronic media and hence to knowledge of such mysteries. This has led to the demise of a social hierarchy based on age. He writes: 'As literacy creates a hierarchical intellectual order, manners create a hierarchical social order. Children must earn adulthood by becoming both literate and well-mannered' (1984: 88). Not only do they no longer earn it, but the very phenomena that open up the adult world to children, especially TV, electronic media, advertising and the hegemony of the visual, works he claims, encourage the irrational and emotive over the conceptual and abstract mode of thought. This complements the notion of *homo economicus*' narcissism; it also induces conformity, rather than originality or critique.

This is also where the link with age patriarchy becomes clear. Goodman's (1960) social critique, though written as these societal changes were beginning, sheds light on this in that he emphasizes the dual role of our personal unwillingness to grow up with the experts and institutions that are happy to encourage this including the nature of education and the absence of meaningful work to 'grow up for'. Today, a variety of factors ranging from the dispositions required to be successful in education including a long professional training to the markedly heavy parental involvement, first institutionalized in behavioural contracts at school but continuing through university for many students, mean that young people experience delay in their maturity and intellectual and emotional independence (Deresiewicz, 2014). In addition, education is itself presented as a consumer good, with all the associated features of narcissism and immaturity noted above. Meanwhile, 'real' work, Goodman points out, belongs to an earlier, or 'heroic' form of capitalism (from which women, as well as the 'feminine' were excluded) and which allowed for 'the ideal... that you risk your soul in a make good or be damned' way (1960: 36). At the other end of the life course old age was once the time when questions of existential meaning could be contemplated within the space of retirement; today the emphasis is on active productive ageing up until the limits of our functioning.

Indeed, late modernity according to Postman, involves a reconfigured stages-of-age 'at one end, infancy, at the other, senility. In between... the adult-child' (1984: 99). This 'childification' or infantilization makes us, of course, more amenable to outside control at all ages by experts, who then assume for themselves the symbolic status of adults. The overlap between feminization and infantilization is apparent in this discourse; indeed an older stress on innate hardiness or resilience has also been replaced by the notion of an essential vulnerability that applies to all age groups and which emerged in media and professional discourse, first in children from around 1990 and then more generally (Furedi, 2007).

In this context, although age-specific norms are less conspicuous than they once were they have been replaced by a hegemonic norm that applies to all age groups equally, in the form of the enterprising and productive self. As Beck and Beck-Gernsheim note:

> You may and you must lead your own independent life, outside the old bonds of family, tribe, religion, origin and class; and you must do this within the new guidelines and rules which the state, the job market, the bureaucracy etc. lay down. (2002: 11)

As noted, this is not an individually shaped life course so much as an individualized one. The impact of our notions of success on agency and, indeed, on the concept of maturity, represent a narrowing and impoverishment. As Neiman suggests: 'when consuming goods rather than satisfying work becomes the focus of our culture, we have created (or acquiesced in) a society of permanent adolescents' (2014: 15). Indeed, the marketing of goods, utilizing psychological techniques, appeals specifically to our irrationality, our fantasies, desires, nostalgia, affect, in a way which infantilizes us in the service of consumption. Within this framework ageing per se is invariably cast as a problem, pointing to the outer boundary in the symbolic grid on the other side of which the abject – dependency, passivity, breakdown of control – resides.

Conclusion

Developmental psychology remains an extremely important influence in terms of shaping the imagery of the life course. The 'stage' idea of development, of which Piaget's framework is an excellent example, directly feeds into the staircase construction of the life course and further substantiates its meaning. We can of course return to earlier stages, as noted, in order to recuperate our wounded child selves so that 'the therapeutic discourse joins the developmental one' (Burman, 2005: 359) thereby facilitating self-normalization and regulation; but not, indeed, to later ones. Further along in time, the staircase rises, then falls away, ultimately into broken darkness But this decline is foretold in the very terms and values selected at the outset. What is looked for, the notion of improvement, then regress, is what is found. Sugarman observes: 'These standards of comparison precede empirical observations' (Sugarman, 2001: 4).

There are other skills and attributes that might be selected as valuable outside the terms of the entrepreneurial self, and that might underpin an altogether different life course. However, since our imaginations have been so invaded by this staircase concept, and the ideal-typical adult into which we will turn at the peak, how can we try to shift our way of thinking about life stages and their relationship with each other? What imagery and concepts could we employ to envision the life course differently?

One suggestion is to stress that all ages have in common the fact that we are 'fundamentally dependent and incomplete' (Lee, 2001: 113); however, this requires recognition of the danger this poses for us in laying us open to intervention by experts who claim to know how to 'complete' us. Invoking the inner child lends itself to being treated – no matter one's age – as an actual child.

An alternative tack is to stress the incommensurability of the qualities and strengths of individual life stages. So for childhood, recognition of the uniqueness of this stage – its elements of magical thinking, similar to the modes of poetry and the tropes of metaphor, capable for example of experiencing a different relationship to time (Hardman, 2001) – permits an alternative to the teleologically informed stage-theory with its standardized model of adulthood waiting at the top (Hardman, 2001) and in turn opens up the possibility of a more heterogeneous adulthood (and old age). Middle age similarly has its unique qualities, with the energy of youth not yet entirely abated and the wisdom of old age also in sight. Gullette (1997) observes, of the experience of herself and her peer-group:

> 'we' grow more resilient, assimilate new concepts faster, stretch our moral ambitions, invent new pleasure for ourselves, control envy and malice better... Mid-life could be a name for that long rich time of life when we possess both knowledge of the workings of the world and maximum power to make change. (1997: 2)

Similarly Woodward (1978), in the case of old age, has identified unique modes of subjectivity that invoke a shift in temporality and can include the meditative mode or 'still point' in T.S. Eliot's words. This emphasizes a state of active, conscious receptivity, characterized by a seamless unity between thinker and universe, antithetical to the Cartesian conception of mind as separate from the universe, and serves as a counterpoint to, but not rejection of, the 'frenzy of agitation' that imparts meaning to the lives of both youth and middle-age individuals (Moody, 1986).

However, acknowledging the presence of unique attributes does not imply a qualitative 'break' with other ages as the developmental psychology model holds but something else: a deepening of certain qualities at different times and contexts, both historically contingent and springing from involvement in certain roles and relationships at particular times of life but not thereby inaccessible as qualities to other ages. Good work, for example, is not the opposite of 'play' and indeed requires the latter for both creativity and innovation (Deresiewicz, 2014) which would also be fed by access to a different mode of time outside clock time. Nor does it imply the essential association of certain life stages with characteristics such as dependency or vulnerability, or alternatively strength and competence. On the contrary, the latter is an effect of power and a feature not of nature but of regulation, division and control.

CHAPTER SUMMARY

- We examined the framework of the modern life course and its construction of ages and stages, looking at its changing construction over time and contrasting it with the medieval concept of the wheel of life.

- We noted how the life course in its shape and trajectory institutionalizes age relations, age ideology and the notion of progress and decline as shaped by the concept of 'development'.

- Specific features associated with late modernity include the co-existence of: (a) fuzzy boundaries between ages; (b) age patriarchy marginalizing non-adult life stages; and (c) a hegemonic master identity of the entrepreneurial or successful self shaping the norms and aims of each individual stage. These features are associated with a differentiation of chronological and symbolic adulthood combined with an infantilization of society more generally.

- We suggested ways of rethinking 'development' and thereby viewing the trajectory of the life course, and the interplay of ages and stages within it, in alternative ways.

Further questions

1. Can we truly understand what it was to be a child one hundred years ago?

2. Is youth the privilege of the rich?

3. Describe and account for the distinction between the third and fourth ages.

Talking point

Futurologists have predicted that children in the West today could actually go on to work to the age of 100 and have 10 different careers spread through 40 different jobs. Meanwhile in Japan the advent of a hyper-aged society (defined as one in which at least 21 per cent of the population is aged 65 and over) combined with low fertility is fundamentally changing the relationship between ages and stages as well as the overall shape of the life course. In particular, where in 1950 the population structure of Japan had the classic pyramid structure, rising to the tip of old age, by 2050 it is likely to take the shape of a reverse pyramid. Furthermore by 2035 the average age of the Japanese population is projected to be 50; there are already more people aged 65 and over than there are children under 15. Within such a context, both 'timetables and time consciousness change', notes Coulmas, and he asks: 'When is the right time to go to school, to get married, to give birth, to retire from work, to receive a pension, to die?' (2007: 130). How would you answer that question?

—— Key texts

The following books provide excellent overviews of the **life course and the organization of ages and stages**: Cole, T. (1992) *The Journey of Life*, Cambridge: Cambridge University Press; Pilcher, R. (1995) *Age and Generation in Modern Britain*, Oxford: Oxford University Press; Mintz, S. (2015) *The Prime of Life: a history of modern adulthood*, Cambridge, MA: Belknap Press of Harvard University Press. For **childhood** see Cunningham, H. (2006) *The Invention of Childhood*, London: BBC; Hendrick, H. (1990) Constructions and reconstructions of British childhood: an interpretative survey, 1800 to the present, in James, A. and Prout, A. (eds) *Constructing and Reconstructing Childhood: contemporary issues in the sociological study of childhood*, Basingstoke: Falmer Press, pp. 35–59; Jenks, C. (2005) *Childhood: key ideas* (second edition), London: Routledge. For **youth** see Furlong, A. and Cartmel, F. (1997) *Young People and Social Change*, Milton Keynes: Open University Press; Jones, G. (2009) *Youth*, Cambridge: Polity. For **mid-life** Gullette's books provide the best introduction and overview interwoven with accounts of age ideology. For **old age** see Gilleard, C. and Higgs, P. (2000) *Cultures of Ageing*, Harlow: Prentice Hall; Katz, S. (1996) *Disciplining Old Age*, Charlottesville, VA: University of Virginia Press; Phillipson, C. (2013) *Ageing: key concepts*, Cambridge: Polity. For **comparisons between youth, childhood, femininity and class** see Hockey, A. and James, A. (1993) *Growing Up and Growing Old*, London: Sage; Firestone, S. (1970) *The Dialectic of Sex*, New York: William Morrow.

Further resources

The Centre for Longitudinal Studies (http://www.cls.ioe.ac.uk/default.aspx) has four longitudinal studies following children born in 1958, 1970, 1989–90, and 2000; it has a large and diverse range of publications on ages and stages and many other aspects comparing the different cohorts for example in terms of timing of life events, features of different life stages and the shifts in gender patterns associated with these.

Figure 4.1   Wheel of the ten ages of man – Psalter of Robert de Lisle (c.1310), f.126v – BL Arundel MS 83.jpg

Note

1. This describes the shift epidemiologically from deaths from infectious disease through deaths from chronic disease to the stage, noted since the late twentieth century, when people are living, not dying, with chronic illness.

5

IDENTITY AND AGE

Background: the dread of old age as a logic of theoretical models

In the previous chapter we observed that the unique experiences, priorities and qualities associated with different ages and stages of the life course are being homogenized within this framework, compressed to fit the mould of the enterprising self: one that emphasizes productivity and consumerism. Whilst this 'one size fits all' identity hides the differences relating to class and gender, this approach to the self is also, importantly, static and contains no suggestion, once one has reached adulthood, of how one changes through the rest of the life course, except through negative increments away from that state. If ageing, then, is the enemy of the self, and this belief is also structured by an increasingly loose and permeable boundary between ages and stages, it is not surprising that a valued identity in adulthood is one that is youthful and resists change with age.

Simone de Beauvoir's writings, her philosophy, fiction and volumes of autobiography, demonstrate the powerful effect of such cultural conceptualizations regarding ageing and the self. Although she was able to defy all the ideological norms attributed to her sex, the prospect of losing herself to old age, as she saw it, of becoming the Other, even to herself, horrified her, no less so than might sharing the fate that befell Gregor Samsa in Kafka's nightmare tale of a man waking up to find he had become a giant cockroach. Indeed, her autobiographical reflections reveal that at each new stage of her life she felt herself threatened by loss of the essential self, meeting each transition with the question: 'How can I change whilst remaining myself?' and finding the answer to be: 'I cannot'(1996: 283) (a question and answer the image of the Hag seems uniquely to symbolize as we suggested in Chapter 1). Ageing through mid-life carrying a more palpable sense of dread, she records the sensation of having 'crossed a frontier' somewhere between the ages of 50 and 54. Unlike the Othering she had already experienced on account of gender, this is both a social Othering and a *self*-Othering, more alienating and objectifying than any male gaze: 'Within me it is the Other – that is to say the person I am for the outsider – who is old: and that Other is myself' (1996: 284).

She writes in *Adieux*, her record of the last years of Sartre's life, of her distress at the fact that not only does he dribble, eat appallingly, wet himself and enjoy the sensation of others 'coddling' him, worst of all is the fact that he often ceases to activate that critical analytic mind that she continued to value above all in herself: 'He liked gazing at the world, doing nothing... he would sit on the balcony for long periods and contemplate the village. I was glad that he did not find idleness wearisome, but it rather wounded my heart that to find pleasure in it he should have to be really "empty" as he had said to the doctor' (1985: 52).

Beauvoir's anguish has cultural roots in the Cartesian framework we have delineated in earlier chapters. Stay young, shrink-wrapping the self in this mode, or decline and lose the self: thus do our models prove inadequate for signposting ageing through the life course or ushering us through its different thresholds. These models serve us far less well, indeed, than those of tribal societies which, with their rites of passage from one state to another, express the existential fact that we are born and die throughout our life in many ways. Van Gennep conveys this notion with crisp and lyrical precision:

> For groups, as well as for individuals, life itself means to separate and to be reunited, to change form and condition, to die and be reborn. It is to act and to cease, to wait and to rest, and then to begin acting again, but in a different way. (1975: 189)

It is our very cultural 'sophistication', the ways we have invented to master the material world, and forget our own mortality, that underpin our ignorance of how to live as beings in time. As we have seen, some of the strongest influences on our views on the self today emerge from the psy disciplines. These emphasize disjunctures in the self during development; adulthood is the goal of development and it is something completely distinct from childhood, as is old age from adulthood, a matter not of degree but kind. Sociological theories do not, by and large, seek to counter this discourse, choosing either to focus theories of identity on socialization processes relating to the malleable infant or on the shaping and maintenance of stable adult identities, all of which emphasize structure over a focus on the 'complexity of the person' (Connell, 1987), 'deriving individuals from the social structures to which they belong' (Cohen, 1994: 6). Thus, theories of socialization from Parsons through to Bourdieu present an account of how the social structure is more or less successfully internalized during childhood in the 'lodging of the system's basic instrumental and expressive drives into the structure of individual personalities' (Jenks, 2005: 17). Similarly, what Foucault has called 'subjectification' is a concept widely used to explain 'character' or 'values' or 'disposition' and as such holds subjectivity at arm's length, as a thing to be explored, as a technology of, rather than for, the self. As a result of such an approach, sociology lacks a developed theory of the 'personality' as compared to psychology and thus cannot readily present alternatives to the rise and fall emplotted by the latter, nor challenge its ageist ideology.

In addressing this, our broad aim in this chapter is to suggest approaches, informed by a more dynamic theory, that induce us to anticipate ageing-through-the-life-course without the dread and resistance generated by, and through, our current cultural models and norms.

AIMS OF THE CHAPTER

- We will look at how the enterprising self as a hegemonic identity impacts on identities traditionally associated with specific ages and stages.

- We will look specifically at two phases of life:

  (i)   successful or 'can-do' youth;

  (ii) successful or 'third age' old age.

- We will then consider alternatives to these dominant approaches, using bio-graphically informed meaning and values as a compass.

- Finally, we consider some sociological concepts upon which we can build in an approach to identity that emphasizes:

  (i)   ages and stages as a continuum rather than a series of radical breaks;

  (ii)   the mutual involvement of continuity and change at all points in the life course;

  (iii) the effect of age-ideological models on the anticipation of age-related change.

The enterprising self: a master identity for all ages

Let us examine in detail the hegemonic identity that is common, with certain varia-tions, to all life stages. This is an identity associated with: (i) work as a role; (ii) productivity as an ethic; (iii) consumerism as a source of self-expression and exis-tential meaning. Sketching the genealogy of late modern subjectification, Nikolas Rose (1998) traces this to nineteenth-century liberalism which first sought to produce 'free' individuals by making them capable of governing themselves as a process of institutional shaping, through families, education, hospitals and workplaces. This sought to align the aims of government with those of citizens. So schools inculcated particular habits of self-mastery, responsibility and rationality and a particular civil sensibility, the base of a 'free' liberal polity. After some deviation via the 'social' approach to freedom during the first half of the twentieth century, there appeared, from the latter part of the twentieth century, a new current seeing self-determination in terms of 'the capacity to realize one's desires in one's secular life, to fulfil ones potential through one's own endeavours, to determine the course of one's own existence through acts of choice' (Rose, 1999: 84). An array of experts including teachers, doctors, psychologists, advertisers and the media, ensure that this theoretically limitless menu is enfolded firmly within a market rationality; the result is a hollowing-out of values which Charles Taylor says 'heads us towards a point where our major remaining value is choice itself' (1992: 69). In this environment there is a cultural turn towards psy disciplines which claim to tell us more about our own self than we know ourselves and to judge the rightness and wrongness of choices on a basis not of morality but of science (Rose, 1999).

Indeed, recent trends in lifespan developmental psychology establish a scientific basis for the enterprising self: these emphasize continued psychological growth throughout the 'life span' (up to a certain age at least) but suggest that universal processes only provide an outline whilst the substance is filled in by individual capital, leading to heterogeneity in developmental outcomes. This brings the socio-economic process of individualization into the heart of theorizing insofar as fulfilment of biological potential is presented as the result of individual competence. The 'enterprising self' as a mode is a perma-identity that treats as irrelevant all differences associated with class, gender and (mostly) age. Likewise, the genealogy of dependence (Fraser and Gordon, 1994), previously discussed, identifies the ways in which structural characteristics over time are assumed to be individual attributes and in turn 'the opposition between the independent personality and the dependent personality maps onto a whole series of hierarchical oppositions and dichotomies central to modern culture' (Fraser and Gordon, 1994: 332), including male/female, public/private, work/care, which similarly become individualized.

In the next section we turn to examine the way the enterprising/successful self is formulated at distinct life stages, and with what consequences.

The successful self through the life course

Another way of framing this inquiry may include: What happens to the qualitative, incommensurable properties of ages and stages in the context of a hegemonic identity such as that of the enterprising self? What happens to perennial questions such as 'Who am I? What is the meaning of my life? What can I expect from different points in my life? How do I grow up and grow old without losing who I am?' One approach suggests that all the different practices and relationships associated with domains as diverse as health, family life, work roles and life stage, are unified in stressing the same qualities and interpellating the individual in the same way or, as du Gay puts it,

> such seemingly diverse forms of conduct as a person's relationship to self, their relationship to their paid work activities, to their leisure activities, their family, environment and so forth all become inscribed with the ethos of the enterprise form. (1996: 184)

For economists like Gary Becker this is because the economic approach is inherent to the way individuals make their decisions in every domain of life. But for others, this results in a flattened and impoverished view of attributes, practices and relationships, with 'success' taking the place of the 'good' in a way that fails to register any goals outside this hegemonic vision. Sandel suggests that this is because, with neoliberalism, we have 'drifted from *having* a market economy to *being* a market society' (Sandel, 2012: 16, original emphasis). Impoverishment results from the fact that markets do not just allocate goods but also generate certain attitudes towards those goods, imprinting our whole ethical system, and our subjectivity, with its particular stamp.

To explore what this means in practice we will discuss the shape the enterprising self takes in youth and old age.

'Can-do' youth

The key image of the successful youth is that of the can-do Girl (Harris, 2004) who achieves success educationally, such an achievement equipping her also with the skills requisite to compete within the neoliberal workforce (McRobbie, 2013; Harris, 2004). Precedents for this model can be found as far back as the 1890s, in the wake of an expansion of educational opportunities for middle-class women. But the origins of her form as she began to emerge in the 1990s were planted in the Sex Discrimination Act (SDA) of 1975 and the efforts that followed thereafter to root out both direct and indirect gender discrimination in schooling (Dyhouse, 2014). Alongside the outperforming of boys educationally, comes a particular brand of self-assertiveness, known as 'Girl Power' which in 2001 the *Oxford English Dictionary* defined as a 'self-reliant attitude amongst girls and young women manifested in ambition, assertiveness and individualism' (Dyhouse, 2014: 210).

That such success is predicated as a quality of femininity is no coincidence: it is in the first instance the product of a feminized education system, based on continuously assessed work and the ongoing diligence, docility and emotional literacy associated with this. The attributes associated with femininity in this environment, which Rosin (2010) calls 'social intelligence, open communication, the ability to sit still and focus' both equip her for her place in a flexibilized labour economy and ensure that she is the quintessential docile subject. She is also the product of successful consumption choices; Harris explains: 'the image of successful individualized girlhood itself is one of the most profitable products being sold to them' (2004: 20). Research by Demos found that girls spend far more of their money than boys on clothes, accessories, toiletries and magazines, whilst boys choose to spend their cash on sports, hobbies and snacks (Darlington et al., 2011).

For success, however, the Girl must combine elements of both traditional femininity and masculinity, including individualized competitiveness, a focus on work and an ambitious desire to succeed, as encapsulated in 'Girl Power', but the latter is depicted in terms of qualities of 'personhood', especially what is required to succeed in the public sphere. This approach succeeds in neutralizing the gender equality agenda, reducing 'rights' to the right to choose, replacing notions of societal change with an emphasis on lifestyle change. This also substitutes for personal change/maturity in a way that has been described as 'adulting' which signifies a play-acting of the role of adult without a subjective sense that one has attained maturity. Thirty-year-old Sophie Lucido Johnson writes in *The Guardian* newspaper that she has come to the conclusion that none of her friends are true adults, that adulthood is a 'myth' (Johnson, 2015) and thus it seems that the horror of adult change can be held at bay indefinitely today, where Beauvoir felt she had no choice but to succumb. Meanwhile, for Johnson and her friends, adulthood is aped by means of 'buying things adults were supposed to have' and for women that includes fresh flowers, white wine, clean linen, an apron and a dishwasher. Laurie Penny irefully condemns the limited vision of success contained therein, and highlights the toothless nature of 'power' in Girl Power, declaring: 'That's why the "career woman" is a neoliberal hero: she triumphs on the market's own terms without overturning any hierarchies' and adds, by way of commentary on the Girl: 'the women of my generation were told that we could "have it all", as long as "it all" was marriage, babies and a career in finance, a cupboard full of beautiful shoes and terminal exhaustion' (2014: 6).

Indeed, Penny protests at exactly the sort of things Goodman noted as a feature of the late 1950s: the meaningless and ultimately corrosive nature of the work on offer. This is possibly more acutely experienced, or at least it is actually articulable, by older workers who have known other ways of doing things but this does not mean its effects on younger workers are benign. Empirical research found that flexible capitalism has inculcated 'internalized flexibility' in young subjects 'which helps them to handle change in a challenging economic environment' (Bradley and Devadson, 2008: 121) (and which enables official critique of older workers as 'inflexible' (Preston, 2015), putting them, not the system, at fault). But there is a darker side to this picture and where 'dislocation has become normalized' (Bradley and Devadson, 2008: 133) for these younger workers, the result is endemic confusion and uncertainty, a permanent state of anxiety at losing control both at work and in a general, psychological sense, and a disjointed sense of time, threatening coherent self-narratives, among other things (Sennett, 1999). Such changes in employment practices, moreover, mean that the difference between labour and work, in the Arendtian sense of the distinction, where labour is about survival and work is the self-defining project of humanity, has been all but lost.

This vision of successful youth is, of course, reliant on the existence of its opposite, and here (in addition to the broader backdrop of troublesome older workers which sets it in relief) we can identify two youthful categories. The first is that of 'at-risk' or failed femininity. The second is that of hegemonic masculinity. The 'at-risk' category for girls is characterized by low literacy, teenage pregnancy, drug and alcohol abuse, educational failure, unemployment and so on. In fact successful girls are equally 'at risk' in terms of the complex negotiations involved in success on the terms being made available to them, for example, involving the paradoxes of gender performance and the embodied dis-ease that may result (discussed further in Chapters 6 and 8 respectively). The second is masculinity, which is problematic at this life stage for different reasons. We have already noted the gender gap educationally and here the losers are overwhelmingly working-class boys of especially white and black ethnicities (Francis, 2010). As Phoenix (2004) points out, the 'enterprising self' that is demanded of young people by the educational system directly contradicts norms of valued masculinity, with the latter implicated in an anti-swot oppositional stance that, whilst shaping hegemonic masculine identities, directly impedes educational success. Of course, this is not to say that boys do not succeed academically; we have already noted that middle-class boys do better than working-class girls. But boys of all classes, if they want to achieve good grades, have to find ways of managing their educational experience such that this aim will not conflict with their presentation of 'masculinity', perceived to lie in defiance and an air of unconcern regarding academic success, emphasis on sporting prowess and so on. At any rate, for boys and girls who fail to 'do' successful youth, the Youth Crime and Justice Section of the 1998 Crime and Disorder Act introduced strict surveillance and disciplinary measures including child curfews and antisocial behaviour orders with an emphasis on prevention pointing to the underbelly of successful youth with its lack of social and cultural capital.

This division between success and failure, however, is extremely unhelpful even for the successful and one of the reasons for this is that it makes failure something to avoid at all costs, thereby minimizing risk taking, which is at the heart of both intellectual success and emotional maturity (Deresiewicz, 2014). It has also shaped a generational mentality that is unusually conformist. But failure is neither irredeemable nor, conversely, can one draw a final line beneath it, even if one wanted to: for those who fail the first time, education is something that can be returned to later in life and this has been a specific educational policy in the UK since 1987, and a key part of the then-planned expansion of higher education (the 'Widening Participation' agenda). Those disadvantaged through socio-economic deprivation, ethnicity and/or disability are targeted including through access courses, designated the 'third route' into university (Reay, 2002). But in practice, this depends not on the purported change in the culture of the educational institutions themselves but on individual transformation, as Reay found in her interviews with mature students. She explains how one student's account of her success (she had tried and failed to take the access route several years previously)

> hinges around her own transformation and draws heavily on individualized explanations of deficit and self improvement – namely that she has worked on herself and is now able to adapt more effectively to higher education culture. (2002: 414)

As noted, developmental approaches to emerging youth individualize 'success' and 'failure'. Côté (2002) describes how the individualization of which the emergent adulthood stage is a part is more or less developed in individual cases and takes the form of either '"default individualization" – or the passive acceptance of mass-marketed and mass-educational pre-packaged identities, which can lead to a deferred membership in an adult community – through degrees of "developmental individualization", or the active, strategic approaches to personal growth and life-projects in an adult community(ies)' (2002: 119). Although Côté stresses individual 'agency' and 'skill' as a determining factor in this differentiation, more sociological models have criticized its lack of sensitivity to constraining features such as class. Bynner puts this succinctly: 'By and large those who have most to start with will extend their transition the longest' (2007: 372), adding that 'the huge diversity of individual experience is constrained by location in the social structure' (p. 378) (leading to predictable patterns and outcomes). Deresiewicz writes that the privileged Ivy League graduates he taught told him they did not wish to be squashed into the confines of an adult role or identity but, by holding back from choosing one career or another, one role over another, one persona over another, they felt they would remain indefinitely 'brimming with potential' in the words of one twenty-two-year-old. We will return to this in the talking point at the end of the chapter.

Successful ageing

The term 'successful ageing', which is found in policy and medical as well as popular discourses, is composed of three separate but complementary strands which delineate medical, psychological and social characteristics. These strands are associated, respectively with Rowe and Kahn (1997; 1987), who coined the term, but also Baltes and colleagues (2003; 1999; 1996; 1990. See Box 5.1 below for a summary) and Butler (2002), who emphasized the social and psychological attributes.

BOX 5.1

The characteristics of successful ageing

Where 'usual' ageing is characterized by functionality but displays deficits, sometimes judged (by both social norms and clinical medicine) as 'normal' ageing, successful ageing is ageing that is both free of deficits and is productive and socially engaged.

Rowe and Kahn's (1987) model includes physical, cognitive, psychological and social elements where excellent functioning in each category is predicated. It inserts an extremely important distinction within the category of 'normal' ageing between *usual* and *successful* ageing, overturning in the process one of the key tenets of geriatric medicine, namely the different norms pertaining to old age (Pickard, 2013). How older people most commonly are – the 'usual' here – is really 'pre-pathological', displaying a range of deficits and decrements. This contrasts with healthy, or 'successful', old age, free of such faults, whether or not the latter impact on function. Although drawing on medical research, it extends its definition to social elements also where successful ageing is conceptualized in terms of active engagement with others and the exhibition of autonomy, not just physiological characteristics. A follow-up paper (1997) extended the criteria of successful ageing in several ways, particularly stressing the 'active engagement with life' component (p. 433). It argues that 'low risk of disease' is as important as the actual presence of disease; and it also requires two further elements: 'interpersonal relations' and 'productive activity'. Robert Butler's (2002) paper links with this in its focus on productivity as an ethics of the self. It includes 'voluntary as well as paid contribution to society and, at its most basic, continuing self-care' (2002: S323). This overlaps with the concept of the third age and in Laslett's description this is achieved, not given: the 'crown of life' claimed by those who lived and planned correctly at earlier stages of the life course and 'above all... a matter of choice' (Laslett, 1991: 152). Thus, the third age represents the outcome of correct choices and reflexive lifestyles, past and present; at the same time it represents the only 'correct choice' for later life that we can make. Finally, the work of Baltes and colleagues focuses on the psychological dimension of successful ageing. Their examples of 'selective optimization with compensation' all concern retaining, albeit in modified form, goals and abilities that made one successful earlier in life. To that extent, successful ageing is formulated within the *homo economicus* model and has pushed aside much of the insight we have from older personality theories that suggest a healthy change in priorities and goals later in life. This means that whilst the latter may continue to figure in lived experience they are becoming invisible to our theoretical models, which, within the concept of a static identity, emphasize what is continued and what is lost from earlier life stages (measurement of which forms the distinction between the third and fourth ages). For example, the approach to wisdom enshrined in this framework is to see it as a form of instrumental rationality, captured through assessment of the mechanics and pragmatics of cognition (Baltes and colleagues, 2003; 1999): not surprisingly, it declines steeply after the age of 75.

Importantly also in all these models of successful ageing, as in our earlier example of youth, is that although there is an emphasis on difference and distinction there is no mention of the social constraints within which one may be operating, nor of the different levels of capital that may be drawn upon to aid 'optimization'. For example, noting the reasons for the heterogeneity in ageing, Baltes and colleagues posit a combination of genetics, lifestyle and disease occurrence; no mention is made of structural factors that can aid or obstruct these attributes. Individual (dis)advantage, however, is evident at mid-life where 'for some individuals mid-life change trajectories are related to... cognitive impairment in old age' (Willis and Schail, 2005: 244) and indeed, conversely, the adaptive qualities of the 'superagers' are also already in evidence in terms of both positive physiological and lifestyle changes.

The fourth age is more likely to be experienced by those with low social and economic capital through the life course and should be seen, in that sense alone, not as rupture but as continuity (this is not to say, of course, that those of privilege can avoid the onslaught of disease or frailty; they cannot, but they are less statistically likely to succumb until they reach older age). Phillipson (2013) suggests that the variegated and enriched leisure and consumption experience enjoyed by the richest pensioners co-exists with the fact that 'the daily reality for many groups within the older population remains that of living on a very narrow range of income, that almost certainly limits participation within the community' (p. 99). Poorer health in mid- and later life is also associated with early age at retirement, experiencing a job loss and more time spent unemployed or in jobs with low control (Glaser et al., 2009) indicating real constraints on a healthy, active participation in the third age, the future consequences of which may be particularly marked for the present younger generations employed in the insecure and 'flexible' service economy. Finally, successful ageing, along with successful youth, appears to imagine no alternative valued identities than those contained in the 'third age' and no valuable choices other than those lifestyle choices relating to diet, exercise and so on: how impoverished a view of existence, as well as of ageing itself, is enshrined in such a vision. Certainly, although most older people characterize themselves as ageing successfully, only a tiny minority meet the criteria set down by Rowe and Kahn (Strawbridge et al., 2002; Sidell, 1995). By contrast, other more sociologically focused psychologists stress the ongoing development that occurs not despite, but rather because of, the challenges, losses and assaults that impact on the self in late old age, including both dementia and adapting to frailty and disability (Coleman and O'Hanlon, 2004) and thereby call into question the distinction between the third and fourth ages, as well as the attributes of successful ageing. Wisdom, for Tornstam (2003; 2011), is conceptualized as a shift of consciousness rather than acquisition of knowledge and on this basis, wisdom, and development/growth in general, increase till 95 years old and only thereafter drop, but only very moderately. Tornstam is suggesting, thus, that older people's reasoning is spoken in a different voice, just as Carol Gilligan found for girls (Friedan, 1993).

The dominant theories, however, all shape a model of the self that is successful insofar as it does not age beyond the prime of life. Expanding Goodman's view of the lack of interest in growing up in a world filled with meaningless but endless productivity, Neiman suggests 'we have not created a world in which reasonable people should want to grow up, or grow old' (2014: 208). Finally, we have to consider how 'successful ageing' does not exist in isolation from, but rather fits with, selfhood over a whole life course. Of course, we can join up the dots in terms of the visions of success at separate points in the life course and impose a unity thereby. But these appear to be less an expression of full and authentic selfhood than a vehicle for the extension of the 'iron cage' across the life course, by way of specific age subjectivities. At all ages:

> the self-control we imagine as the realization of our true or mature self is much more likely to represent the reverse: the development of a self able to consciously flex and adapt itself to the increasingly strident demands of rationalized abstract systems. (MacInnes, 1998: 145)

In this approach, moreover, work (and, more generally, productivity) ceases to be the object of critique and the worker him- or herself becomes instead both the problem and the solution. Setting this in context, a historical sweep shows an immense transformation in both the nature of employment and what is expected of employees, with a massive shift having taken place between the advent of 'Organization Man' in the 1950s and the flexible worker of today. Although the stultifying effects of the requirement to conform and give unswerving loyalty to the corporation are well-documented, there has been a stark decline in work satisfaction and an increase in stress and performance driven both by fear of losing one's job (Mintz, 2015) (apparently more stressful than bland certainty) and by the inability to ever 'leave the office' and switch off completely. More than the actual requirement to have a job, indeed, is the imperative to be 'active' at all times, at all phases of life, in or out of work (if this distinction still has meaning), pre- or post-retirement (Katz, 2000), turning us all into cogs, no matter our age or stage, even if there is no wheel except that located in our own heads.

Success, choice and identity: the limits of consumerism

We have already noted the hollow ring to the enterprising identity that frames the fluidity of age norms noted in the previous chapter just as it makes ideas about what it is to live *well* (as opposed to successfully) increasingly difficult to articulate. If we set our symbolic grid atop this, we can see that ultimately success concerns (self) control: control of boundaries, control of the processes of change, splitting off the abject elements and ensuring the self remains a substance as hard and sharply defined as diamond, the more capable of resisting the softly enfolding embrace of the Hag.

Let us consider briefly the nature and meaning of choice as it is presented to the Girl and to the third-ager respectively. Brumberg's (1997) research shows, through the analysis of personal diaries, that young women in the last century aimed for achievement and growth through cognitive abilities and improvements in their personality, whilst today measures of self-improvement are inordinately centred on bodily perfection: losing weight, using cosmetics and hairstyling, fashion and gyms. Meanwhile, although they may succeed in education, the latter, especially higher education, is geared towards increasing their 'capital' and making them marketable so, as Brown regrets, 'no longer is there an open question of how to craft the self or what paths to travel in life' other than those which will make the student competitive in a world of inequality (2015: 41).[1] Similarly, consumption is the means through which older people have been invited to transform the meaning of later life by refashioning their identity by means of shopping (Gilleard, 1996). But can one really shop for one's identity on the high street? And is this a means of trivializing retirement just as much as Goldman and others argued that work itself was being rendered meaningless? And in that case, are the existential questions now shunted out of the productive life course and into the fourth age (somewhat ironically, given its devaluation and association with lack of agency and capacity)?

We might explore which concepts allow us to understand the difference between living successfully and living well at every stage of life. We can glimpse it in the distinction between what Taylor calls the scientific mode of thinking's insistence on understanding 'human beings in terms continuous with the sciences of extra-human nature' (1985: 80) and the 'thick description' which is necessary to access the 'qualitative distinctions' that people make in terms of what counts in their own, unique lives. We can also draw on Alasdair MacIntyre's invoking of Aristotle. For Aristotle, the 'good' is '*eudaimonia*' or flourishing in terms of one's aims and goals, and what is 'good' is embedded in practices, which include all and any of the common practices of everyday life, including work but also family life and leisure. Such goods cannot be defined externally, as is the case for 'successful' ageing/youth. The 'telos' is also 'internal' to a person's life, binding together the goods in a unique thread of coherence and leading to integrity or coherence as a goal in itself (and an alternative way of viewing 'development'). It is in this context that we can understand the context of 'ageing well'. It is not defined in relation to good health or lifestyle or exercise or cognitive skills; it can only be understood in terms of individual flourishing over a life course, and being true to oneself, displaying what Taylor calls 'authenticity'. Eagleton further clarifies the distinction. He writes: 'The idea of fulfilling your nature is inimical to the capitalist success ethic. Everything in capitalist society must have its point and purpose. If you act well, then you expect a reward.' Aristotle, he explains, sees acting well as an end in its own terms, shaping the type of human being one could become, an idea many people live by today. Eagleton continues:

> Modern capitalist societies are so preoccupied with thinking in terms of means and ends, of which methods will efficiently achieve which goals, that their moral thinking becomes infected by this model as well. What it is to live well thus becomes a matter of acting so as to attain a certain goal. (Eagleton, 2004: 116–23)

The idea of flourishing involves continuities, as well as change, which contrast with both the continuities of successful ageing and the idea of change contained in market flexibility associated with faddish cycles of consumerism and necessary obsolescence; the values of a life remain consistent even though the forms through which they are expressed may change. Thus, if we are going to find alternatives to success that transcend the good/bad binary that defines every life stage, we must start from the perspective of individuals themselves. We explore this next.

Narrating the self through time: building age and temporality into theories of (adult) identity

Narrative identity highlights the perspective of the individual and revolves around the subject's interpretation of his or her life seen as a whole and what is meaningful to him/her in the context of available discourses and material possibilities. This process of working to achieve meaning is not just located at a later point in life, although important and powerful then, as the work of Erikson as well as later life Butler's (1963) 'life review' suggest, but is equally important earlier in the life course and indeed begins at a very early age. Dunn (1988) points out that seeing the self in narrative form occurs from the child's second year and the narrative 'tone' is established early in life (McAdams, 1993). The weaving of narrative identity employs the cultural scripts that we all share and indeed the process itself is given prominence in today's therapeutic culture wherein the life course is often seen as a self-authored book. However, dominant or inauthentic scripts encourage a particular kind of emplotment, with the rise-then-fall trajectory inbuilt and an emphasis on an ageless self. Authentic narrative identity, by contrast, avoids a direct colonization of the self (or 'infolding') through the making of personal moral choices (Frank, 1996). Relatedly, it utilizes time and temporality in an alternative way to that of hegemonic systems such as development, focusing rather on values which lead to an 'orientation in moral space' (Taylor, 1985: 48) viewed in terms of the distance we perceive ourselves to be from realizing our goals relative to our values (i.e. not in terms of a temporal 'ladder' of stages or linear progression). This moral orientation also imparts a sense of 'unification' without which selfhood is reduced 'to a collection of roles learnt, expectations enacted or structural locations occupied' (Connell, 1987: 222). In youth, such personal value orientations are hard to acquire, especially in a world in which grand narratives are optional or lost altogether: those young people in Brannen and Nilsen's 2002 study who were able to discern a plan for their life tended to espouse traditional values; it is not easy for those others who wish to find their own paths to a fulfilled life. Deresiewicz suggests that young people, in thinking about what work to choose – certainly the central decision today – should ask themselves, 'What am I good at? What do I care about?' and a touchstone for this might be: 'Do what you would choose to do anyway even if you didn't get rewarded for it' including what you did spontaneously when you were younger 'before all the spontaneity got beaten out of you' (2014: 97).

However, expressions of value will differ not just in different contexts within the same life stage but also across different life stages; what is involved in a good youth will differ from a good old age as Jung famously pointed out. Thus, Myerhoff's (1978) ethnography of older people attending a Jewish day centre in California in the 1970s found that 'productivity' to give one example, was associated with business success at younger ages but could mean at older ages the ability to give instrumental help to one's less healthy peers or keeping oneself presentable at the day centre, and in being thereby symbolic and expressive, is thus almost the exact opposite of 'successful ageing' which stresses *substantive* continuity. The point is, that a good old age is one that sustains the essential sense of coherence enabling, as MacIntyre puts it, 'an individual to make of her or his life one kind of unity rather than another' (2007: 203). However, this unity will probably not follow what Conway has termed the 'triumphalist' or 'restoration of normality' plot (Conway, 2007) implicit in the idea of agelessness. It will tell of change to the self, and end in a different place to that from which it began. Such a perspective sweeps away distinctions such as the third and fourth ages. Of course this may not be understood within the perspective of our dominant approaches, requiring thus a distinction between the secret or inner history and the judgements of the public world, a quiddity, source of resistance, private space, glimpsed perhaps only by the discerning.

Let us identify 'ageing well' (with its elements of wisdom and growth) in narratives of older people themselves. For Heschel, an informant in Myerhoff's study, this was about 'getting a soul' and as such it requires 'pain' (1978: 197), by which he means a full reckoning with the disappointments and joys of a whole life, as well as the challenges of old age. He explains, 'you get from this the whole thing, the idea of life itself... you get a clarification....' He describes this as a process in which 'choice' has a meaning utterly removed from its neoliberal tenor:

> I call the pain out. After you go through this you discover you got choices.
> You become whole. This is the task of our life. I want to live this kind of
> life, so I can be alive every minute. (1978: 197)

Similarly, individuals in Lloyd et al.'s (2014) study of identity in the fourth age note how individuals continued to display reflexivity and agency, a quality they named 'perseverance' and which was applied to managing their illnesses, including adapting to reduced abilities and increased problems. The authors stress that there was a 'continuation of individual identity, even in their recognition of how dramatically their lives had changed' (2014: 16). One might even suggest a testing and subsequent strengthening of identity at this point, rather than its dimming and faltering, which continues right up until the end.

Below, we consider some methodologies and models that, taking the approach of narrative identity, offer a variety of ways to capture continuity-in-change as an essential feature of identity throughout the life course. They comprise: (i) biographical disruption/narrative reconstruction; (ii) hybridization and metamorphosis; and (iii) post-modern non-linear approaches. As such, all of them encourage us to view ageing without the dread that Beauvoir expressed.

(i) Biographical disruption/narrative reconstruction

One helpful approach derived from sociological analysis of illness narratives is concerned with analysing the processes of construction and reconstruction of both self and identity under the disruption resulting from illness. In illness narratives, people reclaim their selves and restore continuity through an interactive creative assemblage of past as well as present and future. According to Williams (1984) the process of cognitive organization or 'narrative reconstruction' involves the reassembling of past events to explain how all things have led to this particular present. It involves a different version of time to clock-time, a discursive time that is both deeply personal and a resource against the hegemony of clock-time. In the words of Merleau-Ponty:

> Time is... not a real process... it arises from my relation to things. What is past or future for me is present in the world... I do not pass through a series of nows, the images of which I preserve, and which, placed end to end, make a line. With the arrival of every moment, its predecessor undergoes a change. Time is not a line but a network of intentionalities... when time begins to move it moves throughout its whole length. (2004: 478–87)

Heidegger similarly sees the omnipresence of all tenses in the 'now'. Clock-time encourages us to feel that time is a separate substance, both external to our lives and impossible to capture, but the work of narrative reconstruction points to the deeper understanding of present, past and future interpenetrating in the present and inextricable from the self.

(ii) Hybrid and metamorphosis

In this section, I discuss two models which, taken from medieval literary tropes, help us visualize contrasting approaches to identity change through age within a different paradigm to that dominant in modernity. Taken from the work of Caroline Bynum (2001), these are the monster and werewolf or shape-shifter respectively. Bynum describes how these two tropes represented two distinct conceptualizations of change in the twelfth and thirteenth centuries respectively whose contrasting concerns with alterity were generated by different social contexts and espouse wholly different ontologies. As Bynum puts it:

> The hybrid expresses a world of natures, essences or substances (often diverse or contradictory to each other), encountered through paradox; it resists change. Metamorphosis expresses a labile world of flux and transformation, encountered through story. (2001: 29–30)

Hybrid is driven by an explanatory model within the natural sciences and philosophy containing the notion of a teleological logic that like begets like, expressive of the unfolding of a predictable, universal blueprint established by God: oak trees from acorns, particular lives for particular classes of men. Anything that departs from this is considered unnatural and monstrous. It suggests an endpoint, not

constant change. The gargoyles are examples of this hybrid form which includes cen-
taurs, creatures with many bodies and one head or many heads with one body, head
of the fish on a horse body and so on: a griffin with a tail hand, for example, represents
the unnatural addition of one species to another. Such images served as a particular
commentary on the importance of tradition and the status quo and the dangers of
transgressing the natural, social and moral order, offering commentary about people
who marry 'up' or 'down', those who are both statesmen and priests, or who change
social class, thereby combining opposites which should ideally remain unmixed.

Metamorphosis, appearing from around the start of the thirteenth century, is
quite different, admitting the possibility of radical change in the replacing of the
original entity by something altogether different, as in the concept of alchemy or
shape-shifting. This model emerged from a society in ferment characterized by economic growth, crusades and wars, and changes in familial and social structure, all
of which loosened the bonds of tradition. Shape-shifters or werewolves that appear
in literature after 1200 provide examples of this, and represent a trope that 'encap-
sulates graphically and simultaneously the sequence, the before and after, of a self'
(Bynum, 2001: 181). Traces and vestiges of a former self are retained, however, in
the being that the self becomes; without this, there is no 'self' to be discussed, no
identity that endures. Metamorphosis, in other words, addresses the state of becoming, of social death and rebirth, showing a movement in which like the development
of the adult from the child, traces remain within a very different being.

Both hybrid and metamorphosis can be applied to contemporary issues around
identity change. We can look at class change, for example, through the notion of the
hybrid. Lawler (1999) notes the presence in the upwardly mobile women she interviewed of both conscious performance of middle-class style with traces of working-class
sediments remaining at both a conscious and unconscious or practical/tacit level:

> In their interviews, the classed self is expressed by means of a surface/
> depth model: Barbara invokes 'another side' to the self; Frances repre-
> sents her working-class subjectivity as 'forgotten' but 'returning'...
> Although 'depth' subjectivity seems to signify authenticity, then the 'deep'
> self is not necessarily the *real* self... the sedimentations of an earlier habi-
> tus remain to disrupt and fragment a later one.... Thus, the habitus
> claimed is not one that can be fully inhabited. (Lawler, 1999: 16–17,
> original emphasis)

Successful forms of femininity today are similarly composed of hybrid forms including elements of both hyperfemininity and masculinity involving the push and pull of
affect, will and psychic elements, some of which may seem less 'authentic' than others,
and all of which point away from a rational unified self. Masques provide another
example of the hybrid form. This is encapsulated in the 'ageless' (Kaufman, 1986; see
also Conway and Hockey, 1998) or eternally youthful self (Thompson et al., 1991)

trapped inside an older body. All of these examples indicate resistance or obstacles to 'inner' change and a sense of fragmentation. One thing not present in the medieval tropes discussed above, however, is the possibility of moving *from* hybrid *to* metamorphosis but it is certainly possible to see hybrid (sometimes) as a stage on the way to metamorphosis, as well as being an end point (at other times) in itself, characterized by ambiguity. Felski's approach to hybridization holds out this fluid possibility, referring to the holding simultaneously of contrasting identities and involves difference and sameness standing together with neither one privileged or dominant. She lays emphasis on

> fracturing and complicating holistic notions of identity but also addressing connections... by recognizing affiliations, cross-pollinations, echoes and repetitions. (1997: 12)

With regard to metamorphosis, identification is the term Hall gives to the process by which a subject not only is interpellated into a subject position but also invests in that position, through a mixture of social and psychic constituents. There are two parts to this: firstly, a positive embracing of a new subject position, such as a new age identity, which 'entails discursive work, the binding and marking of symbolic boundaries, the production of "frontier-effects"' (1996: 3) and which may correspond to the hybrid. Secondly, there is a setting of barriers and boundaries, excluding some elements and including others. Focusing on age identities, Woodward sees exclusion as 'necessary' to permit us to live in the present and to

> focus on what needs to be done and experienced at the moment rather than losing ourselves in others – or, alternatively, losing ourselves in our past selves and our future selves. (1991: 96)

Jackson makes the same point a little differently:

> The knowledge whereby one lives is not necessarily identical with the knowledge whereby one explains life. Would one ever make a nest if one were mindful that some day one would have to dig a grave? (1996: 2)

or indeed marry the beautiful man/woman if we knew, but *really* knew, that one day s/he would turn into a Hag? Or pass the exams and go onto university if we knew that, bit by bit, it would turn us into the serious, stolid, dull, unfree adult we absolutely did not wish to become? What, after all, is the alternative?

Yet, against this, our perceived inability to move in and out of age identities, or empathize with those of others, is not inherent but is to a degree historically contingent. In the autobiographical and other texts noted earlier in the chapter, Beauvoir made the observation that the child she had been was no longer accessible to her except as a memory. She reflects: 'There are times when I want to believe that I still carry her inside me, that it is possible to tear her free from the wrappings of my memory, smooth her worn eyelashes and sit her down beside me just as she used to be. 'But', she concludes with palpable regret, 'it isn't possible' (1968: 371–2). Had she been writing this today, however, it is likely she might have had a some-what different view, so commonplace has it become (and recommended by experts for its therapeutic properties) to call forth one's inner child. Likewise, especially in today's age regime, it remains considerably harder to see oneself as older than one is, but still this is not impossible: every teenager knows the experience of trying to 'pass' as older through makeup or general swagger and generally feeling exhilarated – and older – when it works. Similarly shifting and contingent are the identities associated with particular ages and stages. If we consider the description by the nineteenth-century social researcher Henry Mayhew of the 'little watercress girl', whom he interviewed for his survey on the London poor, we can see that, although only eight years old, she very much does not see her identity in terms of 'child' but rather as a 'worker'. Mayhew describes how she:

> although only eight years of age, had entirely lost all childish ways, and was, indeed, in thoughts and manner a woman.... At first I treated her as a child, speaking on childish subjects. I asked her about her toys and her games with her companions; but the look of amazement that answered me soon put an end to any attempt at fun on my part. (Mayhew, 1864; quoted in Cunningham, 1991: 108–9)

Explaining that she had 'lost the gift of tears' she displayed a maturely responsible attitude to her earnings and explicitly distanced herself from the identity of 'child' (at least in its middle-class version):

> All my money I earns I put in a club and draws it out to buy clothes with. It's better than spending it in sweet-stuff, for them as has a living to earn. Besides, it's like a child to care for sugar-sticks and not like one who's got a living and vitals to earn. I ain't a child and I shan't be a woman till I'm twenty but I'm past eight, I am. (Cunningham, 1991: 109)

To her, being a child is synonymous with a lack of responsibility, and thus alien to her situation in life: it is a state of mind, connected to a set of material and social circumstances, not a chronological category, much less an incommensurable essence.

(iii) Post-modern journeys through the life course

Deleuze and Guattari (2000) are also helpful in providing some conceptual and sym-bolic tools with which to re-imagine the life course, outside the trope of development, progress and their antithesis. They depict moving through the life course as a non-linear experience, taking the form of a 'rhizomatic' pattern, a movement which is neither to nor from, up nor down, advance nor decline. Rhizomes, sprouting in all directions with no 'main' artery, do not proceed through careful advance plotting but in a more intuitive, organic, spontaneous pattern, mapping broad areas, forming alliances with objects, other people, ideas and so forth and are constantly modifiable despite continuity. They are coloured not by normative timetables or events but by 'plateaux', which are meaningful themes or motifs that have enduring value and can repeat like the motifs in a fugue. This is specifically intended as a contrast to *ends* and *beginnings*; it also allows for the self to fail, to wander and get lost and take up the pattern again later, with Odysseus the archetypal example of this, thus providing an alternative way of viewing one's life history from the expected 'milestones' provided by dominant culture. Within this system, although there will definitely be a perception of age – a consciousness of the dimensions, shape and contours of the map of life and the territory one has covered, physically and cognitively and psychically – it will not be according to a chronology but rather with reference to identifications – aligned with one's unique values or interests and it may or may not approximate to things society judges as 'success'. Kate Bolick, in a literary memoir, talks about experiencing this on the occasion of her fortieth birthday party:

> I was now in possession not only of a future, but also a past. It was almost a physical sensation, as if everything I'd ever thought or done had been embroidered onto the long train of a gown that now trailed behind me wherever I went. (2015: 7)

Again, in order to avoid the language and imagery of development Deleuze and Guattari (2000) talk in terms of changes in speed, intensity, sound and so on, and draw comparisons with music and with non-human animal life.

Conclusion

Following our discussion in Chapter 3 of the way that sociology has ceded the body in old age to biology and medicine, we can say it has similarly ceded the emplotment of movement through the life course to the psychologists, accepting its shape of growth, stability and decline, concentrating attention instead on the middle portion associated with stability, and inadvertently contributing to this mythology. We have seen that whilst the middle portion, that of adulthood, is extending its symbolic reach to other ages, it is doing so in relation to a hegemonic, ageless identity associated with productivity and consumerism. As such it both underplays the impact of structural features on successful identities and provides a context even less conducive to ageing well through the life course than in the days when Beauvoir was writing. In the models offered to us in late modernity, Harry Moody suggests, 'the appeal is always to turn away from outdated images of maturity in favour of a reinvented identity outside time and finitude' (2005: 64; quoted in Andrews, 2009: 74). No wonder, with time conceived of as an enemy, stealthily and remorselessly stealing all of value from us, year by year, stage by stage. But the opposite of a homogeneous 'youthful' identity is not a staccato series of discrete age identities, either those found in developmental models, or in contingent historical constructions. Instead, we can look to the possibility of drawing on the various qualities associated with diverse life stages as we travel through our unique biographies, keeping our subjectivities age-mobile in the sense of not being defined by any, but incorporating all, as and where appropriate.

In *The Coming of Age* Beauvoir observed that the Buddha alone was able to recognize his own fate in that of the old man: only he could take in the entirety of the human state. Accepting this as a worthwhile goal will require a model that resists the ageless model of old age. Such a model will 'not seek to hide the years but rather to recognize what has been gained and what has been lost with the passage of time' and above all will recognize that 'the process of ageing is the process of living' (Andrews, 2009: 75–80).

CHAPTER SUMMARY

- In this chapter we looked at how the hegemonic master identity of the entrepreneurial self works to shape subjectivities at specific ages according to a particular model of 'success' associated with symbolic adulthood.

- In order to counter both the overly static approaches to identity contained herein as well as the association of a valued identity with particular notions of 'success' in an individualized life course, we suggest the use of narrative approaches to identity.

- Starting from the perspective of the individuals themselves, this approach temporalizes identity, includes a tension between continuity and change, and admits a perspective formed outside the framework of age ideology.

- In terms of working with continuity and change within such narratives, we highlight, among others, the models of 'hybrid' and 'metamorphosis' as capturing resistance to, and acquiescence in, change respectively.

Further questions

1. What might it mean to 'age well'?

2. What, according to mainstream psychological theories, happens to the human mind and personality over the life course? Do you find these theories satisfactory?

3. In the neoliberal context, whereby consumerism is elevated to a principle that applies to every domain of life, Seabrook writes this about the poor: 'as more and more aspects of our lives are transformed into market transactions, this process sets vital experiences out of reach of the poor, and at the same time, damages the values they embody' (2013: 212). Discuss in relation to different stages of the life course.

Talking point

We have noted how Ivy League graduates saw their lives at 22 as 'brimming with potential'. But research by Barnardo's suggests that whilst between 14 and 16 all social classes feel positive about their futures, by the age of 22 many have given up: 21 per cent of the sample category aged between 20–22 agreed: 'people like me don't have much of a chance in life' (Hellen, 2015). How might class, gender and other characteristics impact on every age identity?

—— **Key texts** ——————————————————————————————

Good overviews of **sociological theories of identity** are found in Cohen, A.P. (1994) *Self Consciousness: an alternative anthropology of identity*, London: Routledge; Jenkins, R. (2004) *Social Identity: key ideas* (second edition), London: Routledge; Lawler, S. (2008) *Identity: sociological perspectives*, Cambridge: Polity. For a general overview of **identity from a psychological perspective** see Sugarman, L. (2001) *Life-Span Development: frameworks, accounts and strategies* (second edition), Hove: Psychology Press. For discussions of **identity at specific ages or life stages** see Woodhead, M. and Montgomery, H. (2003) (eds) *Understanding Childhood: an interdisciplinary approach*, Milton Keynes: Open University Press; Baltes, P. B. and Baltes, M.M. (1990) *Successful Ageing: perspectives from the behavioural sciences*, Cambridge: Cambridge University Press; Coleman, P. and O'Hanlon, A. (2004) *Ageing and Development: theories and research*, London: Arnold. For **sociological critiques of such theories** see Rose, N. (1989) *Governing the Soul: the shaping of the private self*, London: Routledge; Burman, E. (2007) *Deconstructing Developmental Psychology* (second edition), London: Routledge. For approaches to **narrative identity** an excellent introduction is Frank, A.W. (2010) *Letting Stories Breathe: a socio-narratology*, Chicago: University of Chicago Press. For discussion on **freedom, liberalism, neoliberalism and their influence on the self** see Taylor, C. (1985) *Sources of the Self*, Cambridge: Cambridge University Press; Lukes, S. (2006) [1973] *Individualism*, Colchester: ECPR Press; Rose, N. (1999) *Powers of Freedom: reframing political thought*, Cambridge: Cambridge University Press.

Note

1. Key university policy papers, such as the Browne Review (2009) and the Higher Education White Paper (2011) conceptualize the university within market terms, including fee income, value for money and student choice. The 2012 Wilson Review 'argued that universities were an integral part of the supply chain to business' (Phipps and Young, 2012: 22).

6

AGE AND EMBODIMENT

Background: constructing the rational body

We have argued in the preceding chapters that the age and gender regimes are mutually constitutive. In this chapter we will explore how this works in relation to embodiment through the life course. As also noted, gendered inequalities, inscribed first and foremost on the body, operate throughout the life course and work with and through age categories in order to do this. In previous chapters we have described how 'dependency' is structurally produced yet both individualized and located within the subjectivity: this chapter demonstrates how it is also inscribed upon the body at key points in the life course. The myth of permanence (a key part of age ideology) suggests that these early dispositions, once acquired, will endure. For example, in Bourdieu's approach the bodily hexis constitutes a 'permanent disposition' (Bourdieu, 1990: 70); the principles it embodies are 'below the level of explicit statement and therefore outside the control of logic' (p. 94). Each age is constructed in terms of particular embodied characteristics which are valued more or less highly or considered more or less rational in accordance with the other norms and practices that bear down on particular age groups. In this respect, Connell (2005) talks in terms of 'fixing' mechanisms which work to reduce the limitless discursive fluidity attributed to both men and women in late modernity. The contribution made by this chapter is to suggest that these fixing mechanisms are located at key points in the life course, through which they acquire associations of inevitability. In addition, ageing, as an embodied process, in and of itself produces inequality. Developmental psychologists Bee and Mitchell (1984) summarize the physical changes associated with ageing as 'smaller, slower, weaker, lesser, fewer' (quoted in Sugarman, 2001: 62). In terms of gender, masculinity and (particularly) femininity are youthful attributes which are perceived to decline with age.

AIMS OF THE CHAPTER

- We look at how bodies are shaped and constructed at particular stages of the life course in accordance with the gender-related norms associated with these stages focusing on:

  (i)   children's bodies;

  (ii) gender practices in the context of school days and youth;

  (iii) intersections of class and gender;

  (iv) menstruation;

  (v)   menopause;

  (vi) old age.

- We will then look at ways of resisting and challenging these norms, recognizing that the latter are deep-seated, located as they are in the bodily hexis.

Childish bodies: unique characteristics?

Before looking at the way children's bodies are differentiated from adults', and girls' bodies from boys', I wish to highlight a very early feature of infancy, namely embodied being characterized by intersubjectivity, which is overlooked in the Cartesian emphasis on the individual, atomistic body. Merleau-Ponty (2004) suggests that pre-communicative early life does not differentiate one individual from another but perceives an 'undifferentiated group life' (p. 112) and from this basis arises communication in that we are able to read and interpret the 'corporeal schema' of others because it is open to our understanding. The body, moreover, is and remains, 'open' in ways that the emphasis on the closed 'civilized' body suppresses culturally. Although a key process of socialization involves children learning to separate self from other, this resource remains at the foundation of social being (O'Neill, 2005).

Also, from earliest days, children's bodies are distinguished from adults' bodies according to the framing device of 'development'. Growth and development charts stress the acquisition of 'sucking, rolling over, sitting up, crawling, chewing, hand to eye coordination, walking, talking, running, jumping, bowel and bladder control, hopping, climbing, skipping' (Hockey and James, 1993: 85). These are all perceived as necessary steps on the path to adulthood, hence their absence is considered problematic and they are judged in accordance with an ever-narrowing range of normality. One need only compare the 'landmarks of development' taken from a 1924 publication (Lyddiard, 1924; reproduced in Rose, 1989) with a 2014 equivalent

(Sharma and Cockerill, 2014). The earlier text notes for nine months the landmark 'able to sit erect'. The later has seven such landmarks for this age followed by six pages of detailed accounts of developments in posture; visual, perceptual and fine motor regions; hearing, speech and communication, social behaviour and play, and last but not least, 'self-care and independence' which includes the rudiments of eating alone and trying to manipulate cups and utensils in the process (Sharma and Cockerill, 2014: 18–23). Rose (1989) notes: 'Non-intellectual behaviour [is] thus rendered into thought, disciplined, normalized and made legible, inscribable, calculable' (p. 147). Other ways of judging children's bodies are overlooked within this schema: limitless energy, for example, the unrestrained and uninhibited ability to inhabit one's body in play and dance, suppleness, flexibility, spontaneity and all-round health and vitality. Because of this theoretical emphasis moreover, certain strengths and capabilities of children are often overlooked with the consequence that a view of childhood as vulnerable and needy is maintained, even against the living facts. This has wider consequences in terms of access to power and the structuring of inequality. Hockey and James observe:

> Children who run households, care for disabled parents, engage in prostitution, contribute to family income and take charge of younger siblings reveal the extent to which images of dependency are ideological rather than actual. (1993: 92)

We turn next to the way that, simultaneous with the separation of children's bodies from adult bodies, girls and boys learn to be embodied according to the contrasting norms of masculinity and femininity.

Men and women in the making

Prendergast and Forrest's (1997) study of boys' behaviour at school shows how boys learn to be masculine by literally incorporating gender roles into their bodily performance and gender scripts into their emotional and instrumental repertoires with such learning sustained among their peers and defined in opposition to girls. That is, as Connell (1987) observes: 'My male body does not confer masculinity on me, it receives masculinity (or some fragment thereof) as its social definition' (p. 83). Indeed, in line with the feeling rules and emotion work identified by Hochschild (1979) it suggests that gender is learnt through performance that is enacted first, and to which later the 'appropriate' feelings are added. So, for example, a little boy learns to act aggressively with a toy gun or sword, copying 'activities that he does not understand because they seem to signify excitement or power' (Prendergast and Forrest, 1997: 187). Indeed, one can see in these embodied masculine scripts how the process of individuation and separation from the Mother firstly, and then from femininity more generally, is embodied as well as psychologically inscribed as the body is literally hardened and toughened against the threat of femininity inside and outside. So, for example, playing sports like rugby encourages the physical sense of maleness to grow within the bodies of adolescent boys and lays the foundation of a more general claim, contained within masculinity, of superiority over women and hegemonic masculine domination of other men (Connell, 1987).

Gendered roles at school involve: (i) a particular use of space by boys; (ii) particular bodily valorizations – tallness, hardness or toughness in particular; and (iii) the power of peer pressure in shaping masculine identity. Thus, in Prendergast and Forrest's (1997) study, boys' exuberant physicality dominated public space, as opposed to girls who clustered in small, tight groups on the margins. Bigger boys in particular dominated this – their size and height, and strength and toughness winning them control over the space – and the activity involved pushing, tripping up, and generally pushing each other to the limits. This process continues throughout boyhood. Connell notes that 'certain areas of school life serve as "hot spots" or vortices in the construction of masculinities' (2000: 66) and appear to include school sport and interaction with peers and with teachers, with contrasting responses possessing a strongly classed dimension. The gender-divided curriculum also reinforces traditional associations between masculinity and science and technology, for instance. However, the norms of masculinity can negatively impinge on the ability to function successfully within a school environment for many boys and can easily overlap with symptoms of ADHD. Boys represent the overwhelming number (approximately 75 per cent) of children diagnosed with ADHD (Singh, 2005) and although approached as a 'developmental disorder' consider this description by two psychologists:

> children [with ADHD] seem to have an internal dynamo that compels them to constantly expend energy. They find it almost impossible to sit still: they fidget, run about the room, and climb on chairs, tables, doors, windows, and anything else that can be climbed. (Mitchell and Ziegler, 2007: 100)

The condition is also exhibited in anger, risky behaviour, 'unwillingness to wait in a queue' and general lack of docility; of course all are characteristics traditionally associated with masculinity, but rendered problematic within the context of an environment stressing (inner-generated) docility. We can see the continuation of older discourses here also and can trace a direct lineage with earlier notions of delinquency that were, in turn, based on the aim of transforming children's identities from workers to school pupils (Hendrick, 1990).

Looking at women's use of space and embodied motility, Iris Marion Young (2005) describes women's bodily style from very early days as one of a constricted use of their bodies and inhabiting of the world, characterized by greater inhibition and uncertainty as compared with men's embodiment. This arises from tensions generated by a variety of social pressures that converge on the bodies of girls and young women, including the tension between legal and social freedoms and the continued objectification of women's bodies through the male gaze. The cultivated enfeeblement which arises, imbuing the sinews, the musculature and the bones with femininity-as-weakness, has been termed a 'frailty myth' (Dowling, 2000), involving the ideological construction of women's physiology as 'naturally' weaker than men's. That this is not an inherent characteristic of women's bodies is clear if we consider the fact that women's sporting prowess in terms of speed, strength and endurance have all increased enormously since the mid-1960s: for example, over the period 1964 to 1995 the world record for marathon speeds for women improved by 1 hour 5 minutes, 21 seconds; for men by only 5 minutes 2 seconds (Cashmore, 1990; quoted in Dowling, 2000), the direct result of women being trained with the same techniques as men.

On the face of it, the frailty myth flies against the strong, assertive imagery associated with 'Girl Power'. Closer analysis, however, suggests that the latter has a limited effect on embodiment and/or that it co-exists with opposite trends. Budgeon (2014) notes that today women are 'invited' to incorporate into their subjectivities elements of traditional masculinity (assertiveness, freedom) alongside traditional femininities (affect, feminine appearance, etc). This combination is always 'reassuringly feminine' (McRobbie, 2009) and where it is not – as in the case of women who are masculinized, etc – it is stigmatized. So, for example, the 'crew nights', in which both male and female athletics teams socialize at Oxbridge colleges, are characterized by an overt sexism on the part of the male athletes (Porter, 2013) and an expectation that the women athletes present will conform to the norms of feminine sexuality.

More generally, athletics and sports training, where it takes place, is layered upon an initial gender socialization which results in the fact that, in comparison with men's bodies, women's bodies are stiff and enclosed; their stride is shorter in proportion to their body, their arms held closer to their body, their step less springy and more flat, their legs closer together in sitting or standing. Young (2005) notes three specific modalities of feminine motility: (i) an ambiguous transcendence; (ii) an inhibited intentionality; and (iii) a discontinuous unity with her surroundings. Locked within herself, both physically and symbolically, she does not extend herself into public space, a fact which extends to ambition in work and life but which Erikson (1964), in his theory of woman's 'inner space', essentialized and indeed related to the nature of female sex organs. This constrained physical stance results in a more general inability to 'do' as a competent embodied being in the public world, and in a way that extends to other social roles and practices. By age 15, only half the total number of girls achieve the government's target activity rate for children of 60 minutes of exercise per day and nearly double the number of men than women aged 16–24 regularly take part in sporting activity (Women's Sport and Fitness Foundation, 2007; UK Sport, 2006; both cited in Banyard, 2010). These differences arise from certain basic suppositions that relate to ideological notions concerning gender. They include: (i) sex-based differences viewed as biological resulting in; (ii) different expectations with regard to play and performance; and

(iii) different labelling of activities in terms of gender-appropriateness, relating to factors such as physical power, aggressiveness, exertion, activity and so on. Such differences have significant implications in later life as we will see.

Class and gender hierarchies

Bodies are also inscribed with hierarchical differences that differentiate genders by status, and which include social class inscriptions. Particular bodily characteristics underpin and influence the performance of hegemonic, or dominant, forms of masculinity although the priority of sporting prowess and physical strength in childhood/adolescence can be modified by practices in adolescence such as going to the gym and sculpting a muscular physique, overturning original disadvantages. In adulthood, hegemonic masculinity is principally associated with business, the professions, the military and science (Connell, 1993). Indeed, there is a sharp disjunction between the forms of hegemonic masculinities/social power found in youth and in adulthood. Whilst hegemonic masculinity per se can be seen to encompass two major contrasting versions – muscular machismo and ultra-rational Weberian control – these have often been seen as pertaining to two stages in the life course, namely boyhood and adulthood. However, class underpins the shift from one to the other, enabling middle-class (but not working-class) boys to transition successfully. Indeed, as far as the shift to the rational is concerned, Ehrenreich explains that it is necessary for men to employ 'the verbal means of command and the emotional distance necessary to function in a bureaucratic setting' (1983: 133). Thus, the shift has particular consequences for working-class boys, as Willis' (1977) classic ethnography illustrates. For the 'lads' in his study, masculinity in its hegemonic or tough macho form bestowed greater distinction than the more 'feminized' bookish forms of the conformist boys but simultaneously worked to trap them in their working-class lives. Indeed, despite its detachment from a foundation in industrial manual labour, the macho type of laddishness has remained important in masculine identities (O'Donnell and Sharpe, 2000). Research indicates that contemporary 'lads' have responded with even more pronounced forms of hypermasculinity with machismo spreading to other classes and seen as a way for these school-age boys to 'regain control of their lives' (Arnot, 2004: 28). Indeed Tolson (1977) sees working-class masculinity as comprising real power, for example, in the industrial settings in which it was traditionally deployed (although denigrated by middle-class observers) and contemporary expressions may similarly generate social power for such boys among their youthful working-class peers (but not by adult/middle-class perspectives or in other milieux) (Ehrenreich, 1983).

Recent research suggests a more complex picture in terms of hybrid masculinities and femininities in the new gender regime than that of the gender hierarchy described by Connell (1993; 1987), which originally posited a hegemonic masculinity at the top of the hierarchy with subordinated masculinities and femininities below this. It posits instead a more complex and relational approach involving plural masculinities and femininities involved in relational interactions with each other, but all of which complement hegemonic masculinity. The hybrid femininity we have noted as involving elements of traditional masculinity and femininity is marked off relationally from more traditional femininities that exhibit greater reliance on heterosexual relationships; so the can-do girl is defined by her greater distinction in relation to the girls displaying emphasized femininity without any hybridity. For example, the 'can-do' young women in an ethnographic study by Rich felt that females defined by more traditional characteristics were personally at fault for not taking opportunities open to them or making poor choices (Rich, 2005).

Evidence suggests that both girls and boys who want to do well at school are involved in complex and challenging management strategies of their gender performances, with girls allaying their 'threat' to hegemonic masculinity by hyper-femininity in other aspects of their behaviour such as not speaking out or putting their hand up in class (Renold and Allan, 2006) and boys occupying a careful low-key 'middle position' in which they are seen as neither too academic nor its opposite (Phoenix, 2004). Precisely because of these multiple masculinities and femininities, it has been suggested that differences between boys and girls should not be taken as a clear dividing line and indeed that this multiplicity in itself challenges the idea that boys and girls have clearly distinguishable cultures (Thorne, 1993).

Nevertheless these two gender polarities, even if more complex in empirical reality, shape the way boys and girls are 'seen' and their actions 'read'. There are also gendered attributes common across the varieties of masculinities, as well as across racial and class lines, for example, in the continued expressed desire to dominate girls, either materially or symbolically, in boys 'who had learned something from the gender equality agenda but still retained significantly patriarchal and sexist attitudes and patterns of behaviour' (O'Donnell and Sharpe, 2000: 87). Indeed, hegemonic and subordinated masculinities are not only shaped in relation to class differences but each relate differently to women. Pyke points out that in the absence of legitimated hierarchical ascendancy, working-class men are more overtly masculine, or hyper-masculine, 'relying on blatant, brutal and relentless power strategies in their marriages, including spousal abuse' (1996: 45). However, this also serves the interests of higher-class men in 'deflecting attention from their covert mechanisms of power and enabling them to appear egalitarian by contrast' (p. 545). We might also usefully see these forms as reflective of forms of capitalism: the industrial-era masculinity that equipped a boy for the harsh discipline of factory or army contrasting with the softer but no less coercive consumer capitalism of today (Seabrook, 2013).

Throughout the life course, the relation of classed gender performances is less straightforwardly associated with wellbeing; as we will see in Chapter 8, successful youthful femininities, whilst associated with socio-economic capital, also bring greater risk of certain psychopathologies. In old age this relationship may remain complex; hegemonic masculinities, for example, are not associated with the capacity for caring friendships that may be more important at this point for health and wellbeing. On the other hand, traditional femininities also come with a price and we will suggest in Chapter 8 that emphasized femininities are over-represented in diagnoses of frailty.

Menarche, menstruation and the stigmatizing of female bodies

As we noted, one of the reasons that women are 'physically inhibited, confined, positioned and objectified' (Young, 2005: 42) is because they are objects of the male gaze. This means that, unlike men, whose bodies can more readily 'disappear' into the background, women are thrust into hypervisibility, which is the usual condition of (youthful) femininity, where they remain to mid-life (currently, it seems women commonly feel they become 'invisible' (to the male gaze) at the age of 46 (Smith, 2014)). Young (2005) suggests that it is around the time of menarche (first period) that girls usually first feel the force of this objectifying gaze focused on their breasts which are supposed to conform to particular standards and aesthetics.

The experience of menstruation remains problematic, bodily and socially, despite women's full engagement in education and the workplace. The atmosphere of secrecy and taboo, necessary for concealment, and underpinned by the imparting of imperfect information, means that girls experience this in isolation as an individual-ized process. Indeed, as one girl related in Prendergast's study, it took on all the overtones of trauma:

> Like this girl in primary school, she and her sister had started and… there was blood everywhere, and all the boys were taking the mick. And we used to dread it. I thought that it would be permanent and that you bled all the time. (2000: 109)

We can trace this silence and misinformation historically to the development of middle-class concepts of femininity in which discussions about menstruation (and sex) were removed from the public domain to become the province of physicians alone. Thuren (1994), in a fascinating account of how menstruation practices changed in Spain following the social and political changes that arose in the wake of the death of General Franco, notes that although the powerfully restrictive nature of taboos around menstruation were replaced by a 'problem of etiquette' (Young, 2005), menstruation is still considered a 'hassle'. She explains:

> To have one's first menstruation… is to be ushered into a negative phase of life, in which one will have a monthly practical problem to deal with. This is called 'to become a woman'. To become an *adult* is something very different. What is positive in 'modern society' is to 'become a person',

which is automatic for men while women have to fight for it, and that fight entails, in some sense, to learn NOT to be a woman in the ways womanhood used to be defined. (1994: 15)

Meaning of the menopause

If menarche marks the beginning of a life stage characterized by hypervisibility in several areas of life, menopause marks out its demise. But if menstruation is problematic, its demise is even more so. A fixing mechanism akin to the onset of menstruation, 'menopause' as a discursive event both paradoxically hints at the essential deficit of femaleness and suggests the ending of femininity. However, in Martin's (1987) study, women's lived experience of menopause was very different to its portrayal as a negative event in the literature, both popular and medical. Indeed, Martin's respondents associated it with a 'release of new energy and potentiality', (p. 177) although interestingly, outside observers, including younger women as well as doctors saw menopausal women as 'out of control' (p. 177).

Greer (1991) suggests that the menopause can be liberating insofar as it can precipitate the loosening or freeing up of women from a normative femininity that involves their domination by hegemonic patriarchy. Here, Greer is distinguishing between 'femininity' which she sees, like Butler, as a drag act, and 'femaleness': an essential quality which she defines as 'self-defining female energy, and a female libido that is not expressed merely in response to demands by the male, and a female way of being and of experiencing the world' (1991: 59). Unlike 'femininity', moreover, femaleness is not imprinted with a youthful stamp. However, whilst this sounds like a wonderfully positive differentiation, unfortunately Greer cannot enlighten us further as to what it might actually mean in concrete terms as she says: 'After centuries of conditioning of the female into the condition of perpetual girlishness called femininity, we cannot remember what femaleness is' (1991: 59). Similarly, Daly (1991) urges that women reject 'the state of tameness' and become 'wild' but never expands on what the latter might mean. (I do not mean to imply criticism here, but rather to stress the difficulty of imagining what it is to be female outside the hegemonic order and the artifice of femininity produced within it.)

Utz's (2011) study on the contrasts between the approach of two generations of mothers and daughters reveals a third alternative to either concealment or celebration of menopause, and that is 'control'. This was a common theme expressed by the daughters (born during the boomer generation), but not their mothers, suggesting a refusal on the part of the former to conform to the idea that menopause is the end of women's sexuality, and a desire to continue to control the body as a project of the self. This involved the use of pharmaceuticals to control the body's changes, and as such it joined with other anti-ageing strategies embraced by these women, an approach particularly likely to appear in the narratives of successful professionals (Gullette, 1997). Unlike their mothers, who viewed the menopause as natural, and accepted it as a significant transition event, the daughters saw it as a disease to be treated (with HRT or other remedies),[1] a signal of ageing which for them symbolized a potential loss of control presaging the ultimate loss of control that is death: evidence, perhaps, of the increasing cultural distanciation from the Hag. In this respect it continues the course that many of these women have followed since youth, using the Pill to control their reproduction and seeing the body's 'natural' processes as not something to submit to: truly the daughters of Simone de Beauvoir.

Certainly, the *prominence* given to the menopause in today's society, as compared to earlier generations, suggests its important regulatory role within the gender regime with an equal but opposite weight accorded to an idealized motherhood. Indeed, Gullette suggests, the problematization – and attention given to – menopause is part of a gender backlash, some aspects of which are subtle and others not so. Whilst younger women are regulated by rape, abortion, pornography and violent imagery, mid-life women receive attention from the 'public menopause discourse' (1997: 101). Herein, an ordinary physiological event (or process more accurately) is labelled a deficiency disease. Termed '*the change*' it implies that we are not ordinarily subject to flux in terms of our embodiment (one, in fact, only has to consider the processes involved in digestion to reflect on how *stability* is not the ordinary condition of bodies, whatever age or gender). The discourse also suggests, in a powerful if implicit message, that there is only 'one' change and thus that 'only women age' (Gullette, 1997: 105) and indeed despite terms such as 'male menopause' there is really no equivalent for men; prostate discourses, for example, do not receive anywhere near as much attention, or problematization.

Embodying older age

The discourses of masculinity and femininity that we have been describing have in common the fact that they are associated with a youthful ideal so that older masculinities and femininities are portrayed in terms of deficit and lack. This is especially true for women, as the characteristics that are valued in femininity in many ways evoke a *childlike* persona, weak, vulnerable, in need of protection (Bordo, 1995). By contrast, we can see how masculinity is, in many ways, treated as synonymous with adulthood and indicates a positive relationship with power. Not surprisingly in her research for the *Feminine Mystique*, Friedan identified a 'terrifying blank' (1963: 64) that made women unable to think of themselves over the age of 21. Although that age is likely to have risen in recent years, an age or ages of symbolic dread still apply to many women – whether that be 25 or 30 or 40. Indeed, its very vagueness simply adds to its terror. Penny describes her friends looking towards their thirties in terms of a time for 'hard, adult choices in a way I never hear from my male friends' leading her to suggest: 'the precious core of modern male privilege is time' (2014: 88–90).

A further consequence of the fact that gender norms are associated with younger bodies is that the problems and issues associated with ageing masculinities and femi-ninities are sometimes overlooked by those theorists examining gender inequality earlier in the life course: we do not know whether Connell's hegemonic and sub-ordinated masculinities, for example, remained relevant in old age (for the current older generation), or whether hybrid gender forms are patterned differently in old age and what the relationship is with wellbeing, identity, relationships and so forth. In the next section we will look at how older embodiment is a site in which the norms of the civilized body are perceived to be under threat, leading to greater exter-nal scrutiny of the older person. In this section we will examine how this is evident in relation to: (i) the experience of falling; and (ii) the incontinent body. The aesthet-ics of the older body are also closely related to its being treated as uncivilized, but we will take up this theme in Chapter 8 and concentrate on specifically embodied dimensions of this experience here.

In terms of falling (i), Young suggests that females 'develop a bodily timidity that increases with age' (2005: 43) and although she is talking about growing through childhood and adolescence, this observation is equally relevant for ageing into old age. One way in which this timidity may be accelerated is by the very act of its being interpreted through a lens of decline. For example, Madonna's infamous fall on stage during her performance at the 2015 Brits music awards was related in many public commentaries to her age, rather than to the ordinary dancer's risk (Orr, 2015). Because of the link between menopause and osteoporosis, this discourse tends to be applied to women earlier than men; indeed from the point when they begin to experience a slippage in status and social value. So let us consider the ways in which the modalities that Young (2005) notes regarding women's bodies, which we have discussed earlier, apply to embodied old age (including those of older men). Firstly, (a) ambiguous transcendence: 'a woman frequently does not trust the capac-ity of her body to engage itself in physical relation to things. Consequently, she often lives her body as a burden, which must be dragged and prodded along and at the same time protected' (p. 38); (b) inhibited intentionality: women's bodies 'project an aim to be enacted but at the same time stiffen against the performance of the task' (p. 37); (c) a sense of alienation or apartness from the environment: 'I have observed that women tend to have a latent and sometimes conscious fear of getting hurt, which we bring to a motion' (p. 35). All of these pronouncements apply, more obvi-ously so, to older bodies, highlighting feminization as an embodiment of social disempowerment: the loss of trust in the body as the 'certain grounds of our daily experience' (Kleinman, 1988: 45); the perception of oneself as fragile, liable to break; and characteristics such as kyphosis; unstable and awkward gait. These surely be speak of social marginalization and negative valuation just as much as physical limitations and adumbrate the process of losing one's grip on the world, in a multi-layered metaphorically embodied sense, not just 'poor balance' or faltering step. Many of us will have observed older people negotiating a familiar street with a tread that combines heaviness and uncertainty, resignation and suppressed fury; not, that is, as if the path ahead sprang up around their body in the 'open and unbroken directedness upon the world in action' (p. 30) but rather as if they scarcely felt the right to be there. These modalities remind us of Douglas' view that the body is above all a social body, reflecting social hierarchies and mappings.

Lloyd and colleagues (2014) noted that their 'fourth age' interviewees saw illness as representing a 'step-change' in their identity; but this transformed self-perception arose directly from the discourses available to interpret their experience. For example, in discussions with doctors and family, embodied characteristics can come to symbolize a transition from one status (competent adult) to another (fourth age) and this may in turn be internalized by the older person through the 'at risk' label, which may result in a general state of ontological insecurity (Pickard, 2010). This is marked strongly by age ideology, as Stephen Katz notes: 'bodies that fall down also fall out of the social domain' (2011: 194). The parallels with the experience of falls in childhood here is especially instructive. Kingston observes:

> Children enter the world *metaphorically down*; that is, they spend their early months after birth lying down. From the *down* position, they get *up*; they first learn to crawl, then to walk. The movement is *down-up* considered part of the learning process in order for the child to learn *up* and avoid *down* – conversely older people in later life are *up*, the fall takes them *down*. The movement is *up-down*. (2000: 230; original emphasis)

Whilst this is certainly how normatively aged society perceives and interprets the fall, is this not an ideology that is scarcely borne out when one considers the reality of adult life? Indeed, is life so stable from the period of childhood to late adulthood, that anything that disrupts this is truly anomalous? Do we not all fall, at times, in the physical sense, particularly those who play sport, and in other senses too, upended by a variety of experiences including falling in love/off the wagon/asleep/ about laughing/out of favour and isn't it more accurate, in any case, to describe the movement for most older people as going from *up* to *down* to *up again*? That this general truth is denied for old people only makes sense in the context of a cultural image of old age (fed by psychological and medical discourse) as located on an inexorably *down-ward* path.

Turning now to (ii) (p. 121) we see that what is often called 'incontinence' in the literature actually refers to a continuum, not an either/or status, which ranges from minor accidents through to chronic loss of bladder control. Research by Mitteness and Barker (1995) indicates that it is *management* of incontinence – the performance of continence – that is the crucial indicator of social competence, specifically the ability to conceal this leakiness from public view, not the experience itself (Higgs and Gilleard, 2015). This is especially used to problematize older women's bodies but although urinary incontinence affects older women more than men, diseases of the prostate also render it an important part of the lived experience of older men.

With the less serious manifestations, such as benign prostatic hyperplasia (BPH), which includes frequent need to urinate and dribbling, affecting 50 per cent of men over 50 and rising to 90 per cent between 70 and 80 (Men's Health Resource Centre, 2015), this inherent leakiness underpins the social feminization of the old man's body. However, in practice all bodies are inevitably leaky and young men, for instance, worry about signs of wetness after urination in a way that is not, for them, symbolically marked with decline. Oring notes: 'The fear is not that you have contaminated yourself' (as presumably this is not uncommon) 'but that others will notice' (1979, quoted in Mitteness and Barker, 1995: 196). That is, although leakiness is ordinarily experienced by all ages it is only problematized as a failure of social personhood in old age (and may even place an older person at risk of enforced institutionalization thereby (Mitteness and Barker, 1995)). In fact, as in our earlier example of falls, there is also a pointed contrast between the way children's incontinence is perceived as compared to its presence in older people. Referring to the stigma surrounding incontinence in old people, Herskovits and Mitteness (1994) suggest that they fall liminally between the inability (but potential) of childhood and the capability (and realized competence) of adulthood. The symbolism of this condition is uppermost in the social imagination when judging such occurrences: 'The endpoint of this loss of control is complete disorder and death, which is of course the ultimate failed mastery and lack of productivity' (p. 17). The fact that such a distinction is held *despite* the evidence that it affects all ages draws attention away from the degree to which the construction of adulthood in terms of 'realized competence' is ideological. Moreover, the projection of lack of control onto older bodies marks the latter as the location of the abject, as Kristeva describes it, representing 'what I permanently thrust aside in order to live', a space in which 'I am at the border of my condition as a living being' (1982: 3). It is the concept of precise boundaries that is key to post-Cartesian notions of selfhood; anything suggesting ambiguity is threatening to self.

In relation to our earlier point about if and how different styles of masculinity persist, or not, in old age, it is interesting how attitudes towards prostate cancer can give an opportunity to express hegemonic masculine norms of self. The British TV presenter Michael Parkinson claims: 'If you can pee against a wall from two feet, you haven't got it' (Lott, 2015). A review in the *London Review of Books* (O'Hagan, 2013) relates quasi-competitive and gung-ho dialogue between the elderly Norman Mailer and Philip Roth discussing their need to pee urgently:

> Halfway down the corridor, I was looking for a john and who do I see but Philip Roth. 'Hey, Philip, what you doin' here?' 'Oh, I had to pee,' Roth said. 'Happens to me all the time,' I said. 'You just have to pee.' The previous week I went to see my daughter in Brooklyn and I couldn't make it up the hill and had to stop in a telephone kiosk to pee.' 'Oh, that's happened to me,' Roth said. 'I've done the kiosk thing.' 'Well, Phil,' I said. 'You were always precocious.'

By contrast, the conventions of femininity mean that it is very hard to imagine women boasting about their habits of urination in such a way; such association with masculine swagger enables these men, to some degree, to hold themselves apart from abjection.

Conclusion

The above discussion has indicated how gender norms are formulated in embodied terms throughout the life course enmeshed with other stratifying features, especially age hierarchy. The question is, with this instated in our very bodily hexis, how can individuals hope to challenge this?

Firstly, perhaps, what should be the aim of such a challenge? We have already noted, after all, the limits of our imaginations beyond the current gender hegemony. Certainly, then, the aim cannot be to 'feminize' domains that once were masculine and vice versa, as this does not eliminate hierarchies (and in the case of feminization, has a disempowering effect in any case). One alternative aim is suggested by Derrida in his concept of the ultimate destabilization of all categories, and the resisting of closure (Annandale, 2009) so none attain hegemony. In terms of encouraging this, institutional and practical support is of course also helpful in blunting the extremes. Connell (2000) has suggested that institutions such as schools should continue to play a central role in supporting the formation of more equal gender relationships and more sensitive masculinities. Emphasizing and encouraging women's physical strength and capability is another important approach and can occur through shifts in attitudes towards women's sport. All these positions are self-evident, but the difficulty is their fit with the requirements of femininity and the latter will take time to truly shift, perhaps in an iterative interplay with these practices. Concurrently, and in the meantime, feminist metaphysics and aesthetics can transform the meaning of key embodied experiences for women (and here it is assumed that it is women's bodies which are most regulated and constrained to the point, as we will see in Chapter 8, when young women especially normalize psychopathologies). Familiarity with historical accounts can also help de-naturalize forms of embodiment as they relate to both gender and age. For example, we can certainly imagine that a child's embodiment during the time that children worked and were treated like adults would not be the way it is for children today. Likewise, Duden's (1991) examination of eighteenth-century medical case notes facilitates our understanding of how the most fundamental embodied gender differences are historically contingent. So where we see women's monthly periods as key to both women's difference from men and women's social and biological role, this was not a differentiation made at that time. It was normal never to experience the menses but instead to bleed from other parts of her body; some women never bled unless they were pregnant, and then they bled monthly; men also bled; but women had a disposition to bleed from one location. Nor does menopause have to be seen as 'the change' when it is considered how the body changes on a daily, indeed hourly basis, according to the hormonal cycles associated with digestion, sleep, anxiety, and all affected by emotion, activity, hunger and so on.

Although Duden's examples may appear wildly surreal, overlain with a patina of archaism redolent of fairy tales, in fact modes of femininity and masculinity are still imprinted with the stamp of the eighteenth and nineteenth centuries wherein women were denied space in the public sphere which was the domain of men. Femininity's valorized attributes – childlike physical features, narrowed and constrained bodily movements, delicacy, modesty, refinement, and other characteristics that define a hexis more appropriate to a minor than a major player on the stage of life – not only form the base of women's continuing bodily diffidence but continue to be the prime reason why older women's embodiment is so devalued today. Even small changes in physical exercise and bodily norms will undoubtedly pave the way to a more assured future old age for today's young women. But what if the whole phenomenology of feminine embodiment was shifted to reflect their greater claim on public space, so that it was no longer characterized by the profound inhibitions noted by Young that might have been continuous with the mores of Victorian England but certainly no longer are? Or does the persistence of bodily inhibitions perhaps allude to more profound gendered inequalities still actually at work beneath it all?

In 2015 the women's crews competed for the first time on the same day and over the same course as the men's team in the celebrated Oxford–Cambridge Boat Race, whereas up to that day they had been obliged, by antique rules, to race over a shorter, less demanding stretch of river. But the more difficult journey leading from attitudes exemplified by commentary by a Cambridge rowing captain in 1962, that women's rowing was a 'ghastly sight, an anatomical impossibility (if you are rowing properly that is) and physiologically dangerous' (Ward, 2015) to the race itself, was in the end only made possible by the commercial sponsorship of a female City banker determined to expand women's embodied sense of possibility. It remains true, as we have noted, that the members of such a team, like other high-achieving girls, might well have to negotiate demands that they also exhibit hyperfemininity in other environments (Porter, 2013), and photographs of England's striker Laura Bassett wearing her characteristic bright red nail varnish during matches for the 2015 Women's World Cup for soccer seems to confirm the fact that such femininities are both 'progressive but also consummately and reassuringly feminine' (McRobbie, 2009: 57). Yet still, how differently might an eleven-year-old girl, on the cusp of puberty, envision her own embodied possibilities today when watching these powerful women uninhibitedly, and successfully, engaging in what until just recently was considered a man's sport?

Might the concept and practice of gender as a social institution, decoupled from 'essence', be also rendered sufficiently elastic to accommodate lifelong changes beyond childhood and early adolescence rather than freezing women into extremely youthful modes? Turning to women who are currently old, one of the ways that we can try to shift embodied experience for them is by reinterpreting the signs and marks left by age on the older body. This does not mean ignoring physical problems but it does suggest interpreting bodily attributes symbolically within a universe of meaning in which age ideology is not all-defining (Berg and Gadow, 1978). For example, the slowed-down body is usually interpreted as a body 'wearing out' (reflecting biological theories). However, in line with the concept of the 'still point' in consciousness terms could this not also symbolize a different embodied relationship to time and the world, one defined by other values than speed and efficiency? As noted previously, Coleman and O'Hanlon (2004) extrapolating from the empirical finding that many very old people adapt well to frailty, suggest that 'development' in the sense of growth and learning of new skills, including in embodied terms, may continue into late life, including past the watershed of the fourth age. But our very systems of thought, the linking of 'development' with youth, 'growth' with particular capabilities and not others, render us blind to this possibility. Research with dementia patients, for example, stresses the ongoing embodied communication that older people with dementia maintain, in terms of their corporeal schema (Kontos, 2006). It can be interpreted by sensitive carers and indicates the ongoing significance of Merleau-Ponty's insight that consciousness is revealed through 'the [embodied manner] in which the other deals with the world' (2004: 109), that is, not isolated within a psyche sealed off from everyone else's psyches. This realization, present in the earliest years, in turn should help with recognition of the unique qualities of childhood and indeed links childhood with old age in a way that, with the advent of *homo clausus*, we have lost. O'Neill (2005) comments about Piaget that he

> brings the child to a mature outlook, as if the thoughts of the adult were self-sufficient and disposed of all contradictions. But, in reality, it must be the case that the child's outlook is in some way vindicated against the adult's and against Piaget, and that the unsophisticated thinking of our earliest years remains as an indispensable acquisition underlying that of maturity, if there is to be for the adult one single intersubjective world. (2005: 119)

At the other end of the life course, Sally Gadow (1983) uses the insights from phenomenology to suggest that different states of embodiment in old age should be seen as norms in their own right. We can plot these against the tropes of hybrid and metamorphosis as discussed in the previous chapter. Shifting through painful stages of hybridization as one enters deeper into old age one finally achieves a metamorphosis of meaning in which we enjoy a new relationship to the world, not conditioned by what we lost, or the standards of youth, but, as Gadow puts it, 'the body in… ageing insists that its own reality, complexity and values be supported' (Gadow, 1983: 108). This is a stage in which the body, no longer objectified by the remnants of a youthful perspective, is experienced by the subject her/himself as a 'subject body', totally encompassed in a new existential state. Again, this may involve a slower walking style symbolic of a wholly new relationship to time which makes possible in turn a new relationship with the world (just as the mature body of adulthood leaves behind all memory of the body of childhood and does not feel its loss). Reading this helps us understand the nature of changes that occur throughout our lives, and encourages us not to fear them, as each brings a different phenomenological relationship to the world.

Berg and Gadow (1978) also have an ingenious way of reading the symbolism provided by the older physical body in a non-age-ideological way. They suggest that this hardening and stiffening of joints and movement may be seen as the setting of the once-malleable self in a finished form: 'perhaps the hardening is a final structuring, a settling on what one's character and essence are to be, once and for all' (1978: 86).

We also need to leave behind the either/or binary that decrees you are either 'old' or you are 'young' and in which one of the ways the distinction between young and old is artificially maintained is through use of the civilized rational-body norm. More relevant is to stress continuities and the way ages and stages exist as a continuum with growth and decline characteristic of all stages, even at the most basic cellular level. Gullette observes how her own embodied performance does not observe a consistent age performance whilst it is 'backstage' or out of the public realm. She writes:

> Sometimes I squat like a kid, sometimes I march like a [man], when I'm utterly absorbed by a thought I… fall into a slower, meditative pace… This variety is normal, not inconsistent, but rather, as long as we are not feeling watched, integrated into a whole. (2004: 162)

In this vein, Douglas (1966) reminds us that all categories – not least the category of the rational, civilized body – are leaky and provisional. She warns that 'if we select from the body's image a few aspects which do not offend, we must be prepared to suffer for the distortion' (p. 201). She gives an example of one tribe who 'used to pretend that at initiation their anus was blocked for life. Initiated men were supposed never to need to defecate, unlike women and children, who remained subject to the exigency of their bodies' (p. 201). She concludes: 'Imagine the complications into which this pretence led Chagga man' (p. 201). With that in mind, we can see how our own asserted distinction between rational and non-rational bodies involves us in similar contortions.

But such a shift can also be accompanied by greater strength, power or enjoyment of the body. Here is where it is important to recognize that 'development' as it is understood in Western thought is not the only way in which development can be seen. That is, that growth and decline can actually be seen as proceeding together, and not necessarily in the order that our models would lead us to expect. This is why I will close this chapter by discussing the embodiment of British dentist Dr Charles Eugster, a self-styled '91-year-old body builder' (Eugster, 2011). I think it would be a mistake to read this as a capitulation to hegemonic masculinity in old age; above all the narrator is aware of the fluctuations of his embodiment; it has been weak as a young boy, then strong, then weak and aged, and now strong and aged. This, he also knows, will not last.

When, following a sickly early youth, his tonsils were removed and his health improved, he began to box, row and play rugby: 'I thought back to myself as a frail, sickly boy and vowed never to be like that again.' In his middle years, following divorce from a marriage which had turned him into a sedentary individual, he 'regained' himself by both physical activity and professional focus. Following this resolve, he joined a bodybuilding club and reflects: 'There's no research into body-building for the over-80s, so it's been an experiment. With weight-lifting and protein shakes, my body began to change. It became broader, more v-shaped, and my shoulders and biceps became more defined...' He turned heads as he had hoped, attracting female attention. However, 'Everything I learned was tailored to help my body cope with old age. I took up judo to teach me how to fall properly. My circulation and posture improved, and I was told that there was a chance more muscle mass could protect my brain from Alzheimer's. I stopped thinking about dying. As I approached 90, my focus was on getting my body back.'

Many interesting themes are present in his account: how his self-esteem is based on productivity and enterprise of various kinds; the continuing masculinity of his embodiment in its appearance and 'feel'; a continued growth and development through his 80s and into his 90s (so far). He is also directly challenging the meaning of old age and suggesting that one can defy ideological norms through one's embodiment. He is clear on what he is doing, asserting:

> I'm not chasing youthfulness. I'm chasing health. People have been brain-washed to think that after you're 65, you're finished. We're told that old age is a continuous state of decline, and that we should stop working, slow down and prepare to die. I disagree... I turn 92 this year. It is a frightening prospect – that law of averages is against me, and, yes, one day something will happen and that will be it. But until that day comes, I'm going to carry on working on my abs. (Eugster, 2011)

This autobiographical reflection shows how age, working through gender performance, both is and is not 'drag'. It suggests how one can manipulate the body to ape the appearance associated with youth; but this performance is part of 'youth' as a symbolic state of mind and is vigour in itself. Hence at 91 he looks and feels younger than his age. Being and doing are mutually constitutive: what we feel we will 'get' with certain ages, is how we experience our embodiment, in the normal course of affairs. Age ideology is carried in the hexis and only rare examples, like that of Dr Eugster, can show us how to break it at one end whilst young girls who can watch the Women's Boat Race take place on equal footing with the men's for the first time in 2015, can begin to understand how it can be dislodged at the other end.

CHAPTER SUMMARY

- This chapter demonstrated how gender practices inscribe hierarchical norms on bodies at key points in the life course.

- Working with and through age and infused with class differences, these embodied characteristics construct differences that then appear natural.

- Modes of embodiment embedded in everyday practical logic thus work to instate both difference and inequality between individuals of the same gender, between different genders and between ages.

- In looking at ways to challenge such norms we suggested a number of possibilities such as questioning the clear distinction between growth and decline, reinterpreting the symbolism associated with bodily forms and events and imbuing the concepts of masculinity and femininity with greater elasticity which could grow with the individual over the whole life course.

- In all cases we suggest greater emphasis should be given to the continuities that link bodies at all stages of the life course.

Further questions

1. What do changing concepts of childhood, youth and/or old age suggest about debates on natural versus socially constructed bodies? What age-related features of the body transcend socio-historical context?

2. Do norms of masculinity and femininity change over the life course? With what consequences?

3. Whose bodies move further from the gendered norm in old age: men's or women's?

Talking point

Sam Fussell, a bookish, Oxford- and Ivy League-educated young man and confessed 'geek', in his autobiographical account of constructing for himself a champion bodybuilder's physique, reflects as follows: 'The gym was the one place I had control. I didn't have to speak, I didn't have to listen. I just had to push or pull... It beat the street. It beat my girlfriend... I didn't have to feel. I simply had to lift... This is about looking good, not feeling good... I'd become a bodybuilder to be comfortable with a self I'd invented... But once I'd manufactured all the muscles and the puffery I felt trapped inside the colossal frame' (1992: 62; 184). Taking these examples as a starting point, consider: (i) how shifts in physical norms altering women's use of space and embodied motility might occur at any point in the lifecourse. What processes might shape this? What postures and stances might this involve? And (ii) what effect might these have on the traditional norms of femininity including associations with both fragility and care for others?

—— **Key texts** ——

For **embodiment in childhood and old age** see Hockey, J. and James, A. (1993) *Growing Up and Growing Old*, London: Sage. For **boys' embodiment** see Connell, R. (1987) *Gender and Power: society, the person and sexual politics*, Cambridge: Polity Press; Connell, R.W. (1994) *Masculinities*, Los Angeles: University of California Press; O'Donnell, M. and Sharpe, S. (2000) *Uncertain Masculinities: youth, ethnicity and class in contemporary Britain*, London: Routledge. For **girls' embodiment** see Young, I.M. (2005) *'Throwing Like a Girl' and Other Essays*, Oxford: Oxford University Press. For **an overview of gender** the following provides a helpful overview: Jackson, S. and Scott, S. (2001) *Gender: a sociological reader*, London: Routledge. For a clear summary of theoretical approaches to the **relationality of plural masculinities and femininities** see Budgeon, S. (2014) The dynamics of gender hegemony: femininities, masculinities and social change, *Sociology*, 48(2): 317–24.

Note

1. The association of HRT with health risks is currently being reappraized and it is very possible that we will see the return of HRT to popularity, linked to this trope of 'control'. See also note 1, Chapter 8.

7

SEXUALITY THROUGH THE LIFE COURSE

Background: sexuality as a regulative device

In this chapter we turn our attention to sexuality and I suggest that, as a regulatory and ideological vehicle, sexuality works closely with, and through, gender to establish and maintain not just difference but inequality. As Foucault tells us, it does this through introducing 'sexuality' as a property of the self, in and through which our subjectivities are expressed (and increasingly seen as the site of our true selves). (Hetero)sexuality, and the heterosexual matrix,[1] we will argue, work to ensure the dominance of both men over women and youth over age. Here, we first set out two main approaches to analysing sexuality on which we will draw (Walby, 1990). The first approach (i) considers it a 'drive'; the second and more sociological (ii) sees it as a social construction or learned behaviour. Both introduce useful perspectives to our discussion. The former is the point of view of classic psychoanalysis and the latter includes the diverse perspectives of discourse analysis, symbolic interactionism and radical feminism. In terms of sexuality as a drive, Freud, Marcuse, Reich and others all described sexuality as a biological urge but channelled into particular objects and aims and repressed by civilization (Freud thought this necessary; Marcuse and Reich did not). Drives change over the life course, moreover. According to (ii), sexuality is learned and negotiated, with appropriate scripts followed over the life course. One thing that is clear in all these accounts is that, whatever its origin and combination of biological and social elements that comprise it, in late modern capitalism, sexuality serves as a regulative device through which power flows fixing norms that divide the genders and the ages from each other in complex and minute ways. These benefit both patriarchy and the capitalist economy.

AIMS OF THE CHAPTER

- We begin by discussing the role of sexuality in constructing the category of childhood, defined in opposition to sexuality.

- We will then look at the adult heterosexual regime beginning with youthful sexuality and its relationship to gender roles and age inequality, in particular looking at how it serves to regulate femininity, and hence women, through the beauty myth and the time economy.

- We will then consider how mid-life discourses, focused on the menopause, serve to signal a qualitative break in sexuality and gendered identities. We examine the newer emphasis on retaining or restoring sexuality in later life and its connection with the perpetuation of youthful norms, positioning this as a key 'third age' practice.

- Finally, we consider ways in which different approaches to sexuality can form part of a challenge to the practices and institutions associated with a hegemonic age and gender regime.

Sexuality and childhood: the formation of the gender regime

Freud was one of the first theorists to assert the importance of sex and sexuality in childhood. In his essay on Infantile Sexuality (2000) Freud challenged the general perception that what he called the 'sexual instinct' was absent in childhood, awakening only in puberty and teleologically bound up with reproduction. He emphasized by contrast that sexual drives are inherent because sensations attach themselves to infants' attempts to satisfy biological needs and only later through appropriate social scripts, attaching men and women to the prescribed objects. Although Freud stressed the biological origins of sexuality, many of his insights can be used as the basis of further sociological reflection: for example, his suggestion that women's sexuality is more problematic than men's as it is mediated by a switch from female to male object at puberty, leading to a greater propensity for neurosis. That femininity more generally and feminine sexuality specifically is harmful to the health was a point later argued by many feminists from the 1960s onwards. Meanwhile, Lacan's differentiating between a phallic 'law' and the fleshly penis gives insight into the patriarchal order beyond the family setting. In the 'symbolic order', a discursive realm based on the patriarchal law of the Father, each individual is sexed within language that is already imbued with patriarchal meaning. Moreover, this difference between the phallus and the penis allows both women and men to suffer a sense of lack as indicated by the following quote: 'The fact is the penis isn't a patch on the phallus' (Dyer, 1982: 71; quoted in Plummer, 2004: 179).

With respect to the psychic economy as it is shaped in childhood and youth, Nancy Chodorow (1978; 1989; 1994), working within the 'object relations' school of psychoanalysis (which departs from classical psychoanalytic concern with the oedipal period by emphasizing the importance of the pre-oedipal period in the formation of masculinity and femininity), has focused particularly on the overarching role played by the mother in shaping childhood sexuality and gender identities through 'unconscious psychic structures and processes' (Chodorow, 1978: 4) with lasting implications into adulthood. Chodorow demonstrates theoretically how relational needs and dispositions that underlie the basic difference in male and female gender identities in a 'sexually unequal society' (1978: 173) are formulated in childhood, pivoting on the relationship with the mother (because in families it is women who predominantly mother). The boy's oedipal crisis, requires him to give up his attachment to his mother and to distinguish himself from her in a way that girls, sharing the same sex, need not. Furthermore, in contrast to Freud's approach, masculinity is defined in opposition to the feminine; it is thus complex in a way that Freud did not identify and in this respect, at least, women's sexuality is *less* problematic. However, both girls and boys share an ambivalence to the mother: for both, to different degrees (and because she is the primary care-giver) 'mothers represent regression and lack of autonomy' (Chorodow, 1978: 181). In a boy this leads to a rejection of feminine characteristics in himself and a devaluing of women more generally. This relationship and its psychic structures, Chodorow believes, explains the tenacity of people's commitment to the social organization of gender, present even among the consciously reflexive and self-aware, explaining:

> the intensity of the taboo on homosexuality; why people often cannot change even when they want to; why a 'liberated' man still has difficulty parenting equally or being completely happy about his successful, independent, liberated wife; or why a feminist woman might find it hard to be attracted to a non-macho, non-traditionally masculine man just because he's 'nice' and egalitarian or to be unambivalent about choosing not to have children. (1989: 171)

Chodorow's findings remain relevant in the current social context; whilst families are increasingly fragmented, regardless of the form they maintain they are heavily mother-dominated and some more so than ever, given the rise in lone mothers. Only 1–2 per cent of couples comprise stay-at-home fathers and there are ten times as many stay-at-home mothers (ONS, 2013; Bradley, 2007).

We have already encountered the works of Dinnerstein (1976) and Benjamin (1990) regarding the reproduction of the gender regime through infant–mother relationships and its effect on sexual relationships. Dinnerstein argues that men experience a felt sense of greater vulnerability, especially during heterosexual relationships with women, which can reawaken earlier vulnerabilities regarding 'the unqualified, boundless, helpless neediness of infancy'. The threat lies herein: 'If he lets her, she can shatter his adult sense of power and control' (Dinnerstein, 1976: 66); this explains the rigidly defensive structures of sexism and misogyny, as well as emotional distancing in sexual relationships. However, the little girl's identification with her mother leads to less clearly erected ego boundaries priming young women for particular emotional needs and dependencies. In this context, the figure of the older woman awakens profound feelings of vulnerability and fear, especially in men, conjoining as it does ordinary vulnerability and those associated with death.

Benjamin (1990) focuses on how the process of individuation leads to practices of domination and submission. She posits two ideal-typical patterns of self/other differentiation during infancy. In one model, mutual recognition takes place – emphasizing a separate person who is like us but different – not inferior or Other, simply other. In this model, a tension does of course inhere in terms of the mutual need for self-assertion as well as recognition of independent existence of the other but the tension endures without resolution in a way that tolerates ambiguity, comprising both conflict and co-operation, which is at the essence of intersubjectivity. In the other, standard or Hegelian model, the self feels it is only possible to be a self if the Other is obliterated or alternatively that attunement is only possible if one surrenders to the Other. However, the latter pattern really can be described as failed intersubjectivity; part of the problem is that it is presented as the 'standard' prototype of development in mainstream psychological theory and thus assumes a cultural dominance. It is this latter which serves as the model for sexual submission/masochism and dominance/sadism, binaries which map onto gender differences through social learning and subsequently normalize hierarchical distinctions in a diverse array of other areas, including age, throughout life. For this reason, sexuality constrains women within their own subjectivities and, as Benjamin suggests: 'In our era of sexual equality and liberation, the fantasy of erotic domination returns like the repressed' (1990: 83).

Finally, turning to approaches that highlight the social construction of sexuality, Stevi Jackson (1982) disputes the Freudian concept that children are 'sexual' suggesting that sexuality is not 'innate' but learned behaviour. This means that, although children are capable of sensual pleasure, lacking the cultural meanings imputed to such responses by an adult world they thus lack 'sexuality', or, in Foucauldian terms, they stand outside the discourses that frame sexuality as a mode of understanding the self. However, the insistence with which society ensures that children are kept apart from such knowledge is germane to the way that 'childhood' is constructed as a discrete life stage. Moreover, she suggests, the foundations of sexuality are laid in childhood through the discrete learning of gendered roles, which prepare girls and boys for the unequal practices of heterosexuality.

We will utilize insights from all of the above positions when tracing the practice of gendered sexuality throughout the life course, beginning with youth.

Initiation into the heterosexual regime: the 'male-in-the-head'

Where childhood is 'defined' and constructed in terms of sexual innocence, youth, by contrast, is defined in terms of sexuality, albeit one which young people have not yet learned to 'control'. There is a break with childhood norms for young men however, more than for young women, this constituting a 'hot spot' for the fixing of gender identities. Becoming masculine involves leaving childhood behind primarily through becoming sexual; for young men, heterosexual sex is a marker of the transition to adulthood just as much as the more structural transitions such as leaving home and getting a job (Richardson, 2010). For young women, however, the break between childhood and femininity is less clear, for the emphasis throughout for them is on being sexually 'attractive' rather than 'sexually active' or 'desirous'. In that sense, femininity involves preserving childlike qualities, including passivity (the ability to be chosen, not to choose) and the importance of making oneself desirable whilst masculinity involves rather their repudiation (Jackson, 1982). For example, there is a particular etiquette in which a man is expected to work towards sexual access positioned as a 'natural urge' for men and in which context women are located as 'the objects of the sexual drive of which men experience themselves as subjects' (Hollway, 1984: 64). Part of the rationale behind this – in lay, popular and scientific depictions – has been an emphasis on male adolescent hormonal drives 'compelling' their sexual practice. However, Richardson (2010) and others suggest that the undoubtedly real element of compulsion experienced by many (male) teenagers at this point arises from social pressures, not biological elements, indeed deriving from school-age male peer groups which define sexual activity (with specific characteristics, such as multiple partners) as a key element of masculinity.

It has been suggested that sexuality is 'the mainstay of male identity' in a way that it is not for women (Person, 1980: 605) and heterosexual intercourse is the key means of validating masculine identity; again this is not so much the result of 'drives' as of social pressure and social discourses. Tracing the historical origins of this, it was in Victorian times that, along with the problematization of menstruation and menopause, heterosexual intercourse became the only legitimate form of sexual activity (Smart, 1996). Focused on the penis, it resulted in a 'sexual division of labour' which privileges men's role and physiological needs, starting when he is aroused; finishing at his climax; making her satisfaction his responsibility; and in which 'he is the sexual actor while she is acted upon' (Holland et al., 1998: 6) (and even where she is 'active' this is in the guise of 'pleasing her man'). No wonder that boys tend to think of sex as something they do 'to' girls not 'with' them (Jackson, 1982); this is quite accurate, given the patriarchal and age-related norms inscribed onto feminine bodies in such a practice. In other words, heterosexual sex in many ways symbolically enacts the gender regime itself in microcosm. Although the sex act itself is most powerful in this regard, sex education, formal and informal, also serves to reinforce these norms. So young women are educated (formally and informally) to guard their reputations and protect themselves from danger including unwanted pregnancies, sexually transmitted diseases and sexual violence; young men learn how to 'prove' themselves through the pursuit of sexual pleasure and the making of conquests.[2]

More generally, and insidiously, young women's sexualities are regulated by what Holland et al. (1998) term the 'male-in-the-head', the 'male gaze' that now acquires a sexual component by which young women both judge themselves and judge other women. This gaze both objectifies them (in terms of their bodies) and works on them as subjects (in terms of their moral choices) and the advantage here for young men is that there is no 'female-in-the-head' equivalent which could similarly serve to judge them, a discrepancy underpinning the maintenance of the sexual double standard. Walby suggests that whilst heterosexuality constitutes a patriarchal structure, it has transformed from a system of control and regulation of women's sexual pleasure to one of an obligatory sexual pleasure for women (depicted as a 'freedom' in the post-feminist rhetoric but still incorporating the male-in-the-head). The ultimate consequence of this is their 'more willing incorporation into other aspects of patriar-chal society' (1990: 124). This is a key aspect of what Walby identifies as the shift from private to public patriarchy and also a key aspect of post-feminism.

Closely related to this, the heterosexual regime is regulated and its gendered hier-archy preserved through: (i) the beauty myth; and (ii) the time economy, to which we turn next.

(i) The beauty myth

Naomi Wolf's (1990) brilliant analysis of beauty ideology demonstrates, among other things, that ideology surrounding beauty norms works with and through 'sexuality' to bind and constrain women, despite formal political and legal equality. Women's beauty and sexuality are both constituted within the terms of the 'male gaze', meaning that in a very real sense they do not 'own' their own sexuality. Let us recall the words of Berger:

> *Men act* and *women appear*. Men look at women. Women watch them-selves being looked at. This determines not only most relations between men and women but also the relation of women to themselves. The sur-veyor of woman in herself is male: the surveyed female. Thus she turns herself into an object – and most particularly an object of vision: a sight. (1972: 47; emphasis added)

In addition, Wolf identifies two features as being particularly toxic. These are what she calls 'beauty pornography' and sadomasochism. The former is shorthand for the images found in magazines and advertising in which models, possessing the ideal-type face and body – thin and very young – are depicted in poses suggestive of sexual ecstasy. These imply, Wolf suggests, that, in order to be desirable and hence sexual, one must be beautiful in such ways. Sadomasochistic images, in which, through movies and other media society abounds, suggests that her private submission and submissiveness is what is required for sexual desirability (arising directly from early norms of separation/individuation). Within such a normative context, it is not surprising that almost 20 per cent of school-age girls experience physical and sexual violence from boyfriends and that it is normalized under the discourse of 'boys being boys' (Hlavka, 2014: 3). 'Beauty pornography' claims that women's beauty is synonymous with their sexuality (rather than, as Wolf suggests it should be, the other way round); sadomasochism gives the message that sexual violence, including a rape culture, is elegant, cool and aspirational. This makes women's sexuality a tool for gender (and as we will see, age) hegemony. Moreover, with female sexuality 'equivalent' to beauty, women become alienated from their own bodies and sexualities; their surveillance gaze is trained upon their own bodies and they learn to see themselves from the outside: 'what little girls learn is not the desire for the other, but the desire to be desired' (Wolf, 1990: 157). Even in conditions of youth and physical beauty, acceptability of their own female body cannot be assumed, and this is a feature of the privileging of the male body and the male standard: whilst the old woman is the antithesis of the ideal, the young female body, to remain attractive, must not betray any imputation of 'dirt', including sexual licentiousness as well as lack of attention to hygiene, and remain thus fully ordered. As Menninghaus puts it, 'the female body, the ideal of beauty, needs a ceaseless effort of self-idealization in order not to succumb to its inner propensity to the impure and the disgusting' (2003: 101).

Young women learn to look with distaste upon their own sex organs, moreover, which Segal (1994) identifies as a 'condensed symbol of all that is secret, shameful and unspeakable in our culture' (p. 225). This is further underpinned by the 'rules' of formal aesthetics whereby the female sexual organ 'runs against the canon of the softly taut, uninterrupted, unblemished skin-line [in that]… it has the form of a fold' (Menninghaus, 2003: 75). This, according to the classical canon, is an even more serious defect than wrinkles, warts and pockmarks, being both fold and opening and thus blurring the distinction between outer and inner (Menninghaus, 2003).

As noted, it is a very particular, normative, indeed youthful idea of beauty that is held here and one that ensures women 'lose' their sexuality as they age, meaning that it divides women from each other: older from younger women, and all women from their youthful (and allegedly more beautiful) selves (Gullette, 1997). In this, the male-in-the-head makes itself felt beyond the sexual act, in the way women appraise their own bodies and appearance. Morgan notes: 'Actual men – brothers, fathers, male lovers, male beauty "experts" – and hypothetical men live in the aesthetic imagination of women' (1991: 36). Within the current post-feminist regime, normative femininity is increasingly centred on a woman's body: it is less about codes of behaviour or decorum and more about bodily appearance in which women are schooled to police themselves and others, all this being a key component of 'girlfriend culture' (Winch, 2013).

Let us look here in a little more detail at the Girl, our symbol of late modern youthful success, and her negotiation of sexuality, because there is some discordance between her sexually assertive self-presentation in all the streets and on the television screens of the Western world and this theoretical discussion of her apparent 'constraints'. In fact, one of the constraints is the very obligation she is bound by to present herself as sexually assertive and open constituting a '"technology of sexiness" [which has replaced] "innocence" or "virtue" as the commodity that young women are required to offer in the heterosexual marketplace' (Gill, 2007b: 72). Encouraged to see herself as active and desiring, sexual agency is, however, confined to the 'aestheticization of their physical appearance' (Gill, 2009: 1), such an aesthetic being appraised within the purview of the male gaze, of course. This state of affairs is the 'resolution' of the tension between the (highly misogynistic) sexual revolution of the 1960s.

Needless to say, such hyper-sexualization is strictly time limited, although, ironically, the sexual double standard is not, as Sontag's classic article on the double standard of ageing powerfully exposes. Beauty is youth for women and obliges women to remain as close as possible to youthful norms; ideal feminine beauty indeed is a 'eunuch' trait, 'the look of the very young', characteristic of the weak, feeble, vulnerable' (Sontag, 1972: 201). 'Looking serious', the mark of the 'person', is not considered attractive in a young woman, as anyone who has been instructed to 'Cheer up, love, it might never happen' by random passing men, in cheerfully aggressive tones, as if policing the gender order, can attest.[3] But whilst women are allowed only 'one standard' of beauty, by contrast, men are provided with two equally as valuable models for sexuality: that of the boy and that of the man which latter permits the 'silver fox' as it echoes men's increased status and power at this age. Acceptable age pairings in terms of sexual relationships are rigidly policed: women are expected to be in relationships with older men (giving the latter a clear power advantage) whilst sex between older women and younger men produces, in Sontag's words, an 'involuntary recoil of the flesh' and 'visceral horror' such as underpinned media accounts of, for example, the break-up of the marriage of Hollywood film stars Demi Moore and Ashton Kutcher (and we can recall the opening of *New Moon* as discussed in Chapter 1). Indeed, our earlier discussion has noted the link between ambiguity and the imposition of pollution beliefs, suggesting that reporting of the Moore–Kutcher breakup was infused with a sense of shrill inevitability, and portrayals of Moore as disgusting and desperate arise from this queasy friction between nominal sexual equality and cultural inequality.

Gullette (1998) also suggests that, around mid-life, ongoing sexuality can, in the context of the double standard of ageing, introduce or channel gender conflict into relationships between men and same-age women:

> Having learned that they age sexually nearly as early as women do, fearing competition from female workers as well as male, having lost the absolute superiority of being sole wage earners, men exacerbated the age/gender superiority that we now refer to as the double standard of ageing – discriminating against 'older' women in the workplace and in private life. (p. 26)

'Stella Grey' details the lived consequences of this in her weekly *Guardian* column, in which she relates her dating experiences as a 50-year-old divorcee. In one typical entry, she describes how, after a very enjoyable dinner date with a new man, all seemed to be going well and further meetings had been suggested, until at the end of the meal Stella stands up and as it was the first time Miles, her date, who was also in his 50s, had had a chance to survey her body, 'his eyes went to my hips and thighs, and his smile faltered'. She recounts: 'Miles, who is heavy, with a belly that I could have forgiven, couldn't bring himself to see me again' (Grey, 2015). The understated prose style is quietly heart-breaking for the sympathetic reader: it certainly suggests that Sontag's observations are as relevant today as they were in the 1970s.

As we noted in previous chapters, some have argued that, given the constraints involved in sexual relationships for women, it is not surprising that ceasing to be seen as a sexual being is often seen as liberatory (Greer, 1991). So, the professional women that Trethewey (2001) interviewed at mid-life found both a positive and negative aspect to this 'loss of sexuality'. It 'entails losing the burdensome sexual objectification, and sexual tension that they too often experienced as younger professionals. For others, however, ageing-past-youth brings with it another sort of loss, an "erasure" and pathologizing of their sexuality' (p. 200). Trethewey, in a personal aside, notes her feeling of being disturbed by the choice of one or other of these binary alternatives alone; I share this sentiment.

Although this analysis has been focused on heterosexuality, it is important to note that these experiences are associated with men and women regardless of their sexuality, being associated with gendered practices, and thus also relevant to gay and lesbian men and women. Certainly, the presence of multiple gay identities occupying a vast array of positions that combine traditional male and female roles in inventive ways has potential to disrupt the polarity that lies at the heart of gender performance as well as the male hegemony within that system, for example, by stressing the pleasure of powerlessness and passivity, by stressing sexual fidelity as separate to monogamy, and so on. However, it is all too easy for gay partners to relate to each other in ways that yet repeat and rehash old patterns, including old hierarchies and patterns of domination and submission, as some have identified in gay marriage (Richardson, 2004). Perhaps, as Segal puts it, gay sexualities cannot help but be 'filtered through the symbolic discourses of dominant heterosexual and gender codes' (1994: 204) as the concept of the heterosexual matrix might suggest. Perhaps this also reflects the fact that in our neoliberal economy marriage has become a status symbol and vehicle for conspicuous consumption and display as well as conformity. Moreover, a prominent strand in gay male culture emphasizes hegemonic masculinity and has been described as 'more phallic centred and more male' (Plummer, 2004: 185) in their sexuality than heterosexual men, practising sex stripped of all the restraints and embellishments that derive from both bourgeois 'civilized' culture and relationships with women. There is also evidence that the particular glorification of the young, muscular body in gay culture leads gay men to experience 'accelerated ageing' (Bennett and Thompson, 1991; quoted in Slevin,

2010: 1007). However, there is some indication that lesbian relationships are less age-discriminatory and Segal describes many examples of such relationships that begin, or endure, with genuine physical passion, in later life, born from an attraction to the person not, primarily, the physical envelope (Segal, 2013).

(ii) The time economy, sexuality and the age regime

As we have seen, the beauty ideology we discussed in the last section is closely linked to age. The classical ideal of beauty is one that privileges the closed, civilized body and devalues the body that is old and female most of all. Enlightenment theories of art, or aesthetics, which provide the ongoing foundation of contemporary aesthetics, are closely allied to the conventions of femininity and thus of gender hierarchy more generally. Placing the male youthful gaze at their centre, they highlight the principle of non-interruption of lines as underpinning the ideal, avoiding especially curves, angles, wrinkles, folds and other features that might break the smooth taut sweep. The 'ideal-type' of ugliness, the low extreme that sets the tone for the whole aesthetics, is that of the ugly old woman (Menninghaus, 2003). For these reasons, women's beauty is considered swiftly perishable, unlike that of men's; for example, older women's breasts go against the ideal we noted in the previous chapter, and are read in terms of a 'woman used up' (Young, 2005: 79). The consequences, for the body in deep old age, are profoundly alienating. In an extremely powerful and affecting passage, Twigg writes:

> Culture provides us with almost no images of the ageing body unclothed, so when we do encounter the reality of such, it comes as a visual shock… we have little sense culturally of aesthetic pleasure in old flesh, or of what a beautiful body might look like… older people thus experience their age-ing bodies in the context of a profound cultural silence. (2000: 46)

Indeed, culture encourages older people to apply the youthful gaze upon their own bodies: hence the shame that many old people receiving day care in Twigg's study felt during their experiences of being bathed and dressed by younger care assistants. Hurd Clarke (2011) notes that in her research among older women:

> During the past ten years I have frequently encountered women who have tended to describe the typical older woman's body with words such as 'awful', 'a disaster', 'dumpy', 'droopy', 'fat', 'sagging', 'ugh', 'ugly' and 'yuck'. For example, an 82-year-old woman said: 'The ageing body is a disaster. No question about it. As far as appearance is concerned, it's ugly.' (p. 38)

As we have seen in the previous chapter, ageing is approached as something that must be forestalled for as long as possible, outwardly at least. Negra has suggested that one of the characteristics of post-feminism is the way it defines female life stages within a paradigm of 'time panic'. Women can reverse this problematic relationship to time by 'the minimization of their ambition and reversion to a more essential femininity' (Negra, 2009: 49) before the watershed of menopausal middle-age. Bridget Jones counts calories when it would be just as accurate a description of her mindset to have her counting the tick-tock of her biological clock (Negra, 2009). Yet these and other chick flicks and chick lit characters, Knight (2014) suggests, are also frustratingly immature, featuring 'superannuated 'girls', with a focus on calories and fashion and white wine and dating, rather than 'grown-up women' with 'rich-inner lives': perhaps the discourse of romance can feature no more mature female individual. Not surprisingly, there are virtually no heroines in romantic fiction who are middle-aged or older, even when the novels are written by older women themselves (Greer, 1991). There is, within such discourses, the accompanying message that women's beauty is declining and fading away altogether with the passing of the years and the idea of having 'lost' one's beauty constitutes an aspect of the powerful mid-life nostalgia that we have already identified to be a key part of the age-as-decline ideology. Gullette (1997) suggests that it is training in the so-called 'brief perfection of youth' that sets up the later 'masochistic nostalgia' (p. 59) that taints mid-life and beyond with dark tones of decline and loss. The 'Mirror Scene of Ageing' is definitional to this process. Whilst the Mirror Scene of Youth problematizes young women by reflecting back to them their failure to measure up to their peers, the Mid-life Mirror Scene reveals a self that is 'less perfect than my own younger self used to be' (1997: 67) (even if that younger self felt far from perfect at the time).

Beauvoir depicts this in the volume of her autobiography, *Force of Circumstance*, written when she was 55. Talking about the fear of ageing and the way thoughts of the future oppress her, we might call this the Mirror Scene of Ageing #2, wherein shock is not new, but neither has it abated and one still compares one's face to its youthful version:

> I have but to stand and face my mirror. I thought, one day when I was forty: 'Deep in that looking glass, old age is watching and waiting for me; and it's inevitable one day she'll get me.' She's got me now. I often stop, flabbergasted, at the sight of this incredible thing that serves me as a face... Perhaps the people I pass in the street see merely a woman in her fifties who simply looks her age, no more, no less. But when I look, I see my face as it was, attacked by the pox of time, for which there is no cure. (1968: 672)

Actually, women experience ageing as a loss in one form or another from the very youngest ages. Beauvoir herself, in *Memoirs of a Dutiful Daughter*, remembers dreading the time when she would be too big to fit into her mother's lap; others cling to the image of being a 'little girl' long after they no longer are. The beauty industry certainly uses 'time' and fighting it/beating the clock as a key regulatory device and central mechanism for encouraging sales of creams and potions which can play a trick on time, rather than stop it, in terms of youthful complexions (as if we all, like Bella Swan, had just turned eighteen, with forever-seventeen vampire boyfriends).

However, the ads for anti-ageing creams, serums and supplements all do one thing, Penny points out, which is to 'reinstitute a measure of compliance in women and girls. It tells us that any freedom we may have is time limited' (2014: 90). This reinforces what we have known since, as children, we were introduced to the symbolism of carriages, pumpkins and midnight. So powerful is this message that it contributes to the 'Hag-in-the-head', representing the other extreme in the symbolic regime, positioned at the limits of sexuality. This is a binary pairing. Where the male-in-the-head imprints women's sexual subjectivity with the male gaze, the Hag-in-the-head internalizes the age gaze; it marks the constitutive limit, the threat or warning, the polluted, against which the clean, whole and desirable can be understood. Both speak to women alone.

Wolf (1990) argues convincingly that the effect of such a focus on aesthetics works to constrain women's full and effective participation in the public sphere, as well as their opportunity for successful careers. The effect of the beauty myth in high-profile 'serious' occupations such as TV journalism – with its infamous cut-off point for older women – also possesses 'allegorical force' (p. 34) which serves to limit and constrain expectations for career success by and for women. More generally, *before* the development of non-surgical cosmetic procedures, the women in Hurd Clarke's longitudinal study spoke about wrinkles as an undifferentiated category. After the development of these procedures, however, a fine gradation appeared: wrinkles around the eyes denoting character were tolerable, but across the forehead or encircling the mouth they were not and Hurd Clarke predicts that as procedures become more distinct then new facial flaws will be identified that will further problematize the female face. Certainly, ideas about beauty, sexuality and value provide one reason why women tend to be perceived as being older than their same-aged male counterparts both generally and by employers; they are also considered to be old at a younger age than men.

Most symbolically important of all, in constituting the Hag-in-the-head, is the discourse around menopause. We consider this next.

Menopause: the 'Hag-in-the-head'?

Menopause serves for many women as the constitutive limit against which both femininity and heterosexuality are defined and shaped. Whilst childhood and adulthood are separated by sexuality, menopause stands at the far end, a gateway through which women pass into a post-sexual regime (or at least one shot through with ambiguity, constraint and problematizations). It is associated with functional problems; even if sexual activity continues, it is acceptable within marriage but more problematic outside this state and particularly where a male lover may be younger). Medical discourses play a large part in shaping this negative approach. For example, in terms of its effect on a woman's sexuality, in a review of medical textbooks, Guyton and Hall (2006) note the following description: 'the sexual organs regress to some extent, so that the uterus becomes almost infantile in size, the vagina becomes smaller and the vaginal epithelium becomes thin and easily damaged' (p. 1023). As Niland and Lyons (2011) comment, both this and other texts they analyzed construct 'a view of a woman who is asexual and passive, having regressed not in age but in sexual organs. Indeed, it portrays a woman who has lost claim to being a "woman" because her body parts are no longer "fully developed"' and in that regard she is contrasted negatively against the younger woman as standard.

The medical view stressing the loss of femininity is reinforced by psychoanalytic discourse. Helen Deutsch wrote of menopause 'an incurable narcissistic wound' which takes back all that was given a woman at puberty (1984: 56; quoted in Greer, 1991: 275). Similarly Erikson, linking this to the 'despair' generated by the emptiness of woman's 'inner space' when she is not pregnant wrote: 'Such hurt can be re-experienced in each menstruation; it is a crying to heaven in the mourning over a child; and it becomes a permanent scar in the menopause' (Erikson, 1994: 278). In such a way, whilst the menstrual period is described as a 'wound' and a 'curse', its ending is not rendered a cause for celebration. Jackson's insights would suggest a more socially constructed reading where attitudes to older women's sexuality are based not on changes to organs but on the logic of patriarchy that can be traced all the way back to the construction of childhood as asexual. In terms of the asexuality expected of childhood, boys are expected to grow out of this but girls are supposed to take on a passive dependent style of sexuality; from this starting point it is easy to de-sexualize older women once again, thus emphasizing the centrality of both heterosexual intercourse and reproduction in attitudes towards age. By contrast, Greer suggests that menopause provides an opportunity to reclaim all that was taken from a woman at menarche (although her bodily hexis is already, as we have seen, conditioned by femininity, and hence by the heterosexual matrix). This view urges an embracing of the Hag within as an aspect of woman's true self and involves a variety of approaches to sexuality, including embracing celibacy as well as its opposite, in terms of a revitalized sexuality based on something other than the male-defined sexuality that characterized sex at earlier points in the life course. We return to these themes later in the chapter.

At this point, we should also mention the so-called 'male menopause', which has a separate but parallel historical trajectory and serves to regulate older men's sexuality, although not nearly to the degree it does so in women. Historically, various factors have converged to problematize male sexuality in mid-life, with Gullette suggesting that age anxiety focused on a decline in work and sexuality as the twin foci enabling internalization of the concept of a 'mid-life crisis'. In fact, Gullette asserts, the idea of male menopause has no robust physiological basis but really constitutes 'the loss of some (vaguely defined) past possession of masculinity, such as desire, sensation, strength' (1998: 24). As we have seen this has not impacted on the expectation that mid-life men will take much younger sexual partners, suggesting that it is to mid-life women that most problems are said to accrue.

At this point we turn to a consideration of gender and sexualities in later life.

Sexual relationships in later life

Traditionally, advancing age has been seen to result in a hollowed-out version of gender differences, with masculinity and femininity converging in the figure of the 'asexual' older person. Indeed, UK health policy documents and many health professionals, including GPs, share this assumption, associating 'sexual health' with younger people and often assuming that sex plays no part in the lives of older people (Gott and Hinchcliff, 2003). In fact, such a view is partly responsible for the increase in sexually transmitted diseases in the over-65s, noted by Public Health England in recent years.

Evidence suggests that changes occur physiologically for both men and women as they age but these are not inherently problematic and nor are they so different from problems appearing earlier in life. Specifically, more stimulus of the penis is required to attain a full erection, cycles are longer and slower: a delay of arousal, plateau, orgasm/ejaculation and resolution (Jung and Schill, 2004) (all of these of course could be described in positive terms rather than their being embedded in a paradigm of deficiency). For women, meanwhile, evidence of the impact of ageing is contestable and what is most striking is the degree of continuity between problems and concerns in later life as compared to earlier life (Nussbaum et al., 2004). Some examples from the latter's research include: lack of interest, raised as a problem in their sample in 88 per cent of women under the age of 44, 90 per cent of women aged 45–54, and 85 per cent in those aged 55 and over. Lubrication was raised as a problem in 75 per cent, 74 per cent and 74 per cent respectively in the above categories, to name but a few issues. These findings suggest that phallocentric practices at the heart of heterosexual sex remain potentially problematic for women throughout their sexual lives, a continuity that is 'lost' through the discourse of 'the change'. For example, vaginal dryness, which is one of the issues mentioned above, is frequently associated with the menopause and described as caused by the drop in oestrogen levels. But levels of oestrogen fluctuate regularly during younger women's cycles and it is also linked to pregnancy, breastfeeding, stress and, perhaps most consistently of all, to problems whose source lies not in hormone levels but in the relationship itself.

Moreover, increasingly we can witness a cultural obligation to maintain sexuality as one maintains appearance, health, consumer activity and work roles, all being aspects of the productive self. In emphasizing a youthful mode of practice which does not value qualitative change, it overturns a previous scientific discourse which claimed that the sexes grew more alike, or 'gender neutral' in older age and maintained that this was, in fact, in keeping with socially appropriate roles for older people (who were perceived as socially disengaging more broadly). Facilitated by the availability of Viagra, the result is that 'performing gender becomes a lifelong project for both men and women' (Katz and Marshall, 2004: 91) extending 'sexual freedom' to older age where, as in earlier life, it benefits men more than women and restores the full reach of the heterosexual matrix to this stage. But does continued sexual activity necessarily involve continuing old gender roles and associated sexualities? Or can there be alternative ways to negotiate gender and sexuality in later life?

Contrasting insights emerge from empirical data obtained by interviewing women in mid- and late life (Vares et al., 2007; Potts et al., 2004; 2003). In the case of those older women whose husbands had begun to take Viagra (Potts et al., 2003), there are examples, particularly among women aged 60 and over, of women feeling pressurized into sex when they are ambivalent at best. But comments of women somewhat younger than this (Vares et al., 2007), in their late 40s and older, suggest that in some cases women's sexuality grows more assertive and confident in mid-life. By contrast, several writers have suggested alternative perspectives to youth-orientated gender identity and associated sexualities in later life. Against the notion of freeing oneself up from the shackles of sexuality and the oppressive heterosexual matrix, Segal cautions that sexual intercourse and sexuality should not be confused: 'Sexuality in the form of desire is an all-pervasive aspect of our physicality' (2013: 95). She suggests that a gendered identity can be constructed in later life that embraces sexuality of a reconstituted kind (Segal, 1994). That is, whilst we might cease to have intercourse, sexuality is 'free' to emerge in different ways, as a more diffuse relationship between self and world, akin to childhood's polymorphous perversity (Segal, 2013).

But what about the possibilities for older men in constructing different gendered identities and negotiating different practices regarding sexuality? Ethel Person reminds us that for men, because of early socialization and childcare relationships, 'gender appears to "lean" on sexuality' (1980: 619). Data from studies of the effects of impotence-inducing treatment for prostate cancer suggests that whilst impotence is particularly challenging for younger men, older men are certainly not immune to the threats it poses to gendered identity. An 80-year-old man confessed poignantly:

> I feel I've lost all masculinity. I'm not a man anymore. I mean I'm just not. I mean if I were walking along with my wife, very slowly these days, and somebody accosted her I would sort of run away. I have no masculinity left. (Chapple and Ziebland, 2002: 833)

Unfortunately, the 'meaning' of sexuality to men includes many non-sexual issues serving as a vehicle for domination, the disguising of dependency needs, giving reassurance against castration as well as, at base, the need to overcome a primary female identification (Person, 1980). This indicates that, although presented as 'healthy' and 'necessary' to men's wellbeing, the resumption of sexual activity via Viagra in later life thus has the potential to reinstate older patterns of gender inequality and indeed oppression that may have become somewhat etiolated in more recent years.

In her reflection on ageing and old age, Segal (2013) identifies and addresses what she considers a key question: which gender is more 'tormented' by age in terms of sex and intimacy?. Segal is of the view that men suffer the most. On the one hand, from a position of deficiency all along, one might argue that women are accustomed to suffering assaults on their personhood and in addition have lifelong problems with male-defined sexuality (although this is not suffering less absolutely). In an eightieth birthday interview with Gail Collins in the *New York Times*, Gloria Steinem talked about the advantages of having a 'reduced sex drive: "The brain cells that used to be obsessed are now free for all kinds of great things... I try to tell younger women that, but they don't believe me"' (Collins, 2014). This is very different in tone from that of the ageing heroes or anti-heroes in the fiction of Philip Roth, for example, or the characters in Hanif Kureishi's later novels, all of whom continue to define themselves by youthful modes of sexuality and to suffer accordingly. However, and on the other hand, the beauty myth is particularly cruel to ageing women, and from a very youthful age. Moreover, the male/youthful structure of the look suggests that women are at an ontological disadvantage whereby their appearance, especially when ageing, threatens their very social personhood. Perhaps it would be most accurate to suggest that sexuality, configured as it is within a hierarchical gender regime, causes both men and women to suffer but in different ways and according to a different timing and trajectory.

Conclusion

Having noted how sexualities are embedded in the age and gender regime, the question will then be how the latter can be disrupted, especially in the culture of post-feminism with its intricate mix of objectification and sexual freedom for women. We might begin with Plummer's point that sexualities are 'messy and ambiguous social practices, not fixed and straightforward "drive releases"' (2004: 187). As social practices, that is, they are open to infinite revision, and 'libido', whatever its biological or psychic 'origins', is as much a force for freedom as for subjugation as Reich, Marcuse and Brown have all suggested. The work of Jackson (1982) and others suggests re-examining our attitudes to the way we lay the foundation of sexuality in childhood, because, by keeping children asexual and then encouraging only the male sex to break from these constraints, women are systemically disadvantaged. Both the children's laureate, Malorie Blackman, and the well-known children's author Philip Pullman have called for more depictions of sexual experiences in teen novels where, unlike the online porn that teenage boys in particular access, there can be a 'moral context'. The ramifications that lead from pornography, according to the UN goodwill ambassador for family planning, the Belgian sexologist Goedele Liekens, extend deep through the life course. Firstly, they reinforce boys' dominance in the classroom. Secondly, they foster unsatisfactory relationships. But in Lieken's view, a reshaped sex education can help young people learn about 'sex as a source of comfort and intimacy' rather than as a means of status in a peer group, control and dominance (Driscoll, 2015). Additionally, Dinnerstein has advocated that the sharing of childcare more equally in the home will not only enable gender equality to be established in actuality in terms of work and life opportunities for mothers but also help both men and women let go of toxic psychic associations with the mother's female body that prove so harmful in later life. With that knowledge, we can be aware of the constructed nature of male sexual domination and either refuse to perpetrate it (if one is a man) or challenge it (if one is a woman), making use perhaps of the rich possibilities of fantasy which certainly do not stick to the prescribed script (Jackson, 1999). As far as the former is concerned,

Stoltenberg (1984) suggests that men especially can start to think of their sexualities by means of different metaphors, and ones that more accurately reflect their lived experience. For example, in terms of the male erection, the metaphor has it that 'rigidity means power, rigidity means manhood, and rigidity means the urgency for something called "release of sexual tension"... the truth is that bone-hard erections aren't very comfortable... they feel a little dead... the idea that they feel good... is only a cultural illusion' or what Stoltenberg calls a 'symptom tension artificially induced' (1984: 27). For women, Hollway (1984) suggests that the myth of the powerful penis is an attempt to disguise 'men's vulnerability to women' because of their relationship with the Mother and to her the greatest weapon for challenging this is through the production of alternative accounts of male sexuality.

Meanwhile, mid-life seems to admit a variety of possibilities for interrupting hegemonic norms, such as related by the sample of middle-aged women interviewed by Potts and her colleagues (2004, 2003; Vares et al., 2007). Many stories disrupt expected narratives centring on gender and age and point to the potential of embracing a more dynamic, temporally charged understanding of gender, sexuality, identity and embodiment, one not defined by loss and not structured according to hierarchies and the binary pairing of power/submission, and one that does not, for example, see women's bodies before and after the time of menstruation, as vestigial (Cole and Winkler, 1994).

Aesthetically, given the link between beauty and sexuality in women, we can endeavour to 'see' age differently, by means of stepping outside the youthful gaze. Berg and Gadow suggest developing a gaze outside the age-hegemony that shapes classical aesthetics, using phenomenology as a framework. They ask: why see wrinkles as marring beauty? Why not a meshwork of tracings from the past symbolizing 'a world filled with leaps, windings, countless crossings, immeasurably more intricate and perhaps also more true than the world of one-dimensional thought and self-evident distinctions' (1978: 86). This resonates with another strand of aesthetic theory, moreover, where Ruskin admired the heterogeneity that came with age suggesting that

> a broken stone has necessarily more various forms in it than a whole one; a bent roof has more various curves in it than a straight one, every excrescence or cleft involves some additional complexity of light and shade, and every stain of moss on eaves or wall adds to the delightfulness of colour. (Lowenthal, 1985: 165)

In terms of gendered examples we can think here of flesh that is flaccid and sagging with breasts a prime example. In fact, we have symbols already in existence that challenge its one-way association with decline. The penis and male genitalia are the obvious example: not always the proud thrusting member standing like the wand of an ancient god and terrifying for women to behold as in D.H. Lawrence, but the decidedly more vulnerable organ that Sylvia Plath once memorably described in *The Bell Jar* as akin to turkey neck and turkey gizzards. Babies are wrinkled and flaccid as week-old peaches; silk and other delicate fabrics also have that sense of inward folding and soft collapse and also conjure up images of strength and delicacy, of suppleness and refinement, that can be the basis of an aesthetic of ageing, gendered bodies that lie outside the hierarchies implicit in social roles. Young (2005) notes that certain cultures venerate sagging breasts, seeing them as emblematic of 'much mothering and the wisdom of experience' (pp. 79–80). The imagery exists for us to play with different meanings in a way that is freeing and exciting.

For Greer (1970) and Wolf (1990) the 'beauty' that apparently eludes older women with such devastating consequences is in fact never 'natural' but something women have to labour at and perform throughout the life course; the beauty rules can be challenged and the ideology itself undermined by younger women's candour (as happened with the #nomakeupselfie campaign in 2014). Through mid-life and beyond Greer (1991) notes:

> Even those of us who look good know that the secret marks of age, the witch-marks, are there. The proliferation of moles and wens, the sags and wrinkles, the spurs on our heels, the thinning of our hair, the bristles that sprout on our chin, all are easily hidden, but we know that they are there. (p. 411)

In a powerful message, Lena Dunham describes how her portrayal of imperfect young bodies in the HBO series *Girls* performing clumsy couplings is part of a conscious project to debunk the myths. She notes, 'Between porn and studio romantic comedies, we get the message loud and clear that we are doing it all wrong. Our bedsheets aren't right. Our moves aren't right. Our bodies aren't right.' But she is proving them wrong in her show by showing sex 'as it is' (Dunham, 2014: 103). Similarly the new campaign 'This Girl Can' (http://www.thisgirlcan.co.uk/), a project developed by Sport England to encourage women of all ages to take part in exercise, promotes women's enjoyment of diverse kinds of physical activity from solitary jogging to belly-dancing classes. The current advertisement shown in cinemas and TV during 2015 begins controversially: 'I jiggle therefore I am'. By watching these women and girls, with their fleshy, imperfect, flabby, dimpled bodies – exactly the bodies you see every day, in streets, changing rooms and reflected within one's own mirror – we get the message that we are doing it 'right': as long as we are fully engaged, wholehearted as boys, that is. Findings suggest that young women's enjoyment of exercise is lost past puberty when a concern with their appearance, the 'ugliness' of their flesh, and with not getting sweaty or messing up their hair, takes centre stage (Girlguiding UK, 2012). Watching these women puff, pant and take enormous pleasure in what their bodies can do, oblivious to what they look like, their bodies subject bodies through and through (the 'male gaze' that would turn them into objects has been switched off in their heads, so to speak), and with Dunham's images in my mind also, I cannot be the only one to have experienced a euphoric 'click': the realization that the sight of these bodies inserting themselves unabashedly into the world *is* the (or at least one powerful) definition of beauty. This is a beauty available to many, moreover (whether or not one can dance and even possible if one cannot walk). It is one definition that, connected to vitality and appetite for life, is wonderfully commonplace, and not at all the possession of the elite: as if it ever could be.

In this context, challenging the beauty rules, or at least expanding the possibilities of beauty, starts to seem less Utopian and there is no reason why 'old is beautiful' cannot become a rallying cry to which many of us will respond with enthusiasm. Norms of beauty can, and do, change and all it requires is the cultural and political will to do so, with women posting selfies without makeup and actresses refusing to be airbrushed – all excellent examples pointing in the right direction. Most of all, perhaps the link between highly conventional (and thus restrictive) norms of beauty and sexuality is not helpful for women of any age (being beautiful does not signify enhanced sexual pleasure, for example; moreover, the norms of femininity are contrary to a rich and complex female sexuality that entails maturity, confidence, self-knowledge and experience). Learning to see differently can begin by viewing the female body not as an object but in relationship with others and, like men's bodies, defined by action and knowledge. Finally, as with age ideology entrenched in all other aspects of lived experience we have discussed in previous chapters, perhaps the most potent challenge will be to emphasize the continuity of experience both across the life course and between ages and stages; sexuality is absolutely no exception.

CHAPTER SUMMARY

- In this chapter we discussed how sexuality plays a key part in defining life stages and delineating boundaries between them.

- Childhood as a life stage is constructed as asexual; youth as asexual but uncontrolled and requiring regulation; menopause symbolically marks the end of femininity and problematizes a woman's sexuality.

- Relatedly, we traced the ways in which the heterosexual regime is regulated and its gendered hierarchy maintained through: (i) the beauty myth; and (ii) the time economy, both of which work to control women through setting a limit to beauty, sexuality and femininity.

- Where the third age defines itself as youthful this includes continued sexuality involving a continuation of gendered norms and practices, where once these norms were considered to soften, and the similarities between men and women increase.

- We suggested that challenging these hierarchical norms requires, among other things, revisiting the gender socialization of children, whilst in adulthood one way to start would be by examining our everyday beliefs about what is beautiful and questioning the link between beauty and sexuality.

Further questions

1. What is the link between romantic love and gendered and classed inequality through the life course for both men and women?

2. What is the connection between sexuality and health throughout the life course?

3. How do norms and practices around (hetero)sexuality perpetuate other hierarchies and inequalities throughout the life course?

Talking point

David Sims' celebrated photographs of roses portray them towards the end of their life, as wilting, dying, dehiscent, pink blossoms tinged with sepia, waxy petals coming slowly apart, wrinkled at the edges, anthers splayed, filaments crumpled. Their beauty is of a different order from that of young roses but it is undeniably beauty and for the photographer himself apparently more memorable of all in this form. Use this as inspiration for alternative relationships between ageing, old age and beauty in human bodies. See http://www.visionaireworld.com/96-roses

---

Further reading

For a **general overview of sexuality** see Segal, L. (1994) *Straight Sex: rethinking the politics of pleasure*, Berkeley, CA: University of California Press. Also useful is the edited volume by Weeks, J., Holland, J. and Waites, M. (eds) (2003) *Sexualities and Society: a reader*, Cambridge: Polity. For **sexuality during the life course:** for **childhood** see Jackson, S. (1982) *Childhood and Sexuality*, Oxford: Wiley-Blackwell, also any book by Nancy Chodorow, particularly the 1978 publication *The Reproduction of Mothering*, Berkeley, CA: University of California Press and *Femininities, Masculinities, Sexualities: Freud and beyond*, Kentucky: University of Kentucky Press (1994); for **mid-life:** Greer, G. (1991) *The Change*, London: Hamish Hamilton; for **old age:** Marshall, B.L. and Katz, S. (2012) The embodied life course: post-ageism or the renaturalization of gender? *Societies*, 2: 222–34; Gott, M. (2004) *Sexuality, Sexual Health and Ageing*, Milton Keynes: Open University Press.

Further resources

Stella Grey's *Guardian* Column (http://www.theguardian.com/lifeandstyle/series/mid-life-ex-wife) describes dating and mid-life, with many bittersweet reflections on mid-life sexuality and social capital.

Notes

1. A psycho-social structure, identified by Butler (1990) which establishes the genders in a binary relationship, constitutive of, and by, heterosexual desire, regardless of individual sexual orientation.

2. Although in the UK sexual and relationship education (SRE) is compulsory from age 11, this relates only to biology – reproduction – and sexual health and schools can thereafter determine what else is taught (and parents can choose to withdraw their children from this).

3. Indeed, children, women and older people are all expected to 'smile' emphasizing submission and compliance; Firestone (1970) wrote: 'My "dream" action for the women's liberation movement: a *smile boycott*' (p. 89; original emphasis) and Woodward (2002) talks about the 'damaging effects of the cultural prohibition of anger in older people' (p. 187) as an ideological means of containing any possibility of critique and protest.

8

HEALTH, ILLNESS AND NORMALITY THROUGH THE LIFE COURSE

Background: woman's soul as prison of her body

This chapter continues the discussion, found in Chapters 3, 6 and 7 particularly, on the intersections of the age and gender regime, focusing on where the underlying tensions give rise to bodily problematizations and disorders. Ellen Annandale (2009) suggests that indeed the effect of the complexity of the new gender order has been to introduce a new pattern of health inequalities in which old issues remain interwoven with newer ones. The effect of mixing young women's educational success with the constraints the latter experience in the work place or at home, the complex requirements to balance autonomy and a re-sexualized femininity, all take a toll on health whilst old inequalities related to poverty and oppression remain. For this reason we will concentrate in this chapter on women's bodies because they are both disadvantaged in the gender regime and constitute a key site of new modes of governmentality that apply to all. We focus on specific points across the life course where norms of femininity are in contradiction with requirements of the productive body, or where certain requirements of femininity are in tension with other requirements of femininity. At such points, diagnoses of pathology may be made and the dissonance that results from ambiguity within the gender regime managed by pharmaceuticals or other forms of therapy.

If it is true, as Foucault argued, that the 'soul is the prison of the body' (1977b: 30), then this is particularly true for women. Although both masculinity and femininity involve exaggerations, on the one hand, and, suppressions on the other, of the full range of human attributes, empirical evidence suggests that, through a greater disciplining and resultant docility of soul, women's bodies 'are subject to stricter rules of behaviour: how to act, what to say, what to want' (Penny, 2014: 13). But whilst the social requirements of femininity have been recognized as giving rise to 'gender pain'

(Morris, 1991) I suggest that the intersections of the age and gender regime mean that such pain today has a very particular association with age and stage of life, rendering it also describable as 'age pain': an expression of the sufferings generated by an ageist context which may be compounded by other forms of social suffering. Indeed, health can be perceived as a lens through which to view the lived effects of these structures on women's lives (Annandale, 2009). However, it is not the argument here that women's bodies are inherently more vulnerable; rather it is the social processes associated with the age and gender regimes, particularly clashing configurations (Segal, 2007), that serve to 'enfragile' women, to coin a phrase, in specific ways.

AIMS OF THE CHAPTER

- In this chapter, we will explore how specific tension at three points in the female life course give rise to problematic psychopathological symptoms or syndromes.

- These tensions are associated respectively with: (i) the hypervisibility and hyper-surveillance of the 'Girl' stage; (ii) the ending of Girlhood and resocialization into a narrative of decline in mid-life; and (iii) old age and, for some, entry into the Hag stage.

- We will trace these in relation to eating disorders in youth, menopausal disorders and frailty in old age. All three stages, however, create 'frailty'.

Girls' embodiment and gender pain

We will begin by describing the concept and context of gender pain which I adapt from David Morris to refer to the gender-based suffering embedded in a psychosocial landscape defined by a 'dominator/dominated model of social relations' (1991: 117). Cartesian ontology, in all its ramifications, together with contemporary young women being interpellated as 'active subjects', set up a tension between what Beauvoir would call a woman's 'immanence' and the more masculine ideal of transcendence. This sets her will at war with her body, specifically at war with the unruliness that threatens the viability of the Cartesian project to which she is now, apparently, invited. Young's (2005) observation concerning the uncomfortable conjunction of subjectification and objectification in a woman's embodiment which first arises with the changes of puberty and adolescence, thus has a late-modern 'twist'. Its origins extend far back historically. For example, the state of hunger that many women inhabit through diet and exercise regimes has a parallel in hysteria that affected middle-class girls in the nineteenth century who were also beset by a variety of contradictory and complex choices, though different in nature to today's.

Indeed, although the social landscape of the contemporary Girl departs from this, sediments of previous constructions of femininity remain, and historical and contemporary discourses both position women's bodily wellbeing in opposition to their educational advancement. During the nineteenth century, according to medical discourse, female 'weakness' was predicated on the principle of conservation of energy and in women this had two aspects: (i) she could develop one organ only at the expense of others (hence the dangers of developing the intellect through education or reading) and linked to this; (ii) reproductive organs took the lion's share of the available energy (but not in men, for whom it was quite the opposite: for men the emphasis was on not letting their 'seed' draw from their higher functions). Ehrenreich and English note:

> Because reproduction was woman's grand purpose in life, doctors agreed that women had to concentrate all their energy downward toward the womb. All other activity should be slowed down or stopped during the peak periods of uterine energy demand. At puberty, girls were advised to take a great deal of bed rest in order to help focus their strength on regulating their periods – though this might take years. Too much reading or intellectual stimulation in the fragile stage of adolescence could result in permanent damage to the reproductive organs, and sickly, irritable babies. (2013: 139–40)

These sorts of arguments reappeared during the emergence of the educated and career-orientated New Woman in the 1890s. They also underpinned the psychological theories of adolescence of the early to mid twentieth century propounded by G. Stanley Hall and Erik Erikson, among others. Hall suggests that whilst 'boys grew towards self-knowledge and began to acquire an adult identity' (Dyhouse, 2014: 65), girls never outgrew this stage. Indeed, it was a 'hazardous time' for young women whose potential for cognitive advancement was low and who should therefore be encouraged to acquire skills for suitable refined domesticity. Feminine traits noted by Hall include: 'clothes consciousness, whimsicality, flirtatiousness, fads, fickleness, weeping, giggling and non-intellectualism' (Dyhouse, 2014: 66). Erikson also built on biological notions centred upon girls' future reproductive function – his concept of the psychic 'inner space' of femininity – to posit a more limited development as compared with men, with a 'natural' foundation in women's reproductive role which meant that they did not 'progress' as far beyond adolescence as the male.

The contours of this discourse indicate the extent of the social shift that has occurred over the past decades in order to give rise to the valorizing of the Girl at school and in the work place. To recap, girls have been highlighted as achieving greater educational success than boys, gaining higher marks in almost all subjects and making some headway in traditional 'boys' subjects'. Methods of study – especially continual assessment – suit girls more, but the bigger picture, to which

Burman (2005) draws attention, is that 'the feminization of education occurs... alongside other feminizations' (p. 356) including the work place, and is under-pinned by a 'feminized' subjectivity: docile, self-regulating and emotionally literate in the mode of the 'confessional'. This is linked to a cultural feminization that is deeply disquieting in its disempowering thrust, as Burman suggests: 'The "neo-liberal twist"' regarding the educational and professional success of girls and women lies in an ongoing tendency to 'naturalize and then co-opt women's traditional skills, the skills wrought of subordination, into success strategies, to extend structures of exploitation' (2005: 364). The lived problem for girls lies with the gender norms that they transgress through their educational success in particular, with its association with 'masculine' ambition rather than feminine 'lack'. Ringrose (2007) suggests that the task, then, for girls involves the 'new highly complex and contradictory work of "doing" girl and of performing com-plex dimensions of specifically "bourgeois" success in increasingly neoliberalized sites of schooling and work' (p. 484). This produces a heightened tension, perhaps even an ongoing embodied crisis for girls, compounded by the 'laddish' culture they encounter among male peers in both high schools and universities, including the most elite (Phipps and Young, 2012).

This social thrust conjoins activity and passivity in an uneasy composite. Moreover, in highlighting the feminization of education and employment we have to put this in context with its opposite trend, and speak of 'gender-asymmetry' (Esping-Anderson, 2005). In relation to a feature also noted by Kohli, Esping-Anderson suggests that it is characterized by a 'masculinization of female biographies' involving women taking on male patterns of educational achievement, later marriage and career focus destabilizing the work/care binary (whilst not challenging the primacy of the former). However, men, so far, have not embarked on anything approaching a 'parallel feminization' of their life-course (Esping-Anderson, 2005: 271; quoted in Scott et al., 2010: 12). Beck and Beck-Gernsheim (2002) and (Beck-Gernsheim, 2002) have noted the contradic-tory ongoing requirements that women be responsible for the bulk of care and domestic duties, as well as engaging with public life, meaning that for women, individualization is incomplete and indeed aspects of it are incongruous and paradoxical in a way that can be expressed, by some, only through the body. We have noted, for example, how women outperform men in educational achieve-ments in every class grouping, and now reach graduate level in greater numbers than men. But the fact is that despite this, only 21 companies in the US Fortune 500 list are run by female chief executives (and a meagre four of the 100 FTSE 100 companies in the UK) and women make up a small percentage of those at the top of every company, from stuffy law firms to trendy Silicon Valley start-ups. There are real obstacles, hard for her to pinpoint, but felt at every dimension of the Girl's life.

In the next section, we will look first at the nature of pathologies that affect ado-lescent girls and explore this as a manifestation of gender pain.

The Girl: an excess of enterprise

Frost (2001) suggests that, whilst all young people are experiencing problems with addictions, depression and other mental health issues, young women face unique problems which include body dysmorphic disorder, eating disorders and other forms of self-harm which Frost locates within the general category of 'body hatred'. The International Classification of Diseases (ICD) identifies young women as most likely to suffer from eating disorders and they are still more frequently diagnosed among middle-class girls, with an inverse relationship existing between socio-economic status and weight among young women (Frost, 2001).

Figures released in 2014 showed that hospital admissions for eating disorders were up by 8 per cent in a year, the average age being 15, with nine times as many young women compared to young men being admitted; 76 per cent of admissions were for anorexia and 5 per cent for bulimia (HSCIC, 2014). The National Association of Anorexia Nervosa (ANAD, 2015) indicates that 91 per cent of women surveyed on a college campus had attempted to control their weight through dieting (Shisslak et al., 1995) and that anorexia was the third most common chronic illness among adolescents (Public Health Service's Office in Women's Health, 2000). It is recognized as such a significant problem, dissatisfaction with body weight even identified among six-year-olds (Walter, 2015), that it has generated national campaigns in the UK (the Campaign for Body Confidence) and captured domestic political attention (the All-Party Parliamentary Group on Body Image (2012)) and also international concern ('Endangered Bodies': see http://www.endangeredbodies.org/). Harris suggests that such attention arises from the acknowledgement that much is at stake in terms of the success of young women especially 'maintaining a skilled and acquiescent workforce for the new economy' (Harris, 2004: 34). Thus the management of young women's eating disorders becomes a key aspect of governmentality.

As an expression of gender pain it has multiple layers of signification. Laurie Penny, the journalist and young feminist blogger, draws on her own experiences to describe the role dieting plays in the regulation and self-regulation of young women today, being simultaneously an expression of anger and acquiescence, of agency and subjugation, signalling mastery and control, whilst also expressing suffering and distress. A thin body gives a woman social capital even as it debilitates her, whilst Bordo reminds us also of the psychic origins of the anxiety over 'soft, protuberant body parts' which evoke maternal femininity, and which is part of this fear generated by infant vulnerability. Thus, to be considered attractive today, 'female bodies… must be stripped of all psychic resonance with maternal power' (Bordo, 1995: 208). Bordo also suggests that this indicates a problematization of the unstable production/consumption divide, a feature of late modernity, but for women in particular, 'the regulation of desire [including food and sexuality] becomes especially problematic' (1995: 212). It may also represent a deep protest against growing up which is all the more reasonable on account of the ever-youthful identity of the Girl. Indeed, one of the central attractions of the Girl is that she does not grow up. Penny again: 'It's hard growing up; it's easier to grow sideways, to veer off from becoming a person and just be a girl instead' (Penny, 2014: 49). But we need to explore: Why are these relationships to the body characteristic of this particular age group? How does the intersection of age, class and gender converge in these symptoms? What do they say about age relations and the age system more generally?

Certainly the revolutionary shift in girls' achievement at schools compared to boys, has taken a massive toll on girls' psychological and physiological wellbeing. Middle-class and working-class girls experience complex, if contrasting, role pressures. Generated by the education system and the labour economy, they are reflected in cultural values and focused on appearance and particularly the body. In this section, I will draw extensively from Valerie Walkerdine and colleagues' perceptive and probing research into girls' educational experiences and the interplay of class and femininity therein. Walkerdine et al. (2001) describe the issues that confront (various groups of) girls thus:

> The young women from professional families have to cope with not only the loss of security that the new economy brings, and therefore uncertainty about the reproduction of the middle class, but also their remaking as a new female professional elite at a time of a labour market shift that puts high-flying men elsewhere and devalues the status of the professions.... Young women from erstwhile working class families have to face the realm of work throughout their adult lives, unlike any other generation before them. They face a 'girl power' that tells them they can be what they want in a labour market that cruelly sets limits on any ambition, together with an education system that classifies them as fit for certain kinds of work depending on their academic capabilities. (p. 21)

Here, the slow-track adolescence of middle-class girls subjects them to unique risk factors as their dependency on their families is prolonged if they complete their lengthy education, possibly followed by an internship. Drawing on the work of Alice Miller, Deresiewicz has described the cycle of grandiosity and despair that often accompanies educational success from a young age, when anything other than the highest scores constitutes profound failure and summed up by the comments of this high-achieving schoolgirl: 'Some people see health and happiness as more important than grades and college: I don't' (quoted in Deresiewicz, 2014: 51). Middle-class girls often take their father as compared with their mother as their role model; in terms of gender performance this requires the balancing of feminine and masculine traits, as we have seen, constituting the feminine as a 'site of crisis, anxiety and desire' (Ringrose, 2007: 484) in common with other fragmented habituses; in practical terms this means avoiding early pregnancy and motherhood, which may consequently involve a more brutal separation and individuation from their mothers. As a result, Walkerdine et al. suggest, for middle-class girls (and working-class upwardly mobile girls), their reproductive potential is particularly problematic:

their inscription as the bourgeois subject… counterposes fecundity in a way that simply does not allow the possibility of pregnancy. The two positions are incompatible and that incompatibility must be lived by the girl herself as… a psychic struggle from which she never escapes…. The increase in infertility technologies and methods of assisted conception points precisely to the increase in some demand for motherhood by older women who have been caught inside this struggle in one particular way, the career path of middle-class girls. (Walkerdine et al., 2001: 187)

Other studies also suggest that 'an intrinsic element of the "can-do" experience is thus the delaying of motherhood' (Harris, 2004: 22) into one's thirties and forties. However, a problem arises when the 'more traditional requirement for women to have children at some point still comes to bear on these girls' (Harris, p. 23). Indeed, a key part of the regulatory discourse is that 'they are simultaneously told that they must pursue a career and at the same time factor in children before it is "too late"' (pp. 23–4) with confessional accounts by well-known 'childless career women' (from Germaine Greer and Elizabeth Wurtzel to Liz Jones and Kate Spicer) revealing that the 'moment' when it would have been appropriate to have a child is something (so elusive) that they 'missed' it and, for those who subsequently attempted to do so, they found they could not now get pregnant (and thus only 'know' the moment once it is in the past). Indeed, these sorts of accounts are often used as cautionary tales, along with warnings of early menopause and 'fertility dives' in young women's magazines, to 'warn' young women of the time-limited nature of their reproductive capacity and to impress them, above all, with a sense of 'time panic'. The UK TV presenter Kirstie Allsopp, known for her homely shows on renovating old houses and on crafts and vintage decorative arts, for example, speaking from a position of immense class privilege, suggested she would give the following advice to daughters, had she had them: 'Don't go to university. Start work straight after school, stay at home, save up your deposit – I'll help you. And then we can find you a nice boyfriend and you can have a baby by the time you're 27' (Coren, 2014). (Perhaps it was just as well that she had sons.) Other discourses use time panic to impress upon women the need to work hard and gain success in one's career 'before' one has a family (implicitly, the two are not compatible) whilst being haunted by the fear that this 'before' might extend indefinitely until it is already 'too late'. This joint theme is summed up in the perk Apple and Google have introduced to female employees in the form of paying for egg freezing (Tran, 2014) and this is a trend that the *Elle* magazine columnist, Victoria Coren, feels is beneficial on the whole. Disagreeing with Allsop's push into 'premature motherhood' she reflects: 'The key to true liberation actually lies with egg freezing' (Coren, 2014). If young women are disadvantaged directly through lack of 'time' as compared with men, then buying time is certainly a step towards equalizing this disadvantage under the circumstances.

In such a context, with its peculiar combination of opportunity and (bodily) constraint, and the co-existence of pre- and post-feminist ideals, it is inaccurate, Bordo suggests, to see eating disorders as either disease or protest, rather than as potentially both. McRobbie sees it as a form of 'illegible rage' (2009) with multiple layers of signification including the desire to transcend the female body as established through institutions around reproduction, mothering and domesticity; to control the waywardness associated with female bodies, including their time-limited abilities; whilst simultaneously bringing about a re-entrapment of women in their bodies. It also represents an excessive self-discipline and self-regulation, a working-on-oneself, a triumph of mind over matter, that, in other areas of her life, she has learned, brings success and validation to the Girl. It is thus both an extreme (especially if taken to full-blown anorexia) and the logical conclusion to the enterprising zeal conjured up in her and thus not something that can be switched off by cool logic. Moreover, young women's socialization into the new gender regime has already prepared them for the self-surveillance that is required through, for example, norms around menstruation, and in which they will have absorbed a fundamental paradox, namely that the body is wayward and uncontrollable yet must be controlled as an ongoing project (Moore, 2010). The alienation women may feel from their bodies is, then, a 'normal' alienation. Brumberg (1997) illustrates this with regard to the activity of purchasing jeans, an event generative of torment and self-loathing for many:

> Some girls assume there is something wrong with their bodies when they cannot fit consistently into the same 'standard' size; others will reject a pair of jeans simply because they do not want to wear that size, even though the number has no substantive meaning. (p. 129)

Chronic fatigue can also be considered an expression of gender pain, as with its dual classed and gendered dimension, it particularly applies to the Girl, whether at work or still in education, implying that the effort she needs to make to remain ahead is quite literally exhausting and also perhaps the recognition that her time is short. Lian and Bondevik (2015) observe: 'The silhouette of the upper-class woman of the 1800s, who failed to cope with stress and pressure in expending her energy both in and out of her home, is visible in the background' (p. 12). That is, 'ME [Myalgic Encephalopathy] is a self-inflicted creation of educated wage-earning women who have become too ambitious and perfectionist' (p. 11). Such expressions of illness stamp even the highest-achieving young woman as essentially feminine (and, again, suggest that frailty does not begin in old age). It is also the young woman's 'fault' and the change in tone becomes clear through historical analysis of attitudes towards recognized conditions such as neurasthenia. Originally, the explanation found in the medical literature, as with hysteria, is one of social and emotional pressures but in the twentieth century, this is framed in terms of individual inability to cope. (We might also discuss young women's increased smoking and drinking in similar terms.)

But we cannot get a full picture of women's situation without a brief consideration of men's position here. Firstly, the educational environment, characterized by increased surveillance and ongoing testing, means that many boys are unable to manage this appropriately, given the norms of hegemonic masculinity, and may be diagnosed with ADHD. Indeed, the association of both masculinity and socio-economic disadvantage with this diagnosis indicates that it is working-class masculinity that is being problematized particularly here. However, recognizing that men are also subject to tensions within the gender regime, Gill (2008) suggests that three aspects of hegemonic masculinity underpin their relative immunity from the tension between self and body. These include: the injunction that one should be 'one's own man' and not submit to social pressures; that men should not be vain or narcissistic; that men should not be obsessive. All are themes within hegemonic masculinity. In practice, these motifs of masculine subjectivity serve to protect them against a straightforward capitulation to any perceived pressures (which after all require them to change less than girls). More fundamentally still, perhaps, growing into adulthood is a way of growing into masculinity; for young women, however, in growing into womanhood their concern is that they are, already in life, departing from the feminine ideal. In addition, boys' obsessive bodily self-regulation, where it may be expressed through sporting activity, weight training and bodybuilding, is all about *adding* power, size and strength and *increasing* rather than *reducing* the 'space', literally and symbolically, that one occupies in the world. Furthermore, in schools and universities, 'lad culture', with its macho rituals and sexist overtones, has been found to be as undermining of women as it is supportive of men, serving for them as a 'means by which privileged men police and preserve territory' (Phipps and Young, 2012: 29). Of course, this masculine ethos does generate problems further down the life course for men, as we have noted in Chapter 7 on sexuality. But at this stage at least boys do not experience anything like the contradictory pressures upon them regarding reproduction. Not only is 'time' on their side here but when they do become a father, unlike the 'mummy pay gap' that affects mother's pay adversely in relation to men's, and the fact that women with children are less likely to be hired than women without children, fathers are 19 per cent more likely to be hired than comparably qualified men without children, indicating its association with positive masculine qualities such as authority, responsibility, paternal care and so on (Spar, 2013).

'Menopause': suffering (and) the end of femininity

It arrives at last, now in mid-life, what they most fear: the end of Girlhood, signalled by menopause which serves as a 'bridge', linking the Girl, emblem of the enterprising self, to the frail older woman, its opposite. As Penny puts it, girls 'never really get to grow up, which means they can only ever get old, which is a fearful thing for girl-children' (Penny, 2014: 50–51).What Penny is referring to here is the constricted space of adulthood for women; successful women must often choose, or so it appears, to 'act as men' or else try to employ their sexuality in a way that requires cultivation of feminine norms. Moreover, with mid-life woman, the possibilities associated with the Girl are demonstrated to be time-limited in a very specific way through medical discourse, with ample support in popular culture. We have already discussed various aspects of the role the menopause plays within the age regime over previous chapters; here we will concentrate on how as an embodied 'event' or process it has become medicalized and treated as a disease and/or syndrome. One of the consequences of this, I will argue, is to re-socialize women at mid-life, as they are disembedded from the central role they formerly played in the gender regime and eased into marginalization through decline discourses. Although this does not happen to all women in the same way, possessing, as all other age-related inequality, a strongly classed element, no woman is immune.

In symbolic terms, menopause signals the end of Girlhood and whilst part of a consistent problematization of women's bodies, it possesses factors that are unique to it. For example, discourses around it differ from those problematizing menstruation – such as Premenstrual syndrome (PMS) – in that menopause itself is highlighted as a problem, not just its 'effects' (Lorber and Moore, 2002: 82). In other important aspects, however, it is a continuation of the problematizing of women's reproductive physiology, which is a problem of 'woman' herself throughout the life course. As we saw in Chapter 6, although associated with the youthful and fertile body, menstruation is depicted as something shameful, dirty and embarrassing, signs of which have to be carefully concealed. The same is true of menopause, but with the added negative association with biological decline as well as unproductivity. Martin (1987) shows how in the case of both menstruation and menopause the 'deficiency' lies in some teleological idea of what a woman's body is 'for'. This telos remains embedded within medical discourses and its presence therein continues to define women's reproductive role as central to her social value and purpose; hence, pronouncements such as that by Kirstie Allsopp; and hence the irredeemable stigma of menopause (which can never be reversed).

The difference between menopause as a disease and as a syndrome (with its implications of greater and lesser containment) requires unpicking. Menopause, can be both, or either, of these, depending on the context and what part of a woman's body is being problematized. MacPherson (1981), in research that remains relevant today, shows that the construction of menopause as a disease was boosted by the emergence of hormonal therapy as a treatment. She notes that calling it a 'disease' 'influences millions of women to perceive themselves as ill during their menopausal years and to seek a medical cure' (1981: 111). By contrast, a syndrome has ramifications that extend into everyday life. It is 'a combination of symptoms resulting from a common cause or commonly occurring together' (1985: 12); a general and all-embracing term which gives a wide latitude for linkage and 'without scientific evidence of a direct causal relationship' (p. 12). A review of contemporary medical textbooks used in undergraduate education (Niland and Lyons, 2011) finds menopause treated as a syndrome *and* a disease, discussed in terms of ovarian 'failure' and endocrine 'deficiency'. This means that as well as problematic in itself it is a 'health risk' (for example, presaging the probable onset of osteoporosis). To offset such risk, the recommended treatment is HRT, (although this is to be carefully managed in regular discussion with patients, as a result of the findings that relate it to health issues[1]), a discourse which establishes it as pathological rather than a 'normal' change. Indeed, recent research (Avis et al., 2015) which also received extensive international media coverage, suggests that, contrary to the popular notion that hot flashes associated with the menopause last only a few years, they can in fact continue for up to fourteen years (Anon, 2015). Significantly, the research notes that those who suffer more protracted symptoms are those with less education, of low socio-economic status and non-white ethnicity and who have experienced a greater degree of perceived stress, anxiety and depression preceding the onset of menopause. Moreover, this ill-favoured group also has a greater risk of heart attacks and osteoporosis. In other words, such problems are individualized and associated with mid-life generally and menopause specifically, despite having deep socio-structural origins. More broadly, findings that suggest that problematizations are far from being the lived experience of most women are under-reported and the several studies that found the majority of women having little or no problems with hot flashes (Lorber and Moore, 2002; Martin, 1987) and that nearly a quarter did not have hot flashes at all (Lorber and Moore, 2002) received nowhere near the same press attention.

The creation of 'menopausal syndrome' (MacPherson, 1985), or a discourse in which the 'menopause' is linked to general problematization of the body (regardless of whether or not one experiences problems with the menopause per se, or indeed with one's reproductive system) leads to a more general loss of confidence in the body as a whole, teaching women almost literally to begin to doubt their body's strength and capability and to see themselves as vulnerable and fragile. Osteoporosis is most prominently linked with menopause and is usually discussed in terms of risk of fractures but not all women with fractures have osteoporosis and not all women with osteoporosis have fractures, meaning 'there is no simple relation between bone mineral density and incidence of osteoporosis' (Lock, 1993: 355). Moreover, the standard against which osteoporosis is measured is taken from the bone density of young women (Lock, 1993) so that, for women's bodies, 'normality means youth' and 'specifically... normal means to be of reproductive age' (p. 377). This makes women's mid-life bodies by definition problematic (but only if we agree with the initial assumption, of course). However, if we look a little more carefully at this we will find that osteoporosis is a logical consequence of embodied femininity. Indeed, data indicates that the feminization of society is leading to gender convergence in men's rates of osteoporosis (IOF, 2015). Currently, 1 in 3 women over 50 experience osteoporotic fractures and 1 in 5 men. But there is a projected increase of 310 per cent in men and 240 per cent in women by 2050. By 2025 the estimated number of hip fractures occurring worldwide in men will be similar to that observed in women in 1990 (IOF, 2015). Factors underpinning this are associated with a feminized culture and society: physical inactivity; sedentary lifestyle; reduced muscle strength; low body weight. Class factors also play a part; for example smoking features too. Early prevention (for women and men) is of the kind we have noted in Chapter 6 as bringing about a different kind of female embodiment: more exercise from childhood throughout life to improve muscle mass and less emphasis on slenderness and other feminine traits (IOF, 2015).

The disjunction between lived experience and ideological discourses of this kind, as well as the fact that other factors are clearly implicated in health experiences at this time, suggest an intent to 'control' the middle-aged female body in a variety of ways (Gullette, 1997; Lock, 1993; Martin, 1987). Both during menstruation ('not pregnant') and menopause ('and will never (again) be pregnant') women have evaded the structures of patriarchal control. Menopausal women, moreover, are doubly threatening in that they are potentially at the height of their powers, socially and economically. Menopause discourses thus serve to naturalize age ideology. For disadvantaged women their ideological purpose is partly to disguise other forms of inequality (Martin sees the 'hot flash' itself as a body metaphor for social embarrassment, frustration and repressed anger at one's repeated humiliation). For middle-class professional women, it undermines their confidence in themselves and justifies unequal treatment by employers – passing a woman over for promotion at best or redundancy at worst, promoting men and younger people above her 'naturally' – and successful mid-life then involves 'managing' this condition in a way that enables one to distance oneself from others less able. It is also an attempt to 'control' an ambiguous social category: female but not able to reproduce; neither old nor young and so on. For all women, however, menopause is potentially problematic in terms of their femininity, which is essentially associated with the reproductive body and they have to find a way to reconfigure their femininity in as satisfactory a way as possible. For some, viewing it as a disease to control can then be helpful (and we will discuss this further in relation to Mariella Frostrup, in Chapter 9, who made a vocal and public complaint when her health insurance company refused to treat it as an illness). Finally, and perhaps most importantly, medical 'control' of the ageing woman's body results from deep fear of the Hag. As Margaret Lock puts it, the increasing division of menopause into pre-, peri- and post-menopausal, complete with measurements of bodily functions and hormone levels, as well as being a 'heuristic device' with little correspondence to the heterogeneity of lived experiences among women themselves, actually serves to 'essentialize' women at this stage of their lives turning her from a flesh-and-blood reality into a symbol, a 'universal figure who smells faintly of old age, decrepitude and death' (1993: xxxii).

That this ever-increasing distancing and problematization is a product of an age ideology specifically connected with this phase of late modernity can be seen by comparison both to other cultures and to other depictions of menopause historically in Western societies. In both instances, women are often depicted as arriving, through menopause, at a valued state of biological maturity; the nineteenth-century physicians Tilt and Aldrich both wrote of its link with growth and development in women (although this was not a view widely shared at the time (Greer, 1991)). Moreover, in Peru, according to research reported by Lorber and Moore (2002), women experience an increase in status enjoying 'full adulthood' for the first time (p. 81). Similarly, lacking an equivalent concept of 'menopause' in Japan, women do not report symptoms in any way like those experienced by Western women, very few reporting even one hot flash (Lock, 1993). Such evidence reminds us both that we should take care to avoid universalizing bodily experiences, as is the practice of Western biomedicine, and that it is possible to imagine other ways of experiencing and perceiving the midlife woman's body within the context of other age and gender regimes. It also reminds us that we should see menopausal problems as arising from 'local biologies', including a greater or lesser investment in traditional femininities associated with classes and historical eras alerting us too to the complex mixtures of equality and inequality, new and old, as they manifest in health (Annandale, 2009).

Before moving on to the relationship between embodied femininity and frailty in old age let us pause here to consider medical views on ageing more generally as they form the context in which frailty is viewed.

The science of ageing: what causes our bodies to age?

Perhaps the most influential theory of biogerontology today is that associated with Thomas Kirkwood, who argues against the idea of any pre-programming, as found in developmental theories, and suggests that ageing is to be understood through the 'disposable soma theory', the result of genetic *oversight* or *neglect* of the later part of the life course through concentration on the reproductive potential of the individual via the germinal line. Ageing is the result of the accumulation of damage rather than the reaching of some inherent limit; it 'evolved not through genes *doing* something, but because of genes *not doing* things' (2008: 120–21; original emphasis).

Although this does not contain notions of inevitability, as in developmental theories, and might seem on first glance more positive in terms of challenging age ideology, nevertheless three important consequences stem from this and not all of them helpful. The first is the association between ageing and disease, with the 'effects' of ageing, as we think of them now, being inseparable aetiologically from the effects of chronic disease. There is but a small step to the second consequence, which renders ageing, because of its link with disease and lifestyle, a matter of individual responsibility. Kirkwood suggests that these agentic factors include nutrition, lifestyle (exercise etc), socio-economic status and work (2008: 123). This fits the distinction between biological and chronological ageing. Contemporary evidence, for example, by Lowsky et al. (2013) found that a significant number of adults aged over 50 years were healthy, including those aged 85 and over, which suggests 'significant variation in how people experience ageing today' (2013: 646), a variation easily linked in other discourses to worthy personal characteristics. The third consequence makes ageing inherently negative; indeed none of the various theories of ageing – from compression of morbidity, to extension of morbidity, and from lifespan extension to disposable soma (see Moody and Sasser, 2015) – suggest that the old body can be viewed in a positive light in terms of any strengths or new capacities whatsoever. Its functioning is measured in terms of a direct comparison with younger bodies and in terms that leave no possibility other than that of decline. There is no physiological or clinical equivalent of gerotranscendence,[2] for example. Moreover, in the new approach for monitoring chronic disease an older distinction, between 'involution', or the 'natural' decremental changes associated with the processes of ageing per se, and pathology, has been lost entirely and the distinctiveness of older bodies has been subsumed into a statistical regime which treats all aged bodies as commensurable and indeed measurable by the same standard (Pickard, 2013). Measuring physiological functioning by the same standard as mid-life bodies and younger has led to the emergence of new 'diseases': where previously kidneys with lower functionality, to give an example, were considered ageing and hence normal they are now, with the same degree of function, labelled pathological and treatable. More important still is the role this plays in the clinical separation of chronological from biological age, and hence in the shaping of the third and fourth age. The individual him/herself only appears in terms of their actions in regard of leading a responsible life that will, purportedly, 'slow down ageing'. Indeed 'slowing down ageing' is discussed in the medical literature in terms of 'taking on time itself' (Farrelly, 2008). In so doing it problematizes ageing ontologically – our current biological design is not 'optimal' (p. 147) – for reasons of economic productivity. One example is found in this passage from a paper published in the *British Medical Journal*:

> By extending the lifespan when higher levels of physical and mental capacity are expressed, people would remain in the workforce longer, personal income and savings would increase, age entitlement programmes would face less pressure from shifting demographies and national economies would flourish. (Farrelly, 2008: 148)

These factors, as well as the intricacies of the gender regime and the bodily contortions and stylizations of femininity, as we have discussed in previous pages, all form the context in which frailty can be understood, as we will see next.

The frail older body: identifying (and preventing) the fourth age

Frailty was, until recently, considered a common characteristic of old age, associated with the need for social, rather than medical care and a key characteristic structuring the identity of the 'old-age pensioner'; it was not until the late 1990s that medicine began to approach it in terms of a distinct diagnosis representing discrete pathology. However, the new clinical diagnosis reflects norms associated with changed material and social conditions in which old age, like any other age, is embedded but which are not peculiar to old age itself. Associated with these new norms are new kinds of divisions between the civilized and the abject, the '*affiliated* and the *marginalized*' (Miller and Rose, 2008: 98; original emphasis) where the latter refers to dependence and lack of agency. 'Frailty' marks this division between the third and fourth ages in the form of a medical label. However, the fact that it is as much a 'moral' as a 'medical' category is indicated in the latter's indeterminacy which has meant that mechanisms for identifying it are constantly expanding in terms of potential identifiers: one tool (the Frailty Index, or FI, as we see below) went from about 11 potential components in 2004 to 92 (and could potentially expand beyond those) a fuzziness indicative of 'diagnostic slipperiness' (Lorber and Moore, 2002: 78). If we consider how a diagnosis is made and who the older people thus labelled are, we find that two main frailty instruments have developed since the late 1990s. These are firstly: (i) the phenotype approach (Fried et al., 2001) which focuses on attributes of the body, specifically three or more of the following characteristics: shrinking; weakness (measured by grip strength); self-reported exhaustion suggesting poor endurance and low energy; slow walking speed; and low physical activity (Fried et al., 2001). Secondly, (ii) the Frailty Index (FI) (Rockwood et al., 1999) looks at any factor that could be considered a deficit with frailty based on the accumulation of such deficits up to the potential maximum number so far of 92, as noted). These factors are diverse in nature, extending from the seemingly trivial (such as headaches, constipation and restlessness) through to cancer, diabetes and heart attacks. Counting deficits gives the individual a number indicative of their degree of frailty or, to be more accurate, gives the professionals managing them a number indicative of how likely the old person is to fall, be hospitalized or die. In both instruments, frailty is defined in terms of vulnerability, seen as the potential for future adverse outcomes, especially mortality, but also for events like falls, hospital admission and worsening disability. In both cases, conditions that are part and parcel of embodied experience through the life course – weak grip for some, exhaustion for others, constipation, insomnia or headaches intermittently for all – are given a problematic status *because* they are connected to the old body.

The diagnosis configures the old body as ontologically problematic in a complementary manner to the psychological deficiency inherent in the 'incomplete ontogeny' of the mind defined by Baltes and colleagues (and which connects to the cognitive element identified in frailty (e.g. Rolfson et al., 2013)). This links with the work of bio-gerontologists which emphasizes the evolutionary origin of ageing as a kind of unthought-through event for an organism whose sole genetic purpose is to survive to reproduce. But lifestyle as well as medical expertise come into play here and there is a large emphasis within the medical publications on the positive role the individual can play through 'self-care'. The message is that biological age-ing can be improved by a combination of individual effort and professional expertise (Ferrucci et al., 2004) (although interventions for frail older people, including the introduction of exercise programmes, have had limited success). In these discourses the problematic ontology of the ageing body is established in two main ways: firstly through depictions of the old body as inevitably frail – by the age of 95, no matter how much care you have taken of yourself, and how much capital you have employed in this purpose, ultimately you will most likely be frail as, with some individual exceptions, this is an ontological fact of the old human body (Rockwood, 2005). Secondly, even if you are not (yet) frail, and are indeed chronologically advanced but characterized as robust, or functioning well with chronic diseases, or one of the other pre-frail categories, you may still harbour one or several of the manifold 'deficits' that suggest you are inexorably, if impercepti-bly, beginning your descent into decrepitude.

Inevitably, despite the emphasis on the ontological riskiness of old age generi-cally, the medical emphasis on individual effort and lifestyle inevitably means that some individuals and groups are more likely to be seen as frail than others. Research employing either one of the diagnostic tools, or their variants, identifies the latter as predominantly (although not exclusively) females who are poor, with low educational achievement indicative generally of a mixture of personal and social deprivation (Fried et al., 2001). Race is implicated but only in its association with socio-economic disadvantage (Szanton et al., 2010). Thus, whatever other functions they perform, the technologies of frailty add a clinical problematization to a group already possessing numerous other disadvantages and inequalities, accumulated through manifold disadvantages associated with earlier points in the life course. They also take the generic lifelong problematization of women's bodies to a culmination in old age and in three respects in particular: (i) in clinical terms, where the normal body is the (youthful) male body; (ii) in terms of current notions of valued femininity, where emphasized femininity is, today, associated with unde-sirable traits (a shift that has occured since the current generation of old women's youth); and (iii) in terms of socio-economic disadvantage accruing to working-class women leading to a 'poverty gap in old age' (Thane, 2006).

Indeed, gender and age work together to 'naturalize' social inequalities and hier-archies within this diagnostic category created by a toxic stew of patriarchy and capitalism. Starting with the gender aspect: if it is true that women's bodies, espe-cially in old age, are weaker than men's, then previous discussions in this book all indicate that this is not a product of 'pure' biology but rather a continuation of learned frailty present among women leading both directly and indirectly to frailty in old age. We have noted how an ongoing frailty myth is intrinsic to conceptualiza-tions of femininity throughout the life course in which the binary pairing of men's *strength* and women's *frailty* is an integral element of the gender hierarchy (Dowling, 2000).

BOX 8.1

The frailty myth

We saw in the previous chapter that the 'frailty myth' comprises the ideological construction of women's bodies as weaker than men's. Presented as natural, it is the result of specific social practices and norms, which together result in modes of femininity involving embodied constraint, weakness, self-objectification and hesitancy. These same tropes, in different, and exaggerated forms, appear again in 'frailty' diagnoses in old age.

These learned differences are obscured by scientific explanations highlighting the role of sex hormones, particularly the difference between oestrogen and testosterone, which suggest essential biological differences, as witnessed in discussions regarding osteoporosis. Thus, when we turn to gendered explanations of frailty found within the clinical discourses what we find is an essentializing of 'sex' differences between men and women, including variations on the evolutionary telos (see: Hubbard and Rockwood, 2011; Fried et al., 2001). These include suggestions that women's 'physiological investment in reproduction' (Hubbard and Rockwood, 2011: 205) underpins late life frailty although smaller family size means that their life expectancies '*may be longer than predicted by evolutionary design*' (Hubbard and Rockwood, 2011: 203; emphasis added) (meaning that evolution intended them primarily to reproduce, which could presumably give them a shorter life span than men, when the menopause is taken into consideration). This anti-evolutionary trajectory ensures they live on, but in a state of frailty. Indeed, not only are older women overwhelmingly more likely to be frail than men but also one study found they have an estimated 20 per cent lesser chance of dying at a given time than men of the same chronological age and degree of frailty (Goggins et al., 2005) including in the most frail categories. This is not, however, a positive thing, according to medical texts, nor even the lesser of two evils: the implication of the compression-of-morbidity thesis implies that death itself is a preferable outcome to frailty. (Nevertheless, the fact of the longevity of older women, including living in a state of frailty, indicates that one of the key regulative devices for women in the age and gender regime – that of time panic – might be better directed at men, unless of course one agrees that women are first and foremost baby incubators.)

A brief genealogical sweep will reveal how older attitudes towards the female body also leave their traces in this approach. We have already noted how female biology was considered to enfeeble the woman's intellectual capabilities in Victorian medicine but the link with class was also important. Whilst the construction of class distinctions in the nineteenth century were centred upon the difference between working-class and middle-class *female* bodies (Skeggs, 2004; Nead, 1988), 'frailty' featured as a key element of the process, and here it was a symbol of distinction, indicative of bourgeois femininity which was characterized by a mixture of 'dependency, delicacy and fragility' (Nead, 1988: 28) featuring lack of appetite, enervation and anxiety. The current category of frailty exhibits both discontinuities and transformations from this position – the greater presence of frailty as the opposite of the productive self in disadvantaged, as opposed to bourgeois, women; its problematic as opposed to aspirational status. But nevertheless, this background remains important to understanding it.

Moving to the present, if we examine the characteristics of the 'phenotype' we can see that the characteristics that identify a body type as frail do so with regard to the absence of qualities traditionally associated with masculinity: so frail bodies lack energy, strength, stamina, speed; they are weak, enervated, listless, passive, fragile, lacking will and motivation: all in ways consistent with the performance of femininity. Thus, it might be apposite to consider the degree to which, in practice and seen as a continuum, *frailty is a normal condition for older women*. Indeed, frailty indices are not only less valid for women as indicators of risk than for men but also may even be capturing and problematizing a state that is 'normal' among certain women, that while of course intensified in old age yet expresses a continuity of lived experience that the label of 'frailty' does not by any means convey. This is the association between *femininity* and frailty (Dowling, 2000) which starts in the earliest days of the life course. However, the greater preponderance of the condition among women has a somewhat different root cause than that of biology: unless girls are able to achieve peak bone mass density in their adolescence – which is highly unlikely given femininity's requirements, including a preference for dieting over strength training – they are likely candidates for osteoporosis but here again we should look not to innate differences but to learned repertoires. Particularly telling is frailty's relationship with instrumental activities of daily living (IADLs), but not activities of daily living (ADLs). ADLs are the basic tasks of everyday life such as eating, bathing, dressing and toileting, difficulty with which is indicative of disability; IADLs are activities related to *independent living* such as preparing meals, managing money, shopping for groceries or personal items, performing light or heavy housework, doing laundry and using a telephone and thus are associated with classed and gendered norms. Sixty per cent of Fried et al.'s (2001) frail sample had difficulty with IADLs but only 27 per cent of them also had difficulty with ADLs which suggests an association between frailty and the normative values of independence, autonomy and maintenance of the enterprising self, quite distinct, in other words, from disability and chronic illness (as is recognized in the medical literature (Fried et al., 2004)). Frailty interventions, then, are above all about encouraging '"independent living" used interchangeably with "successful", "healthy" and "productive" ageing' (Katz and Marshall, 2004: 63).

Similarly, class aspects are individualized in the contemporary discourses of frailty. Most frailty technologies explicitly recognize the association between structural disadvantage and frailty and this is directly addressed in the social vulnerability index by some of the authors associated with the frailty index (FI). Although distinct from frailty they suggest this is part of the complex interplay of 'social' and 'medical' factors that relate to health in old age (Andrew and Keefe, 2014). These include factors such as: possessing no telephone; inability to get to places beyond walking distance; lack of positive feelings towards housing, finance, neighbourhood, current income, etc. (again women have a higher social vulnerability score than men in general). We can of course speculate as to whether factors listed as health deficits in the FI such as anxiety, sleeplessness, depression, inability to go out, impaired abstract thinking and impaired judgement, also arise from social vulnerability. We might suggest too that certain tropes characteristic of femininity itself make social, material and physical vulnerability, and relatedly frailty, more likely.

Following the limited success of interventions aimed at the latter part of life, attention has been turned to prevention further down the life course and here epidemiologists (e.g. Kuh and colleagues, 2007) suggest that factors such as the mother's diet during pregnancy, nutrition and education in the earliest childhood years, adult lifestyles, obesity and unemployment are all associated with frailty and thus suggest the benefit of lifestyle changes at 'sensitive periods'. In this, 'frailty' as a discourse is not alone in individualizing disadvantage but joins other preventive discourses (Leibing and Kampf, 2013) associated with cardiovascular health, Alzheimer's disease and prostate cancer, among other conditions. These conditions, it is maintained, can be prevented by lifestyle changes earlier in the life course, all of which translate social factors into a biological mechanism so that structural features 'drift out of sight' (Leibing and Kampf, 2013: 17). The 'problematic nature' of syndromes associated with female embodiment earlier in the life course might also lead to frailty: eating disorders and menopause are both directly linked to osteoporosis and the latter is also closely associated with frailty.

We might then stop to ponder what exactly the unique elements of age pain associated with frailty may be. What if we recognized that the fatigue, enervation and slowed-down state of being is a familiar trope for women throughout the ages, a series of symptoms that have meant different things at different times but which all suggest disempowerment, intractable contradictions and obstacles in the way of claiming full personhood? What, in other words, if this condition was more akin to eating disorders in young women, which has hitherto been recognized? Or ME, or menopausal syndrome? Here, after all, is the same combination of rationality and irrationality, of order and control; both an exaggerated manifestation of 'femininity' and a somatic protest. All conditions share similarities with the way in which Showalter (1997: 7) describes hysteria, for example, as a 'body language for people who otherwise might not be able to speak or even to admit what they feel'?.

Even so, the label of frailty and its medical depiction maps only crudely onto the lived experience of the old body. As we noted in previous chapters, ethnographic data indicates the presence among 'frail' individuals of a variety of positive factors: frailty co-exists with strength, health with disease, decline with the possibility of growth, autonomy with dependence. So whether we highlight its link to gender problematization, to its inherent relationship with femininity, or to class, there is something more, something that remains unexplained. As Higgs and Gilleard (2015) point out, frailty is not simply the opposite of successful ageing (which would be ageing with disease or disability and thus fairly easily defined) but something qualitatively different, something feared and reviled that 'unsuccessful ageing' does not capture, which is adumbrated just as vividly in Larkin's poem 'Old Fools'[3] whom the poet observes sitting through 'days of thin continuous dreaming, watching the light move... [with] these... the first signs: not knowing how, not hearing who, the power of choosing gone' as in the sophisticated diagnostic tools of geriatric medicine. Indeed, it boils down, as everything, it seems, must today, to a matter of choice, and the revulsion towards older women who have, most of all, lost the ability to make the productive choice that is the keystone of competent human personhood today. The old, frail, poor woman is the abject, signalling the boundary of selfhood and the ultimate logic of the age system, 'the ground of fixity from which others can become mobile' (Skeggs, 2004: 25–6). Such labelling, then, delineates the fourth age, a medical mapping of the symbolic space of the Hag, as well as the attempt at controlling and managing such a site, presenting it as something that can be avoided by self-care or careful expert management. In such a way the wildness of death is tamed, in the eyes of the experts, by ever-closer prediction and isolation of its processes.

Conclusion

In this chapter a focus on women's experiences of (ill) health has enabled us to view the intersection of the age and gender regimes in ways that further illustrate their mutual implication. In youthful eating disorders, ME, menopause and frailty, the body speaks eloquently of experiences of oppression, frustration and repressed anger, a combination of age and gender pain. We might also note the growth of smoking and drinking excessively in women, all aspects of the performance of liberated Girlhood, which have resulted, in recent years, in new linkages between health, illness and the gender regime. In all these ways health is not only a product of the age and gender regimes but also serves as a lens in its own right through which to view socio-structural and cultural changes.

In all this, we might also remember the jointly productive and oppressive role of medicine in shaping women's experience of their own bodies. Ehrenreich and English (1973) point out, for example, that the medical system both shapes and reflects sexist ideology about the body; but at the same time it is the source of many of women's freedoms. There is no doubt that women do suffer from debilitating symptoms of menopause, for example, or sharp anxiety or frailty, whose symbolic dimensions do not obviate the need for material relief. This links with our earlier observations that the 'essence of femaleness' is unknown, at any age, but that it suffers from its relationship with femininity. Ehrenreich and English argue: 'There is no "correct line" on our bodies. There is no way to determine our "real needs", our "real" strengths and liabilities, in a sexist society' (1973: 92). We can make exactly the same case for the strengths and liabilities of each age group.

CHAPTER SUMMARY

- This chapter focuses on the intersections of the age and gender regimes at points in the life course where a concentration of tensions arising from the combination of freedom and constraint, or new opportunities and old obstacles, underpins the emergence of psycho-pathological disorders, especially for women.

- Because of their deep association with key points in women's life course, this chapter suggests that to the concept of 'gender pain' we add that of 'age pain' as an explanatory concept.

- The chapter also suggests that depictions of the body as a vulnerable product of individual life choices made throughout the life course has wider repercussions, again explicable in the differentiation between symbolic and chronological adulthood.

Further questions

1. What do specific illnesses tell us about the (gendered) norms and expectations associated with particular stages of the life course?

2. Many women feel that the menopause causes symptoms, sometimes severe, that require treatment; others feel it is 'natural' and thus not an illness; many help-sites advising on menopause feel that women should not 'suffer needlessly' by turning down HRT as a matter of course owing to possible side effects that may not present much risk for them. These three separate positions can be reconciled within the 'body as situation' framework. Discuss and in so doing make reference to the concepts of gender pain and age pain.

3. Which illnesses or pathologies may be considered to reflect tensions in the gender regime for men at different points in the life course?

Talking point

Although it is clear that age regulates the gender regime as women age, this regulation appears early in life, operating through complex and subtle channels. Research by Demos, for example (Darlington et al., 2011), notes that girls become less happy as they age through their teenage years and twice as many teenage girls as boys suffer from 'teenage angst'. When asked about the disadvantages of being a girl, almost half of girls (aged 7–21) named 'pressure to look attractive'; 52 per cent that 'girls are expected to cook and clean'; and 67 per cent named 'periods, body changes, pains of being pregnant and giving birth'. Meanwhile, girls as young as 7–8 felt that 'girls have less chance to play at sports and games than boys do' and aged 9–10 identified one disadvantage to be that 'girls are expected to be mature and responsible'. The authors of the report asked: 'Why is the self-esteem of girls lower than that of boys?' Use the model of the situated body to explain this.

—— Key texts ——

For **gender pain** see Morris, D.B. (1991) *The Culture of Pain*, Berkeley: University of California Press. For the pressures on **young women** see the following ethnographic study Walkerdine, V., Lucey, H. and Melody, J. (2001) *Growing Up Girl: psychosocial explorations of gender and class*, London: Palgrave; or this firsthand experience: Penny, L. (2014) *Unspeakable Things: sex, lies and revolution*, London: Bloomsbury. Emily Martin and Margaret Lock both present ethnographic research into **key points in a woman's reproductive life course**: Martin, E. (1987) *The Woman in the Body*, Milton Keynes: Open University Press; Lock, M. (1993) *Encounters with Ageing*, Cambridge: Cambridge University Press; see also Ehrenreich, B. and English, D. (1973) *For Her Own Good: 150 years of the experts' advice to women*, London: Pluto Press. The following account considers **the fourth age** in all its ramifications: Higgs, P. and Gilleard, C. (2015) *Rethinking Old Age: theorizing the fourth age*, London: Palgrave Macmillan. The connection between **women's health and inequalities throughout the life course** is examined in Annandale, E. (2009) *Women's Health and Social Change,* London: Routledge.

Further resources

Useful reports on the anxieties and stresses experienced by young women include: Darlington et al. (2011) *Through the Looking Glass*, London: Demos; available at http://www.demos.co.uk/publications/throughthelookingglass

A report prepared by Phipps and Young (2012) for the National Union of Students on the culture of sexism in universities which is challenging for girls in higher education is available at http://www.nus.org.uk/Global/Campaigns/That%27s%20what%20she%20said%20full%20report%20Final%20web.pdf

Girls' Attitudes Surveys are regularly repeated on a cross-section of girls and young women in the UK and cover attitudes to a variety of issues from education to health, wellbeing and social life; they are available at http://girlsattitudes.girlguiding.org.uk/video/girls_attitudes_video.aspx. Since 2012 they have also included the attitudes of a sample of boys.

Notes

1. Two studies, the US Women's Health Initiative (WHI) and the UK Million Women Study (MWS) published data in 2002 and 2003 respectively, linking HRT use to increased instances of breast cancer and heart disease, among other things. This led to a fall in the overall number of women taking HRT of 66 per cent. Subsequently, however, research published in 2012, and more recently corroborated in 2015, suggests that these negative results may have been overstated and inaccurate and indeed that the 'benefits outweigh the risks'; a new generation of HRT has also appeared which is less 'risky' (see http://www.womens-health-concern.org/help-and-advice/factsheets/hrt-know-benefits-risks/). Certainly, on an NHS advice page for menopausal women, the first listed treatment for those with 'severe' symptoms of menopause is HRT (see http://www.nhs.uk/conditions/menopause/Pages/Treatment.aspx; accessed 18 October, 2015). See also Elgot, J. (2015) Using HRT to treat menopause is safe, *The Guardian*, 19 October.

2. Tornstam defines his theory of gerotranscendence as follows: it 'suggests that human ageing includes a potential to mature into a new outlook on and understanding of life. Gerotranscendence implies a shift in metaperspective, from a materialistic and rational view of the world to a more cosmic and transcendent one, normally accompanied by an increase in life satisfaction' (Tornstam, 2011: 166).

3. From *High Windows* (1974) London: Faber and Faber.

9

REPRESENTING AGES AND STAGES

Background

In this chapter we will look at the depiction of ages and stages in visual and textual media, also examining their relationship with lived experience. What we might consider to be our automatic response to visual or symbolic depictions of age is in fact filtered through an ideological lens and involves relationships of power and inequality. Representations not only reflect our views on age but shape them and also misrepresent them and as such are a key site of struggle and resistance, of hegemony and transformation. Skeggs notes: 'A daily class struggle is waged through challenging the values generated through representation' (2004: 117–18). This chapter will demonstrate that exactly the same claim can be made for age relations and that there is much at stake in how ages and stages are portrayed, who gets to portray them and how these are linked to other aspects of social inequality and difference.

Most importantly, we will be extending our previous discussions concerning the male gaze and the age gaze to the arena of representations.

AIMS OF THE CHAPTER

- We will first review methodology that can help us identify, deconstruct and ultimately challenge the way that representations work ideologically, including through our automatic responses and intuitions.

- We will then look at the variety of representations of particular ages and life stages that have appeared, disappeared and co-exist historically, exploring what they say not just about these ages but (particularly, perhaps) about the standard adult (the bearer of 'the look').

- We will end by looking at methods of resistance, including that of developing a different age 'gaze'.

Conceptual and methodological approaches to representation

This section will not present an extensive account of methodology; for that, Rose (2012) and Hall (2013) are recommended. Here, I briefly aim to review the main approaches that will be useful in our understanding of how ages and stages are represented which are all broadly social constructionist in approach. In general terms, social constructionist views hold that all signs are arbitrary and the meaning depends on the relation between a word/sound/image and a concept which is fixed by a code. One important question arising from this is the question of how far our experience is actually shaped by our words and concepts (Hall et al., 2013). That is, if we do not have the words for it, do we *experience* it? Foucault made this and similar questions a central theme in his critical work where he argued that discourse (not just words, but the system in which those words are given meaning and the practices associated with that system) makes possible certain experiences just as it rules out others. The most important point, perhaps, is one we take from Marx, which is that representation is at once reflective and constitutive of lived reality. Pollock (2003) expresses this succinctly:

> Representation can… be understood as 'articulating' in a visible or socially palpable form social processes which determine the representation but then are actually affected and altered by the form, practices and effects of representation. (2003: 8)

Difference and hierarchy

We also draw on the work of Saussure and Barthes in semiotics and on the postmodern philosophy of Derrida. One of the important elements of semiotics is the idea that 'difference' is essential to meaning; signifiers, or the names that 'represent' the things (signified) do not have meaning in or of themselves. Since meaning is relational, it is defined against what it is not; young is not old; man is not woman; each derives their meaning from contrast with the other. Derrida also stressed that the binary relationship that contains this meaning is one of power; the association is not neutral and one is always dominant (Hall, 2013): for example, the male gender is dominant over the female as is youth over age. Below is an example of the way childhood and old age are depicted in road signs, at once depicting them by bodily characteristics and relationships to other age groups whilst indicating their shared marginalized status (involving dependence and vulnerability) with respect to age-normative (adult) society: the solitary, straight-standing, autonomous individual which is an absent presence in each case.

Both difference and hierarchy are then at the basis of all our classification systems, and, as we know from Douglas, what threatens this classification are objects or concepts

that do not fit comfortably within any one category or which fit into more than one, thereby threatening not just the validity of these categories but also potentially of this whole system of classification. These classifications not only order, but they may equally also distort. Whilst we cannot make sense of the world without 'typifications', as Schutz called them, these can easily be replaced by stereotypes which, Hall (2013) note, '*reduces, essentializes, naturalizes and fixes "difference"*' (p. 258; original emphasis) in a way harmful for the object of stereotyping. An example of how this works with older people, through metonymy, is suggested by Hockey and James as follows:

> One or two physical features – such as incontinence, lack of rational speech or faltering step – are taken as defining criteria for the whole body. Thus, for example, the elderly person who has poor bladder control becomes seen as incontinent. (1993: 94)

We can also draw on 'figurative methodology' (Tyler, 2008) to describe the ways in which 'at different historical and cultural moments specific "social types" become over determined' (p. 18), which, especially if they are repeated across a range and variety of media, are generative, as well as reflective, of social experience. Particularly important is the way such figures always derive their meaning from another figure related as a binary opposite.

Foucauldian discourse analysis

Foucault's analysis of discourse enabled a distanciation of our taken-for-granted assumptions and the assembling of a history of the present. In this process, archaeology (analysis of discourse) and genealogy (identification of the relations of power in which such discourse is shaped and embedded) together form the key methodology (Dreyfus and Rabinow, 1982). Foucault's focus is not, unlike the semioticians, on the words themselves but on the general system in which meanings are based and in which representations across all the various categories of scientific and lay knowledge derive. It is discourse that governs the way a topic can be meaningfully talked about and thought about and it rules out other ways of constructing these topics or mentalities. He was also interested in the points when the 'discursive regime' changed, from privileging one major paradigm of meaning to another, and this analysis makes it possible to identify who benefits from particular 'ways of seeing'. One way of tracing changes is by focusing on metaphor which provides an overarching unity between various domains in the form of a metaphoric 'flow' of ideas (Figlio, 1976: 26), which shift in accordance with the overarching tropes of governmentality in which they are embedded. For example, in late modernity tropes related to capitalist production are found in a variety of domains including medicine, psychology, economics and so on.

Feminist analysis

Broadly speaking, feminist epistemology approaches representations through a lens that views language as inherently patriarchal. As we have noted, feminists writing in the 1970s considered psychoanalysis to be particularly helpful in decoding representations, seeing, for example, processes of cinema as dream-like and mimicking those of the unconscious (Kaplan, 1983), and thus providing a screen to display elements of the 'patriarchal unconscious'. Psychoanalysis adds to the social and cultural shaping of subjectivity a further recognition of the role of the psyche which, along with conscious aspects, together form the 'regime of representation' or 'the formation of visual codes and their institutional circulation' (Pollock, 2003). Building on Mulvey, Kaplan suggests that the cinema is structured around three specifically male gazes which all objectify women. These are: (i) the look of the camera; (ii) the look of the male characters within the narrative; and (iii) the look of the male spectator. These all position women as objects of this look. However, although it can be pointed out, following Sartre and others, that everyone is objectified, and that all gazes, including female gazes, objectify others, the difference in the dynamic of the male gaze is that it carries with it a connotation of power – of action and possession – which is absent from the female gaze (Kaplan, 1983).

Other techniques are also assembled in ways that produce women as Other in various complex ways including the concepts of castration, fetishism and voyeurism (Hollows, 2000). The notion of castration symbolizes the way woman's difference from man signifies an inferiority or 'lack' in relation to man. She thus signifies the threat that they might become like her: above all, powerless and also lacking in certain positive attributes of masculinity. Fetishism and voyeurism serve to reduce this threat. Fetishism makes a woman safe by reducing her to a part that can induce pleasure – hair, breasts, legs and so on. Voyeurism reduces the threat by means of a detached 'controlling' gaze. According to Hollows, all these modes are employed by cinema. Elements of age can also be fetishized but where, for the woman's body, this is associated with a feminine mystique that comprises connotations of pleasure and sexuality, for the old body this is associated with dread and revulsion and this difference is precisely captured in Friedan's comparison of the 'feminine mystique' and the age mystique (Friedan, 1993).

Meanwhile, the contradictions set up by more empowered women, both on screen and as viewers are met by 'strategies of containment and discipline' (Doane, 1987; quoted in Hollows, 2000: 54) so that there is frequently, for example, a narrative in which an independent or powerful woman's situation is analyzed and found to be problematic in some crucial way and a solution then found through a masculine gaze (as channelled through female or male actors), which may include a medical gaze. From her identification of the various forms of the male gaze, Kaplan (1983) poses several key questions including: Is the gaze necessarily male? Could we structure things so that women own the gaze? And in what ways could the latter occur outside the binary relations of dominant/submissive or oppressed that currently pattern that gaze? Her analysis then suggests that, although women can own and be the agents of the gaze, the structure of the unconscious (shaped by our socio-cultural environment) means that thereby the woman assumes the masculine position; that is, the 'female dominant' position is merely a substitution of female for male in the 'masculine' role, not something qualitatively different.

All of these important insights can be used in a parallel way to deconstruct age relations recognizing a particularly pertinent question to be: *is the male gaze as identified above also necessarily youthful?* Wearing's (2007) analysis of recent films and TV shows suggests a similar picture in that, whilst older women may own the gaze, this requires their rejuvenation, especially through their (hetero)sexuality. Positive ageing, as it appears in these media, involves what Wearing calls the '"girling" of older women' and what Whelehan relates more generally to the 'girling of popular culture' (2013: 78). Alluding to the blurring of chronological points and age norms Wearing notes: 'If chronological boundaries are indeed blurring this only happens in one direction; that is 'younger women... are not encouraged to "aspire" to age' (p. 294). Paralleling Kaplan's analysis, then, this suggests that when older women own and activate the gaze, they do so through assuming the youthful position.

Ideology and advertising

Given the importance of consumption in late modernity, advertising occupies a central position for the production and distillation of representations, being as influential on people's lives today as are education and religion (Gill, 2009). It has also been a key component in shaping post-feminism, collapsing the binaries of second-wave feminism, for example, housewife versus career woman, 'fast' girl versus good girl, and melding them together into a framework of '"freedom" through consumption' (Gill, 2007a: 81). The male gaze is the absent presence throughout, in whose real or imagined orbit all choices are made. Goldman (2000) notes, 'reframing feminism through the commodity form turns the political discourse of feminism into the discourse of style' (2000: 11). This indeed is how hegemonies work, as Williams (1977) notes, identifying resistance and neutralizing it through incorporation. In such a way feminism becomes consumerism; social control and power condense to control over one's weight, appearance and general sexual desirability, in competition with other women, which also involves a strict emphasis on agelessness. The age gaze is a key constituent of what Goldman calls feminine 'terror' (p. 123) and among other things comprises the fear of being invisible to the youthful gaze. In setting women against each other, and against their past selves, such body-based competition, moreover, 'does nothing to challenge the male power to scrutinize and judge' (Goldman, 2000: 129); nor indeed does it challenge the age gaze and age relations. Furthermore, post-feminism works through nostalgia, a trope featuring prominently in cinema and other media (Munford and Waters, 2014) in which retro-chick, especially an obsession with 1950s-style domesticity, re-enchants the pre-feminist era in the present. This recognizes the fact that psyches of current adults were formed in, or contain many elements of, pre-femininist eras; it also taps into our fears and losses associated with growing up. Negra (2009) notes too the plot line of women leaving then returning to their family home: what she calls 'retreatism'. There are parallels also in nostalgic imagery of older people associated with a previous regime of old age, before the current third/fourth age distinction.

Representations of ages and stages

In this section, we move away from theoretical discussion to consider the way different ages are represented concretely in fields ranging from social policy to children's stories and popular photography. We will see that normative age groups, taking the hegemonic perspective, work through the problems and issues they are most concerned with through a focus on marginalized or minority age groups, and a projection of their own concerns onto these groups: seeing them as crystallizing 'human nature', showing them what they 'really are' beneath the layers of civilization, or what they have lost or may yet become; or else as symptomatic of the changing structures of society in some way, whose consequences they can only perceive when projected outwards onto these other, or rather Other, age groups. All of these points are true of childhood, to which we turn first.

(i) Representations of childhood

Children and childhood have been depicted by means of a variety of themes historically, all of which contribute towards the construction of a childhood altogether distinct from adulthood and which take their starting point to be the child as basic building block of the adult. All themes still circulate in contemporary society but arose originally in a specific historical context. These include:

(a) The Dionysian, or 'evil' child: like Hobbesian adults, children need discipline for both they and society to be rendered safe and anarchy forestalled.

(b) The innocent or Romantic child, as found in Blake and Rousseau, indicating the essential goodness of human nature.

(c) The blank slate, or tabula rasa, highly impressionable, leading to, among others James Mill (father of John Stuart Mill), stressing the absolute importance of education and a conducive early environment.

(d) The savage child: the theory of recapitulation suggested that, in growing up, the child proceeds through all the stages of civilization that modern societies have passed through. A child has reached the stage of a savage, indicating a natural hierarchy from childhood up to (Western) adulthood. This is linked to (e) below.

(e) The naturally developing child, following a blueprint for 'normal' development, as found in the ideas of Piaget. Like the Darwinian theories linked to recapitulation, there is a strong element of biological determinism present within such theories but most important is the way in which, by stressing the distinction between the 'figurative' thought of childhood with the 'operative' intelligence associated with adulthood, Piagetian psychology establishes a 'natural' separation between childhood and adulthood.

(f) The Freudian child: this links with previous theories in that the id resembles the 'evil child' idea but takes the form of the unconscious. The ego resembles the child as tabula rasa. It is also our inner child or essential self, before being claimed by the hegemonic order, represented by the superego (James et al., 1998).

(g) The 'abused child': this has been mythologized to serve a number of themes serving variously as symbolic of the fragmentation of family life, of sexual laxity, alienation, vulnerability and patriarchal violence (Jenks, 2005).

As we have seen, the dominant class has traditionally perceived childhood as an entry point into controlling the dangerous working class. Hendrick (1990) shows how representations of childhood and 'children' in political and social discourses including the 'factory' child, the 'delinquent' child, the 'schooled' child, the 'psycho-medical' child and the 'welfare' child, between them shifted the image of children from workers to school pupils, from independent to dependent, and from precocious and knowledgeable worker to age-graded and 'ignorant' child (whose malleable mind was amenable to being imprinted with middle-class 'education' and its associated norms). Across these tropes children may be consistently presented as either potential victims or threats, both sides of the binary implicitly containing the other (Hendrick, 1990). So, across a long historical sweep, efforts to 'save' children from factories or chimney sweeping, from 'problem' families or from social exclusion or from ADHD, all implicitly refer to the 'threat' such children would otherwise pose to the dominant order. The language of risk, individualization and responsibilization is only the latest version of the same approach, which links children to the 'destiny of the nation' (Rose, 1989: 121). Meanwhile, Higonnet's (1998) study into the visual depiction of childhood shows how the romantic, innocent view of childhood – as found still today on chocolate boxes and sweet tins – often featuring the work of Sir Joshua Reynolds, is now, in keeping with 'end of childhood' theme, being joined by what she terms the 'Knowing

Child' and these children 'have bodies and passions of their own. They are also often aware of adult bodies and passions, whether as mimics or as witnesses' (1998: 207). These do not necessarily replace the innocent child but rather co-exist with it, each gaining meaning from the other in the good/bad binary that marks every age group. The knowing child, as bad child, also possesses a class association: feral children indulging in anti-social behaviour, precocious girls who will go on to swell the statistics of teenage motherhood, children who murder other children, all hail from this source.

Most importantly, perhaps, these depictions serve as a repository of attributes that adulthood denies or represses in itself. Today, this is often seen in terms of the 'inner child', where the child comes to assume the form of a trope for the 'true self. This may be particularly keenly felt in mid-life, through a form of nostalgia' (Gullette, 1998), which encourages the ideas that the best years of life lie in the past, an affect which is the fulcrum of age ideology. This can be both personal, relating to the individual's own biography, or more general, relating to the feeling that society has lost something in modernity, and that progress brings with it loss. Cunningham writes thus of it:

> The more adults and adult society seemed bleak, urbanized and alien-
> ated, the more childhood came to be seen as properly a garden, enclosing
> within the safety of its walls a way of life which was in touch with nature
> and which preserved the rude virtues of earlier periods of the history of
> mankind. (1991: 43; quoted in Jenks, 2005: 58)

Increasingly, this 'inner child' is talked about in therapeutic terms signifying that it is lost, or damaged, and requires healing, not least if we are to live our adult lives 'authentically', within a rationalized and disenchanted world. Indeed, well before Freud cast this idea in his own stamp, this idea of lasting damage is present in the Wordsworthian notion that the 'child is the father of the man', a notion given vividly concrete form in the Barnardo's campaign of 1999–2000 ('Giving children back their future'). Created by the advertising agency Bartle Bogle Hegarty, it depicts damaged young adults as tiny babies and toddlers surrounded by the sordid para-phernalia of their current (adult) lives – syringes, empty liquor bottles – which links with a developmental trajectory of individual loss and recuperation, also present in the prominent contemporary trope of the abused child. Here, although it has a mat-erial reality, of course, the fact that child abuse has always existed and yet has only recently come to such prominence suggests a more symbolic significance:

> The post-modern diffusion of authority has not led to democracy but to
> an experience of powerlessness. Children... figure largely as symbolic
> representations of this welter of uncertainty both literally and metaphori-
> cally. (Jenks, 2005: 115)

Healing the child still resident within the adult is posited as the key to solving present problems. This is so powerful because, in children and childhood, literally and sym-bolically, is distilled the meaning that has otherwise been lost from a meaningless universe, a 'worship' of childhood whose origins can be traced back to the mid-nineteenth century, which accompanied the onset of scepticism in religion that was shared by many writers of children's books, leading to portrayals of childhood as a displaced form of heaven (Cunningham, 1991). Today, with meaning further divested from public institutions, combined with the erosion of trust and authority therefrom, this displacement has continued apace and Jenks suggests: 'The trust that was previously anticipated from marriage, partnership, friendship, class solidarity and so on is now invested more generally in the child' (2005: 111), constituting a 'private type of re-enchantment' in an individualized society, in the words of Beck (1992: 118; quoted in Jenks, 2005: 112). This underlines the affective aspect of age patriarchy where the attempt to protect the space of childhood serves the psychic needs and fantasies of adults.

But what, finally, of representations of our Girl as a child, symbol of success in today's world? Matilda, in the movie of the same name, based on the children's book by Roald Dahl, is an interesting example of the constraints and possibilities she embodies (and a younger version of Amélie, noted earlier). Matilda, a girl of around nine or ten, develops superpowers as a result of diligently cultivating an extraordinary intelligence through sneaking off to the library and refusing to sit round the TV with her lower-middle-class parents who treat her like an outsider. However, she uses these skills not to win any prizes in school but to help those she cares for, particularly her teacher, Miss Honey, who has been ousted from her family home by her evil aunt who is also headmistress of the school, the fearsome Miss Trunchbull. Matilda starts by little acts of appropriation, retrieving Miss Honey's beloved childhood doll, and some-time thereafter employs her skills to help Miss Honey regain her rightful inheritance, in the form of the big house she had lived in as a girl before her parents died. Finally, Matilda's skills secure her own rise into the middle class, to which she goes alone, leaving her family behind after Miss Honey agrees to adopt her. Having righted such wrongs, thereafter she never uses her superpowers again: no need, we are told, because both Matilda and Miss Honey have now got what they always wanted in the form of a loving family. (Would this have been the ending for a boy hero?)

(ii) Representations of youth

If childhood represents the past from the point of view of adults (Jenks, 2005), youth represents the unfolding of the future, its shape and tone serving as a barometer or litmus test whereby yesterday's changes and yesterday's policies are gradually making themselves felt in a forward-moving arc:

> Youth… is expected to reflect the cycle of booms and troughs in the economy; shifts in cultural values over sexuality, morality and family life; and in changes in class relations, concepts of nationhood and in occupational structures. (Griffin, 1993: 197–8)

If we start by taking a historical view, adolescence emerged as an object of science as well as a discourse in social policy in the USA in the late eighteenth to early nineteenth century with the two-volume work of G. Stanley Hall (1905) most closely associated with this (Dyhouse, 2014). This discourse represented adolescence as crucial to the nation's future (a male adolescence, moreover, that contrasts strikingly with the image of the Girl). This was to be effected through the young men who were to be encouraged to attain both strong wills and powerful bodies in order to ensure the prosperity of the nation. Hall's approach was that of an evolutionary psychologist and he saw the job of scientists and educators to help avoid the possibility of white males being arrested in their development where women, like savages in the theory of recapitulation, occupied a lower rung (Dyhouse, 2014; Jones, 2009).

As we have noted throughout the book, today's fascination is with the Girl and Gornick suggests she represents both the anxieties and possibilities generated by a series of work-based and wider social changes, especially the replacement of manual production with service work creating a feminized sector as the mainstay of the neoliberal economy. Similarly, there have been shifts from production to consumption and to a psychological culture promoting emotional literacy (Burman, 2005) which also contributes to the 'feminization of neoliberal subjectivity' (Gornick, 2006: 5). As with all other ages, there are binary discourses brought to bear on Girlhood which are both mutually antithetical and at the same time complementary, revealing the truth of and through each. In particular, the binary couplet serves to show the range of the Girl's socially constructed power: her possibilities at one end and their limit at the other, which also links with the strategies of containment as noted by Doane (1987), cited earlier. We can identify several binary couplets here, with the first being 'Girl Power' versus 'Reviving Ophelia' (Gornick, 2006). Although representing contrasting significations, Gornick demonstrates that they actually work together 'to articulate a complex of fiction and fantasy, regulation and persuasion' (2006: 2). 'Girl Power' – whilst its meaning is highly contestable – privileges a femininity that is angry, assertive, consumer-based, action-orientated and 'sexy' such as represented in its early days by Xena and Buffy as well as the Spice Girls and, in recent years, by a whole range of action heroines, featuring in *Divergent, The Hunger Games* and so on. *Reviving Ophelia*, the title of the 1994 book by Mary Pipher, by contrast, talks about girlhood in terms of its vulnerability. Pipher points out that at puberty girls are pressured into becoming 'female impersonators' pleasing others according to the ideals of femininity thereby losing their 'authentic' pre-pubertal selves. Girls are victims both of media representations and of their own bodies as hormones and organs and skin all work against them and 'calmness is replaced by anxiety' (Pipher, 1994: 27). This echoes Gilligan's work (1982) which claimed that girls undergo a 'crisis in self-esteem' in adolescence from which they never fully recover. The reason is that this is the time when she connects her life with a culture and tradition in which 'personhood' has always been 'male'. Indeed, this is quite dramatically demonstrated in Hall's (1905) older representation of girls as akin to the 'irrational' and hence dangerous to young men. According to Hall, women were normally subject to psychological constraints, but where they were 'precocious' they were dangerous as witches or vampires for boys whom they tempted into the ways of vice (Dyhouse, 2014). Gornick explains: 'fragile and vulnerable, Ophelia is shadow twin to the idealized empowered girl. She will need help and intervention in order to turn herself into the correct neo-liberal version of successful girlhood' (2006: 15). Gornick suggests that one representation is the middle-class ideal, the other symbolizes those who may not be so successful at such transformation. However, as we have seen in previous chapters, this is also, and most crucially, co-present within each girl, especially perhaps in the 'successful' Girl. As such they 'bespeak the two central and interrelated contradictions of the times' and among other things 'they suggest that the individual produced by means of such solutions is both a leverage for change as well as a closure on what it is possible to become' (Gornick, 2006: 19).

Another binary is the Ladette versus what we might call the 'Crazy Girl'. The Ladette, who began to appear in the media from the mid-1990s, is an independent, successful and assertive young woman (aged between 16 and about 30) who claims her 'right to use public space, to be heard and seen, and to engage in pleasures that are considered relatively unproblematic for boys and young men' (Jackson and Tinkler, 2007: 267). And here's the rub: unless kept in check she threatens the hegemonic gender order. Three discourses are therefore used to contain her: health (her drinking, smoking and 'casual sex' puts her at risk); her 'biological clock' – although she prefers her career, female friends and liberated sexual encounters, 'representations of ladettes... encourage women to "settle down" with a man and have children' (2007: 258) (and there are many high-profile ladettes celebrated for eventually doing exactly that). Thirdly, there is the risk of excess, represented by the Crazy Girl, always teetering on the brink of self-destruction. In the media these figures have been represented by such celebrities as Tracey Emin and Courtney Love with the latter illustrating in particular how fine is the line that, for the Girl, divides triumph from that worst of all fates: making a 'spectacle' of herself. Kate Moss is increasingly positioned in that territory, as a result of her ageing whilst refusing to settle down. Meanwhile, the death of Amy Winehouse, who epitomized the Crazy Girl, only serves to reinforce this warning. These binaries are clearly age regulative showing that, if nothing else, time and age will serve to put a brake on her dangerous ambitions. Relatedly, there are two tropes which shadow the Girl, being related to the theme of her 'biological clock' as noted above. The first is that of the teenage mum, antithetical to all the Girl represents, and something that, in her days and nights of adventuring, must be avoided. But this exists in a close binary with that of the woman who has 'left it too late' thereby serving as a warning to young women that they too need to fulfil their reproductive duties or risk a stigmatization as great as that befalling the chav mum (Tyler, 2008).

(iii) Representations of mid-life

In previous sections, we discussed the importance of menopause in marking the limit of femininity and we can expect to find this depiction in representations of mid-life. Here, we will concentrate on two themes that appear frequently in various media stories featuring the subject of mid-life or mid-life individuals: (i) denigration of mid-life former sex symbols, and (ii) confessional accounts of menopause.

With regard to (i) Madonna provides us with a vivid example. It is not difficult to find examples of virulent misogynist and ageist remarks concerning her appearance, especially focused on her continued self-display in a variety of sexual poses. Here, we find insulting nicknames directed at her in social media and online articles, such as 'Vadgesaurus' and 'Oldonna' (Gorton and Garde-Hansen, 2012). Of course, she is to some extent trapped in the bind of her early success: whilst it is particularly those women who once traded on their sexuality who are vulnerable to being abused in this way (Whelehan, 2013) the dynamics of this backlash are embedded in the gender regime, and have their origins in the valorization of the Girl and in the emphasis on liberation through sexuality earlier in the life course. It is this very emphasis that underpins the fact that in today's gender regime any continued expressions of sexuality by older women are considered more taboo than ever: what is, for one group, considered empowering is, for another, grotesque and hence the parts of Madonna's anatomy rendered 'abject'. So the young sexual rebel morphs, earlier than others, into the Hag. Comments were mostly hugely derogatory about Madonna's pictures in *Interview Magazine* when she posed with a prosthetic breast-top (most people commenting did not seem to realize they were not her own breasts). They include: 'Put 'em away Madonna, you're, like, 90' and 'Looks like an old dairy cow that has been milked every day for fifty years' (Freeth, 2014). In an interview with Ellen DeGeneres, Madonna expressed frustration at the interest people take in the age of her sexual partners. Responding to Ellen's question about her youngest-ever lover, she said 'The youngest was, in the last six years, 22.' She went on to ask the reasonable question: 'Why is everyone so obsessed? Age is a number. Until you're walking with a Zimmer frame you can do whatever you want' (Pearson, 2015). She might have added: and men do not receive anything like the negative critical attention for doing the same thing, with male celebrities as diverse in their characteristics as Donald Trump and Woody Allen, Nelson Mandela and Pablo Picasso, Buzz Aldrin and Laurence Olivier all taking much younger partners (again indicating the wholly different symbolic meaning of the so-called 'male menopause' in comparison to the female version). However, although the public response to several leaked, unairbrushed shots of Madonna have also been hugely offensive on numerous online sites, there have been positive and sympathetic responses too, praising the authentic beauty of the original snaps and regretting that she does not use these instead. And *Guardian* columnist Deborah Orr, in an article already cited concerning Madonna's 'fall' on the stage at the Brit Awards in 2015 declared:

> Madonna is a more inspiring figure now, as she declares the sexual worth of women in their 50s, than she was when declaring the sexual worth of a woman aged 28. That never seemed terribly radical to me. (Orr, 2015)

Unfortunately, however, Madonna is still proclaiming her sexual worth in terms entirely derived from the heterosexual regime, rather than subverting or challenging this, and the problem is, as we have noted, that these terms are by definition age-defined and temporally limited. So we find in Madonna's case a mature and experienced professional woman incongruously wearing babydoll dresses and singing in high-pitched adolescent tones about the sort of romantic problems a 20-year-old might identify with. Although she is known for appearing in man drag, she might be better off playing this youthful femininity as drag because to play it 'straight' puts her in the company of Beauvoir's tragic ageing women who emphasize their femininity, despite having acquired personhood, independence and rich experience with the passage of time:

> she exaggerates her femininity, she adorns herself, she uses perfume, she makes herself all charm, all grace, pure immanence.... And she enacts this comedy with a certain sincerity. (1997: 590)

The second theme (ii) is that of public discussions of the menopause. An example of the latter is provided by Mariella Frostrup, a presenter of highbrow arts programmes on TV and radio and celebrated for her wit, elegance and beauty. In 2014, Frostrup decided to speak out about her experience of menopause owing to a dispute in which she was involved with her private health insurance company which refused her request for menopausal syndrome to be treated as they maintained this was 'natural' not a disease (Glennie, 2014; Kinchen, 2014). In the course of discussing this, she describes her symptoms in the following terms:

> Like a lot of people my age, I had been suffering from sleeplessness and strange anxiety about things, like the Ocado shopping list – stuff that doesn't really matter in the great scheme of things. I wake at 2am and think: 'Did I put carrots on the list?'. (Kinchen, 2014)

The publicity her statements attracted pleased her hugely and she enthused to the *Sunday Times* interviewer: 'Menopause, menopause, menopause, menopause... Now I've seen the reaction it gets I want to say it all the time' (Kinchen, 2014). Clearly, she feels she is striking a resounding blow on behalf of liberation for women. But Gullette (1997), for one, is not so sure. What the menopause confessional actually does, suggests Gullette, drawing upon a Foucauldian framework, like any confessional practice, is enfold us deeper in the regime of mid-life ageing. The 'confessional tone' that surrounds such discourse suggests liberation because 'silence implies taboo, feminism breaks silence; ergo, women need to speak menopause' (1997: 99). However, far from being taboo, 'it's in real danger of becoming obligatory. And what it obliges us to do is "prepare" ourselves early for the marker event as a disaster foretold' (p. 99).

An ad on US primetime TV leaves us in no doubt about the nature of this disaster. This is the ad for Osphenia ('Painful sex after menopause isn't sexy' as a magazine spread for the same product declares) which claims to treat problematic sex directly caused by the menopause with pharma. The women in the ad smile sadly; they are gorgeous but faded, and, like witches with long, grey hair and silk slips, the impression they give of being ghostly versions of their younger selves is intensified by their being filmed behind veil-like layers of gauzy chiffon. This chiffon has multiple layers of potential meaning; it suggests something of the traditional striptease, but in soft-focus because after all these are erotic ghosts who would dissolve in an over-abundance of light; there is also a certain Miss Haversham feel about them too, reminiscent of old wedding veils, except that wedding rings are clearly visible on their fingers, as is compulsory for acceptable mid-life sexuality. (Could one be jilted on a more symbolic level by the event of menopause?) The message reinforces the connection between sex, age and pain and hence the unnaturalness of sex for older women (although we have seen that this is a feature of younger women's sexual experience also) even whilst holding out possibility of a cure

To return to Frostrup, she is linking events that can, surely, be associated with the combined demands of juggling a successful career, young family and, clearly, ongoing responsibility for aspects of traditional domesticity – witnessed by the worries over the carrots – with the 'menopause'. Would she not be better employed turning her incisive intelligence to pondering the question of why she is worrying about carrots at 2am when she has a remarkably successful career to focus on? Perhaps her husband might wake up and worry about them instead? Drawing attention to her own irrationality in this way seems dangerously close to apologizing for having it all, a form of penance even, a claim to an essential vulnerable femininity (as offered by many other illness narratives), rather than taking the next step of claiming the greater power that beckons at mid-life for women such as herself. Indeed, such admissions of vulnerability provide an alternative, and acceptable, mode of asserting femininity for older women (as compared with the stigmatized 're-sexualization' attempted by Madonna). The menopause discourse certainly provides us with an example of the way post-feminism utilizes older truths from the second wave of feminist struggle in softly convoluted representations that draw us back into patriarchal strategies through our own 'free will'.

(iv) Representations of old age

As we have seen throughout this book, old age in late modernity is represented by two contradictory yet complementary discourses, one of which presents itself as not-old age and the other as abject or deep old age. Taken at face value it is the contradictory and clashing nature of these discourses when juxtaposed that is most striking. These representations, although currently manifest in the distinction between the third and fourth ages, have a longer history in terms of the splitting of old age that Cole (1992; 1986) traces back to the nineteenth century. Essentially, the 'good' was split from the 'bad' as if the attributes related to both could never co-exist: 'Rather than acknowledge ambiguity and contingency in ageing, Victorians split old age into: sin, decay and dependence on the one hand; virtue, self-reliance and health on the other' (1986: 123). Of course, this says more about the adult self's attitudes towards control and its limits in embodied vulnerability and finitude than it does about the lived experience of old age.

Two important features stand out in terms of the common representations of old age in media and policy discourses: firstly, the relationality of the third and fourth ages, with the boundaries being especially important to establish and maintain; secondly, policy does at times, in line with the ends of making citizens more self-steering and responsibilized, distinguish between both ages. So, strikingly different images appear in policy papers of 'successful' ageing discussing the newly raised retirement age because of increased health and longevity as compared with those that describe how older people are suffering from multi-morbidity and blocking hospital beds (Pickard, 2011). The paradox is captured by the Department of Health (2006), which celebrates old age but makes this provisional on productive or successful ageing. However, it is also true that the 'old age as burden' discourse absorbs both the third and fourth ages. In the following section we will trace the burden of old-age discourse and examine continuities and shifts in this discourse over time, focusing on the version as it appears in the the UK; the US version has a similar trajectory, with different socio-historical details (see Cole (1986) for these details). Both culminate in the 'generational equity' debate, or 'generation war' (which we will discuss further in Chapter 10). After this we will return to media images, including both those rare depictions of deep old age and those aimed at the difficult relational boundary.

The burden of old age

Ageing has been treated as a burden in policy and media discourses from the start of modernity, albeit for different reasons and in different contexts. We can trace this to the Poor Law of 1601 when 'old age' only became identifiable to government when it became a problem requiring poor relief. The old were generally considered 'deserving' and thus worthy of relief but this was not automatic and the later establishment of pensions in 1908 at a rate below subsistence levels continued this distinction, intended to ensure that people were thrifty during their lives and did not squander their wages (a view reinforced by the 1948 Pensions Act) (Thane, 2000). Following the establishment of the welfare state, Phillipson (2013) identifies the following shifts in the discourse as follows. Firstly, in the 1940s, the emphasis was on the changing demographic of the population in the context of a declining birth rate. Richard and Kay Titmuss wrote of something 'vast and almost terrifying in its grim relentless development' and spoke of society being in danger of losing 'the mental attitude that is essential for social progress' (1942; quoted in Phillipson, 2013: 24). There was also concern about the potential conflict of interest between worker and pensioner. The debate receded for the next two decades but the normative expectation, as illustrated by Erikson's concept of 'generativity', was that older people would be committed to furthering the interests and knowledge of the young. However, a more conflictual rhetoric returned in the 1970s and 1980s and at that point the greater importance of spending on children was emphasized. In the 1970s and 1980s, reflecting on the size of the pension provision 'burden', Phillipson notes, 'older people were depicted as a "selfish welfare generation"… or "greedy geezers"' (p. 24), taking resources away from the young. This was the concern that informed health policy and ethics discourses such as the highly influential ethical manifesto by Daniel Callahan (1987) which recommended that healthcare should not be provided to people who have 'lived out a natural life span' (1987: 60). He originally suggested the limit would be around the age of 80; but since entering his 80s he has somewhat softened his position. He clearly saw the contribution that older people are able to offer society as lying not in self-development, nor the self-indulgence that one might imagine would come after a lifetime's deferred gratification combining hard work and the obligatory saving, but rather in the contribution they can continue to make to younger generations (including those not yet born). In the 1990s, meanwhile, the context in which such questions were framed was that of the risk society, in which ageing appeared to be another risk, both at the societal and personal level. By the 2000s, Phillipson suggests, both the notion of 'economic burden' and 'cultural anxiety' fused into a 'moral panic' about the ageing of the boomer generation with its large demographic apparently threatening all other generations. In addition to its size, they began to be depicted for the first time as 'politically powerful, selfish, and potentially dangerous' (Cole, 1986: 377–8).

Since the Great Recession of 2008, and the onset of retrenchment and austerity policies, this message has grown more strident. An example is provided by the establishment of the Intergenerational Foundation which has constructed an 'Intergenerational Fairness Index' through which to view policy and practice. Its aim as an organization is to 'protect the rights of younger and future generations' against the 'entitled' older generations. Prominent on its web pages is a quote from Laurence Kotlikoff, who was based at the World Bank in the 1990s, who praises the index and comments: 'The UK, like other developed economies, has engaged in fiscal, educational, health and environmental child abuse' (Intergenerational Foundation, 2015).

We can identify several consistent themes through these discourses, as well as important shifts between older and contemporary discourses. Firstly (i) the fear of the nation being overwhelmed by a tidal wave of ageing people links with fears of degeneracy, with the old obstructing progress and the nation's productivity. Whilst in the nineteenth century this generally related to working-class children and young people, now it is particularly targeted at the old and the oldest old, those aged 80 or 85 and above (Higgs and Gilleard, 2015). In that context, there is repeated talk about health and social care, as well as informal care, supplies being unequal to the task, given the demographic situation. Relatedly, (ii) children (and young people) are prioritized and associated with the 'future' over the old who are the 'past' (and therefore obsolete/valueless). Where once this related to producing a nation fit for competing internationally, in the factories, the colonial outposts, and the battle-fields, now consumerism and technical innovation in the field of media and communications is probably intended. Thirdly, (iii) is the fear of ageing as decline (of societies and individuals). Where in older versions, represented by the statement of the Titmusses, this was focused on social progress, now the focus is on risk: Mullan (2002) suggests that this is an aspect of a more generalized anxiety, in which one's personal fears are seemingly crystallized in the risk that ageing appears to pose for the self. Fourthly, (iv) in a way that is new for this discourse in welfare policy but has cultural resonances elsewhere, for example in psychoanalytic discourses as well as fairy tales, is the fear of the older generation eating up the younger genera-tion – or at least the resources and opportunities that the younger generation require to establish an independent life. (New variants on this theme include a focus on education and housing, with older generations portrayed as having had access to such resources in a way that is more problematic for younger generations.) The co-existence of the extreme neediness with the bloated-with-privilege themes suggests that this is one place where the discourse has absorbed both the third and fourth ages and thus, from a chronological perspective, does not distinguish between them. From an ideological perspective, the role and value of old age is ambivalent at best, problematic at worst, and the good and bad depictions are readily conflated in policy whereby age is being used as a smokescreen to avoid apportioning blame elsewhere. Which brings us to the representations of the difficult line between the third and fourth ages.

Representing the third and fourth ages

In the following section, we look at media depictions of 'ageing' per se and at the boundary between ageing and being or appearing 'old'. We can see, firstly, how the long shadow of the Hag trickles ever further back into the years associated with youth, including advertisements aimed at 30- and even 20-somethings that play on the fear of ageing that figures so prominently in the post-feminist regime. 'Wrinkled or wonderful?', 'Grey or gorgeous?' is the choice one is offered in the Dove adver-tisements, for example. Moving up the age range we find that advertisements for the holiday cruise company Saga (aimed at the 'over-50s') do not interpellate their target group as old: there is a youthful agelessness in the depiction of older couples holi-daying with style and money. Indeed, in these ads greater chronological age is linked to maturity and freedom, an elegant sexuality, a moneyed savoir-faire. This, of course, is not 'old age' but privilege. In fact, this youthful distinction can extend into advanced ages, with the qualifier being health, elegant self-presentation and money. These ingredients are all present in the advertisements for a high-end fashion com-pany, Cole Haan, which feature successful men and women celebrities to signal a claim to classical beauty in its 85th 'birthday' campaign 'Born in 1928'. The models it selected were also born in 1928, with Maya Angelou, the former astronaut Jim Lovell and photographer Elliott Erwitt among them, and all exude a particular combination of elegance, intelligence and stylishness. The message seems to be that it is cultural capital and wealth that above all endows old age with a certain kind of beauty, the type that keeps one within the parameters of the third age. This is the acceptable 'look of age' (Lowenthal, 1985) which is also appreciated in classical ruins and listed buildings but not otherwise.

On the rare occasions that deep old age is depicted (Lovgren, 2012) it is an old age beyond the possibility of salvaging: whether wearing its good or bad face, it is old age as Other. These images fall into two main types, associated with either negative or positive imagery, with a third emerging variant. The first comprises the 'tragedy' view of old people depicting illness and fragility and summed up by adverts for fall alarms and stair lifts, some of which feature old people in the most abject of conditions: calling for help that no one hears; lying in a twisted heap at the bottom of steep stairs, both suggesting that old age has turned their home into a prison. Indeed, wheelchairs, stairlifts and fall alarms serve as fetishes in some of these adverts, standing in for one's worst fears and at the same time offering the hope of technical mastery over them. The poignancy of such scenes is highlighted by the presence in some advertisements of glimpses of ordinary life continuing outside, scenes in which the old person would once have partaken too. In an ad for a fall alarm, as one family takes their Labrador for a walk they pass by an old woman's kitchen window; what they cannot see is that, on the other side of that window, she is lying crumpled and helpless on the kitchen floor following a fall. She is thus set apart from the 'happy family' circle in a very literal sense. As the camera sweeps slowly over a space in which well-used pots and pans hang, we are meant to recall days (in our own lives?) when those same pans, so lifeless and cold now, were used to cook a meal for her children – the adult viewers – with loving care. The children (we) are grown up; the pans are all cold. These advertisements are indeed mostly aimed at the adult children, their appeal pitched in terms of peace of mind knowing poor old Mum or Dad will be safe with this gadget, their own ontological security thereby assured, up to a point at least (but see below).

The second type features cuddly old grandmothers and grandfathers who exude both a protectiveness for, and similarity with, children. These representations are steeped in nostalgia, associated with an imagery of old age that hails back to the era of institutional retirement and employed to evoke old values, and a sense of what we have lost. This is the old age of my grandmother, not my own mother at 82. One example is that of the 'nanas who knit' featuring old-fashioned grannies with neatly waved white hair, horn-rimmed spectacles and floral pinnies. Overseen by a curmudgeonly old male boss, they 'knit' a breakfast cereal enjoyed by children and adults alike. But what both the 'nanas who knit' and those who fall, or who die of heart attacks, have in common is that they represent 'real' old age, age as the Other, a de-sexualized, marginalized, powerless category. But their differences are equally clear. The nanas who knit, or the grandpa featured hard at play with his grandchildren, in another advert for childish breakfast cereal, in cowboys and Indians, hula hoops, and other nostalgic games, all hail from a previous regime of old age. Their presence encourages the adult viewer (if not actually younger then one that at any rate takes the 'youthful gaze') to relive these former times of irresponsibility and playfulness, now long gone. These old people, as a type, may no longer exist but both the sweet old dears and the jolly old boys remain in the realm of story-telling, fantasy, and nostalgia, and it is their presence that conjures up the enchanted gardens in which our (inner) children may play.

A third and more recent version of this is associated with the retro-trend in entertainment represented by a resurgence of traditional arts and crafts with Mary Berry and the *Great British Bake Off* situated at the apex of this. Berry is a nannyish grandmother, sweet and doll-like but yet bossy and sternly matriarchal in a way that reassures and comforts, especially those whose early lives were populated by powerful older women, whether as family, teachers, or fantasy figures. However, this infantilization of the viewer also serves the inequality agenda, suggesting the 'all in it together' discourse with its familial and nostalgic references, reminiscent of the war-time coming-together of families and communities. In reality this is associated with a nostalgic romanticization of current 'austerity' policies suggesting rather that in fact it 'has been used to sugar-coat a free-market nationalism that isn't sweet at all' (Williams, 2015).

By contrast, the first type – the decrepit old people – are from today's fourth age and they interpellate their adult children as adults, making them responsible not only for their own children but also for their elderly parents too – the 'burden of old age' as felt at a strictly personal level. But the burden, for the mid-lifers, is above all resident in the loss of the child in themselves, combined with the unwanted adult knowledge of vulnerability, decay and death, the finitude of days sounding with the hollow ring of empty pans. Stay young and healthy, is the message; for no one would choose the alternative as it is presented in such scenes.

(In) conclusion: age as drag

As we have illustrated throughout this chapter, representations, whether in the form of images and metaphors in policy, science or everyday speech, are key elements in the ideological dominance of certain groups over others, specifically (symbolic) adult groups over non-adults who project their own problems, fantasies and fears onto these ages. However, this is not the end of the matter: it is by the very fact of being structurally inferior that children and older people derive the capacity to 'see through' the age system (Hockey and James, 1993) and by their alterity they can be viewed not as incomplete or deficient but as potential agents for change (Jenks, 2005).

Imagery of old and young playing together may evoke the kind of reflection that Goodman (1960) articulates as follows:

During childhood, they played games with fierce intensity, giving themselves as a sacrifice to the game, for playing with the chief business of
growth, finding and making themselves in the world. Now when they are
too old merely to play, to what shall they give themselves with fierce
intensity? (p. 421)

Politically, the message may be, as he goes on, that the promise of childhood is not
fulfilled in adulthood because of the wasteful and oppressive structures of capitalism, resulting finally in a decrepit old age. I end this chapter not with a conclusion
but with a challenge, in the form of representations which unseat the usual assumptions and meanings associated with particular ages as well as the expected
relationship of ages with each other. I will call this 'age as drag'. But first this
requires a brief exposition.

Certainly transgression can serve as a hegemonic force, reconfirming and reacti-
vating the prevailing order even as it mocks its rules; but it undoubtedly has a
slippery and subversive potential also. A good example of the tensions therein is
provided by Butler's notion of drag. She quotes Esther Newton:

At its most complex, [drag] is a double inversion that says, 'appearance
is an illusion'. Drag says, 'my "outside" appearance is feminine, but my
essence "inside"… is masculine.' At the same time it symbolizes the opposite inversion; 'my appearance "outside"… is masculine but my essence
"inside"… is feminine.' (1990: 186)

Butler goes on: 'As much as drag creates a unified picture of "woman"… it also
reveals the distinctiveness of those aspects of gendered experience which are falsely
naturalized as a unity through the regulatory fiction of heterosexual coherence' and
which are 'denaturalized and mobilized through their paradoxic recontextualiza-
tion' (1990: 187–8). Yet, she affirms, 'parody by itself is not subversive, and [so]
there must be a way to understand what makes certain kinds of parodic repetitions
effectively disruptive, truly troubling, and which repetitions become domesticated
and recirculated as instruments of cultural hegemony' (p. 189). Can we distinguish
the challenging from the conservative?

Below, as a step in this direction, I offer what I consider to be contrasting
examples of 'conservative' and 'disruptive' parodies of the age regime. However,
in classifying them, both images initially gave me pause as it was not at all clear
into which category I should place them. Indeed, where Butler's theory of performativity stresses the instability of gender because of its need to be reproduced
constantly in everyday practices, the identification of this instability is potentially subversive as well as conservative, like the idea of transgression itself
(Deutscher, 1997).

Image A: The photograph on page 197 shows the model Heidi Klum attending
a Hallowe'en party in fancy dress as a 'wrinkled old lady' (Carpenter, 2013).

Klum has chosen to abandon the more traditional witch's garb in favour of the (more?) ghoulish image of herself as Hag. The photograph reveals an incredibly life-like transformation, as if she had aged, like H. Rider Haggard's Ayesha, some 40 years in one evening, with the help of liver spots on her hands, bumpy varicose veins on her legs, bags beneath her eyes, sagging jowls and deep hollows in her neck. This, we are told, is the work of Oscar-winning make-up artists. There is a grotesque display of sexuality hinted at here, ambiguous in its depiction: not only is she wearing a tight, short skirt and a low neckline but her open mouth is both typical of the drooling mannerisms of the old, yet a tad lascivious; the finger-pointing is again stereotypical of this age group yet possibly raised in an obscene gesture. However, it is the response that this image is designed to elicit – embarrassed, somewhat horrified amusement – serving to distance us as readers from this figure, rather than encourage us to see ourselves therein, that finally suggests that, in this case, the drag act is anything but subversive. Just like the Rabelaisian carnival celebration of the grotesque, the poor and the ugly, Klum can only indulge in her spectacle of age because in the world of Order she is known for a youthful beauty that has earned her a fortune. The performance draws attention to the disjunction between the 'real' Heidi and this Hag; it does not so much suggest the arbitrary quality of the rules of age and beauty as remind us why they are (rightly) there. In addition, as the newspaper articles point out, Klum is behaving in a very 'ungrannyish' way: dancing with energetic abandon, drinking, hoiking up her skirt in a display of raucous hedonism far removed from the behaviour we would normally associate with old ladies (who only reveal such traits in the midst of dementia). It may unsettle but the dissonance does not, in the end, lead us to see things of which we were not previously aware, nor question the conventions of society. Rather its clear depiction of this spectacle as a form of Hallowe'en grotesquery, its mutant 'raunch' femininity marked off from everyday life, more starkly suggests that it is literally 'pumpkin time' – the loss of femininity at midnight – reinforcing the seemliness of things as they are normally done.

Image B: A contrasting example of 'disruptive' parody includes the extraordinary series of photographs by Zachary Scott that accompanied an article on psychologist Ellen Langer's experiments, in the *New York Times* (Grierson, 2014). These experiments were attempts to see if older people could 'trick' themselves psychosomatically into believing they were younger and thereby 'cure' themselves of illnesses associated with their personal expectations of their septuagenarian bodies, inculcated as we all are with ideas of time running out (Adam, 1995). Told to act 'as if' it were 22 years previously, by the end of the project the individuals indeed exhibited huge changes in their physiological and mental functioning. The photographs by Scott, designed to illustrate the suggestion that 'age is all in the mind' feature children dressed in the clothes associated with and adopting the poses and expressions of old people. However, depending on one's gaze, you see them as either young dressed as old or as the epitome of the 'child is father of the man' idea, suggesting that we carry age identities, including our 'inner child' with us through the life course. These pictures prompt a wealth of feeling too about the 'real self' the idea of the qualitative relationship between change and continuity, authenticity, development, socialization into age-appropriate identities and so on. Moreover, these pictures are truly provocative as they occupy an ambiguous category of neither one thing nor the other. Although they repeat a traditional motif that views old people as child-like, there is nothing of the belittling stereotype about them and indeed a subversive note is sounded in the reversing of this trope in making children into old people. Like a Gestalt image one sees now the child, now the old person, until the gaze is blurred and the mind struggles to distinguish the difference between both. Take an initial glance and the photographs appear to be portraying the expressions of old people but look again and they are indistinguishable from the expressions worn by young children. When you try to decide *in what* exactly the look of age resides, it is elusive. Is it in grey hair, particular styles of dress, ways of sitting, folding the hands, or stiffening the shoulders? Or a more subtle stiffening of bones and loosening of collagen that the eye recognizes beneath the fabric of the dress and the surface of the skin? In the end we are left with this: we know that these are children dressed up as septuagenarians but we do not know why we know.[1] Age drag is powerful here because it is able to highlight the paradoxical truths of age, real and illusory. Destabilizing categories in a Derridean fashion, it points to both the 'essence' and the 'construction' of age identities, neither fixing on one nor the other, in the play of mobile subjectivities discussed earlier in the work of Ferguson: neither an aged attempt at youthfulness, nor an old age that is quite separate and discontinuous from other ages, nor simply the product of social constructions, but all three.

It has been suggested indeed that it is the ability not just to understand but to accept paradox that is the essence of wisdom, the summation of post-formal rationality that falls outside the framework of development, classically conceived. Piaget stopped at the stage of formal rationality making it the apex of the developmental journey and equivalent to the attainment of adulthood itself. But subsequently, certain psychologists have suggested a further developmental journey, which is the 'ability to live with complexity and tolerate a high level of ambiguity' (Sugarman, 2001: 86). Achieved not through further clarification of logic but rather its opposite, namely intuitive thought underpinned by practical and ethical understanding, this ability seems to call the whole developmental trajectory, with its steps of qualitative transformation, into question. These characteristics of the older mind are also reminiscent of the terms used to describe children's thinking. They imply too that the fullest flowering of post-formal rationality lies not in adulthood but in old age with its qualitatively different form of cognition that has much in common with childhood's magical thinking but with the added richness of experience, of a long life lived: that receptive stillness that Sartre knew when sitting in the sunlight apparently 'doing nothing'; the qualitative condition Tornstam labelled gerotranscendence; Eliot's 'in my beginning is my end'. From this place, far out at either end of the life course, one can perhaps see most deeply into the life course, and perceive also the ideological quality of the age system spread before or behind one. Is it the confusion between young and old that unsettles us so about these pictures? Or is it rather the knowingness of this gaze, confronting us adults with that sense of what we have lost and not yet regained?

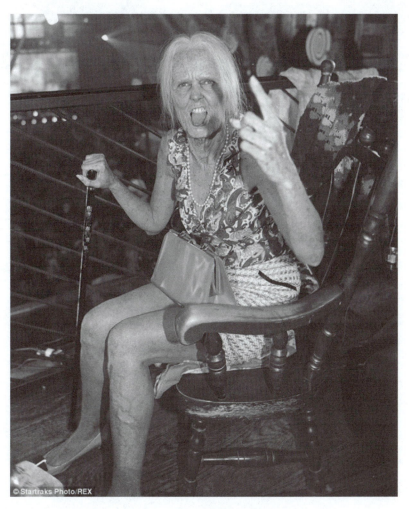

Image A   Heidi Klum dressed as an old lady, Hallowe'en 2013

Image B   Photographs by Zachary Scott illustrating Grierson, N. (2014) What if age is nothing but a mind-set? *New York Times*, 22 October

CHAPTER SUMMARY

- In this chapter we extended previous discussions about the male gaze and the age gaze to the arena of representations.

- Representations of all life stages, we noted, are portrayed from the perspective of the adult gaze.

- These representations often evoke, in the form of caricature or stereotype, characteristics which cannot be owned by adults except in fantasy or nostalgia and which thus reveal much that is denied or hidden about, and to, the adult self.

- We looked at methods for identifying and critiquing age ideology, including semiotics, discourse analysis, Foucauldian analysis and feminist approaches.

- We suggested that 'age drag' representations contain subversive potential.

Further questions

1. Using figurative methodology, choose a trope that, appearing across a range of media, represents popular social beliefs about up to two different life stages and discuss.

2. How do binary pairings in terms of representations in the media work to construct the possibilities and limitations of one or more age and stage?

3. In what ways can women make a 'spectacle' of themselves across the life course?

Talking point

Shulamith Firestone (1970) points out that children, women and the proletariat were all separated from adult groups by dress, activities and reputed characteristics expressive of their social inferiority. Hockey and James (1993) have similarly drawn attention to the parallel depictions of children and older people, with older people called 'little old ladies', 'old dears' or 'old boys' which naturalize the effects of power. Using representations in the media and advertising, describe how these features remain and are modified in contemporary depictions of non-adult stages.

— Key texts —

For **theoretical and practical guides on representations** the following are all-encompassing introductory texts: Hall, S., Evans, J. and Nixon, S. (eds) *Representation* (second edition), London: Open University Press and Sage Publications; Rose, G. (2012) *Visual Methodologies: an introduction to researching with visual methods* (third edition), London: Sage. On **post-feminism and the media** see Gill, R. (2007) *Gender and the Media*, Cambridge: Polity Press. For **depictions of life stages** see the essays in James, A. and Prout, A. (eds) (1990) *Constructing and Reconstructing Childhood*, Basingstoke: Falmer Press; Griffin, C. (1993) *Representations of Youth*, Cambridge: Polity; Featherstone, M. and Wernick, A. (eds) (1995) *Images of Ageing: cultural representations of later life,* London: Routledge. For **comparisons between depictions of childhood and old age** see Hockey, J. and James, A. (1993) *Growing Up and Growing Old*, London: Sage.

Further resources

The cosmetics firm Dove has a campaign for both 'real' women of all ages which has drawn praise and critique alike. The site can be located via Google with the search terms 'Dove compaign'.

The following are links to YouTube videos containing some of the representations of old age discussed in the advertisements described in the chapter.

- https://www.youtube.com/watch?v=-o7X1hJwBJA (Shreddies Knitting Nanas)
- http://www.youtube.com/watch?v=yjA5hWOM9Ck (Weetabix advert, grandpa playing with children)
- http://www.youtube.com/watch?v=J4JzxG0cnpg (Life Alert commercial, 2014)

Note

1. Even when we use cosmetic surgery to give us the smooth, taut skin of a younger person, to lift our breasts or eyelids and so forth, 'youth' can never be restored; what we have is an old face/body with a facelift, not a 'young person'. Perhaps indeed the latter's 'blank page' comprises both a smoothly unlined exterior *and* interior: not, indeed , something to which those marked by time should – or could (?) – aspire.

10

AGES AND GENERATIONS IN INTERACTION

Background

In this chapter we will look at age relations and suggest that the concept of 'generations', especially as it is used in the media, casts age relations in a conflictual light that quickly becomes naturalized. We will demonstrate how 'generations' link conceptually with class and gender regimes and the struggles associated with them, obscuring the latter and highlighting age relations as the major problem. Similarly, the systemically 'conflictual' relationship between women and children is presented not as an issue within the gender regime – the conflicting demands of individualization on women, the clash between 'personhood' and 'motherhood' underpinned by social policy, for example – but as a generational struggle. It is framed by one of the key tools we have already encountered, that of developmental psychology, by which this mother–infant relationship is held responsible for shaping the infant's life course, long after infancy; indeed today increasingly deep into adulthood. Through this relationship, moreover, the norms and practices of the gender hierarchy are reproduced, from the denigration of the 'feminine' that takes place in earliest childhood, to the psychic 'splitting' that constitutes gender socialization, to the ongoing challenges and problems of individuation throughout the life course. In such a way, the cultural dread of the Mother and fear of the Hag is reproduced on a personal level, despite the many social and political changes associated with gender equality.

AIMS OF THE CHAPTER

- We examine generations as a socio-structural tool, a concept for viewing age relations through a particular (age-ideological) lens.

- We then look at the related concept of 'intergenerational justice'.

(Continued)

(Continued)

- We identify social structural factors as they impinge on generations, including the roles of individualization and social policy.

- We consider how age and gender ideology work through the concept of the 'good mother'.

- Finally, we look at the co-operative interplay of generations through multi-age care-giving through the life course.

Generations as a socio-structural analytic device

In this chapter I will follow Pilcher (1995) in differentiating the concepts of generations, cohorts and family units. Thus, I use the term 'generation' to refer to the socio-structural organization of individuals and populations according to 'levels' determined by chronological age (childhood, adulthood, youth and so on). 'Cohort' will mean defined populations that share certain historical characteristics (and often have labels, such as the 'sixties generation', given to them, and are associated with particular (arbitrary) age ranges (born in the same year or decade). In practice, cohorts are often used interchangeably with generations. 'Family structures' will invoke generations through the medium of roles – parent, child, grandparent generation – which of course may not coincide with chronologically organized generations because grandparents could be individuals in their thirties.

BOX 10.1

Generation and cohort

Generation: refers to population 'levels' such as childhood, adulthood, old age; it also refers to the specific historical periods in which people occupying those levels were born.

Cohorts: refers to people born within (arbitrary) age ranges (same year or decade).

Mannheim's (1952) discussion of generations is the best-known approach to this field within sociology. Mannheim uses the concept in a way that overlaps with the term 'cohort' and his particular contribution is to emphasize age as a form of social stratification. Suggesting that cohorts act very much like classes in terms of their role in shaping consciousness, he sees the coming and going of generations as key to social reproduction, vehicles of both continuity and transformation, but, in his view, this requires the 'biological rhythm of birth and death' (1952: 168). Here, as noted, we can see that this model implicitly overlooks the more social process of death-and-rebirth that we have suggested is a part of the life course for all. But, before we critique this in more detail, let us look at how he defines generations and the social role they fulfil.

Firstly, they are far more than the sum total of individuals born in the same period (usually a period of around thirty years distinguishes one generation from another). Mannheim indeed compares them to classes, in terms of the way they locate individuals socially and open up certain possibilities and experiences to them whilst shutting down others. In addition, there is a similarity with the idea of classes-in-themselves and classes-for-themselves, with the latter, when applied to generations, indicating self-conscious awareness of their group identity. The latter tends to occur in 'generational units', with separate units contrasting and possibly even antagonistic, in terms of their political affiliations, lifestyles, material interests. That is, Mannheim acknowledges the importance of class, place and other cultural characteristics in shaping cohorts. As Mannheim puts it, those units belong to the same generations but 'work up the material of their common experiences in different specific ways' (1952: 184). This intersects somewhat with what Mannheim calls a 'stratification' of 'consciousness' and 'experience'. This is made up of a dialectic between ongoing experiences and the all-important, defining early experiences which coalesce into a 'natural view' of the world and shape subjectivity in a particular mould, meaning that individuals born at a particular historical moment will invariably have more in common with each other than with those generations that either precede or follow them. In relation to the latter point, where generations are characterized by principles (aspirations, sensibility) unique to them, they share a 'generational entelechy'.

However, not all generations have a particular style initiated by and associated with them and, where they do, Mannheim stresses that invariably social and cultural triggers are involved. This is why he believes generations often come to be associated with political movements or develop in reaction to events or to previous generations. Thus, generations/cohorts may acquire different labels which sum up the flavour of the particular zeitgeist in which they are formed: boomers, Thatcher's children, 'slackers', millennials and so on, all with attributed characteristics that in fact can be seen to be emergent from the combination of social and economic circumstances in which they came to adulthood, and which are always relational, that is, defined in contrast to previous generations.[1]

Without generational influx, Mannheim says, in what he calls an 'imaginary immortal' society, society would be 'stuck' in a particular register. This notion very much depends on the idea, dominant in psychology and other disciplines, of the way in which the significance of the early years outweighs in importance that of other life stages. This social rhythm, driven by the ebb and flow of generations, is a dialectic underpinning the possibility of historical progress:

The continuous emergence of new human beings certainly results in some loss of accumulated cultural possessions; but on the other hand, it alone makes a fresh selection possible when it becomes necessary; it facilitates re-evaluation of our inventory and teaches us both to forget that which is no longer useful and to covet that which has yet to be won. (pp. 171–2)

The role of intergenerational conflict is thereby presented as necessary to social reproduction itself and thus fits within the frameworks provided by both Freud and Marx. However, amplified in the contemporary media, such emphasis on conflict and discontinuity obscures the equally powerful connections, continuity and co-operation that exists between the generations.

Critiquing 'generational war'

In addition to the centrality of conflict contained within it, the concept of generations is infused with a taken-for-granted age ideology that privileges the youthful perspective. In this, youth symbolizes progress, energy, creativity and hope for the future. Relatedly, it lends itself to the old age as a burden paradigm. As noted in Chapter 9, the latter strongly implies that older generations could, in particular circumstances, such as the longevity revolution heralded by anti-ageing medicine, present obstacles to younger generations in a number of dimensions, including education, housing, jobs and the funding of older people's pensions. Indeed these themes underlie the arguments about social justice that appear frequently in the popular press, as well as in policy journals, and increasingly so in the context of 'austerity' (see Box 10.2 below for some examples taken from the UK press).

It is seldom if ever the case, however, that a social problem affects one age group only and indeed it will have unique consequences for classed, gendered and ethnic groups of all ages. Indeed, whilst stressing difference *between* generations it over-stresses similarities *within* them. So, for example, as we have previously observed, the 'winners' in terms of globalization and employment changes are not the mid-life generation per se but rather middle-class professional mid-life men (Roberts, 2011). Whilst this monolithic structure is not the way Mannheim himself saw the concept of generations, as we noted, highlighting the role of class, place and other cultural characteristics in shaping generational units, certainly the complexity of this original position tends to get lost in many media representations (and popular views).

What is the empirical evidence for such intergenerational strife in general and for the negative role of older people in this in particular? Let us begin by examining some of the claims that the old are a social, financial and medical burden on the young. We will begin by returning to the work of Callahan (1987) who was so convinced that older people threaten the greater good of society with their potentially limitless demands for healthcare that he advocated that such care should terminate 'after a person has lived out a natural life span' after which treatment should be limited to relief of suffering. From the arguments in the previous chapters we will recognize the need to be wary of making claims about the length of a natural life span or of its possibilities, in the face of the structural inequalities that impinge on a person's potential from the earliest years, the advent of medical advances and the fact of individual priorities and plans. Moreover, the idea is only sustainable in the kind of life course that follows a uniform and linear progression. Callahan's views also assume the premise that Eriksonian 'generativity' or service to younger generations is *the* meaning of this stage of the life course, and thus contributes to the moral economy, in which moral arguments are often used to justify (and obscure) what are in fact political priorities (see Minkler and Estes (1998) for a fuller discussion of this concept). These sorts of arguments can then justify, for example, the UK's inadequate public pensions.

Let us next consider the structural linking of old people's gain and younger people's loss, which runs like a constant refrain through these arguments. Mullan (2002) challenges what he calls the causal relationship between the social and economic difficulties of the West and the fact of population ageing. At the centre of this argument there are usually two claims: firstly that older people have health problems that result in elevated costs for healthcare systems and social care agencies, and secondly that they are not productive and so depend on the labour of others.

Against the first point: most old people are neither ill, disabled nor dependent; moreover expected improvements in healthcare and life style are likely to result in future generations of older people being healthier still (Mullan, 2002; see also Lowsky et al., 2013), although there are clear class differences here. Secondly, looking at the depictions of old people's lack of productivity as a problem, there have been several recent persuasive criticisms of the technical measurements routinely used to measure such productivity, such as the standard dependency ratios which measure productivity and unproductivity in terms of stages (working age compared with the rest). Given the new flexible nature of the labour regime, the extension of higher education, and the continuation of many older people in employment past the previously constituted 'retirement' age, it would be more accurate to measure those in employment and self-employment as opposed to 'the working age population' (Mullan, 2002). Similarly, Spijker and MacInnes (2013) suggest a tool that takes the more accurate elderly dependency ratio to be the sum of men and women with a remaining life expectancy of up to 15 years divided by the number of people in employment. Using this measure shows dependency to have fallen by one-third over the past four decades and they predict that it will fall still further. Even these more sensitive tools conceptualize dependency in narrow economically active terms, however. In fact, older people contribute to society in a variety of ways not strictly related to employment. For a start, they are important consumers: indeed agentic old age is dependent upon consumerist practices. Moreover, in terms of exchanges within the family, grandparents' contribution to the employment of their children, through care of their grandchildren, is substantial: research has found that one-third of families – and half of all single parents – rely on grandparents, sometimes to an extent which is onerous or deleterious to grandparents' health, wellbeing and financial welfare, especially among the disadvantaged (Glaser et al, 2010). The UK government has acknowledged this by introducing National Insurance credits towards their state pensions for all those caring for grandchildren under the age of 12 as well as introducing from 2018 'grandparental leave' which gives grandparents in employment the right to paid leave for up to a year shared with a parent (the British Chancellor of the Exchequer stating explicitly that this was to encourage grandparents not to leave the workforce permanently). Childcare by grandmothers helps more women enter work, as well as work longer hours, especially in lower-income households (Gray, 2005).

In addition, Higgs and Gilleard (2015) cogently refute the 'problem' of the ageing of the ageing. Although ageing of the ageing (those aged 80 and over) is certainly proceeding apace (up from 5 per cent of the total population aged 65 and above in 1961, to 15 per cent by 2011) the consequences are by no means as disastrous as some predictions suggest. So, for example, whilst most people over 80 have some form of multi-morbidity this may have a minor effect on functionality and there may even be an 'age barrier' beyond which the idea of progressive disability no longer pertains (Higgs and Gilleard, 2015). Other charges that are frequently levelled at them include that they enjoy an unfair advantage in terms of housing stock and property value and that they have also enjoyed the benefits of free education now denied the young. However, surely the blame should be laid not upon older people but, among other things, on the short-sighted government policies which have meant that social housing, sold off during the Thatcher years, was never replaced with no building programmes initiated? And that education, despite its being paid for out of individual loans, is not complemented by an employment market willing to pay graduate salaries (or indeed provide sufficient graduate-level jobs to meet the demand)? It seems, then, that it is the *concept* of generations that should constitute the focus of critical attention just as much as what it identifies and this analysis could be informed by some of the following questions, namely: Is antagonism between generations a given? Might differences co-exist with common concern? Who gains by emphasizing the divisions between generations? Who loses? (See also Basting, 1998.)

Taking the last question first, concerning who loses from pitting one generation against another, this affects all ages and stages in that such divisions mean that we fail to see how poor conditions of employment and inadequate care structures are all aspects of a de-responsibilized capitalism that sees people through the life course as increasingly decontextualized sources of labour to whom employers owe no obligation or ongoing concern. Women lose in particular, as perennial questions such as 'Who will care for the childless boomers?' indicate taken-for-granted assumptions that responsibility for caring for older people will continue to fall, by default, to their children, specifically their daughters, in the absence of state support. Those who gain, on the other hand, are big business, corporate finance, transnational capitalism and their representatives including the World Bank and the IMF, as well as all who benefit from a scaled-down social infrastructure. Not only do these corporations comprise, and serve, those mainly concentrated in the mid-life age group but also they constitute symbolic 'adulthood', as we have noted previously. Reconstructing the class struggles as an age war – between young and old – effectively lets such individuals and causes step out of sight. That is, the changes in employment conditions, the rolling-back of the state, and the individualization of society are all part of late modern capitalism's neopatriarchal neoliberal thrust; and a rhetoric blaming intergenerational war, as well as proclaiming that the class war is dead and gender equality achieved, serves as a superstructure to legitimize this and stifle opposition. Depicting older people as burdens more generally discourages all and any dependence on the state (Mullan, 2002); it also encourages an attitude of pessimism towards the future and lowered personal expectations, thus further normalizing inequality. The media, in producing these stories, plays a significant role here and as Dorling notes, the top 1 per cent 'own newspapers and TV channels, and they spread myths to offset the growing consensus among the 99 per cent' (2014: 23). Whilst many young people adopt this perspective as evident in readers' online responses to numerous persistent online press articles, British Social Attitudes Surveys repeatedly find high support among the young generation for pensions, even though they are not supportive of benefits in general for the working-age population (but also perhaps reflecting a view of old age as needy and vulnerable).

We turn next to examine alternative ways to conceptualize intergenerational relationships.

Generations in context: the life course model

One way to overcome some of the problems associated with the concept of generations is by adopting a life course perspective. Taking the comparison of pensioner wealth versus child poverty, as crudely constructed in media and other representations: pensioners are well off today comparatively; or at least in the UK there has been a striking fall in poverty from the 1960s when a third of the poor were old and today less than one-tenth of those in poverty are in households where all adults are retired (Lansley and Mack, 2015). However, this is one of the 'echoes' of past policy initiatives intended to reverse the earlier experience of dire poverty in old age, including free universal benefits such as bus passes and so on. Most importantly, pensioner comparative 'wealth' and child poverty are not related; the strongest predictor of poverty in old age is poverty and deprivation in childhood and, relatedly, poor employment conditions especially for women (Esping-Andersen and Sarasa, 2002). Moreover, today the public transfer of resources to old people is accompanied by private interfamilial transfers from older to younger family members, and in this case the two facts *are* interrelated (Kohli, 1999), making for closer intergenerational ties and loyalties. Indeed, far from favouring the old, the age regime structurally and ideologically discriminates against them, the impact being felt among particular classes and gender so that over 20 per cent of those who live in poverty are pensioners rising to over 30 per cent if they are single women (Segal, 2013) (17 per cent of the total population in the UK is aged 65 and above according to World Bank figures). However, it is also the case, as we noted in Chapter 2, that changes to the work economy have deeply impacted on long-held notions of inter-generational continuity and solidarity. Furthermore, even such critics as David Willetts (2010), who has written a popular book about the intergenerational conflict arguing that the baby boomer generation has 'stolen the future', suggests that it mat-ters less which cohort or generation an individual belongs to than which point in the life course s/he is currently at, noting: 'The events that matter in your life, what you think of public spending programmes, even how happy you are, depend on the stage you are at in your life' (2010: 119). Willetts also notes the following 'paradox,' which really revolves around position in the life course:

> It is older people who are the most future-oriented. They are thinking about the world their children and grand-children will inherit. It is young people who have the luxury of living in the present because when you are young you think that the present will carry on forever. (p. 118)

The life course perspective makes a crude conflict-of-interest argument between the generations difficult to sustain, emphasizing as it does 'the fact that individuals occupy a variety of age-based social statuses over time: the elderly are not some separate entity, but are our future selves' (Pilcher, 1995: 133). Erikson's theory of identity reveals another facet of this, suggesting that in the psychology of the indi-vidual the ages and stages are not discontinuous but key earlier conflicts/challenges are nested within later ones, like the dolls within a Russian matryoshka, with the identity task at each stage involving a two-fold revisiting of those challenges in the context of the present as well as a unique task pertaining to the challenges at the cur-rent life stage. The life course perspective further helps identify how dependence and independence are both *constructed* as features of particular stages of the life course, suggesting that individuals will almost invariably experience *both* positions during their life.

Picking up this point, we can consider Cole's (1989) observation that debates about intergenerational justice are all really concerned with something more pro-found, namely the loss of meaning in the life course in general and old age in particular. Questions such as:

> Should we be devoting much of our biomedical research and technology to the diseases of ageing?... what 'good' are old people anyway? What do they contribute to the rest of society? Are there any special virtues or obligations particular to old age? (Cole, 1989: 379)

stem from this ontological hollowingout in the sense of the loss of 'shared horizons' (Taylor, 1985). Cole observes that the disenchantment of the life course – its bureauc-ratization in the twentieth century, as well as its current fragmentation – has made old age in particular meaningless and depressing. This meaninglessness is only addressed in a 'positive' manner by attempts to deny it altogether in the eternal sunlight of the endlessly youthful third age – hence the increasing 'danger' presented by the fourth age as depicted in press and policy documents. A life course approach would, as Cole (1989) suggests, enable 'redistribution' to be conceived not just in financial terms but also in terms of the redistribution of meaning, with old age accorded as important and rich a meaning as youth, each being aspects of a full life. This of course means challenging the dominance of age ideology whence originates the kind of metaphors found in an article written by the former cabinet minister Chris Huhne and published in the *Guardian* newspaper: 'The interests of the young are at risk of being marginalized, whilst the old *ride proud*... Policy after policy – affecting some crucial decisions for our future – is feeling the *hot breath of grey power*.... The cost of pandering to pensioners is *social arthritis*... someone needs to fight the *selfish, short-sighted old*. They are the *past*, not the future' (Huhne, 2013; emphasis added). Ideologically, this same view both presents the young as particularly vulnerable and is just as likely, on the other hand, to trivialize their problems, whereby the structural disadvantages experienced by youth today can be downplayed in the 'fortunate to be young' rhetoric.

Bjerrum Nielsen (2004) suggests that whilst a *diachronic*, or time-based perspective on generations (such as that associated with Mannheim) tends to 'fix' generations in 'young' or 'old' categories without giving much sense of how they are involved in interplay, in the *synchronic* perspective older generations are depicted as if they have always been that way, for example, the parents or grandparents generation. This is, again, where a life course perspective – defined by Hareven as moving away from a focus on stages to a concern 'with an understanding of the place of that stage in an entire life course continuum' (Hareven, 1982: xiii; quoted in Pilcher, 1995) – has an advantage in that it can accommodate relationships between ages as well as convey the sense of a dynamic individual movement through the stages and ages, rather than fixing it at one point (as the concept of young versus old implies).

A focus on governmentality adds a further dimension to the life course perspective, enabling an insight into how all ages and stages are imbued with an (albeit unevenly shared) mentality that may shift over the course of a life time: for example, those older people, who would not have analyzed their decisions and acts according to a framework of 'consumerism' or 'the enterprising self' in their youth, today may make sense of many aspects of their old age through that perspective. So, whilst we can see the third age as a generational consciousness (Gilleard and Higgs, 2002) facilitated by social, cultural and economic conditions (which may not converge in such a way for future generations, as we discuss below), it also helps to see its emergence specifically from within the coils of a governmentality associated with the conditions of late modern capitalism. Relatedly, Bjerrum Nielsen (2004) has explored shifts in feminine subjectivity down through three generations of women. Through interviews with the grandmother, mother and daughter of one family unit, she identifies historical shifts on multiple levels, including in socio-structural, material and cultural framing of women's lives. This reveals itself in the way in which the space of girlhood is mapped out contrastingly in each of the three generations by means of the following polarities:

nice girl versus cheap girl (for grandmother); boring girls versus popular girls (for mother); autonomous (self-actualizing) versus girls over-reliant on heterosexual success for granddaughter (corresponding perhaps to hybrid and emphasized femininities). One thing this does not explore, however, is how shifts in (govern)mentalities also introduce a sense of divisions between one's younger and older selves so that the grandmother's view of herself in old age shares something with the granddaughter's view of her youth, in contrast to the way she viewed her own youth at the time. A personal example: my own approach to education when I was an undergraduate was one of infinite expansion of the mind and knowledge of the world for its own sake and today I catch myself looking back at this youthful self with some incredulity, indeed self-reproach, caught up as I am (in my unguarded moments at least) in the rationale of *homo economicus*. This narrative reconstruction imbues the whole of my life course with a neoliberal mentality that does not make sense for the earlier part – a process which adds substance to the commonplace wisdom of the past as a foreign country but one that can make us strangers to ourselves.

This contextual approach to generations, blending stage, historical cohort, social structure and governmentality, also reveals how for youth there may be a general amplification of the consequences of shifts that affect whole societies. One example is that of the disengagement of younger people from the formal political system, including voting and party membership, which is more pronounced both than in older generations and than in any previous generation of younger people (Flanagan, 2009). But a mixture of life course position, structural changes and the shift in governmentality, all converge on this phenomenon. These include: a switch from party politics to lifestyle politics in an era of the 'politics of self-actualization' (Giddens, 1991); the attention needed to make complex transitions into an uncertain job market (Harris, 2009); the demise of party politics in the service-based economy which have particularly affected working-class youth's engagement with politics, UK politics being traditionally rooted in social class (Furlong and Cartmel, 1997); and the rise of new social movements as an alternative to traditional party-based allegiances as a result of both latter events. Relatedly, if we look at the intergenerational conflict discourses, we find a notably conservative impulse in the younger generation: not so much the positing of alternative societies so much as a bitterness at perceived obstacles to getting onto the ladder (of property, regular employment, etc.) and into the mainstream. All these points are suggestive of wider issues such as the hegemonic market rationality that instils a conformity into subjects, and with it a changing relationship of self to demos, which transforms the nature of the demos itself.

Similarly, today's 'third age' as a majority experience is likely to be a special case (Lansley and Mack, 2015). All indications suggest that the rate of poverty in old age will rise in the future, overturning the gains of recent decades. Poverty and Social Exclusion (PSE) analysis (survey data from a major survey of poverty and social exclusion in the UK: see http://www.poverty.ac.uk/pse-research) shows that of those who are not retired, 54 per cent of the poorest fifth and 41 per cent of the next fifth cannot afford to make any payments into a pension scheme, boding ill for a wealthy and agentic future old age.

To sum up then, the concept of 'generations' needs to be supplemented both by a life course dynamic and by an understanding of the discourses of governmentality; but in addition, the heterogeneity within generational groups requires highlighting. Only then can it be a useful explanatory tool for seeing age relations outside an age-ideological perspective.

In the next section, we move on to explore the dynamics between different ages, roles and stages within the family context. We will look particularly at how gender and age inequality is embedded in care-giving interactions and explore how the dual tugs of individualization and interdependency impact on women's experience throughout the life course, thereby highlighting key tensions and inequalities at the heart of the age and gender regimes.

Family forms, public principles and the structuring of generational conflict

Families exist in a wider social context, of course, and against the claims of family are the pull of competing norms deriving largely from the work place, as well as more generally in the cultural context of individualization. Beck-Gernsheim (2002: ix) observes: 'the crucial feature of these new regulations is that they enjoin the individual to lead a life of his or her own beyond any ties to the family or other groups – or sometimes even to shake off such ties and to act without referring to them'; indeed, even perhaps to see them as an obstacle to work success or personal growth. At the same time, the emphasis given by official discourses on the key role of mothers in particular, and families in general, suggests that conflict between generations may be built into the structure of society embedded in a series of micro-tensions and counter-tensions characteristic of clashing configurations. This structuring of generational 'conflict' arises from the paradoxical demands of: (i) individualization; (ii) the ongoing inequalities of the gender regime; and (iii) relatedly, the reliance of the capitalist state on unpaid female domestic and care-giving labour.

Dalley (1988) suggests that policy is not merely pro-family but rather 'as an ideo-logical construct, "the family" underlies all contemporary forms of social organisation of daily living'. Moreover, she continues, it is a two-way process: 'The internal pattern of replication... is then reproduced in the public sphere; the ideology underpinning domestic relations becomes a major organizing principle upon which social relations outside the domestic group are based' (1988: 21) which includes the expectations on women to emotionally 'service' men within work situations through their emotional labour. Likewise, the role of women as mothers is extended 'naturally' into other roles including the concept of women's jobs in 'caring' professions. But in practice, not all work places are flexible and childcare is both expensive and not compatible with round-the-clock commitments to work. Ward et al. (1996) note that the average cost to women for childcare where their youngest child is under five years old is a quarter of their net earnings. Care-giving to older family members or friends similarly mostly falls to women and is presented as a 'natural' part of 'family life'.

We turn next to the relationship between motherhood and child development.

'Good mothers' and the development of children over the life course

Age and gender inequality work powerfully through the ideology of the good mother. We can trace this back to the nineteenth century when middle-class women retreated from streets and public spaces into domestic roles and children, quickly or slowly, depending on their age and class, followed them into the home and the school. Indeed, as we have seen in earlier chapters, the association between childhood and femininity became essentialized in many ways, with (especially genteel) femininity coming to share many characteristics with childhood.

One of the key figures in sculpting the ideology of motherhood through establishing scientific norms for childcare is that of John Bowlby who established mothers as absolutely primary in child development. His work was highly influential in the mid-twentieth century when it appeared and enjoys a lingering influence today. At the time, it justified the political arguments for women returning to the home, following the end of World War Two, thus being inextricably part of an ideological agenda for restoring the traditional gender regime which had been 'denaturalized' whilst men were away fighting. Bowlby (1971) made it a cornerstone of his work – arising from research on mainly institutionalized children – that separation of children from their mothers was inherently traumatic and damaging, no matter the nature of that separation (brief, regular, intermittent, permanent). As Burman summarizes: 'The good mother must therefore be always available and always attentive' and appropriate attachment arises from 'mothers' rapid and appropriate responsiveness to children's demands of hunger, discomfort and boredom' (Burman, 2007: 132–9). Segal (2007: 9) notes how the 'good mother' was framed in relation to her opposite, the 'working mother', observing that she occupied the same place in the 'demonology' of mid-twentieth century society that masturbation had occupied in Victorian times. Paradoxically, the endless attachment of the mother requires the equal and opposite movement to independence of the child in an irreconcilable clash of generations implicit in this model of child development.

The ideology of the 'good mother' asserts itself in contemporary discourses around breast feeding.[2] The ideological importance given to the latter is apparent in the enormous range of arguments in its favour, including not only physical effects in terms of the baby's lifelong health but also suggestions that it increases social capital throughout the life course where breast feeding is even associated with increased upward social mobility in the child and decreased downward mobility (Sacker et al., 2012). Criticisms of this evidence have largely focused on the difference between causation and correlation; breast feeding is practised most by middle-class mothers who already have the requisite degrees of social capital to ensure mobility, health and so on (factors associated with increased breast feeding include higher social class, and being older (Oakley et al., 2013)). Currently, there is an imperative not just to breastfeed today but to breast feed for a prolonged period, with which many women, even if they aspire to, struggle to comply (Hoddinott et al., 2012). Where only 45 per cent of women reported they were breastfeeding without formula at one week after birth and less than 1 per cent at six months (Oakley et al., 2013) this sets up women to experience motherhood within a deficit framework from the start (and is far from the 'good enough' mothering of Winnicott, for example). This is despite the contestability of the evidence underlying such an extreme position (see Fewtrell et al., 2011). As Beck-Gernsheim (2002) points out, this imperative also runs contrary to the fact that women are also called upon to be workers, an activity with which breast feeding is not tremendously compatible (along with inadequate and expensive childcare facilities in the UK and US, including the fact that school timetables and work days do not synchronize). Any possibility that this is an oversight or coincidence is belied by the fact that 'working mothers' (there is no real term for fathers who work) still receive a bad press for the so-called effect it has on their children, which suggests enduring ambivalence about women in public life. (The irritating persistence of the term 'career women' further indicates this). Secondly, this elevates the role of the mother above all other parent/family carers who might also wish to develop links with the baby and it is a contributory factor in the fact that fathers continue to play a subsidiary role in childcare in the UK and other Western countries.

Meanwhile, 'healthy' development in childhood and beyond is based on separation (often conflictual and at least symbolically violent) of child from mother, and repudiation of aspects associated with her, particularly, but not exclusively, by boys. Chodorow notes:

> Both sexes learn to feel negatively towards their mother during the oedipal period. A girl's negative feelings, however, are not so much contempt and devaluation as fear and hostility.... A boy's contempt serves to free him not only from his mother but also from the femininity within himself. It therefore becomes entangled with the issue of masculinity and is generalized to all women. A girl's hostility remains tied more to her relationship with her mother (and/or becomes involved in self-depreciation). (1978: 182)

However, the power of patriarchy allows men to institutionalize their dominance more broadly. Burman (2007) notes that in (non-psychoanalytic) developmental terms, separation also involves a repudiation of the feminine. Drawing on Gilligan (1982) she suggests

> the trajectory of development moves from *attachment*, a stereotypically feminine quality, to a culturally masculine *detachment*.... There is thus a double repudiation of femininity, as both motor of developmental advance and aspect of personal experience, structured within the achievement of autonomy. (Burman, 2007: 142, original emphasis)

This equation of masculinity with detachment from the mother spills over into the feminized schooling environment and is an explanatory factor for the fact that many boys are diagnosed with ADHD. However, although we have already noted the requirement for boys to take on certain feminized qualities, which may be challenging for some in the light of this masculine style of individuation, attributes such as self-care, responsibility to others and therapeutic self-knowledge are subsidiary to the autonomy and detachment of the strongly individualized self. Indeed, 'softer' qualities are co-opted as useful management techniques for 'controlling' others as in 'the indirect, the covert, the velvet glove' (Burman, 2005: 357). As I have stressed throughout this book, however, the development of selfhood can be seen differently if we use a contrasting theoretical lens and here we draw again on the groundbreaking work of Jessica Benjamin (1994). She suggests that the account of early life we find in mainstream psychoanalysis, including that of Chodorow, whilst accurate, is partial because it does not include the reality of intersubjectivity, being the 'capacity to differentiate and to recognize other subjects' (1994: 134) as well as that of struggle and dreams of omnipotence. A capacity for mutual recognition, of infant and mother as separate individuals, can be fostered in a way which replaces the need to survive by repudiation and domination of the mother-figure. However, Benjamin also notes that this requires work on the part of the mother, as well as the infant, so that both can see the other as separate from the fantasy figure they have idealized – the perfect mother and perfect child. A fantasy of omnipotence is not the problem; rather 'it is the loss of balance between omnipotence and recognition, between fantasy and reality, that is the problem' (1994: 137). It is mutual recognition, moreover, that is required as a solution, not complementarity by which Benjamin means the switching of roles: now I dominate; now you do; now I am subject and you object, now we switch. Mutuality, by contrast, is a case of reflexively understanding the other's position so that there is a 'space between the mother and child that allows differentiation of self and other, fantasy and reality' (p. 138) and, we might add, includes both conflict and co-operation. This requires a very different approach to the anxieties inculcated through separation on the part of mothers: one that departs from self-sacrifice and being there always for children (in reality, if not in fantasy).

Segal (2007) draws attention to the way this focus on motherhood obfuscates the nature of capitalist relations and their specifically classed constraints. Focusing on modes of masculinity in the 1950s, she notes the phenomenon of talented young men who focused their frustration on wives and mothers as representatives of some stultifying conventional norm that was really an invisible structural constraint. Segal points out that wife/mother blaming was encouraged by the ideology of capitalism which in the 1950s proclaimed a 'myth of classlessness' which persuaded educated working-class men that the constraints they felt emanated from women. Here, we can see a parallel in the way both intergenerational conflict – framed as hostility towards the older generation as well as vice versa – and gender conflict divert attention from the capitalist system as the source of inequality.

Relationships between mother and children are shaped and patterned by class. With 'girlhood' and 'girls' subject to elevated expectations to 'achieve', as we have seen, a pattern is set up whereby middle-class girls follow their fathers as role models and thereby aim to be different to their mothers who may not have had careers. Gullette (1997) notes that the problematization of mothers is indefinitely prolonged in modern Western societies far more than either child development or psychoanalytic theories postulate. It extends potentially endlessly over the life course, with 'mother', both in her actions in the past and today, the attributed source of so much lifelong disappointment, unrealized potential and failure to achieve what we want, again standing as a screen behind which deep structural inequalities and constraints go unnoticed and unremarked. Gullette notes that a forced and brutal individualization – specifically the requirement to be a competitive, atomistic individual demanded of us by employment practices – works with, and through, a prolonged psychic dependency on the mother. This is indeed another perspective on the social infantilization process identified by Postman and others. Because of this, she says,

> some may maintain an ongoing fantasy of maternal protection (this serves the system, making it more bearable, without threatening it with change). Even when they know rationally that the psychic Mother of childhood cannot protect them, they may hold onto it as a symbol because in a heartless system that seems the only haven. In the crucial years when emerging adults adjust to the workplace and don't yet have a reliable partner, they are caught, able neither to utilize the sweet Mother for real protection nor abandon it. (1997:129)

This is complicated by parents' (especially mothers') willingness to maintain this attachment and to take responsibility, guide and advise their offspring deep into young adulthood and beyond, with middle-class parents often fully involved in their educational life through university. However, at the same time there are pressures on young people to reject the child-like role and take on the independent role expected by the work regime and indeed to identify with the Father which means that the balance between autonomy and connectedness is fraught. 'People have to be "individuated" for the sake of work relationships ... – resocialized out of childlike trust and ... into a more isolated wariness, egoistic competitiveness, and acceptance of powerlessness' writes Gullette (1997: 128). This is then a pressure to 'over-individuate'. In an essay describing her experience of motherhood to teenage daughters, the writer Rachel Cusk (who achieved a degree of notoriety for an earlier autobiographical account of her ambivalent feelings towards pregnancy and motherhood) describes overhearing her daughters' friends discussing their parents:

> Their mothers are known as 'she'... I was slightly puzzled by her status which was somewhere between servant and family pet. She's such a doormat, one of them says. When I forget something I need for school,

> I just text her and she comes all the way across town with it. She's so…
> pathetic. I don't know what Dad sees in her. Why doesn't she get a job?…
> Dad, meanwhile, is revered for his importance in the world… unlike 'she',
> their fathers are hard-working, clever, successful, cool. (Cusk, 2015)

Gullette also points out that 'mother-blaming' arose within the course of feminism as women rejected their mothers' lot: so, for example, the 'third wave' of feminism is depicted as both reaction to, and rejection of, second-wave feminism with acrimony on both sides. Gillis and Munford state: 'the trouble with this model [of waves] is that generations are set up in competition with one another… This… competitive generational model does not allow for a collective memory of female-based thought, empowerment and activism' (2006: 176). They suggest that 'the generational account of feminism – which third wave feminism is perpetuating – should be understood as merely another tool of the backlash' (Gillis and Munford, 2006: 177–8; see also Faludi, 1992).

  For many reasons, then, the mother–child developmental model, as it is depicted in classical psychoanalytic traditions, is not particularly helpful, either for a different kind of maturity, or as a foundation for a different kind of age relations. A girl's detachment from her mother is not discussed with sufficient nuance in the psychoanalytic literature, other than to make the point of its partial and incomplete nature, which is not helpful in this historical context where women have been taking on masculine biographies in a way that departs from their mothers' generation. In addition, not only does it identify early life as the only time of importance in personality formation but it treats the older kith and kin as irrelevant to socialization and obsolescent in psychic terms. This is where (i) adding another generation(s) and (ii) extending the gaze beyond the 'nuclear-family-with-a-child-living-at-home' phase, would layer ages and stages adding a texture of richness and complexity to psychoanalytic accounts of the whole life course (Woodward, 1999). Regarding (i) Woodward builds on her own experience of an 'emotional attunement and mutual recognition' (1999: 149) with her grandmother as a little girl: 'missing were the stormy emotions of envy, fear, hostility, guilt, and jealousy intrinsic to the nuclear family of Freudian psychoanalysis' she writes (p. 148). A theoretical construct that represents more generations would also allot a place to the old woman in psychoanalytic theory, where Freud wrote of women past child-bearing age as 'elderly' and sexually invisible: 'post-historical' (p. 150) as Woodward reminds us. This would also reflect the reality of grandparental involvement for thousands of families, as we have noted, although at the same time this is carefully circumscribed, in expert discourses, with developmental models stressing that whilst helpful, this contribution should not be more than supplementary to mothers' care: 'the quality of maternal care in the home' remains the single most important influence 'on children's emotional and behavioural development' (Stein et al., 2012: 677). In such discourses extended grandparental involvement is linked to hyperactivity, among other things (Ferguson, 2008); however, hyperactivity is common in the context of disadvantaged social situations, themselves more likely to use grandparental care, calling into question the causative nature of grandparents' care itself .

In terms of (ii) Wendy Lustbader (2011) takes Gullette's theory of second individuation further and shows it to be an ongoing process that continues up until, and even after, parental death. She notes that youth 'obscures' the personhood of parents and grandparents, covering them in the mystique of their parental omnipotence, 'then, somewhere in our thirties and forties, we start to get glimpses of our parents and grandparents as actual people in the world. This is the beginning of knowing them beyond the role they played for us.' The obscuring, of course, works both ways, but 'both parties become more visible to each other through the approach of death'. She finishes: 'Gratitude towards parents, in its fullest contours, is almost always belated. Long after a parent has died, understanding keeps on coming' (2011: 22–4).

Care-giving throughout the life course

Whilst the relationship between generations has been depicted in terms of friction, and the old as an obstacle to the progress of the young, this has its counterpart in family relationships (the third aspect of the generation concept). Oft-asked questions in this vein include: What are the limits of carers' responsibility and of the compact between generations therein? How can we balance the 'rights' of carer and care-receiver? In health care policy: how do we facilitate the care-receivers' autonomy by setting up care-receivers as employers of their care-givers? And, bespeaking of the entrepreneurial self, how do people learn to self-care preventatively through life and also 'manage' their self-care in the midst of chronic illness (in order to preserve autonomy)? However, alternative perspectives arising from empirical data will reveal another set of practices, from ongoing intergenerational interdependence, to a general sharing in values, suggesting that there are more interconnections and mutual involvement than a focus on conflict or antagonism, or on making assessments according to the keystone of 'independence', can do justice. One example of this is that of caregiving that extends across generations. The problem is that, because of the ontology that we have inherited from Descartes, including an accentuation of traits of independence and self-actualization, together with other influences such as the Kantian separation of moral reasoning as an autonomous sphere containing universal principles, we are taught to see it not as interdependence but as dependence *versus* independence. Tronto (1993) has explained how one consequences of the separation of morality from politics early in modernity was to relegate moral sentiments to the private realm associated with women and accord lesser importance to each of the latter. This, meanwhile, helps preserve the image of the powerful, public, 'self-made man' (Tronto, 1993). It also categorizes care and care-givers according to how far they are from this ideal. So, for example, care-giving for older people is defined differently than care for children, as in the following definition by Carers UK which defines carers as those who 'provide unpaid care by looking after an ill, frail or disabled family member, friend or partner' (Carers UK, 2012). And whilst Carers UK has come up with this definition with good intent, nevertheless, it contains at its heart a normative distinction, a definition that separates it from care given to children, despite the considerable overlap in the nature of the tasks involved; it is a definition that also separates this form of care for the care (financial, emotional, practical) that, as we have seen, many parents extend to their children well into the latter's adult lives. This implies, within the developmental arc with which we are familiar, that what is normal or unremarkable in childhood, is problematic, or remarkable, later in life. However, if we look at who carers are, we will find that whilst they are mostly middle-aged women, there are also on the one hand many older people caring for other older people, and on the other there are child carers. People at all points in the life course, then, are both giving and receiving care (as defined by Carers UK as well as more broadly). It is unfortunate that feminism contributed towards partitioning off this form of care from the care for children. Historically, as a political movement it focused attention on the inequities of women's domestic labour within the home, by which it meant childcare and housewifedom, and it was not until the groundbreaking work of Finch and Groves (1980) that this concern was extended to other duties, such as the care of older relatives. However, feminist approaches still discriminate against older women, for example by emphasizing the 'burden' placed on mid-life women by these obligations, overlooking all lifelong interconnections in terms of care given and received.

Both the invisibility of care and normative assumptions about who cares and why, within families and age groups, means the fact that many young carers are caring for their parents, siblings or grandparents may be overlooked. Where children and young people 'transgress' social roles by providing care for their parents, this often results in a lack of recognition and support from social and healthcare organizations in their care-giving role. It has been suggested that there may be up to 700,000 young carers in the UK, four times as many as registered officially in the census (Children's Society, 2013). Whilst social services fail to identify them, further factors keep them hidden, including families fearing they may be taken into care if identified and young carers themselves fearing stigmatization from peers. In combination, these factors result in the fact that 'children are often not "seen" as part of an adult's assessment for support and disabled adults not recognized as parents' (Children's Society, 2013). Despite a commitment by the 2008 Carers Strategy to protect children from 'inappropriate caring roles' research found that many missed school, which impacted on their employment prospects, and they often felt unable to leave home because of their parent's need for care and assistance.

These normative assumptions also contribute to the jarring imperatives of individualization on the one hand and affective ties and moral obligations to others on the other, which, combined with not just paid employment but the requirement to develop oneself as an individual, lie at the heart of the clashing configurations characteristic of late modernity, for women in particular. Fine (2012) suggests that in practice such conflicts – which see both disabled people and carers as having 'rights' and 'choice' – can be resolved, 'within the public sphere' (p. 7). However, women's subjectivities, shaped by the experience of being mothered by a woman, and by the compulsory altruism that is still a part and parcel of policy rhetoric, propel them towards self-sacrifice, or at least to service, more than do men's, and whilst there is policy which increasingly (but in a limited way) recognizes the individual rights of carers, at least for support and respite and some self-actualization (e.g. through the Carers (Recognition and Services) Act 1995 and the Carers' Strategy) ultimately the role of care-giver is not one that in the most part is either chosen or perceived as voluntary (as Carers UK acknowledges). Whether or not it can be made to be part of an individualized and self-actualized life project is then very much dependent on the social, cultural and economic capital of the carers involved (Pickard, 2010).

However, interdependence and care also co-exist in creative tension with individuation, a creative tension that is (albeit exacerbated by institutions and intellectual theories) part of the paradox and ambiguity of lived experience. That is, it is important that interdependence not be viewed as the opposite of autonomy (as feminist epistemology tends to suggest). Not only is emotional and intellectual independence the ability to grow as a unique individual, involving some measure of self-determination, a requirement of true maturity, it is also essential for combating the strongly infantilizing tendencies of society, including one's (often middle-class) over-solicitous parents. Kate Bolick puts it thus:

> Obviously I was independent; independence was my generation's birth right. Yet all through my comings and goings I'd been looked after, listened to, accompanied, coddled, whether by parents or boyfriends; essentially, I'd led the life of a child. It wasn't merely that my identity was constructed entirely out of my relationships with other people – my relationships *were* my identity. My relationships took the place of myself.... I wondered: Who was I on my own? How could I possibly become an adult if I didn't know how to answer that? (2015: 72)

This adds complex layers to the meaning of the feminization of the workforce and reminds us of the opportunity that paid work offers women, in whatever poor conditions, to claim a personhood of their own. Though with time and normalization it is easy to see such low-paid work as oppressive, we can remind ourselves of the exhilaration on the part of women for whom the experience of earning money of their own was a new one; for example, women in South Wales who took over the breadwinner role following the coalmine closures of the 1980s found that they were in fact happier to submit to the tyranny of the workplace than to the tyranny of individual men (Seabrook, 2013).

Conclusion

Is there a way that we might see age relations differently from that picture presented in policy, in the media and in our conceptual thinking, with its stress on conflict and division, on struggle and competition over limited goods and resources, whether these be jobs, benefits, health or beauty? One way forward might be not to deny conflict between ages and stages altogether, yet to identify the underpinning causes of this, as well as to give greater attention to the commonalities. Although there are contingent, manipulated causes that we have already noted, in that governments and others benefit from the impression of an essential conflict of interests based on age, this is not to deny that there is also something more profound about conflict of this kind, as illustrated by dramas like King Lear (and grasped at this level also by Freudian theory, with its emphasis on universal and eternal struggle between the parent–child generation (Moody, 2007); the 'progress' Mannheim thinks can only result from new generations is one Freud (2000) felt could only occur through the psychic separation from the parental generation). The experience of a violent rending-asunder, moreover, is something that can be felt even through the most gentle and loving of separations. This suggests that a sensitive portrayal, somewhere between denial and exaggeration of conflict, is what is needed (Moody, 2007) one that recognizes the interplay and balance required. Above all, we should not seek to filter out paradox. Our intellectual models require fine-tuning so as to help us both look for and understand the ubiquity of ambivalence, plurality and something other than an either/or classification in our lived experience

I have suggested that the life course perspective has most potential, reconfigured to give greater emphasis to its dynamic character, seeing stages as akin to shifting perspectives or motifs; a carousel rather than either a wheel or staircase, in that there is movement up and down as well as round and round. In acknowledging the contradictory character of our relationships and holding, rather than attempting to resolves the tensions, therein, the effect will be to enrich our understanding of the shades and nuances in our relationships with others over time, opening up an entirely different vision for age relations.

BOX 10.2

Examples of intergenerational conflict arguments

Recession is worse for the young than the old:

http://www.theguardian.com/commentisfree/2013/jun/14/pensioners-better-off-young-people-suffering

Policy supports the old over the young:

Harris, J. (2015) 'They want more than we did' – how the Tories made age our biggest divide, *The Guardian* 17 July, accessible at http://www.theguardian.com/society/2015/jul/17/old-young-age-divide-christchurch

Sodha, S. (2015) Baby boomers versus the rest: is age the great new divide? *The Observer*, 12 April.

And the opposite view:

Wilson, D. (2014) Why I fear our next war will be against our own children, *Daily Mail*, 17 July, accessible at http://www.dailymail.co.uk/news/article-2631251/Why-I-fear-war-against-children-A-drain-society-Clogging-homes-Soaking-state-cash-routine-insults-hurled-pensioners-resentful-young-Now-one-senior-writer-enough.html

CHAPTER SUMMARY

- This chapter looked at the consequences of the concept of 'generation', ana-lysing relationships between ages and stages on the macro and micro levels.

- We focused on the concept of intergenerational justice and theoretical models of the mother–child relationship, highlighting how in each case an emphasis on the conflictual nature of these relationships obscures other structural systems of inequality.

- The chapter suggests that the use of other models would help identify the presence of co-operation as well as conflict and of commonality as well as difference in interests between ages that, by their rich complexity and mutual interdependence, will help undermine age ideology.

Further questions

1. How does age and class ideology work through generational discourses and practices?

2. Choosing a generation (such as the boomers, Generation X, etc.), discuss the usefulness of this concept in terms of understanding identity, inequality and dif-ference with other generations.

3. Describe an example in the media of policy discussions conducted in terms of generational fairness.

Talking point

In the UK whilst some of the wealthiest people are aged 65 and over, so too are some of the poorest (Phillipson, 2013). We also find that in the UK nearly all the top 1 per cent of earners and half the next 9 per cent go to private schools and only 1 per cent of the remaining 90 per cent have ever attended private school (Dorling, 2014). Children from the top group are six times more likely to go to university and six times more likely to stay in the top group than are those born at the bottom likely to rise to the top (Roberts, 2011). Meanwhile, consider this generational discourse by novelist and journalist Tim Lott who calculated his 'baby boomer' generation had a large set of social and economic advantages over his teenage children's generation but that in the end this was trumped by one (obvious, uncontestable) factor in the latter's favour: 'Because apart from anything else, my children have one immense advantage over old people, despite my generationally-assisted wealth. They're not old' (Lott, 2015). How does this example of the 'fortunate to be young' theme work ideologically when juxtaposed with the above indication of intra-generational inequality?

—— Key texts ————————————————————————————

The following books provide an introduction to the main issues of importance regarding the **relationship between class, generations and life course**: Gilleard, C. and Higgs, P. (2005) *Contexts of Ageing: class, cohort and community*, Cambridge: Polity Press; Callahan, D. (1987) *Setting Limits: medical goals in an ageing society*, New York: Simon and Schuster; Mullan, P. (2002) *The Imaginary Time Bomb: why an ageing population is not a social problem*, London: I.B. Tauris; Willetts, D. (2010) *The Pinch: how the baby boomers took their children's future – and why they should give it back*, London: Atlantic Books. **Families and care-giving** are discussed in Dalley, G. (1988) *Ideologies of Caring*, London: Macmillan Education; and **mother–child relationships** in Chodorow, N. (1994) *Femininities, Masculinities, Sexualities: Freud and beyond*, Kentucky: University of Kentucky Press; also for a depiction of these relationships later in life see Gullette, M. (1997) *Declining to Decline*, Charlottesville: University of Virginia Press, especially Chapter 7 'My mother at mid-life'.

Further resources

The Intergenerational Foundation website is a source of information for some of the debates noted above: see http://www.if.org.uk/

Notes

1. These identities are both socially and historically contingent as we can see if we compare them with the identifying/labelling of generations in Japan where the 1960s generation/cohort is called the 'first baby boomer generation; the 1970s 'the apathy generation'; the 1980s: the 'new species' (individualistic) generation; the 1990s: 'the second baby boomer generation' (Coulmas, 2007).

2. Elisabeth Badinter is a vocal proponent of the 'good mother' as gender backlash position. Interestingly, she focuses on France where the fertility rate is an impressive 2.0 children per woman, as compared with the UK's 1.8 and several other European countries' 1.4 (including Spain, Germany, Italy). She sees 'good motherhood' as regressive, rendering 'equality of the sexes impossible and women's freedom irrelevant': see http://www.theguardian.com/world/2010/feb/12/france-feminism-elisabeth-badinter

11

TELLING OUR OWN STORIES: DEVELOPING AGE CONSCIOUSNESS AND AUTHENTIC AGE IDENTITIES

Background: age ideology, my grandmother and I

In the first chapter I suggested that my own interest in age studies developed from my relationship with my grandmother. One of the powerful things it introduced for me was the knowledge of contradiction between my lived experience and the explanatory models I possessed. An example is the way that very early on in life I learned to associate age with fragility, vulnerability, decline and illness. Although Nana demonstrated all the signs of impressive physical robustness – she was digging her own flowerbeds at the age of eighty and carrying a full coalscuttle in from the shed – my parents often spoke in front of me about her 'bad heart'. On her part, I watched how my grandmother would talk about her dizzy spells, her breathlessness and her enfeeblement, especially when my parents and I hadn't called round to see her in a while. She used such means to draw attention to herself and it gave her a certain tragic power in her relationship with my parents, a way of staking a claim on their time. I saw how it sometimes (but only if used in moderation) achieved its intended purpose of conjuring up my mother's kindest face, my father's taciturn solicitude. Secondly, although my grandmother established for me some wonderfully positive age associations, these were overwhelmed discursively in the overall impression I had of ageing as something to pity and dread, as I shaped my perceptions of her in accordance with the narratives and images I picked up around me. On the one hand, whilst my parents trailed a wake of chaos around them, the scent of cigarettes and perfume just a little too brash, the words spoken a little too loudly after the occasional drunken party, the slammed door shuddering in its wooden frame, I took refuge in the tranquillity of my grandmother's kitchen. Here was a haven beyond the whirling carnival of life, beyond the clamouring demands of family, work, sound and fury and I would often muse about whether it were possible to go straight from being a child to being old like her, missing out what lay in between (which frankly didn't appeal). On the other, part of the reassuring aspect of my grandmother's company, without a doubt, was that it encouraged me to see the ageing process as a straight line that extended in one direction only, the generations marching forward in lockstep, but with me tucked safely in at the back of the line. '*Nothing to worry about yet*', went the reassuring whisper in my ear. The deal seemed clear: accept the terms of the age system and you would be protected from the embrace of the Hag, for now at least.

Age ideology meant that none of us – not me, not my parents and not even my grandmother – thought to question the meaning of age and stage. My parents were not immune themselves to feelings of vulnerability; all that power and glamour and busyness I perceived in their grown-up lives perhaps only intermittently distracted them from the foreknowledge of their own decline. I remember how devastated I was when the hand-made birthday card I had spent hours decorating for my father was met with a somewhat frosty reception and a look upon his face that was inscrutable, sealed and unsmiling. 'Dear Daddy,' I had written, the big shaky letters newly joined up, sparkling with clumpy red glitter, 'Happy forty-second birthday!' Later, my mother explained his reaction to me. 'It's not nice to mention someone's age,' she said. 'Not when you're a grown-up.' 'But why not?' I asked, fighting back tears, and absolutely not understanding what I had done wrong because every year on my birthday the big snowdrift of cards, courtesy of kind relatives, that lay on the doormat waiting for me to scoop them up, proclaimed my age; some even had stickers and badges on them with which I might declare my new age to others. 'It's alright when you're seven,' explained my mother, patiently. 'But grown-ups don't want to be reminded.' I still didn't understand; but I never forgot. Indeed, I returned to this moment many times subsequently in my life, turning it over in my mind as birthday after birthday came and went until the day came when I finally understood.

AIMS OF THE CHAPTER

- We will consider the nature of age consciousness, why it is helpful in challenging age ideology and how to develop it.

- We will look at methodologies and techniques for developing age consciousness through autobiographical reflection, highlighting the practice of keeping an age diary.

(Continued)

(Continued)

- We will then critically examine some literary examples of autobiographical reflection on age, encompassing a range of perspectives which may include both succumbing to age ideology and challenging it in the same piece.

- We will identify some tropes in contemporary fiction that may further assist in generating an age consciousness outside the assumptions that underpin development and other modernist paradigms.

What is age consciousness?

How could the individual members of my family have thought differently? How could we have used this disparity between what we saw and what we were encouraged to believe, to critique and challenge the 'truths' handed down to us? In this next section I am going to suggest that such a challenge will elude us where our own age identities are uncertain and that the key lies in developing an authentic age consciousness. Gullette (1997; 2004) suggests that age consciousness signifies subjective awareness of one's age, at all parts of the life course, without this being determined (though it might be influenced) by dominant stereotypes. It is in parts intuitive, reflexive, taken-for-granted, critical, shared with others and unique, relating to the characteristics of particular 'presents' in one's life understood with reference to one's personal past, and projections for the future. One of the main distinctions of this reflexive practice that I will highlight is that between authentic and inauthentic elements of our age identities. To take the latter first, 'inauthentic' age consciousness comprises the many (sometimes contradictory) age associations we are 'given' by society and accept as 'natural', the way things, apparently, are: the clichéd messages that tell us, for example, that the days of youth are the best life has to offer and the time to 'accomplish' the things that, at some other point (once 40 but perhaps later than that today) located 'over the hill' of life will be 'too late'. When we are tired or angry it is too easy to grab one of the ready-to-wear assumptions just within reach from the rail of tired old cultural clichés, as when we blame aches and pains on our age, or fall into snap judgements on strangers. Thinking get out of the way 'stupid old bag!' when an old lady slows us down on a crowded pavement, reveals not just a burst of impatience but a whole worldview of who, and what, is good and valuable, or else ridiculous and irrelevant; who has right of passage through the day. These age-related ideas are very similar to the messages that once told us that a woman's 'natural' place was in the home, specifically the kitchen and they are equally as ideological in origin and purpose. This message is 'a voice in our head', persistent, even if we are frustrated by it. If, after critical reflection, some of these messages make sense to us, all well and good; but we want to avoid their being unconsciously adopted, and thereby used to manipulate us, by becoming the 'default position' in terms of an 'age code' which we take for granted (Gullette, 1997). Age consciousness can also help us avoid the infantilization that so many cultural themes conspire to encourage: not just the meaningless work and framework of consumerism but the small things we may not even notice like the trend for adult colouring books or the adult craze for skateboarding as if one were being encouraged to respond to adversity or austerity by creeping back into the refuge of one's own childhood (Burkeman, 2015). Age consciousness, however, is not a construction existing in discourse alone; it is real, and tangible, in relation to the journey of one's life. The aim is not to deconstruct it away but rather to find out what it really is, at any one point in time. In the movie *Sideways*, the character Maya's discussion of the 'life of wine', provides an interesting metaphor for what we are trying to locate in our own lives, when she explains: 'I like how wine continues to evolve. Like if I opened a bottle of wine today it would taste different than if I'd opened it on any other day, because a bottle of wine is actually alive. And it's constantly evolving and gaining complexity.' If we opened the 'bottle of our life' today, how would it taste? How would that differ from its taste this time last year? Ten years ago/twenty years from now? Maya's description also calls to mind the medieval sensibility's 'agedness of the soul' a judgement of substance not form, and one freed from the linear notion of progress.

Whatever the messages of age ideology, in practice one might come into one's own at 70, or at 21, or at 35; one's personal trajectory might soar then descend, only to rise again, all the while particular themes weaving in and out of the foreground like a contrapuntal harmony or fugue, or it may gently drift along steadily for most of life; one may find order in one's life according to work, or relationships, or bodily events or ideas and causes; reaching 50 may be a crisis for some but a great achievement for those whose parent(s) died before that age. But however we understand it, almost undoubtedly our old age will be better than we expect (Lustbader, 2011). When, on a vacationing coach excursion overseas, everyone was asked to say a few words about themselves, Wendy Lustbader spontaneously decided to 'speak the truth about age':

> I called out to a bus full of world travellers, all between the ages of eighteen and twenty-four. 'These are the worst years of your lives.' Relief spread across the rows of faces at this stark and unexpected pronouncement.... My husband and I could have been the parents of everyone else on the bus, including the driver. 'Everything gets better – you just have to get through your twenties,' I emphasized, urging them to be patient with these years of struggle. At the next rest stop, I was swarmed by the thankful.... One person after another declared gratitude, each marvelling at having never heard anyone say this before. Praise of youth had been pushed at them constantly, from all directions. 'If this is really the best,' said a 20-year-old from Denmark, 'I don't even want the rest of it.' (2011: 1–2)

My mother is not untypical of an older woman who, freed from onerous caring duties that had gone on for more than half her life when my dad died, experienced an enormous enjoyment of life and growth and freedom in her early 80s. Within months of my dad's death, she moved cities, buying a flat within walking distance of a much cherished Buddhist study group. She began a life more free and fulfilling than anything she had ever experienced before, including in her youth in misogynistic, socially restricted Francoist Spain. She had escaped from this via marriage to my English dad, who was diagnosed with a degenerative disease seven years into the marriage, and who became a lifelong invalid shortly thereafter. For most of her life, she cared for him, and was a wonderful mother, and on top of that brought in the only money that came into our household during my childhood, staying up late to read her books after everyone else had gone to bed. So suddenly, at 82, she found herself with a life crammed with friends and solitary reflection, with serious study and gay frivolity, with excitement and with meditative equipoise. She was free to please herself, to put herself first. Unfazed by the fact that most of her neighbours in the apartment block were in their twenties and thirties, she made friends with many of them, who visited her for tea, sympathy and life advice. It was as if, in her widowhood, fifty years had fallen off her shoulders overnight, like a too-heavy cloak. It was almost like a life lived backwards, the gaiety and fun all coming last. 'Think of me as a person,' she pleaded with me one day, 'not your mother' giving me permission, in my forties, to grow up.

Experience and the standpoint of age(s)

Dorothy Smith observes: 'A disjuncture can arise between the world as it is known directly in experience and as it is shared with others, and the ideas and images fabricated externally to that everyday world and provided as a means to think and image it' (1987: 55). She goes on to explain that addressing this gap lies at the heart of consciousness-raising as it was originally practised in gender studies and second-wave feminism of the 1960s and 1970s.

This process of consciousness-raising is just as crucial to generating knowledge of age oppression as it was to gender oppression in second-wave feminism. This is made clear by the following quote from Betty Friedan, in her search for positive experiences of growing old. She recounts:

> I started my quest for the fountain of age by simply looking for people who seemed to be 'vitally ageing' as compared to the image of deterioration and decline that seemed to be the norm.... I had myself so accepted the image of deterioration and decline that I expected such vitally ageing people to be *exceptional*. Even though our society's dread of age, its dreary or blanked-out image of the ageing, seemed to deny their very existence, even with so many elements of society seeming to conspire to prevent them from continuing to use their human abilities after sixty-five, I found that *they were everywhere*. (1993: 70; original emphases)

However, lived experience cannot thereby be approached 'naively'; it is important to interpret it, or in other words, to politicize it, if it is to be more than simply of 'therapeutic' value to the individual concerned. Standpoints emerge from subjectivities crafted from structural and ideological factors across the life course without which there could be no 'I' to experience them, and thus we begin our view of the world from an identity position, whatever that, or rather those, may be. At the same time this is never just *the result* of these external inscriptions. Nevertheless, awareness of a disjunction between lived experience and official discourses may not necessarily result in a revolutionary consciousness, and indeed it may rather be the case that we experience ourselves as 'split'; in the case of women in a hegemonic gender regime this may mean holding a 'youthful gaze' whilst being old ourselves within the terms of that gaze (and which is akin to the idea of the fragmented class consciousness discussed in an earlier chapter). Rowbotham writes in her book *Woman's Consciousness Man's World*:

> We were allowed to play with their words, their ideas, their culture as long as we pretended we were men.... One part of ourselves mocked another.... Part of us leapt over into their world, part of us stayed behind at home. (1973: 30)

Hollway elaborates on the process in her own autobiographical account:

> To compete with men… necessitated a negative definition of myself as a woman and it reproduced the signifier 'woman' unchanged. Women were a group I put myself outside of. When I made generalizations about women (almost always derogatory) I did not include myself in the group I was talking about. (1984: 229)

We can see this same rejection in older people regarding their age. In conversation with the interviewer in a study of life in old age an 86-year-old said:

> 'See a poor old soul wi' a walkin' stick… you know you do see some terrible poor old souls…' She, however, did not think of herself as old 'and I've no intention of doing it,' she said, 'I have intentions of staying as young as I feel,' and she concluded 'I don't feel my age.' (Thompson et al., 1991: 129)

And the following is an extract from Sharon Kaufman's interview with Ethel, aged 84.

> SK: I want to know what it feels like to be over 70.

> Ethel: I'm not over 70. People tell me I look 60 or 65. And I feel like that too. I don't feel over 70 (presents a picture of herself at age 29).

> SK: Do you relate to that woman?

> Ethel: I feel the same now as I did then, oh yes. (Kaufman, 1986: 12)

In such cases, rejecting one's age can be shorthand for rejecting the derisory judge-ments that accompany this age and instead stressing continuity of self that withstands the ageist society's efforts to undo those threads. It is equivalent to claim-ing the 'male' point of view, for personhood is both male and youthful. That is how I read the following account of Sadie, aged 80, a participant in an ethnographic study of beauty practices in old age, looking at a photograph of herself aged 32 or 33. She says: 'I don't think I look too different. I really don't, because my features are about the same... I don't think I've changed that much' (Furman, 1999: 13).

Telling our own stories

Much of what I have been saying concerns the importance of choice – choosing what to accept about an age identity and what to reject – and, as I am only too aware, the irony of this is that it fits seamlessly with the tenets of an individualized society where the necessity to choose is a mode through which we are governed. This is the society in which Beck and Beck-Gernsheim write: 'Life, death, gender, corporeality, identity, religion, marriage, parenthood, social ties – all are becoming decidable down to the small print' (2002: 5) – and Giddens, of course, went on to suggest ageing itself as a choice. It is then important to consider carefully not just the act of choosing but the substance of the choices made, with reference to their potential to increase personal liberation, empowerment and flourishing on the one hand, or else to function as a technology of the self implicated in practices of domination, on the other. In this context the decision to opt for Botox in one's thirties or even twenties or a facelift in one's fifties, or to diet constantly or exercise compulsively, is a complex act, and can only derive its meaning in the context of an individual's life, culture, social position-ing, biographical history and views of the good life (Bordo, 1995). But how, then, given the pressure to remain youthful, does that shape age consciousness?

Standpoint theory's central claim is that 'all knowledge springs from experience and that women's experience carries with it special knowledge and that this knowledge is necessary to challenge oppression' (Skeggs, 1997: 25). This approach was developed by Hartsock (1983) and others in a Marxist orientation suggesting that a position of subordination, oppression or marginalization privileges the oppressed with the lucid-ity necessary to see through bourgeois mystification. Although their focus was on gender, it also suggests that the perspective of old age, particularly where it intersects with other experiences of oppression relating to class and gender, might also enable such lucidity. However, it is as well to correct the impression that such understanding *only* comes with the passage of time and thus is itself dependent on achieving a certain age. *All* age stages admit unique insights not readily accessible to others. For example, my autobiographical experience with my grandmother suggests the insights that childhood can bring, including an understanding of the affinity between youth and age, my tacit insight into the way the 'second age' of adulthood regulated both of us, whilst I was able to see myself in my grandmother and perceive our commonalities across the passage of time, in a way my parents could not (or perhaps, no longer could or would). Having said that it, remains true that it is harder for the privileged to critique a system in which they are accorded status and distinction as are the young and those in their prime-of-life within the parameters of our own ageist society.

It is similar to feminist consciousness-raising, but it is not the same. Indeed, there is a big difference in that one was once young and one day one will be old. This means that one's age consciousness is not fixed: it has experienced the world from the standpoint of a child and from a young person, it has been labelled differently and labelled others differently, many times over. In addition, age does not exist in a vacuum: I am a woman, professional, white and healthy at that. But still this essential mobility, this experience of being one thing then being something entirely different, separated by the passage of time, yet unified by my experience of being me, is something I have found incredibly useful in helping me understand the constructedness of so many of our social categories, our judgements, our truths.

Putting all this together, the generating of authentic age consciousness will also facilitate us, in this age of extraordinary subjectivity, as Skeggs calls it, in *telling our own stories*. In the process of challenging age ideology throughout the life course, telling stories of a positive old age is especially important, according to Andrews (1999; 2009). There are two reasons for this, she suggests: (i) so that older people will be able to articulate their own tales with confidence and not assume they are alone in feeling and experiencing as they do, as the earlier quote from Friedan suggested; (ii) to prepare younger people for their own inexorable ageing into old age so that they will not see this in the way Beauvoir captures when she writes: 'An absurd inner voice whispers that *that* will never happen to us – when *that* happens it will no longer be ourselves that it happens to' (1970: 11). A successful story of ageing possesses, Andrews suggests (2009), the following characteristics. Firstly, it helps bridge the gap between the old and the not-yet-old, and encourages individuals to view old age as part and parcel of the wholeness of the life course. Secondly, it diminishes the boundaries between self and others and between past and present in one's own life. In other words, it emphasizes continuity-in-change relationality and the process of life as one of becoming. It is especially the not-yet-old who need to go in search of models of successful ageing, in order that they may begin to start building towards their own, starting with the selves they create at younger ages. It is true that age ideology remains difficult to challenge. If resistance is possible, for example, it is not easy to know what this might amount to. Gullette suggests that at least:

> *After* age theory, people will know better what degree of decline, if any, they're experiencing... Decline... would not be default narrative... I might or might not rank myself higher on many measures: I might or might not tell a progress story about it. (1997: 216–17, original emphasis)

Generating age consciousness by itself aids us in at least realizing that we have the power to make choices over the plots we live by, whether or not we actually have the courage to do so.

Tools and techniques for developing age consciousness

Having set out this explanatory framework, we are now in a position to discuss ways of developing age consciousness. One of the most powerful methods, according to Gullette (1997; 2004), is that of keeping an age diary. We look at this first and then consider specific techniques which can be used both within the context of the age diary and everyday life.

1. The age diary

The journal is a place to record observations and reflections about occasions in everyday life wherein age reveals itself as a salient factor in interchanges with others or in events that you witnessed or took part in or assessments that you made about situations or events. These may include your reaction to a character in a film or book in terms both of the age of that character and the author's depiction of that age. It may also be a way for you to deconstruct the factors that go into your habitual assumptions and expectations regarding the way you interact with same and other-age others. Examples of questions you might ask yourself include: How are your interactions with others of a different or similar age characterized by differences in language use or other conversational styles? How does 'difference' make itself apparent for example in: (a) expectations of roles; (b) assumptions/stereotypes made about each other; (c) emotions generated; (d) comparative physical appearance/self-presentation of individuals of different ages? These sorts of reflections will result in a growing consciousness of the role age and other factors are playing, separately and in combination.

2. Switching age perspectives with others

A helpful exercise is to switch perspective with one's mother or grandmother or daughter, one's middle-aged lecturer or the very old neighbour next door and see what difference this makes to the way one judges events. This could include events in the news, policy, gossip, or major life decisions.

3. Return to a movie/book that was important at a particular time in one's life

What difference does the passage of time make in terms of the content/resonance of the book or film? How does it help recapture a former age consciousness as well as crystalize one's current consciousness by contrast and comparison? Can one more easily see the way one was 'meant to feel' at that time which may have contrasted with the way one actually felt? How do/did you perceive other life stages through the prism of the characters/scenes?

4. Reflect on age-autobiographical writing

In this section I will discuss age-autobiographical reflections written at specific periods in three writers' lives: early mid-life and looking back to youth (Elizabeth Wurtzel); late-middle age and both looking back to youth and ahead to old age (Simone de Beauvoir); old age, looking back through the life course (Donald Hall). The aim is that, through critical but sensitive attention to this material, one might proceed more easily to critical thinking about one's own age autobiography and indeed I will close this section with some questions that can get you thinking about this.

Elizabeth Wurtzel: 'The end of the Age of Beauty'

At the age of 41 looking back over her life so far, Elizabeth Wurtzel in an auto-biographical piece published in *Elle* magazine (2009), who acquired youthful fame with her feisty memoir of depression at Harvard and beyond, *Prozac Nation*, high-lights a number of themes common to the post-feminist gender regime. In particular we see the way age regulates the gender regime, dividing older from younger women and older women from their younger selves. Like the Ivy League graduates we met earlier who confessed to William Deresiewicz that they could not bear to limit their identities by choosing one definite career path over another, preferring the fluidity of possibility, Wurtzel similarly could not bring herself to choose a husband. She could not commit to the wonderful boyfriend she had in her twenties although his good humour balanced her own darkness, sweetening her melancholy, in a way, she now feels, might have saved her from a lot of the turmoil she later endured. It was the treacherous sense of 'potential' inherent to (gilded) youth that obstructed her good sense and she reflects:

> I was temporarily credentialed with this delicate, yummy thing – youth,
> beauty, whatever – and my window of opportunity for making the most
> of it was so small, so brief. I wanted to smash through that glass pane
> and enjoy it, make it last, feel released.

With commitment an 'iron maiden', she omitted to cash in her winning hand, which was youth. In fact, in describing her life, Wurtzel's plot does not follow a uniform 'growth' or 'coming to maturity' plot; she was, she says, a 'terrifically brooding and mature teenager, then a whiny and puerile adult' and only now in her 40s does she feel she has come of age and blossomed into her true self. Unfortunately, however, despite being an infinitely better proposition for any man, a 'stable adult professional' with passion but without her former craziness, no longer 'deeply depressed, drugged, sensitive and nasty all at once', yet she has lost her main value: that of youth. She reflects:

> by the time you've got all this great wisdom, you don't get to be young
> anymore. And in this world, that's just about the worst thing that can
> happen – especially to a woman... I am sadly 41. I am past my perfect years.

This is both true and staggeringly untrue, of course; true, in the conventional, ideological sense, for a woman in the terms of the age and gender regime; yet contradicted by all that Wurtzel has just said about herself. Yet she persists with the notion that she has squandered something priceless: 'Oh, to be 25 again and get it right,' she mourns, and like Beauvoir in the next piece we can see that she is still not done with the youthful gaze and its particular judgement on who she is and might become.

Simone de Beauvoir: 'the horror of becoming old'

We have already noted in earlier chapters how Simone de Beauvoir dreaded ageing and old age from a very early point in her life. In her memoir *Force of Circumstance* (1968: 670–74), written when she was 55, she tackles many interesting themes relating to age and ageing, including: the way strangers of various ages label her and she them; her view of other life stages; the age markers that indicate that she is moving to a different point in the age hierarchy; her deepest, unconscious feelings towards age alongside her conscious, rational ones. One theme she touches on is her sense of temporality, of moving through the life course in a way that has a tangible, embodied aspect which she describes through spatial metaphors as if she were moving along a mapped-out road, with a sense of a future massed up ahead and a past behind. Interestingly, she discusses how she had always lived for the future, for the moment of greatest success which she felt was always a way ahead of her; suddenly, at mid-life, she feels it is behind her. The point is that never was it something experienced immediately, in the here-and-now. In this, she has much in common with the contemporary 'Girl', the successful young woman for many of whom the moment of motherhood is always ahead of them; until the day it is behind them. Thus she writes:

> I have lived stretched out towards the future and now I am recapitulating, looking back over the past. It's as though the present somehow got left out. For years I thought my work still lay ahead, and now I find it is behind me: there was no moment when it took place.

Beginning a book gives her a sense of renewal: 'I am a beginner again…. Creation is adventure, it is youth and liberty', but when the project is completed, time swallows her up again, 'I collide again with my age.'

   As with so many aspects of the situated body, the body situated in time is gendered through and through and is another indication of time inequality, of the way that women can never quite be at home in hegemonic time. The present is never something experienced as 'possessed', or mastered by even successful women such as Beauvoir, but eludes them, in various important ways. Time oppresses her; she is terrified of the future; she has a repetitive dream in which she is a young woman again, who wakes from a nightmare in which she had dreamt she was in her 50s. What huge relief to wake to the discovery that she is only thirty! But then – crueller than cruel – she wakes in real life and realizes that it is no nightmare; she *is* fifty-four. This is a nightmare for her because she feels that it signifies that all the sensual things of life, those pleasures and intensities connected with embodiment, with sexuality, are over; never again will she have a lover, or enjoy a strenuous mountain walk, or the ecstatic fatigue that follows; 'it's strange,' she reflects, 'not to be a body anymore' and we know from her concept of the 'situated body' that she means this as a social fact, yet one lived and experienced as a biological fact also.

Although she describes how she has accepted the fate of ageing – 'not my body alone but my imagination too has accepted that' – it is still the gaze of youth she directs upon her body-self; thus, this transformation is accompanied by an inevitable sense of loss. With such a gaze trained upon the future she feels 'the only thing that can happen now at the same time new and important is misfortune'. These are the words she puts into the mouth of the (unnamed) heroine of her tragic novella *The Woman Destroyed*:

> What nonsense, this intoxicating notion of progress, of upward move-ment, that I had cherished, for now the moment of collapse was at hand! It had already begun. And now it would be very fast and very slow: we were going to turn into really old people. (Beauvoir, 2006: 60)

At the end of this novella, the narrator seems poised on the brink of a decision: either to accept the inevitability of ageing by shifting her subjectivity, discarding the youthful gaze that has been her viewpoint till now, or else hold onto this viewpoint whilst submitting to the judgement of her youthful gaze:

> Would the dread of ageing take hold of me again? Do not look too far ahead. Ahead there were the horrors of death and farewells: it was false teeth, sciatica, infirmity, intellectual barrenness, loneliness in a strange world that we would no longer understand and that would carry on without us. Shall I succeed in not lifting my gaze to those horizons? (2006: 70–71)

In Beauvoir's memoir the same question is posed but not yet resolved.

Donald Hall: 'age and the beard'

Reflecting on his life (see Hall 2014: 51–59), from the vantage point of his mid-80s, former US poet laureate Donald Hall employs the feature of his beard to symbolize the waxing and waning of his authentic, masculine identity across the flux and flow of his life. He explains how he has grown a beard three times in his life, cutting it off twice; the present beard is both final and definitive and he intends to 'carry it into the grave'. Each time it is a woman who has instigated the growing of the beard; his first wife Kirby inspired the first beard. The beard, at this time, was also a sign of independent thinking that won him the respect of his departmental chair who went, in a summer, from addressing the clean-shaven version as 'Hall' to acknowledging the bearded version as 'Professor Hall'. This beard he shaved off, however, at the same time as he signed the divorce papers for his marriage to Kirby, reflecting that 'I shaved because the world had altered'.

He grew back the beard, on the occasion of his second marriage to Jane, who 'looked at old photographs and decided that I should grow a beard again', recognizing some essential self in this image. After thirteen years of this beard he decided, for change's sake, to shave it off one Christmas day, delighting in the way this act shocked his family – all, that is, except his discerning son who seemed to understand that it marked a shift in his father's identity, to something mid-life and sedate, a turn to a domesticated masculinity, a mature paterfamilias but still one capable of unpredictability. But then, still young, Jane died; Donald took solace in the arms of a succession of women, a practice through which he expressed his own will to life. The beard, expressive of the same impulse, made a return, nudged into existence by a new lover, who having again seen an old snapshot, told him, 'You'll look Mephistophelian'. Yet this new beard was a shadow of its former self, a trim goatee that she insisted was neatly smoothed over cheeks and chin. This, and later, relationships ended. In time, recovering finally from his grief, he grew back the big version of the beard.

Now, many years later, and in the company of a woman who is his true match, his 'Old Lady of the Mountains', his beard symbolizes all the strength and power of his true self, despite the ailing body, today wheelchair bound, which Linda wheels through airports during their frequent travels:

> When I turned eighty and rubbed testosterone onto my chest, my beard roared like a lion and lengthened four inches. The hair on my head grew longer and more jumbled, and with Linda's encouragement I never restrained its fury.... Declining more swiftly toward the grave, I make certain that everyone knows... that no posthumous razor may scrape my blue face.

As we noted in the metaphor suggested by Berg and Gadow in Chapter 6, where the 'hardening' or 'ossifying' of the body in old age is a symbol of the body-self finally settling into its true character, 'once and for all', so the beard 'fixes' Donald Hall, not in the sense of a trap, or a prison, but in the sense of a commitment to being who he truly is. Unlike Beauvoir and Wurtzel, it seems, Hall has lost his body several times, only to find it, gloriously, in late life.

Below, and drawing on all the commentary and age-autobiographical examples so far, I suggest some of the following questions may help with thinking critically about your own age autobiography:

How do you decide between what is authentic and what is not authentic in your age consciousness?

What has the 'voice in your head' directed you to do/not do in terms of age and time?

Do you ever feel 'split' in terms of your age consciousness?

What choices have filled you with a sense of flourishing and how have these related to hegemonic messages about age and stage?

Do you feel you are telling your own story – or someone else's?

How have you felt about each stage of your life before, during, and after experiencing it?

Can we recognize any contradictions between 'official' stories and our own experiences? If so – what do we do?

How do factors such as our gender and class work to open up and close down possibilities for true self-authorship/self-expression through the life course?

If you are female, how has the desire to have children affected your view of time and age? How have events like menstruation and menopause impacted on your view of yourself?

How can we draw together the various threads of our life, forging continuity between different points in our life, against the multiple fragmentary tendencies we experience?

5. Reflecting on contemporary tales

In this final section, and continuing themes also found in Chapter 5, I want to explore some tropes in contemporary fiction that can assist with developing an age consciousness outside the paradigm of development. One such derives from Philip Pullman's *His Dark Materials* where he uses 'daemons', which are animal forms 'attached' to a person but representing elements of their personality, associated with the opposite gender, that are not normally brought to the forefront of consciousness, as in the Jungian concept of animus/anima. This is particularly interesting in children, where the daemon is mercurial and constantly changing its form, representing aspects of the emerging personality which may or may not be representative of the character of the child when s/he grows up – these remain possibilities only at this stage – but are at any rate completely outside the parameters of progress, normality, advancement or retardation. The daemon finally 'settles' at a point in adolescence when s/he first feels a 'lover's touch' – an interesting way of seeing the gender regime as 'fixing' personality in gendered form. The gender fixing is also something portrayed in Angela Carter's fairy tales, where the trope of shape-shifting is used to great effect to articulate the transformative nature of both ageing and sexuality, which changes children to adults, and certain adults into the Other. In the story the Erl-King from her collection *The Bloody Chamber* (1981) the female character is irresistibly drawn to the werewolf Erl-King's embraces but she is afraid she will be trapped by it like the other girls before her who have been turned into birds and are imprisoned in the cages that hang suspended from branches of his forest dwelling. This is metamorphosis as a trap, fixing her in the male gaze as irrevocably Other. 'Your green eye is a reducing chamber,' she reflects. 'If I look into it long enough, I will become as small as my own reflection, I will diminish to a point and vanish. I will be drawn down into that black whirlpool and be consumed by you' (p. 90). She resists and, indeed, murders him, freeing herself and the other girls. Another tale in the collection, The Courtship of Mr Lyon, a variant on *Beauty and the Beast*, could be representing the Otherness of old age: 'She found his bewildering difference from herself almost intolerable' (p. 45) and Beauty is shocked when she discovers he walks on all fours. However, Beauty is both perceptive and sensitive and comes to realize that he appears grotesque to her only because his beauty is of a different order to that of youth and cannot be judged through the same gaze. Eventually, at the end of the story, in what could be a falling-away of Otherness which begins in compassion and ends up in a gaze that recognizes him as an individual not as an old man, Carter writes: 'When her lips touched the meat-hook claws, they drew back into their pads and she saw how he had always kept his fists clenched but now, painfully, tentatively, at last began to stretch out his fingers. Her tears fell on his face like snow and, under their soft transformation, the bones showed through the pelt, the flesh through the wide, tawny brow. And then it was no longer a lion in her arms but a man' (p. 51). Recognition of sameness in the old is of course fostered by intimacy and biographical knowledge where strangers and 'the old' are so much easier to objectify.

We have noted earlier Bynum's suggestion that metamorphosis is an excellent model with which to confront the 'promise and horror of change' (2001: 179). Metamorphosis deals in real change, 'not mere fluctuations of appearance, the adding and subtracting of qualities or "skins" but the replacement of one existing substance for another' (p. 177). This is real change; yet it is change-with-continuity, retaining traces of what the new being emerged from. Shape-shifting, unlike Pullman's daemons which are 'fixed' at childhood, could be used to depict the meaning of multiple changes throughout life, a process emphasizing not metamorphosis but metamorphos*es* as an ongoing experience of ageing through the life course.

The clear contrast to this is that of the vampire. The vampire is a hybrid: vampires have young faces on old shoulders, eternally fixed at a point in youth, and thereafter float through life beyond the predations of time, and without human vulnerabilities (although another type of vampire is the old person – supernatural or otherwise – who preys on young victims and seeks renewed vitality from them).

Their strength is more like armour, or a hyper-rational carapace, keeping them unchangeable as well as invulnerable. Perhaps it is the fear of growing up that propels young people in particular towards fascination with this trope, where, in a society terrified of ageing, they aspire to remain young and beautiful and sexual whilst time itself, perceived as a relentless march forward into old age, is frozen. Perhaps the popularity of this trope is also reflective of the feeling for young people that they are stuck in a limbo state between being old and being young as emerging adulthood prolongs this liminality. Stafford, in an autobiographical piece published in *The Guardian* newspaper (2015), writes:

> I am failing at being an adult. I don't see myself buying a house anytime soon or investing in property. I don't want to have kids any time soon.... Since turning 25, I find myself having daily anxieties about not being the kind of adult my parents or grandparents were. The Great Recession made us boomerang back home or stay in school to remain afloat during the storm. While this situation seemed to make us too reliant on parents or other support systems, it isn't like millennials weren't trying.... We aren't complete failures, we're just delayed and it's not really our fault.

Such literary forms are important in mediating change in that they can serve as ways of articulating experience for which no words or concepts may yet exist (Williams, 1977) including our swirling and inchoate hopes and fears. This is how new structures of feeling emerge: in the imagination, the psyche, the realm of the fireside tale. Being symbolic, every generation can use these forms anew, adapting them to the particular concerns of the day. And of great importance in this is the role of metaphor which, on the one hand is a key means of transmitting ideological assumptions, as we have seen, but, on the other, serves continuity-in-change in that it is capable of holding paradox and contradiction in exactly that creative tension that is so hard for our classifications to tolerate. How this works in people's lives is described powerfully by Becker:

> The use of metaphor is one way in which people impart elasticity to their personal frameworks of meaning.... People combine different explanatory systems by metaphor.... By reworking their understandings of self and world they remain within the bounds of a cultural discourse, yet the meanings they attach to many of the parameters of a cultural discourse gradually change. Metaphor mediates this process. (Becker, 1997: 65)

As with age drag, such metaphors should inform us of what we don't know, or reveal new ways of seeing old commonplaces, never falling into stereotypes (which are normally not how we think, if we reflect). Indeed, no better source exists for such originality and surprise than our own lives.

CHAPTER SUMMARY

- In this chapter we suggested that an authentic age consciousness is necessary for critiquing and challenging age ideology and we considered some practical techniques for developing this, which would form the basis of an individual, but not individualized, life course.

- We concluded by identifying some tropes in contemporary fiction that depict age identities and age consciousness in ways outside the framework of psychological development and which link with the hybrid and metamorphosis concepts of identity discussed in Chapter 5.

Further questions

1. How much is the fear of growing old(er) a 'fact of life', of being human and how much is it peculiar to our current society? In considering this, reflect on how this process may differ for women and men, for those of different classes and race.

2. F.W. Du Bois talked about double-consciousness in the lives of Blacks; how can we apply this principle in relation to age? How does it intersect with other forms of consciousness? Can any be said to take precedence and, if so, when and how?

3. Movies and books that feature road trips are often vehicles for life reviews; not all of these take place at the 'end' of the life course, for example *Wild* and *Sideways* are about feeling lost in youth and mid-life respectively. Selecting one 'life review' movie, discuss in relation to the themes in this chapter.

Talking point

A book published in 2015 (Toledano, 2015) featured a series of self-portraits by a 45-year-old photographer (utilizing make-up and prosthetics) which imagined a series of 95-year-old future selves. He consulted fortune tellers, numerologists and palm readers, took a DNA test and read insurance company statistics and only thereafter set about imagining his possible futures. A selection of photography plus some commentary about the book is available here: http://www.theguardian.com/artanddesign/gallery/2015/jul/11/the-many-lives-of-phillip-toledano-in-pictures. How helpful (or not) do you think this is as a way of generating age consciousness? Empathy with others? A sense of your own future trajectory?

Further reading

Margaret Gullette has pioneered the concept of **age consciousness** and any one of her books are outstanding for exploring this further, e.g. Gullette, M. (1997) *Declining to Decline*, Charlottesville: University of Virginia Press; Gullette, M.M. (2004) *Aged by Culture*, Chicago: University of Chicago Press. Kathleen Woodward explores **age consciousness in and of old age** in Woodward, K. (1991) *Ageing and its Discontents: Freud and other fictions,* Bloomington: University of Indiana Press. Books on **gender consciousness** can also be helpful as parallels: see for example Rowbotham, S. (1973) *Woman's Consciousness, Man's World*, London: Pelican; and Smith, D. (1987) *The Everyday World as Problematic: a feminist sociology,* Toronto: University of Toronto Press. The **experience of young adulthood** as a state of mind as well as a series of practical accomplishments are captured in Brown, K.W. (2013*) Adulting: how to become a grown-up in 468 easy(ish) steps*, New York: Grand Central Publishing. **Women's mid-life age consciousness** is stunningly depicted in Rinaldi, R. (2015) *The Wild Oats Project: one woman's mid-life quest for passion at any cost*, London: Hodder and Stoughton. **Mid-life ageing** looking forward into old age is depicted in Manheimer, R.J. (1999) *A Map to the End of Time: wayfarings with friends and philosophers*, New York: W.W. Norton and Company. For a candid account of **deep old age** see Athill, D. (2008) *Somewhere Towards the End*, London: Granta. Texts telling '**stories of old age**' from a variety of points of view include: Blythe, R. (1979) *The View in Winter*, New York: Harcourt Brace Jovanovitch; Cole, T.R. and Minkler, M.G. (eds) (1995) *The Oxford Book of Ageing: reflections on the journey of life,* Oxford: Oxford University Press.

Further resources

- There are interesting blogs that are sources for age-conscious reflection at particular stages.

- For youth: Laurie Penny's *Penny Red* (http://laurie-penny.com/) is excellent.

- Helen Walmsley-Johnson writes about being an older woman in her 'Vintage Years' column in *The Guardian* (http://www.theguardian.com/profile/invisible-woman).

- Again at *The Guardian* Tim Lott writes from a consciously late mid-life perspective on life, self and others (http://www.theguardian.com/profile/tim-lott).

- The following *New York Times* articles discuss literature revisited later in life, the authors using the poem or novel as a prism to identify different age consciousnesses as well as the interplay of continuity and change in their lives:

  (i) Levine, L. (2015) 'The Love Song of J. Alfred Prufrock', *New York Times*, 9 August.

  (ii) Kirsch, A. and Heller, Z. (2014) 'Which books from your past do you read now with ambivalence?' *New York Times*, 15 April.

12

CONCLUDING THOUGHTS

Overview of arguments covered in the chapters of the book

Each of the chapters in this book has sought, according to different themes, to demonstrate how the age system serves both to produce hierarchies of its own and to naturalize existing social inequalities by presenting them as inevitable: whether associated with youth, mid-life or old age. In doing so, we have seen how age interlocks with gender and class to form a formidable meshwork of stratification as well as to render individuals governable through their freedom (Rose, 1999). Through the chapters we also looked at the analytic concepts and tools at our disposal as sociologists which may, with certain modifications, serve to highlight and critique age inequalities and the age ideology that underpin them, as well as point the way towards a different perception and experience of age. Our conclusions are, by way of brief summary, theme by theme, as follows:

- We identified parallels and intersections between the age and class systems seeing them as two socially constructed systems establishing deeply entrenched forms of mutually implicated social inequality. In particular, the intersections between the two help naturalize both systems and their supporting ideologies.

- Similarly, the depiction of ageing and old age as a pre- (or post-)social phenomenon was demonstrated to be ideological than 'natural' by means of applying the theoretical and methodological approaches of gender studies. This also indicated the inextricable linkage of the age and gender regimes socio-politically, as well as epistemologically, indicating that gender equality requires age equality and vice versa.

- We looked at the ideological nature of the life course, underpinned by scientific approaches to development and, in late modernity, by the individualization of the life course. Although presenting as a fluidity of age norms and a freeing-up of agency, the latter co-exists with, and indeed facilitates, a strengthened age patriarchy indicated in the separation between symbolic and chronological adulthood. Challenging these structures involves both rethinking the notion of the 'developmental trajectory' and emphasizing an individual, as opposed to individual*ized*, life course.

- We explored theoretical approaches to adult identity, suggesting that sociology utilizes an a-temporal or static approach to adult identity. Whilst this cedes hegemony to psychological theories of development of the other stages, framed by the normative arc of growth–stasis–decline, in turn this feeds the cultural dread of ageing and the fear of losing the self. I suggested that a more fruitful approach to thinking about the relationship of self and time might be through that of narrative identity which accommodates the lived experience of continuity-with-change and permits a clearer view of the distinction between living 'well' and living 'successfully' through the life course.

- We saw bodies as sites through which the age and gender regimes work to 'fix' hierarchies through 'natural' embodied differences centred upon key points throughout the life course. A reworking of gender as both a concept and practice is key to challenging both these systems together with an ontological emphasis on the continuities, as compared to the differences, that link bodies at all stages of the life course.

- Similarly, in the case of sexuality, I suggested that the heterosexual regime uses age as one of the ways to fix hierarchies and regulate women in particular. I suggested some approaches to resistance, including rethinking gender socialization in childhood, challenging the 'beauty rules' that define beauty *as* youth and challenging the connection for women of sexuality as beauty.

- We looked at some of the psychopathologies that are diagnosed at specific points in the life course for women and suggested that we view these as somatic expressions of both gender pain and age pain generated by the contradictions of femininity within the current gender order. Health and illness thereby serve as a lens through which we might view the age and gender regimes, and vice versa.

- We looked at representations of the various ages and life stages, including policy and media depictions and suggested that images (textual and/or visual) by which non-adult life stages are depicted serve rather as mirrors in which we as adults project our own fears and longings. 'Age drag' might unsettle these assumptions, loosening the connection between certain characteristics and age or stage, and facilitating integration of these characteristics within the adult self.

- We explored how analytic concepts that are employed to depict age relations generate conflict and discontinuity, with the concept of 'generations' key. I suggested that a more satisfactory framework would involve a revitalized view of the life course that emphasizes its dynamic nature, including movement through the life course and interplay between ages and stages, whilst retaining the reality of both conflict and co-operation as a lived experience of age relations.

- Whilst age drag might shake up our taken-for-granted and stereotypical assumptions about age properties, we also looked at techniques for developing an authentic age consciousness that would form, and be formed by, an individual biographical narrative in which we 'tell our own stories' of age. We reflected on how certain literary tropes may aid us in this telling.

In the following sections, and drawing on these arguments, I will return to the critical questions I posed at the start of the book, namely: (i) how do we imbue ages and stages with meaning beyond those associated with current hierarchies and polarities? and (ii) how do we re-imagine the meaning of old age? In the terms of our argument, it will make more sense to discuss (ii) first.

Re-imagining the meaning of old age

In re-imagining the meaning of old age we will clearly wish to leave aside its current problematization and devaluation, its association with fear and dread, and its depiction as a burden to the rest of society. Whilst this imagery and rhetoric disconnects old age from the rest of the life course, an alternative starting point could be to examine it as an integral part of the life course and one fundamentally continuous with the rest. However, as this latter approach has emerged in social policy and medical discourses historically, it has always included the further assumption that old age is *the same* as at earlier points in the life course, as in our current third-age discourses. These two positions indicate the outer limits of the social imagination of societies through modernity (Phillipson, 2013). In the search for an approach that emphasizes both continuity and uniqueness we can unravel several strands and interconnected themes. These include viewing old age as (1) the concentration of the logic of the previous life stages; (2) a unique standpoint or perspective; and (3) illuminating/expressing what has been 'split off' from adulthood. We look at each of these in turn.

(1) Regarding the 'same as all the other life stages but more so' perspective: a real alternative to seeing old people as the Other is seeing them as a distillation of who we (at all ages) truly are. This has two aspects. Firstly, in the structural dimension, it represents the logic of the accumulated inequalities of class, gender and so on that have borne down upon each stage culminating at this point where the consequences are plain to see. Secondly, and more existentially, there is 'ageing as a crystal through which experiences common to all persons are the most clearly identified, becoming – like colours through a prism – purified and intensified' (Gadow, 1986: 238). This is old age as the 'essential' self, what remains when the roles and responsibilities of earlier life are divested, a self that has been formed in engagement with enduring dilemmas such as how to balance love and work, freedom and responsibility, strength and vulnerability, and which now stand out starkly against, as it were, the dark backcloth of looming finitude.

of *homo economicus* (Brown, 2015) and lay claim to our own values and priorities. We can also shift tempo in embodied terms, with a 'slowing-down' that enables a quality of attentiveness not usually experienced in the midst of the rush and frenzy of earlier points in the life course (although other marginalized people at any age might experience it), in the form of the meditative mode. These characteristics can be seen as irrational, childish, even tragic from the perspective of earlier stages in the life course; but they can also form aspects of a more integrated life for younger adults. Indeed, to Simone Weil, the quality of attentiveness, or attention, in her words, was of such prime importance, forming the basis of authentic relationships and of an authentic insight into 'reality', that she believed it should be taught at school (Tronto, 1993). Why leave this to the latter part of life, to the time when our bodies force us into it?

Having highlighted general truths about old age, it is important to recognize that old age will always be inextricably bound up with a person's unique subjectivity and biographical history, a fact that the earlier institutionalization of old age obscured. As Kaufman puts it, of the old people she interviewed in her study, they 'do not perceive meaning in ageing itself; rather, they perceive meaning in being themselves in old age' (1986: 6). Old people, it is commonly observed, are more unlike each other than any other group, and a life time of experience produces individuals more, not less, unique. Indeed, it is the ability to be oneself in the fullest possible sense at all points in the life course that is the aim of a re-imagined old age, free from an age and gender ideology that cripples the full range of human expression, an ideological system of which attitudes towards old age form the pinnacle. It is by recognizing this uniqueness that we can also perceive the continuities between life stages. In this endeavour we can export the insight we have from biology, that we are constantly growing and dying, and are young and old at the same time, at a cellular and organic level, into the social domain, where we are always older and younger in comparison to others and where our own pasts and imagined futures give rise to multiple age identities within the present. Here, as with gender, we can play with the different characteristics and perspectives admitted by each stage whilst avoiding reifying them, subverting the hierarchies contained within the age system in a Derridean fashion by asserting the commonalities between ages and stages and their qualities and characteristics so that one shall not attain its value at the expense of the others. As with the various alternatives to male-ordered subjectivity this involves both recognition of 'the complex mix of possibility and constraint in each [age/stage] and a strategic effort to pursue the promise of each with full consciousness of the shadow each one casts' (Ferguson, 1993: 182). With this, in contrast to the dominance of natality, which as we have previously noted is part of the tendency to privilege youth over age, we might draw instead from Heidegger's philosophy which privileges the experience of death, as well as articulating time as non-linear, holding that we are all aware of our finitude at every moment, although we do all we can to distract ourselves from this (both at a personal and socio-cultural level). If death were to be faced fully and appreciated truly, as a lived reality rather than an intellectual 'fact', this knowledge would instantly reduce the divisions between young and old, because instead of seeing *only* the old body as a dying body (Katz, 1996) such recognition would apply to all bodies. In acknowledging the multi-dimensionality of temporal existence, 'development' at once becomes understandable as a renewal of past just as much as of present and future, a feature of frailty and dementia, as much as learning to walk and talk, and as indicative of the energy present in dying as of the process of growing from childhood (Heine, 1985).

Before moving on, I want to suggest that there is one society actively embracing a re-visioning of old age in the light of its demographic transition. As we noted earlier, Japan has long been attempting to shape what it terms an 'ideal longevity society' in which old age is both a valued life stage and integral to the functioning of society. A brief summary of what this entails is suggested in Box 12.1, below.

Re-imagined ages and stages

The source of a vital new meaning of old age lies not at the final point of the life course but from reconsidered norms and values as lived *throughout* the life course: new ways of seeing and experiencing embodiment, selfhood, sexuality and identity that allow us to grow and transform according to new cultural and symbolic repertoires. As I suggested at the start of this book, this does not require rejecting the Enlightenment philosophies and methodologies that were partly responsible for taking us such a distance from the Hag in the first place, but rather using them thoughtfully, excavating those that have been submerged, revisiting their original aim and purpose and modulating their excesses so that our incomplete and imperfect individuation can be brought to a rich completion. To illustrate this point: whilst reason is a requirement of freedom, rationalization, as an excessive application of reason, tends not to free but to enslave, not to facilitate maturity, but ensure infantilization. But used wisely these philosophical methodologies can help in the process of re-enchanting the life course which will involve most of all revisiting what we value in adulthood, wherein the nature and meaning of work, and the definition of maturity, are key.

The role and meaning of work

As Max Weber described, coming to see the self in terms of the work one does was a theme utilized early on in capitalism to link economic achievement with the meaning of life. But since then the work ethic has lost the expansiveness of the vocation and its centrality to the good life, one that infused the mundane with significance and the making of money with spiritual values, and it has contracted to a materialist domain, contributing in turn to an ever-narrower meaning of human existence. For many, work remains a source of satisfaction and fulfilment and for many women especially, paid work, no matter of how humble a kind, or to what ends of capitalist enterprise, has yet been a vehicle of personal liberation from the tyranny of fathers and husbands and a source of identity separate from the family. It is not work, per se, but the 'bullshit' jobs – those designed for the purpose of regulation and control (Graeber, 2015), as well as the expansion of work to fill all 'leisure' times, and the enfolding of once-noble vocations into a bureaucratic-market ethic, that require challenging.

The increasing spread of the rationality of neoliberalism threatens to turn the whole life course into a 'journey of entrepreneurialism', a materialist version of the pilgrimage, but with financial success replacing spiritual wealth. The change is described by Wendy Brown as one in which, where in earlier liberal regimes the market, 'truth' and implicitly the 'good' were aligned, today the market provides the sole truth, and the 'good' becomes increasingly meaningless in any other terms. A consequence for the subject is that, 'narrowed down to market conduct, divested of association with mastering the conditions of life, existential freedom, or securing the rule of the demos… no longer is there an open question of how to craft the self or what paths to travel in life' (Brown, 2015: 41). This is mirrored in the goals of education, from primary school to university and beyond, where, upon graduation, the most elite students take up positions in finance and banking. It also has a dramatic effect on the age system because with such intensification of the values of entrepreneurialism and productivity there is little or no value perceived in anything but 'youth'. The expansion of work into more and more of our 'free' time occurs alongside the ideological separation of the private and public worlds, which has removed 'care' from public life and relegated it to the invisible private domain (although work has also invaded the private space: technological advance has allowed us to literally function as disembodied workers, with the 'home office' as a sterilized space emptied out of all messy human substance beyond the computer screen). This furthers the illusion of the autonomous successful self performing in public roles whilst distorting our ontological picture of human being.

This public/private division further underpins the intricate meshing of the age and gender regimes. For example, Brown (2015) suggests that one of the ways in which gender hegemony is intensified in neoliberalism is that the ontology of *homo economicus*, which views the self in terms of human capital, and is the practical meaning of de-gendering in our current regime, means that the role women play in the domestic and care-giving economies at all stages of the life course is lost from language. Brown notes: 'When there is only capital (human, corporate, finance) what disappears analytically is the already liminal labour of the household… and the gendered division of labour *between* market and household' (2015: 106; original emphasis). It thus becomes literally impossible to understand women's structural disadvantage. Recognizing the centrality of care, alongside work, in life, is thus essential in challenging the hierarchies that elevate some ages (considered to be more independent) over others, and contain millions of women in positions of relative powerlessness (considered to be 'naturally' caring/care-givers), with particularly detrimental material effects in their old age. In addition, 'good' work in the sense, not of Goodman's definition but rather of work that has meaning to the worker, extends into the domain of old age in a way that stands apart from debates around either retirement or an 'active' old age. Nor should 'good work' be considered a middle-class privilege or something only professionals can aspire to. A 1974 oral history found even those in unskilled occupations achieving pride and meaning in their work, whereas a repeat study in 2004 found a prevalence of negative comments, concerning stress, alienation and insecurity, across classes and professions (Mintz, 2015).[1] Indeed, the impulse to self-fulfilment sits outside the good/bad division of every life stage, taking its meaning rather from the concept of *eudaimonia*, as possible for a carpenter as for a philosopher, a cleaner or waitress as for a teacher or doctor.

These are aspects of what would form, not just a critique of the current work economy, but a wholesale shift in societal mentality which may include, among other things, what Seabrook calls:

> the retrieval of another version of wealth [which]... is something we practice daily, since it lies in the freely given, the acts of mercy and char- ity, the performance of duty, the endurance of patience of those who care for the infirm, sick and old, all the gifts of humanity not subject to the transaction or the exchange, all that is shared voluntarily, the ability to see ourselves in others. (2013: 225)

The home and private life are an obvious source of these alternative values, whence they might colonize the space of work, where currently it is a one-way colonization in the other direction.

But this shift would also require a shift in the meaning of maturity, to which we turn next.

New meanings of maturity

Despite the portrayal of development in scientific terms, what constitutes maturity has always been contestable. During the height of the institutional life course matu- rity was synonymous with conformity in work and private life, comprising 'rigid, restrictive role definitions' (Mintz, 2015: 331), perceived by many as 'physical, sex- ual and mental compromise, and the loss of the joys and freedom of youth' (2015: 4). Havighurst's (1953) developmental tasks that led to maturity include selecting a mate, starting a family, managing a home, getting started in an occupation and tak- ing on civic responsibilities (Ehrenreich, 1983). For Levinson et al. (1978) these included: formulating an ambition, or 'Dream', forming an occupation, sexual rela- tionship, marriage and family. Its inherent conformity to mainstream values and their hierarchies is clearly demonstrated by, for example, the suggestion that two 'Dreams' in one household would lead to friction unless the wife's Dream is that of being a homemaker (Sugarman, 2001). Meanwhile, men who refused to shoulder their responsibilities in these aspects were categorized as immature and/or homo- sexual (Ehrenreich, 1983). Unsurprisingly many forms of resistance arose in reaction to this, from the Beats to *Playboy* to feminism, all of which involved rejection of this version of maturity (for requiring of men simply that they 'obey' the dictates of the system and of women that they sacrifice their growth to their femininity which was, in fact, in contradiction to maturity.) However, the emphasis on narcissism and the indulgence of consumerism and the emotional/irrational from the late 1960s and 1970s were not only a rejection of conformity but also of maturity itself and indeed the emphasis in psychology and other discourses transformed into the goal of staying youthful. David Riesman in *The Lonely Crowd* describes the change in terms of a shift from an inner-directed to an other-directed personality; Ehrenreich (1983) sees this as representing a further 'feminization' of personality; psychoanalysis attributes it to a declining oedipal authority leading to a resurgence of the 'primitive, sadistic, self-destructive impulses of earliest childhood' (Zaretsky, 2004: 312–13).

Today, maturity rarely features in official discourse where ubiquitous is the dual aim of 'success' and youthfulness, fed and shaped by a whole host of socio-cultural changes including changes in employment, in medical narratives and in popular culture which have impacted on the aspiration of all age groups. For example, Laslett (1991) defines the second age as one of maturity which he defines as 'responsibility', 'earning' and 'saving' and which alone makes the third age (characterized by youthfulness and success) possible. Conversely, these changes also underpin, when things go wrong, the labelling of not just youth but all generations as 'lost',[2] with the implication that they are 'lost' in the sense that children are lost, abandoned even, in need of direction and protection. It has also been suggested that the characteristics of 'emerging adulthood' are present in all life stages wherein 'instability, uncertainty, and a desire to grow, but not grow up and settle down, persist into adults' thirties, forties, fifties and sixties' (Mintz, 2015: 69). How then, might we salvage the concept of maturity as a valuable goal and this time invest it with meaning outside both institutionalized life stages and market society? What might be its characteristics?

Starting at the beginning, the discussion in the previous chapters of this book suggest the foundation for mature individuals, as for a reconfigured age system, lies in a self-fashioned from a process of individuation from infancy, characterized by continued co-operative interdependence (Benjamin, 1990), admitting a place for conflict but of a type other than the ruthless, competitive individualism that our child development models assume. Such norms of individuation will avoid the gender positioning that arose from the configurations of centuries past, when, to use Berger's words, women were under the 'tutelage' of men. A key consequence will be the transformation of the male gaze, as it configures women's embodied use of public space and women's relationship to self and others, so enabling the political and legal equality women have won to be extended fully through the social and cultural sphere. More generally, if individuation occurs in a way that does not require the projection of certain qualities onto the bodies and selves of others, but rather willingly learns to incorporate these paradoxical elements within the self, more realistic norms for the body throughout the life, and especially in old age, can also be established. This includes a reworked form of aesthetics which can see beauty in old age as well as youth, health as inherent to old bodies as well as young, and strength, caring and competence to childhood as well as adulthood.

We will look also to education to make adults out of young men and young women, rather than producing the child-adults Postman identified. Currently, we have a 'credentialism' that, beginning in school, continues as a characteristic of adulthood where 'the purpose of life,' writes Deresiewicz, 'becomes the accumulation of gold stars' (2014: 16). By contrast, an education for a mature human being necessarily is the sort that goes beyond the narrow ethos of job training, or 'building human capital' which reduces the 'very project of higher education to its income generating promise' (Brown, 2015: 182–8), instead rewarding curiosity for its own sake, regardless of any immediate utility, and sharpening the critical abilities therein. Unlike the docility produced by current practices, the aim of such an education, like Rousseau's in *Emile*, is to produce the sort of citizen who can think for themselves – what Kant defined as true rationality in the sense of 'man's release from his self-incurred tutelage' or 'man's inability to make use of his understanding without direction from another' (Kant (1963: 3); quoted in Dean (1994: 47); see also Neiman (2014)) and which also requires that women be free of the tutelage of the male gaze and older people of the age gaze. For Kant 'maturity consists of throwing off the "fetters of an *ever-lasting* tutelage", which means that one will not allow a book to do one's understanding, a pastor to be one's conscience, and a physician to decide one's diet...' (Dean, 1994: 47; emphasis added) nor any other expert to claim that they know us better than we know ourselves. Descartes' *Meditations* are similarly concerned with growing up intellectually, and emotionally; the main message is that, as children 'we assumed that what we felt was a measure of external reality; now, as mature Cartesian doubters, we reverse that prejudice. We assume nothing.... We begin afresh. For Descartes... the state of childhood *can* be revoked, through a deliberate and methodical reversal of all the prejudices acquired within it, and a beginning anew with reason as one's only parent' (Bordo, 1999: 59; original emphasis). Moreover this is a lifelong process not confined to the school room as it mostly is today where in the UK higher education neither tailors courses specifically to older people nor actively seeks to recruit them through the Widening Participation agenda. At the same time, laying stress on an education for life does not imply that one needs to be 'old' to be mature. Erikson's notion of stage-based tasks linked to a fulfilment of the potential of each life stage implied that there was not just one meaning of maturity that applied to one's whole life, but that it had different meanings, and would take different forms, at different ages.

Finally, the assumption upon which this ideal of maturity is built, and what makes it possible, is the Enlightenment distinction, held by Marx and Weber and with a direct lineage through St Augustine to the Greeks, between the outer and the inner, what Brown calls a 'political exterior and subjective interior' (2015: 101) with the latter capable of difference from, and resistance to, the former. This is because, despite the brilliant arguments of post-structuralists like Foucault, the self is more than an effect of power: it is a 'soulful space', the location and source of true age consciousness; and because if there is nothing with which we can resist, then we are doomed to always remain children.

This is not to deny the inevitability of some resistance to growing up and growing old and one based on recognition that growth and change always involve losses as well as gains. It is as well, then, to remind ourselves of the dangers of the temptations to remain 'young'. Reflecting on his discussions with the Ivy League graduates Deresiewicz observes:

> I remember that dilemma… the desire to remain forever on the threshold of adulthood, the grief at having to surrender your sense of limitless possibility – and I remember how I got past it: by recognizing that it wasn't finally a choice between one thing and everything, but one thing and nothing. If I didn't commit to something, I would never be anything. (2014: 126–7)

The same arrested selfhood is a consequence of the failure to accept ageing and death; Norman Brown points out that, in psychoanalytic terms, individuality is only possible with acceptance of death, because only death bestows uniqueness and true differentiation; repression of death is a flight from true maturity. Today, it is the promise of lifespan extension and the achievements of more mundane medicine that sweeps death out of sight and out of mind. But as we noted in the first chapter, when discussing Bella Swan, the heroine of *Twilight*, to refuse ageing and death is to refuse life: in rejecting the Hag in the mirror, she was rejecting her own self.[3]

'The last of life, for which the first was made'

The previous section sketched the outlines of a different genealogy of adulthood, rooted in an age system which permits us to grow up and grow old in a way that is divested of its current associations with horror and tragedy. In considering the part that being old may play in this reconfigured age system, I return one final time to the example of Beauvoir, whose words have echoed throughout the pages of this book. She felt the coming of age when she was still in her twenties; she dreaded it acutely and underwent something of a collapse in confidence in her mid-life, as we saw in Chapter 11, when all she could see ahead was loss and decline (Moi, 2008; Woodward, 1988). But let us take the story further. As the years continued to pass, as anticipation ceased and the moment of old age was upon her, it seemed she found that things were not as she had dreaded (Moi, 2008). Indeed, there were many positive experiences, including romantic love and friendship, pleasure in writing and friendships and political causes: unanticipated, perhaps, but all of them continuous with who she had always been. Going back to the time of *Force of Circumstance*, it is clear that, despite the desolate mourning for her lost youth, she also recognized the whole concept of development as ideological: 'There comes a moment when one knows one is no longer getting ready for anything and one understands that the idea of advance towards a goal was a delusion all along' (Beauvoir, 1968: 491). What she had *not* yet done here, perhaps, was turn her dread of ageing upon its head, by seeing that *not only* youthful hope *but also* mid-life despair *and* the dread of age are all delusions, ideologically constructed; that although having some essence in embodied tempos and rhythms and hormonal shifts, their cultural weight derives from the myths that bind us, like fairy tales that prepare us for the rivalry of mother-figures, the liberation of a kiss from a man, until we too become the dreaded Hag jealous of her daughter (or male-equivalent drama). When she concludes in the closing lines of the memoir that, although the promises of youth were all kept: 'I realize with stupor, how much I was gypped' (1968: 674) this is the moment when, not just the promise of youth, but the whole edifice of the age system crumbles into dust at her feet. We might speculate how later, when her pessimism had faded away, and the dust had settled, she might have realized that the spell of the age gaze had also been broken releasing her to live the rest of her life as a free woman.

But she did not write about this and I wish to try to fill in some of the blanks left by Beauvoir's story with the following reflection by a retired doctor, reflecting on his life in a long letter to a medical journal, which, I think, illuminates the nature of one's perception of oneself when the age gaze has completely melted away, which for him was deep in his old age, in fact in his 'fourth age'. He verbalizes much of what Sartre had wordlessly conveyed in his appreciation of 'emptiness' (causing Beauvoir, viewing old age at the time from the outside, so much dismay):

> I feel like an old man. I don't work and what's more, I don't walk. It's strange but it doesn't bother me. Suddenly fifty years of work is enough. I no longer take care of patients, and I no longer accuse myself of not understanding them or knowing how to help them.... It's for others to take up the banner. I'm through with my practice and with problems.
>
> I sit in the sun, watching the leaves fall in the pool. I think, I dream, I draw. I feel liberated from the world of reality. I still love, in a tranquil way, and I still feel loved by my family and friends.
>
> I have time. I don't know how much time remains to me, but I'm not in a hurry. I'm not in a hurry to arrive – even to the end. It can wait, and when it comes, I will try to accept it, without any illusions. It won't be easy. I live for and in the moment, and I want to stay here a little bit longer, in tranquillity. I consider [old] age a success in itself. Now I understand better. (Woodward, 1991: 180)

Where Postman talked about the 'mystery' of adulthood that was being eroded by the breaking of barriers between childhood and adulthood, this passage crystallizes the mystery of old age. In both cases, however, contra Postman, it cannot be usurped, or snatched unearned, or indeed transmitted or acquired because the mystery is that of 'maturity', a dynamic property that is different at every age; that is inseparable from the metamorphoses that accompany change throughout life; and that binds each of them with a thread of continuity. Similarly, we might talk of the mystery of childhood as a kind of maturity, but different from the medieval *puer senex*, because rather than transcending the stage of childhood, it is rather inseparable from, and bound up with, the child's consciousness. Dr Grotjohn's reflections return us to the question we posed at the start of the book, suggested by the Hag, namely: '*How can*

I change whilst remaining myself?' His words suggest that time is not something separate from us, something external that we can buy or lose, or be defeated by, but which runs through us like our own blood. The alarms or school bells that punctuate the days are not signalling 'time' but reifying modes of regulation and order. To attempt to escape time and resist change by transcending age identities is, then, to refuse to grow into ourselves, to be trapped within the age system such as it is today, to grow old without maturity. The answer to this question seems to be, then, not '*you cannot*' as all our cultural messages harshly proclaim, but its opposite: that it is only by changing through time and age that you can ever become yourself. This would be the understanding of a new age system.

I have set out in this chapter an ideal picture of old age and all ages and a suggestion of what age and the experience of travelling through the life course might contribute to individual and social flourishing, rather than serving the purpose of control, division and limit. In that sense it is very far from the age system in place today. To get from one to the other will require sweeping socio-political change. Certainly the critique of the age system feeds into a wider movement for social justice because the age gaze, like the male gaze and the class gaze, are all 'reducing chambers' in Angela Carter's words, making millions of us who are forced to look into it as small as our own reflections. But in this sense, Beauvoir was quite right: as it is framed materially, socially and intellectually today, it is old age that most of all exposes the failure of our entire civilization; in all these domains it demands nothing less than a revolution.

BOX 12.1

Japan's ideal longevity society

Japan provides a fascinating example of a society which is working towards realizing a vision of an 'ideal longevity society' in which all ages partake. Comprising a combination of discourses and practices, it combines a different view of work as well as a more positive view of old age. Hinging on the concept of *ikigai*, which refers to a (whole) life of meaning and purpose in which work or service is seen as key, this incorporates all life stages in a framework that is not determined by neoliberalism (although it might be twisted to fit the framework, as is currently increasingly occurring). The configuring of work as service enables a symbolic continuity to be asserted which links pre- and post-retirement periods. Changes in policies include obligations placed upon employers to re-hire workers after retirement; long-term care insurance, payable by all those aged between 40 and 65, for the first time establishes care-giving as a social and collective responsibility, rather than a private familial responsibility. Moreover, the Japanese government has been deliberately employing positive terms to describe ageing and asserting a positive view of an ageing society ever since the 1972 speech by then Prime Minister Kakuei Tanaka who introduced the new fact of the ageing society with the words: 'It is… our duty to take care of those who brought about the present prosperity with their sweat and travail' (Coulmas, 2007). So, in the decades since the 1980s the 'ageing society' was renamed the 'society for longevity'; the 'age of silver' changed to the 'age of gold'; and the 'age of fruition' became the 'age of maturity', all terms associated with a shift in the meaning and role of old age more widely in society from dependence to activity and from marginalization to a valued and still-productive place. At the same time, when discussing old age, Japanese society openly focuses on the idea of a peaceful death. Its valuation of maturity goes hand in hand with an acceptance of life's limits, on the one hand, and the notion, on the other, that, with ancestorhood, death is neither the end of development, nor the end of service; a view that has survived both urbanization and late modernity. Problems and challenges that Japan faces notwithstanding, the contrast with the 'burden of old age' and 'generational war' discourses of the West is instructive to say the least.

Notes

1. This is most obviously applied to the younger generation because of their difficulty in finding stable jobs and establishing lives of their own. But it has also been used to describe other generations whose grip on (symbolic) adulthood in these risky times has been viewed as less than certain. *The Washington Post* highlights the 'regressing' tendency of the 'older Millennials', aged 25–34 (Rampell, 2015). Mid-life men (aged 40–54), positioned between the 'baby boomers' and the 'digital natives' have been described as having 'lost their way', especially with regard to their masculinity, insofar as they are caught between the 'old' and the 'new' (Cavendish, 2015). Similarly, the generation of women aged 43–54 has been described as 'lost' from the business world; an article in the *Huffington Post* (Gordon, 2015) suggests that, since the recession of 2008, a million women of that age group have been lost to the workforce, suggesting they are more disposable to employees than men of the same age. Finally, an article in *Psychology Today* asks, 'Is the "older generation" a new lost generation?' (Weinstein, 2013).

2. 'Alongside the predictable complaints about annoying co-workers, abusive bosses, and underpay, many expressed pride in their work. A bookbinder said that he loved repairing books because "a book is a life". A gravedigger made sure that the edges were square because "a human body is goin' into this grave". Said a waitress, "when I put a plate down, you don't hear a sound. If I drop a fork, there is a certain way I pick it up. I know they can see how delicately I can do it.

I'm on stage"' (see Terkel, S. (1974). *Working: people talk about what they do all day and how they feel about what they do*, New York: Pantheon, quoted in Mintz (2015: 233)). This can be compared with the following statement by a Cornell undergraduate, bound for more elevated tasks, but still deriving no meaning or satisfaction from this: 'I hate all my activities, I hate all my classes, I hated everything I did in high school, I expect to hate my job, and this is just how it's going to be for the rest of my life' (Deresiewicz, 2014: 11).

3. According to Norman Brown (1959), in psychoanalytic terms our repression of the knowledge of death links us to an infantile past; but the 'instinctual unity of living and dying' (p. 101) is thereby disrupted, meaning that it is not only the death instinct that is repressed but the life instinct also. To refuse death means to refuse life.

REFERENCES

Adam, B. (1990) *Time and social theory*, Cambridge: Polity Press.

Adam, B. (1995) *Timewatch: the social analysis of time*, Cambridge: Polity Press.

Ainsworth, S. and Hardy, C. (2008) The enterprising self: an unsuitable job for an older worker, *Organization* 15(3): 389–405.

All Party Parliamentary Group on Body Image (2012) *Reflections on Body Image*, London: National Children's Bureau.

ANAD (National Association of Anorexia Nervosa and Associated Disorders) (2015) information site accessed at http://www.anad.org/get-information/about-eating-disorders/eating-disorders-statistics/ January 1 2015.

Andrew, M.K. and Keefe, J.M. (2014) Social vulnerability from a social ecology perspective: a cohort study of older adults from the National Population Health Survey of Canada, *BMC Geriatrics,* 14: 90.

Andrews, M. (1999) The seductiveness of agelessness, *Ageing and Society* 19(3): 301–18.

Andrews, M. (2009) The narrative complexity of successful ageing, *International Journal of Sociology and Social Policy*, 29(1/2): 73–83.

Annandale, E. (2009) *Women's Health and Social Change*, London: Routledge.

Anon (2014) Authors, teachers and parents launch revolt over 'exam factory' schools, *The Independent*, 3 October.

Anon (2015) How Kate Moss is proof you end up with the face you deserve, *Daily Mail*, 25 September.

Arber, S. and Cooper, H. (2000) Gender and inequalities in health across the life course. In Annandale, E. and Hunt, K. (eds) *Gender Inequalities in Health*, Milton Keynes: Open University Press, pp. 123–49.

Aries, P. (1962) *Centuries of Childhood*, London: Jonathan Cape.

Arnett, J.J. (2000) *Emerging Adulthood: the winding road from the late teens through the twenties*, New York: Oxford University Press.

Arnot, M. (2004) Male working-class identities and social justice. In Dolby, N. and Dimitriadis, G. with Willis, P. (eds) *Learning to Labour in New Times*, London: Routledge, pp. 15–34.

Athill, D. (2008) *Somewhere Towards the End*, London: Granta.

Avis, N.E., Crawford, S.L., Greendale, G., Bromberger, J.T., Everson-Rose, S.A., Gold, E.B., Hess, R., Joffe, H., Kravitz, H.M., Tepper, P.G. and Thurston, R.C. (2015) Duration of menopausal vasomotor symptoms over the menopause transition, *JAMA Internal Medicine*, 175(4): 531–9. doi:10.1001/jamainternmed.2014.8063.

Bakhtin, M. (1984) *Rabelais and His World*, Bloomington: Indiana University Press.

Baltes, M. and Carstensen, L. (1996) The process of successful ageing, *Ageing and Society*, 16: 397–422.

Baltes, P. B. and Baltes, M.M. (1990) *Successful Ageing: perspectives from the behavioural sciences*, Cambridge: Cambridge University Press.

Baltes, P. and Smith, J. (2003) New frontiers in the future of ageing: from successful ageing of the young old to the dilemmas of the fourth age, *Gerontology*, 49: 123–35.

Baltes, P.B., Staudinger, U.M. and Lindenerger, U. (1999) Lifespan psychology: theory and application to intellectual functioning, *Annual Review of Psychology*, 50: 471–507.

Banyard, K. (2010) *The Equality Illusion: the truth about women and men today*, London: Faber and Faber.

Basting, A.D. (1998) *The Stages of Age: performing age in contemporary American culture*, Ann Arbor: University of Michigan Press.

Bauman, Z. (2000) Foreword: individually, together. In Beck, U. and Beck-Gernsheim, E. (2000) *Individualization: institutionalized individualism and its social and political consequences*, London: Sage, pp. 14–19.

Bauman, Z. (2001) Consuming life, *Journal of Consumer Culture*, 1(9): 9–29.

Beauvoir, S. de (1965) [1964] *A Very Easy Death*, New York: Pantheon.

Beauvoir, S. de (1968) [1963] *Force of Circumstance*, Harmondsworth: Penguin.

Beauvoir, S. de (1970) [1948] *The Ethics of Ambiguity*, New York: The Citadel Press.

Beauvoir, S. de (1985) [1981] *Adieux: a farewell to Sartre*, Harmondsworth: Penguin.

Beauvoir, S. de (1996) [1970] *The Coming of Age*, New York: Norton.

Beauvoir , S. de (1997) [1949] *The Second Sex*, London: Vintage.

Beauvoir, S. de (2001) [1958] *Memoires of a Dutiful Daughter*, New York: Harper Perennial.

Beauvoir, S. de (2006) [1969] *The Woman Destroyed*, novella published in the collection *The Age of Discretion*, London: Harper Perennial.

Beck, U. (1992) *Risk Society: towards a new modernity*, London: Sage.

Beck, U. and Beck-Gernsheim, E. (2002) *Individualization: institutionalized individualism and its social and political consequences*, London: Sage.

Beck-Gernsheim, E. (2002) *Reinventing the Family*, Cambridge: Polity.

Becker, G. (1997) *Disrupted Lives: how people create meaning in a chaotic world*, Berkeley, University of California Press.

Bee, H.L. and Mitchell, S.K. (1984) *The Developing Person: a life-span approach* (second edition), San Francisco: HarperCollins.

Benjamin, J. (1990) *The Bonds of Love: psychoanalysis, feminism and the problem of domination*, London: Virago.

Benjamin, J. (1994) The omnipotent mother: a psychoanalytic study of fantasy. In Bassin, D., Honey, M. and Kaplan, M.M. (eds) *Representations of Motherhood*, New Haven: Yale University Press, pp. 129–46.

Berg, G. and Gadow, S. (1978) Towards more human meanings of ageing: ideals and images from philosophy and art. In Spicker, S.F., Woodward, K.M. and Tassel, D.D. van (eds) *Ageing and the Elderly*, Atlantic Highlands, NJ: Humanities Press, pp. 83–92.

Berger, J. (1972) *Ways of Seeing*, London: BBC and Penguin Books.

Bjerrum Nielsen, H. (2004) Noisy Girls: new subjectivities and old gender discourses, *Young* 12(1): 9–30.

Bolick, K. (2015) *Spinster: making a life of one's own*, New York: Corsair.

Bordo, S. (1986) The Cartesian masculinisation of thought, *Signs* 11(3): 439–56.

Bordo, S. (1995) *Unbearable Weight*, Berkeley: University of California.

Bordo, S. (1999) Selections from the flight to objectivity. In Bordo, S. (ed.) *Feminist Interpretations of René Descartes*, Philadelphia: Penn State University Press, pp. 48–69.

Bourdieu, P. (1984) *Distinction*, London: Routledge and Kegan Paul.

Bourdieu, P. (1990) *The Logic of Practice*, Cambridge: Polity.

Bourdieu, P. (1993) *Sociology in Question*, London: Theory, Culture and Society.

Bourdieu, P. (2000) *Pascalian Meditations*, Cambridge: Polity.

Bourdieu, P. (2001) [1998] *Masculine Domination*, Cambridge: Polity.

Bowlby, J. (1971) *Attachment and Loss, vol. 1*, Harmondsworth: Penguin.

Bradley, H. (1996) *Fragmented Identities*, Cambridge: Polity.

Bradley, H. (2007) *Gender: key concepts*, Cambridge: Polity.

Bradley, H. and Devadson, R. (2008) Fractured transitions: young adults' pathways into contemporary labour markets, *Sociology*, 42(1): 119–36.

Brannen, J. and Nilsen, A. (2002) Young people's time perspectives from youth to adulthood, *Sociology* 36(3): 513–37.

Brown, N.O. (1959) *Life Against Death*, Middletown, CT: Wesleyan University Press.

Brown, W. (2015) *Undoing the Demos: neoliberalism's stealth revolution*, New York: Zone Books.

Brumberg, J.J. (1997) *The Body Project: an intimate history of American girls*, New York: Vintage.

Buchholz, S., Hofacher, D., Mills, M., Blossfield, H.-P., Kurz, K. and Hofmeister, H. (2009) Lifecourses in the globalization process: the development of social inequalities in modern societies, *European Sociological Review*, 25(1): 53–71.

Budgeon, S. (2014) The dynamics of gender hegemony: femininities, masculinities and social change, *Sociology*, 48(2): 317–24.

Burkeman, O. (2015) The cult of youth cheats young and old alike. Let's reclaim adulthood. *The Guardian*, 12 May.

Burman, E. (2005) Childhood, neo-liberalism and the feminization of education, *Gender and Education*, 17(4): 351–67.

Burman, E. (2007) *Deconstructing Developmental Psychology* (second edition), London: Routledge.

Burrow, J.A. (1988) *The Ages of Man: a study in medieval writing and thought*, Oxford: Oxford University Press.

Bury, M. and Wadsworth, M. (2003) The 'biological clock'? Ageing, health and the body across the life course. In Williams, S.J., Birke, L. and Bendelow, G. (2003) *Debating Biology: sociological reflections on health, medicine and society*, London: Routledge, pp. 109–19.

Butler, J. (1990) *Gender Trouble*, London: Routledge.

Butler, J. (1993) *Bodies that Matter*, London: Routledge.

Butler, R.N. (1963) The life review: an interpretation of reminiscence in the aged, *Psychiatry*, 26: 65–76.

Butler, R.N. (2002) The study of productive ageing, *Journal of Gerontology: Social Sciences*, 57B(6): S323.

Butler, R.N., Miller, R.A., Perry, D., Carnes, B.A., Williams, T.F., Cassel, C., Brody, J., Bernard, M.A., Partridge, L., Kirkwood, T., Martin, G.M. and Olshansky, S.J. (2008) New model of health promotion and disease prevention for the twenty-first century, *British Medical Journal*, 337: 149–50.

Bynner, J. (2007) Rethinking the youth phase of the life course: the case for emerging adulthood?, *Journal of Youth Studies*, 8(4): 367–84.

Bynum, C.W. (2001) *Metamorphosis and Identity*, New York: Zone Books.

Calasanti, T. and Slevin, K.F. (2001) *Gender, Social Inequalities and Aging*, Walnut Creek, CA: AltaMira Press.

Calasanti, T.M. and Slevin, K.F. (2006) Introduction: age matters. In Calasanti, T.M. and Slevin, K.F. (eds) *Age Matters: realigning feminist thinking*, London: Routledge, pp. 1–17.

Callahan, D. (1987) *Setting Limits: medical goals in an ageing society*, New York: Simon and Schuster.

Campbell, B. (2013) *End of Equality: the only way is women's liberation*, London: Seagull.

Carers UK (2012) *Facts about Carers: policy briefing December 2012*, London: Carers UK.

Carpenter, C. (2013) That's not very old lady like! Heidi Klum is a granny gone wild as she lets loose inside her annual Halloween bash, *Daily Mail*, 1 November.

Carter, A. (1981) *The Bloody Chamber*, Harmondsworth: King Penguin.

Cavendish, L. (2015) Why do so many middle-aged men feel so lost? *Daily Telegraph*, 27 February.

Chapple, A. and Ziebland, S. (2002) Prostate cancer: embodied experience and perceptions of masculinity, *Sociology of Health and Illness*, 24(6): 820–84.

Children's Society (2013) *Hidden from View: the experiences of young carers in England*, London: Children's Society.

Chodorow, N. (1978) *The Reproduction of Mothering*, Berkeley: University of California Press.

Chodorow, N. (1989) *Feminism and Psychoanalytic Theory*, New Haven: Yale University Press.

Chodorow, N. (1994) *Femininities, Masculinities, Sexualities: Freud and beyond*, Kentucky: University of Kentucky Press.

Cohen, A.P. (1994) *Self-Consciousness: an alternative anthropology of identity*, London: Routledge.

Cole, T.R. (1986) The 'enlightened' view of ageing: Victorian morality in a new key. In Cole, T.R. and Gadow, S. (eds) *What Does it Mean to Grow Old?*, Durham, NC: Duke University Press, pp. 115–30.

Cole, T.R. (1989) Generational equity in America: a cultural historian's perspective, *Social Science and Medicine*, 29(3): 377–83.

Cole, T.R. (1992) *The Journey of Life*, Cambridge: Cambridge University Press.

Cole, T.R. and Winkler, M.G. (1994) *The Oxford Book of Aging: reflections on the journey of life*, Oxford: Oxford University Press.

Coleman, P. and O'Hanlon, A. (2004) *Ageing and Development: theories and research*, London: Arnold.

Collins, G. (2014) This is what 80 looks like, *New York Times*, 22 March.

Connell, R.W. (1987) *Gender and Power: society, the person and sexual politics*, Cambridge: Polity Press.

Connell, R.W. (1993) *Masculinities*, Los Angeles: University of California Press.

Connell, R.W. (2000) *The Men and the Boys*, Cambridge: Polity.

Connell, R.W. (2005) Change among the gatekeepers: men, masculinities, and gender equality in the global arena, *Signs*, 30(3): 1801–25.

Conway, K. (2007) *Illness and the Limits of Expression*, Ann Arbor: University of Michigan Press.

Conway, S. and Hockey, J. (1998) Resisting the 'mask' of old age? The social meaning of lay health beliefs in later life, *Ageing and Society*, 18(4): 469–94.

Coren, V. (2014) We need to talk about work vs Motherhood, *Elle*, October.

Côté, J.E. (2002) The role of identity capital in the transition to adulthood: the individualization thesis examined, *Journal of Youth Studies*, 5(2).

Coulmas, F. (2007) *Population Decline and Ageing in Japan: the social consequences*, London: Routledge.

Cumming, E. and Henry, W. (1961) *Growing Old: the process of disengagement*, New York: Basic Books.

Cummings, D. (2013) Some thoughts on education and political priorities, accessed at http://static.guim.co.uk/ni/1381763590219/-Some-thoughts-on-education.pdf, December.

Cunningham, H. (1991) *The Children of the Poor: representations of childhood since the seventeenth century*, Oxford: Blackwell.

Cunningham, H. (2006) *The Invention of Childhood*, London: BBC.

Cusk, R. (2015) Mothers and daughters: a modern tragedy, *Sunday Times*, 5 April.

Dalley, G. (1988) *Ideologies of Caring*, Basingstoke: Macmillan Education.

Daly, M. (1991) *Gyn/Ecology: the metaethics of radical feminism*, London: The Women's Press.

Darlington, R., Margo, J. and Sternberg, S. with Burks, B.K. (2011) *Through the Looking Glass: teenage girls' self-esteem is more than skin-deep*, London: Demos.

Davies, K. (1994) The tensions between process time and clock time in care-work: the example of day nurseries, *Time and Society*, 3(3): 277–303.

Dean, M. (1994) *Critical and Effective Histories: Foucault's methods and historical sociology*, London: Routledge.

Deleuze, G. and Guattari, F. (2000) *Thousand Plateaus*, London: Continuum International Publishing.

Delphy, C. (1993) Rethinking sex and gender, *Women's Studies International Forum* 16(1): 1–9.

Department for Education and Employment (1997) *Excellence in Schools*, London: DfEE.

Department for Education and Skills (2007) *Gender and Education: the evidence on pupils in England*, available at www.dfes.gov.uk/research.

Department of Health (2006) *A New Ambition for Old Age: next steps in implementing the National Service Framework for Older People*, London: HMSO.

Deresiewicz, W. (2014) *Excellent Sheep: the miseducation of the American elite and the way to a meaningful life*, New York: Free Press.

Deutsch, H. (1984) The menopause, *International Journal of Psychoanalysis*, 65(1): 55–62.

Deutscher, P. (1997) *Yielding Gender*. London: Routledge.

Dill, K. (2014) Report: CEOS earn 331 times as much as average workers, *Forbes*, 15 April.

Dinnerstein, D. (1976) *The Mermaid and the Minotaur: sexual arrangements and human malaise*, New York: Harper & Row.

Doane, M.A. (1987) *The Desire to Desire*, London: Routledge.

Dorling, D. (2014) *Inequality and the One Per Cent*, London: Verso.

Douglas, M. (1966) *Purity and Danger*, London: Routledge and Kegan Paul.

Dove, M. (1986) *The Perfect Age of Man's Life*, Cambridge: Cambridge University Press.

Dowling, C. (2000) *The Frailty Myth: redefining the physical potential of women and girls*, New York: Random House.

Dreyfus, H. and Rabinow, P. (1982) *Michel Foucault: beyond structuralism and hermeneutics*, London: Harvester Wheatsheaf.

Driscoll, M. (2015) The naughty aunt wooing teenagers away from porn, *Sunday Times*, 26 July.

Du Gay, P. (1996) *Consumption and Identity at Work*, London: Sage.

Duden, B. (1991) *The Woman Beneath the Skin: a doctor's patients in eighteenth-century Germany*, London: Harvard University Press.

Duncan, C. and Loretto, W. (2004) Never the right age? Gender and age-based discrimination in employment, *Gender, Work and Organisation*, 11(1): 95–115.

Dunham, L. (2014) *Not that Kind of Girl*, New York: Fourth Estate.

Dunn, J. (1988) *The Beginning of Social Understanding*, Oxford: Blackwell.

Dunne, J. (1993) *Back to the Rough Ground: practical judgement and the lure of technique*, Indiana: University of Notre Dame Press.

Dyer, R. (1982, September/October) Don't look now: the male pin-up, *Screen*, 23 (3/4): 61–73.

Dyhouse, C. (2014) *Girl Trouble: panic and progress in the history of young women*, London: Zed Books.

Eagleton, T. (2004) *After Theory*, Harmondsworth: Penguin.

Ehrenreich, B. (1983) *The Hearts of Men: American dreams and the flight from commitment*, London: Pluto Press.

Ehrenreich, B. (2015) 'Rise of the Robots' and 'Shadow Work', Sunday Book Review, *New York Times*, 11 May.

Ehrenreich, B. and English, D. (2013) *Complaints and Disorders: the sexual politics of sickness*, New York: Anchor Books.

Eisenstein, H. (2005) A dangerous liaison? Feminism and corporate globalization, *Science and Society*, 69(3): 487–518.

Elias, N. (1978) [1939] *The Civilizing Process, volume 1: the history of manners*, Oxford: Basil Blackwell.

Erikson, E.H. (1964) Inner and Outer Space: reflections on womanhood, *Daedaulus*, 93(2): 582–606.

Erikson, E.H. (1994) [1968] *Identity: youth and crisis*, New York: Norton.

Erikson, E.H. and Erikson, J.M. (1997) *The Life Cycle Completed: extended version*, New York: Norton.

Esping-Anderson, G. (2005) Final remarks. In Boeri, T., Del Boca, D. and Pissarides, C. (eds) *Women at Work: an economic perspective*, Oxford: Oxford University Press.

Esping-Andersen, G. and Sarasa, S. (2002) The generational conflict reconsidered, *Journal of European Social Policy*, 12(1): 5–21.

Estes, C.L. (1979) *The Ageing Enterprise*, San Francisco: Josey-Bass.

Estes, C.L. (2001) *Social Policy and Ageing*, Thousand Oaks, CA: Sage.

Eugster, C. (2011) Experience: I am a 91-year-old body builder, *The Guardian*, 2 April.

Faludi, S. *Backlash: the undeclared war against women*, New York: Vintage.

Farrelly, C. (2008) Has the time come to take on time itself? *British Medical Journal*, 337: 147–8.

Fausto-Sterling, A. (2003) The problem with sex/gender and nature/nurture. In Williams, S.J., Birke, L. and Bendelow, G. (eds) *Debating Biology: sociological reflections on health, medicine and society*, London: Routledge, pp. 123–32.

Felski, R. (1997) The doxa of difference, *Signs: Journal of Women in Culture and Society*, 23(1): 1–23.

Fennell, G., Phillipson, C. and Evers, H. (1988) *The Sociology of Old Age*, Milton Keynes: Open University Press.

Ferguson, E., Maughan, B. and Golding, G. (2008) Which children receive grand-parental care and what effect does it have? *Journal of Child Psychology and Psychiatry*, 49(2): 161–9.

Ferguson, K.E. (1993) *The Man Question: visions of subjectivity in feminist theory*, Berkeley: University of California Press.

Ferrucci, L., Guralnik, J.M., Studenski, S., Fried, L.P., Cutler, G.B. and Walston, J.D. (2004) Designing randomized controlled trials aimed at preventing or delaying functional decline and disability in frail, older persons: a consensus report, *Journal of the American Geriatrics Society*, 52(4): 625–35.

Fewtrell, M., Wilson, D.C., Booth, I. and Lucas, A. (2011) Six months of exclusive breast feeding: how good is the evidence? *British Medical Journal*, 342: c5955.

Figlio, K.M. (1976) The metaphor of organization: an historiographical perspective on the bio-medical sciences of the early 19th century, *History of Science*, 14(1): 17–53.

Finch, J. and Groves, D. (1980). Community care and the family: a case for equal opportunities? *Journal of Social Policy*, 9(4): 487–511.

Finch, L. (1993) *The Classing Gaze: sexuality, class and surveillance*, St Leonard's, NSW: Allen and Unwin.

Fine, M.D. (2012) Individualising care: the transformation of personal support in old age, *Ageing and Society*, 33(3): 421–36.

Firestone, S. (1970) *The Dialectic of Sex*, New York: William Morrow.

Flanagan, C. (2009) Young people's civic engagement and political development. In Furlong, A. (ed.) *Handbook of Youth and Young Adulthood: new perspectives and new agenda*, London: Routledge, pp. 293–300.

Formosa, M. and Higgs, P. (2013) Introduction. In Formosa, M. and Higgs, P. (eds) *Social Class in Later Life: power identity and lifestyle*, Bristol: Policy Press.

Foster, L. (2013) Pension reform should focus on women, poverty and social exclusion, available at http://www.poverty.ac.uk/editorial/putting-women-centre-pension-reform, accessed 17 August 2015.

Foucault, M. (1977a) A preface to transgression. In Bouchard, D.F. (ed.) *Language, Counter-Memory, Practice: selected essays and interviews*, Oxford: Basil Blackwell, pp. 29–52.

Foucault, M. (1977b) [1975] *Discipline and Punish*, Harmondsworth: Penguin.

Foucault, M. (1982) On Governmentality. In Burchell, G., Gordon, C. and Miller, P. (eds) *The Foucault Effect: studies in governmentality*, Chicago: University of Chicago Press, pp. 119–50.

Foucault, M. (2002) *The Order of Things*, Oxford: Routledge.

Francis, B. (2010) Girls' achievement: contesting the positioning of girls as the relational 'achievers' to boys' underachievement. In Jackson, C., Paechter, C. and Renold, E. (eds) *Girls and Education: continuing concerns, new agendas*, Milton Keynes: Open University Press, pp. 21–37.

Frank, A.W. (1996) Reconciliatory alchemy: bodies, narratives and power, *Body and Society*, 2(3): 53–71.

Frank, A.W. (2010) *Letting Stories Breathe: a socio-narratology*, Chicago: University of Chicago Press.

Fraser, N. (2009) Feminism, capitalism and the cunning of history, *New Left Review*, 56, Mar/Apr, 97–117.

Fraser, N. and Gordon, L. (1994) A genealogy of dependency: tracing a keyword of the US welfare state, *Signs*, 19(2): 309–36.

Freeth, B. (2014) Where did Madonna get THOSE boobs? Internet pokes fun at superstar after that shocking breast-baring photoshoot. *Daily Mail*, http://www.dailymail.co.uk/tvshowbiz/article-2858453/Madonna-mocked-online-bizarre-topless-photoshoot.html, accessed 4 December.

Freud, S. (2000) [1895] *Three Essays on the Theory of Sexuality*, New York: Basic Books.

Fried, L.P., Tangen, C.M., Walston, J., Newman, A., Hirsch, L., Gottdiener, J., et al. (2001) Frailty in older adults: evidence for a phenotype, *Journal of Gerontology: Medical Sciences*, 56(3): 146–56.

Fried, L.P., Ferrucci, L., Darer, J., Williamson, J. and Anderson, G. (2004) Untangling the concepts of disability, frailty and comorbidity: implications for improved targeting and care, *Journal of Gerontology: Medical Sciences*, 59(3): 255–63.

Friedan, B. (1963) *The Feminine Mystique*, New York: Norton.

Friedan, B. (1993) *The Fountain of Age*, New York: Vintage.

Frost, L. (2001) *Young Women and the Body: a feminist sociology*, London: Palgrave Macmillan.

Furedi, F. (2007) From the narrative of the Blitz to the rhetoric of vulnerability, *Cultural Sociology*, 1(2): 235–54.

Furlong, A. (2013) *Youth Studies: an introduction*, London: Routledge.

Furlong, A. and Cartmel, F. (1997) *Young People and Social Change*, Milton Keynes: Open University Press.

Furman, F.K. (1999) There are no old venues: older women's responses to their ageing bodies. In Walker, M. (ed.) *Mother Time: women, ageing and ethics*, Boston: Rowman and Littlefield, pp. 7–22.

Fussell, S.W. (1992) *Muscle: the confessions of an unlikely bodybuilder*, New York: Abacus.

Gadow, S.A. (1983) Body and Self: a dialectic. In Kestenbaum, V. (ed.) *The Humanity of the Ill*, Knoxville: University of Tennessee Press, pp. 86–100.

Gadow, S.A. (1986) Frailty and Strength: the dialectic of aging. In Cole, T.R and Gadow, S.A. (eds) *What Does it Mean to Grow Old? Reflection from the humanities*, Durham, NC: Duke University Press, pp. 237–43.

Giddens, A. (1991) *Modernity and Self-Identity*, Cambridge: Polity.

Gill, R.C. (2007a) *Gender and the Media*, Cambridge: Polity.

Gill, R.C. (2007b) Critical respect: the difficulties and dilemmas of agency and 'choice' for feminism: a reply to Duits and van Zoonen, *European Journal of Women's Studies*, 14(1): 69–80.

Gill, R.C. (2008) Body talk: negotiating body image and masculinity, in Riley, S., Burns, M., Frith, H., Wiggins, S. and Markula, P. (eds) *Critical Bodies: representations, identities and practices of weight and body management*, London: Palgrave Macmillan, pp. 101–16.

Gill, R.C. (2009) Supersexualize me! Advertising and the midriffs. In Attwood, F. (ed.) *Mainstreaming Sex: the sexualisation of culture*, London: I.B. Tauris, pp. 93–99.

Gilleard, C. (1996) Consumption and identity in later life: toward a cultural gerontology, *Ageing and Society*, 16(4): 489–98.

Gilleard, C. and Higgs, P. (2000) *Cultures of Ageing*, Harlow: Prentice Hall.

Gilleard, C. and Higgs, P. (2002) The third age: class, cohort or generation? *Ageing and Society*, 22(3): 369–80.

Gilleard, C. and Higgs, P. (2005) *Contexts of Ageing: class, cohort and community*, Cambridge: Polity.

Gilligan, C. (1982) *In a Different Voice: psychological theory and women's development*, Cambridge, MA: Harvard University Press.

Gillis, S. and Munford, R. (2006) Genealogies and Generations: the politics and praxis of third wave feminism, *Women's History Review*, 13(2): 165–82.

Glaser, K., Nicholls, M., Stuchbury, R., Price, D. and Gjonca, E. (2009) *Life Course Influences in Later Life: summary of the findings*, available at http://justageing.equalityhumanrights.com/wp-content/uploads/2009/10/life-course-influences.pdf

Glaser, K., Montserrat, E.R., Waginger, U., Price, D., Stuchbury, R. and Tinker, A. (2010) *Grandparenting in Europe* (Grandparents Plus), available at http://www.grandparentsplus.org.uk/reports-and-publications

Glennie, A. (2014) Medical insurers won't pay for my menopause treatment, says angry Mariella Frostrup, *Daily Mail*, 26 November.

Goggins, W.B., Woo, J., Sham, A. and Ho, S.C. (2005) Frailty index a measure of biological age in a Chinese population, *Journals of Gerontology A: Biol Sci Med Sci* 60: 1046–5.

Goldman, R. (2000) *Reading Ads Socially* (third edition), London: Routledge.

Goodman, P. (1960) *Growing Up Absurd: problems of youth in the organized society*, New York: Vintage Books.

Gordon, J. (2015) Are we creating a lost generation of women? *Huffington Post*, 20 January.

Gornick, M. (2006) Between 'girl power' and 'reviving Ophelia': constituting the neoliberal girl subject, *NWSA Journal*, 18(2): 1–23.

Gorton, K. and Garde-Hansen, J. (2012) From old media whore to new media troll, *Feminist Media Studies*, 13(2): 288–301.

Gott, M. and Hinchcliff, S. (2003) How important is sex in later life? The view of older people, *Social Science and Medicine*, 56(8): 1617–28.

Graeber, D. (2015) *The Utopia of Rules: on technology, stupidity and the secret joys of bureaucracy*, New York: Melville House Publishing.

Gray, A. (2005) The changing availability of grandparents as carers and its implications for childcare policy in the UK, *Journal of Social Policy*, 34(4): 557–77.

Greer, G. (1970) *The Female Eunuch*, London: MacGibbon and Kee.

Greer, G. (1991) *The Change*, London: Hamish Hamilton.

Grey, S. (2015) I've learned not to make snap judgements. Sexual chemistry can surprise you, *The Guardian*, 20 June.

Grierson, B. (2014) What if age is nothing but a mind-set? *New York Times*, 22 October.

Griffin, C. (1993) *Representations of Youth*, Cambridge: Polity.

Grosz, E. (1990) The body of signification. In Fletcher, J. and Benjamin, A. (eds) *Abjection, Melancholia and Love: the work of Julia Kristeva*, London: Routledge, pp. 80–103.

Guillemard, A.-M. (1997) Rewriting social policy and changes within the life course organisation: a European perspective, *Canadian Journal on Aging*, 16(3): 441–64.

Gullette, M.M. (1997) *Declining to Decline*, Charlottesville: University of Virginia Press.

Gullette, M.M. (1998) Mid-life discourses in the twentieth century United States: an essay on the sexuality, ideology and politics of 'middle-ageism'. In Schweder, R.A. (ed.) *Welcome to Middle Age! (And other cultural fictions)*, Chicago: University of Chicago Press, pp. 3–44.

Gullette, M.M. (2004) *Aged by Culture*, Chicago: University of Chicago Press.

Guyton, A.C. and Hall, J.E. (2006) *Textbook of Medical Physiology* (11th edition), Philadelphia: Elsevier Saunders.

Hall, D. (2014) *Essays After Eighty*, Boston and New York: Houghton Mifflin Harcourt.

Hall, G.S. (1905) *Adolescence: its psychology and its relations to physiology, anthropology, sociology, sex, crime, religion and education*, New York: Appleton.

Hall, S. (1996) Who needs 'identity'? In Hall, S. and du Gay, P. (eds) *Questions of Cultural Identity*, London: Sage, pp. 1–17.

Hall, S. (2013) The work of representation. In Hall, S., Evans, J. and Nixon, S. (eds) *Representation* (second edition), London: Open University Press and Sage Publications, pp. 1–59.

Harding, S. (2004) Rethinking standpoint epistemology: what is 'strong' objectivity? In Harding, S. (ed.) *The Feminist Standpoint Theory Reader*. London: Routledge, pp. 127–40.

Hardman, C. (2001) Can there be an anthropology of children? *Childhood*, 8(4): 501–17.

Hareven, T. (1982) Preface. In Hareven, T. and Adams, K. (eds) *Ageing and Life Course Transitions*, London: Routledge.

Harris, A. (2004) *Future Girl: young women in the twenty-first century*, London: Routledge.

Harris, A. (2009) Young people, politics and citizenship. In Furlong, A. (ed.) *Handbook of Youth and Young Adulthood: new perspectives and new agenda*, London: Routledge, pp. 301–6.

Harris, J. (2015) 'They want more than we did' – how the Tories made age our biggest divide, *The Guardian* 17 July, accessible at http://www.theguardian.com/society/2015/jul/17/old-young-age-divide-christchurch

Hartstock, N.C.M. (1983) The feminist standpoint: developing the ground for a specifically feminist historical materialism. In Harding, S. and Hintikha, M.B. (eds), *Discovering Reality*. Dordecht: Reidel, pp. 283–310.

Havighurst, R.J. (1953) *Human Development and Education*, New York: Longmans.

Haylett, C. (2001) Illegitimate subjects? Abject whites, neoliberal modernisation, and middle-class multiculturalism, *Environment and Planning D: Society and Space*, 19: 351–70.

Hazan, H. (2009) Essential others: anthropology and the return of the savage, *International Journal of Sociology and Social Policy*, 29(1/2): 60–72.

Health and Social Care Information Centre (HSCIC) (2015) Eating Disorders: Hospital admissions up by 8 per cent in a year; report accessed at http://www.hscic.gov.uk/article/3880/Eating-disorders-Hospital-admissions-up-by-8-per-cent-in-a-year on 25 January 2015.

Heine, S. (1985) *Existential and Ontological Dimensions of Time in Heidegger and Dogen*, New York: SUNY Press.

Hellen, N. (2015) We're optimists at 16 – but feel doomed by 22, *Sunday Times*, 4 October.

Hendrick, H. (1990) Constructions and reconstructions of British childhood: an interpretative survey, 1800 to the present. In James, A. and Prout, A. (eds) *Constructing and Reconstructing Childhood: contemporary issues in the sociological study of childhood*, Basingstoke: Falmer Press, pp. 35–59.

Hendrick, H. (2003) *Child Welfare: historical dimensions, contemporary debates*, Bristol: Policy Press.

Herskovits, E. and Mitteness, L. (1994) Transgressions and sickness in old age, *Journal of Ageing Studies*, 8(3): 327–40.

Higgs, P. and Gilleard, C. (2006) Departing the margins: social class and later life in second modernity, *Journal of Sociology*, 42 (3): 219–41.

Higgs, P. and Gilleard, C. (2015) *Rethinking Old Age: theorizing the fourth age*, London: Palgrave Macmillan.

Higonnet, A. (1998) *Pictures of Innocence: the history and crisis of ideal childhood*, London: Thames and Hudson.

Hlavka, H.R. (2014) Normalizing sexual violence: young women account for harassment and abuse, *Gender and Society*, 28(3): 69–80.

Hochschild, A.R. (1979) Emotion work, feeling rules and social structure, *American Journal of Sociology*, 85(3): 551–75.

Hockey, J. and James, A. (1993) *Growing Up and Growing Old,* London: Sage.

Hoddinott, P., Craig, L.C.A., Britten, J., McInnes, R.M. (2012) A serial qualitative interview study of infant feeding experiences: idealism meets realism, *British Medical Journal*, (2012) 2: e000504, doi: 10.1136/bmjopen-2011-000504

Holland, J., Ramazanoglu, C., Sharpe, S. and Thomson, R. (1998) *The Male in the Head: young people, heterosexuality and power*, London: Tufnell Press.

Hollows, J. (2000) *Feminism, Femininity and Popular Culture*, Manchester: Manchester University Press.

Hollway, L. (1984) Women's power in heterosexual sex, *Women's Studies International Forum*, 7(1): 63–8.

Hood-Williams, J. (1990) Patriarchy for children: on the stability of power relations in children's lives. In Chisholm, L., Büchner, P. and Brown, P. (eds) *Childhood, Youth and Social Change: a comparative perspective*, Basingstoke: Falmer, pp. 111–22.

Howson, A. (2005) *Embodying Gender*, London: Sage.

Hubbard, R.E. and Rockwood, K. (2011) Frailty in older women, *Maturitas*, 69: 203–7.

Huhne, C. (2013) Someone needs to fight the selfish short-sighted old, *The Guardian*, Comment is Free, 22 December.

Hunt, S. (2001) *The Life Course: a sociological introduction*, London: Palgrave Macmillan.

Hunt, E. (2015) How old do I look: another way to feel bad about yourself online, *The Guardian*, 1 May.

Hurd Clarke, L. (2011) *Facing Age: women growing older in anti-ageing culture*, London: Rowman and Littlefield.

International Osteoporosis Foundation (IOF) (2015) Facts and Statistics. http://www.iofbonehealth.org/facts-statistics accessed 4 April 2015.

Itzin, C. and Phillipson, C. (1995) Gendered ageism: a double jeopardy for women in organizations. In Itzin, C. and Newman, J. (eds) *Gender, Culture and Organizational Change: putting theory into practice*, London: Routledge, pp. 81–90.

Jackson, M. (1996) (ed.) *Things as They Are: new directions in phenomenological anthropology*, Bloomington: Indiana University Press.

Jackson, S. (1982) *Childhood and Sexuality*, Oxford: Wiley-Blackwell.

Jackson, S. (1999) *Heterosexuality in Question*, London: Sage.

Jackson, C. and Tinkler, P. (2007) 'Ladettes' and 'Modern Girls': 'troublesome' young femininities, *Sociological Review*, 55(2): 251–72.

James, A. and James, A. (2012) *Key Concepts in Childhood Studies* (second edition), London: Sage.

James, A. and Prout, A. (eds) (1990) *Constructing and Reconstructing Childhood*, Basingstoke: Falmer Press.

James, A., Jenks, C. and Prout, A. (1998) *Theorizing Childhood*, Cambridge: Polity.

Jenkins, R. (2002) *Pierre Bourdieu* (second edition), London: Routledge.

Jenkins, R. (2004) *Social Identity: key ideas* (second edition), London: Routledge.

Jenks, C. (2003) *Transgression: key ideas*, London: Routledge.

Jenks, C. (2005) *Childhood: key ideas* (second edition), London: Routledge.

Johnson, B. (2013) The Third Margaret Thatcher Lecture, downloaded at http://www.cps.org.uk/files/factsheets/original/131128144200-Thatcherlecturev2.pdf

Johnson, S.L. (2015) How do you know you've really become an adult? An illustrated essay, *The Guardian*, 3 October.

Jones, G. (2009) *Youth*, Cambridge: Polity.

Jung, A. and Schill, W.-B. (2004) Male sexuality with advancing age, *European Journal of Obstetrics and Gynecology and Reproductive Biology*, 113: 123–5.

Kant, I. (1963) *On History*, New York: Bobbs-Merrill.

Kaplan. E.A. (1983) *Women and Film: both sides of the camera*, London: Routledge.

Katz, S. (1996) *Disciplining Old Age*, Charlottesville: University of Virginia Press.

Katz, S. (2000) Busy bodies: activity, aging, and the management of everyday life, *Journal of Ageing Studies*, 14: 135–52.

Katz, S. (2011) Hold on! Falling, embodiment and the materiality of old age. In M. Casper and P. Currah (eds) *Corpus: an interdisciplinary reader on bodies and knowledge*, New York: Palgrave Macmillan, pp. 187–205.

Katz, S. and Marshall, B.L. (2004) Is the functional 'normal'? Ageing, sexuality and the bio-marking of successful living, *History of the Human Sciences*, 17(1): 53–7.

Kaufman, S.R. (1986) *The Ageless Self*, Madison: University of Wisconsin Press.

Kaufman, S.R. (1994) The social construction of frailty: an anthropological perspective, *Journal of Aging Studies*, 8 (1): 54–8.

Kinchen, R. (2014) I'm glad my hot flushes are causing a few blushes, *Sunday Times*, 30 November.

King, N. (2006) The lengthening list of oppressions: age relations and the feminist study of inequality. In Calasanti, T.M. and Slevin, K.F. (eds) *Age Matters: realigning feminist thinking*, London: Routledge, pp. 47–74.

Kingston, K. (2000) Falls in later life: status passage and preferred identities as a new orientation, *Health (London)*, 4(2): 216–33.

Kirkwood, T. (2008) Understanding ageing from an evolutionary perspective, *Journal of Internal Medicine*, 263: 117–27.

Kleinman, A. (1988) *The Illness Narratives: suffering, healing and the human condition*, New York: Basic Books.

Knight, I. (2014) Chick lit is in its death throes, *The Guardian*, 24 October.

Kohli, M. (1999) Private and public transfers between generations: linking the family and the state, *European Societies*, 1(1): 81–104.

Kohli, M. (2007) The institutionalization of the life course, *Research in Human Development*, 4(3–4): 253–71.

Kontos P. (2006) Embodied selfhood: an ethnographic exploration of Alzheimer's disease. In Cohen, L. and Leibing, A. (eds) *Thinking about Dementia: culture, loss, and the anthropology of senility*, Cambridge: Cambridge University Press, pp. 195–217.

Kristeva, J. (1982) *Powers of Horror: an essay on abjection*, New York: Columbia University Press.

Kuh, D. and the New Dynamics of Ageing (NDA) Preparatory Network (2007) A life course approach to health aging, frailty and capability, *Journal of Gerontology: Medical Sciences*, 62(7): 717–21.

Lansley, S. and Mack, J. (2015) *Breadline Britain: the rise of mass poverty*, London: Oneworld Publications.

Laqueur, T. (1990) *Making Sex: body and gender from the Greeks to Freud*, Cambridge, MA: Harvard University Press.

Laslett, P. (1991) *A Fresh Map of Life: the emergence of the third age*, Cambridge, MA: Harvard University Press.

Lawler, S. (1999) Getting out and getting away: women's narratives of class mobility, *Feminist Review*, 63: 3–24.

Lawler, S. (2000) *Mothering the Self: mothers, daughters, subjects*, London: Routledge.

Lawler, S. (2005) Disgusted subjects: the making of middle-class identities, *Sociological Review*, 53(3): 429–46.

Lawler, S. (2008) *Identity: sociological perspectives*, Cambridge: Polity.

Leach, P. (1977) *Baby and Child*, London: Michael Joseph.

Lee, N. (2001) *Childhood and Society: growing up in an age of uncertainty*, Milton Keynes: Open University Press.

Leibing, A. and Kampf, A. (2013) Neither body nor brain: comparing preventive attitudes to prostate cancer and Alzheimer's disease, *Body and Society*, early view: published online 19 March.

Leonard, D. (1990) Persons in their own right: children and sociology in the UK. In Chisholm, L., Büchner, P. and Brown, P. (eds) *Childhood, Youth and Social Change: a comparative perspective*, Basingstoke: Falmer Press, pp. 40–48.

Levin, J. (2013) *Blurring the Boundaries: the declining significance of age*, London: Routledge.

Levinson, D., Darrow, D.N, Klein, E.B. and Levinson, M. (1978) *The Seasons of a Man's Life*, New York: Knopf.

Levy, A. (2005) *Female Chauvinist Pigs: women and the rise of raunch culture*, New York: Free Press.

Lian, O.S. and Bondevik, H. (2015) Medical constructions of long term exhaustion, past and present, *Sociology of Health and Illness*, 37(6): 920–35. doi: 10.1111/1467–9566.12249.

Lloyd, L., Calnan, M., Cameron, A.M., Seymour, J. and Smith, R. (2014) Identity in the fourth age: perseverance, adaptation and maintaining dignity, *Ageing and Society*, 34(1): 1–19.

Lock, M. (1993) *Encounters with Ageing*, Cambridge: Cambridge University Press.

Lorber, J. (2000) Using gender to undo gender: a feminist degendering movement, *Feminist Theory*, 1(1): 79–95.

Lorber, J. and Moore, L.J. (2002) *The Social Construction of Illness* (second edition), Maryland: AltaMira Press.

Loretto, W., Duncan, C. and White, P.L. (2000) Ageism and employment: controversies, ambiguities and younger peoples perceptions, *Ageing and Society*, 20(3): 279–302.

Lott, T. (2015) We oldies aren't the lucky ones, Children today have much better lives, *The Guardian*, 27 March.

Lovgren, K. (2012) 'They see themselves as young': the market addressing the older consumer. In Ylanne, V. (ed.) *Representing Ageing: images and identities*, London: Palgrave Macmillan, pp. 53–67.

Lowenthal, D. (1985) *The Past is a Foreign Country*, Cambridge: Cambridge University Press.

Lowsky, D.J., Olshansky, S.J., Bhattacharya, J. and Goldman, D.P. (2013) Heterogeneity in healthy ageing, *Journal of Gerontology: Biological Sciences*, 69(6): 640–49.

Lustbader, W. (2011) *Life Gets Better: the unexpected pleasures of growing older*, New York: Tarcher/Penguin.

Lyddiard, M. (1924) *The Mothercraft Manual*, London: Churchill.

Lynott, R.J. and Lynott, P.P. (1996) Tracing the course of theoretical development in the sociology of ageing, *Gerontologist*, 36(6): 749–60.

MacInnes, J. (1998) *The End of Masculinity: the confusion of sexual genesis and sexual difference in modern society*, Milton Keynes: Open University Press.

MacIntyre, A. (2007) [1981] *After Virtue: a study in moral theory* (third edition), London: Duckworth.

MacPherson, K.I. (1981) Menopause as disease: the social construction of a metaphor, *Advances in Nursing Science*, 3: 95–113.

MacPherson, K.I. (1985) Osteoporosis and menopause: a feminist analysis of the social construction of a syndrome, *Advances in Nursing Science*, 7(4): 11–22.

Mannheim, K. (1952) [1927] The problem of generations. In *Essays on the Sociology of Knowledge*, London: Routledge and Kegan Paul.

Manton, K.G. (1982) Changing concepts of morbidity and mortality in the elderly population, *Memorial Fund Quarterly*, 60(2): 183–91.

Marshall, B.L. and Katz, S. (2006) From androgyny to androgens. In Calasanti, T.M. and Slevin, K.F. (eds) *Age matters: realigning feminist thinking*, New York and London: Routledge, pp. 75–97.

Marshall, B.L. and Katz, S. (2012) The embodied life course: post-ageism or the renaturalization of gender? *Societies*, 2: 222–34.

Martin, E. (1987) *The Woman in the Body*, Milton Keynes: Open University Press.

Marx, K. (1976) *Capital, Volume One*, New York: Vintage Books.

Marx, K. and Engels, F. (2010) [1848] *The Communist Manifesto*, London: Vintage.

McAdams, D.P. (1993) *The Stories We Live By*, London: Morrow/HarperCollins.

McRobbie, A. (2004) Notes on 'What Not to Wear' and post-feminist symbolic violence, in Adkins, L. and Skeggs, B. (eds) *Feminism after Bourdieu*, Oxford: Blackwell, pp. 99–109.

McRobbie, A. (2009) *The Aftermath of Feminism: gender, culture and social change*, London: Sage.

McRobbie, A. (2013) Top girls? Young women and the post-feminist sexual contract, *Cultural Studies*, 21(4–5): 718–37.

Menninghaus, W. (2003) *Disgust: theory and history of a strong sensation*, New York: State University of New York Press.

Merleau-Ponty, M. (2004) *Phenomenology of Perception*, London: Routledge.

Miller, P. and Rose, N. (2008) *Governing the Present*, Cambridge: Polity.

Mills, C.W. (1959) *The Sociological Imagination*, Harmondsworth: Penguin.

Minkler, M.M. and Estes, C.L. (1998) *Critical Gerontology: perspectives from political and moral economy*, Amityville, NY: Bayville.

Mintz, S. (2015) *The Prime of Life: a history of modern adulthood*, Cambridge, MA: Belknap Press of Harvard University Press.

Mitchell, P. and Ziegler, F. (2007) *Fundamentals of Developmental Psychology*, Hove: Psychology Press.

Mitteness, L.S. and Barker, J.C. (1995) Stigmatizing a 'normal' condition: urinary incontinence in late life, *Medical Anthropology Quarterly*, 9(2): 188–210.

Moi, T. (1995) *What is a Woman? And Other Essays*, Oxford: Oxford University Press.

Moi, T. (2008) *Simone de Beauvoir: the making of an intellectual woman* (second edition), Oxford: Oxford University Press.

Moody, H.R. (1986) The meaning of life and the meaning of old age. In Cole, T.R. and Gadow, S. (eds) *What Does it Mean to Grow Old?* Durham, NC: Duke University Press, pp. 9–40.

Moody, H.R. (2007) Ageing, generational opposition, and the future of the family. In Pruchno, R.A. and Smyer, M.A. (eds) *Challenges of an Ageing Society*, Baltimore: Johns Hopkins Press, pp. 175–89.

Moody, H.R. and Sasser, J.R. (2015) *Ageing: concepts and controversies* (eighth edition), Thousand Oaks, CA and London: Sage.

Moore, S. (2009) 'No matter what I did I would still end up in the same position': Age as a factor defining older women's experience of labour market participation, *Work, Employment & Society*, 23(4): 655–71.

Moore, S.E.H. (2010) Is the healthy body gendered? *Body and Society*, 16(2): 95–118.

Morgan, D. (2004) Class and masculinity. In Kimmel, M., Hearn, J.R. and Connell, R.W. (eds) *Handbook of Studies on Men and Masculinities*, London: Sage, pp. 165–77.

Morgan, K.P. (1991) Women and the knife: cosmetic surgery and the colonization of women's bodies, *Hypatia*, 6(3): 25–53.

Morris, D.B. (1991) *The Culture of Pain*, Berkeley: University of California Press.

Mullan, P. (2002) *The Imaginary Time Bomb: why an ageing population is not a social problem*, London: I.B. Tauris.

Mulvey, L. (1975) Visual pleasure and narrative cinema, *Screen*, 16(3): 6–18.

Munford, R. and Waters, W. (2014) *Feminism and Popular Culture: investigating the postfeminist mystique*, London: I.B. Tauris.

Myerhoff, B. (1978) *Number Our Days*, New York: Simon and Schuster.

Nead, L. (1988) *Myths of Sexuality: representations of women in Victorian Britain*, Oxford: Basil Blackwell.

Negra, D. (2009) *What a Girl Wants? Fantasizing the reclamation of self in postfeminism*, New York: Routledge.

Neilsen, H.B. (2004) Noisy girls: new subjectivities and old gender discourses, *Young*, 12(1): 9–30.

Neiman, S. (2014) *Why Grow Up?* Harmondsworth: Penguin.

Neugarten, B. (1965) *Norms, Age Constraints and Adult Socialization*, Glenview, IL: Scott Foreman.

Niland, P. and Lyons, A.C. (2011) Uncertainty in medicine: meanings of menopause and hormone replacement therapy in medical textbooks, *Social Science and Medicine*, 73: 1238–45.

Norton, M. and West, S. (2014) *Age UK Poverty Evidence Review*, London: Age UK.

Nussbaum, M.R.H., Helton, M.R. and Ray, N. (2004) The changing nature of women's sexual health concerns through the mid-life years, *Maturitas*, 49: 283–91.

O'Donnell, M. and Sharpe, S. (2000) *Uncertain Masculinities: youth, ethnicity and class in contemporary Britain*, London: Routledge.

O'Hagan, A. (2013) The Reviewer's Song, *London Review of Books*, 35(21).

O'Neill, J. (2005) Embodiment and child development: a phenomenological approach. In Jenks, C. (ed.) *Childhood: critical concepts in sociology*, London: Routledge, pp. 113–24.

Oakley, A. (1972) *Sex, Gender and Society*, London: Temple Smith.

Oakley, L.L., Renfrew, M.J., Kurinczuk, J.J.and Quigley, M.A. (2013) Factors associated with breastfeeding in England: an analysis by primary caretrust. *BMJ Open*, 3: e002765. doi:10.1136/bmjopen-2013–002765

Oberg, P. and Tornstam, L. (1999) Body images among men and women of different ages, *Ageing and Society*, 19(5): 629–44.

Office of National Statistics (2013) *Families and Households*, online publication accessible at http://www.ons.gov.uk/ons/rel/family-demography/families-and-households/2013/stb-families.html

Oliffe, J. (2005) Construction of masculinity following prostatectomy – induced impotence, *Social Science and Medicine*, 60(10): 2249–59.

Olshansky, S.J. and Ault, A.B. (1986) The fourth stage of the epidemiologic transition: the age of delayed degenerative diseases, *Milbank Quarterly*, 64(3): 355–91.

Orr, D. (2015) Madonna's fall doesn't make her ancient – it reveals her as more radical than ever, *The Guardian*, 28 February.

Parsons, J. (1991) [1951] *The Social System*, London: Routledge.

Pearson, J. (2015) 'I fell into the deepest depression'. Madonna says that sending Lourdes, 18, to college was 'devastating' on Ellen Show, *Daily Mail*, 17 March.

Penny, L. (2014) *Unspeakable Things: sex, lies and revolution*, London: Bloomsbury.

Person, E.S. (1980) Sexuality as the mainstay of identity: psychoanalytic perspectives, *Signs*, 5(4): 605–30.

Phillipson, C. (1982) *Capitalism and the Construction of Old Age*, London: Macmillan.

Phillipson, C. (2013) *Ageing: key concepts*, Cambridge: Polity.

Phipps, A. and Young, I. (2012) *That's What She Said: women students' experience of 'lad culture' in higher education*, project report, London: NUS.

Phoenix, A. (2004) Neoliberalism and masculinity: racialization and the contradictions of schooling for 11–14 year olds, *Youth and Society*, 36(2): 227–46.

Piaget, J. (1972) [1927] *Psychology and Epistemology*, (trans P. Wells), Harmondsworth: Penguin.

Pickard, S. (2010) The role of governmentality in the establishment, maintenance and demise of professional jurisdictions: the case of geriatric medicine, *Sociology of Health and Illness*, 32(7): 1–15.

Pickard, S. (2011) Health, illness and normality: the case of old age, *Biosocieties*, 6: 323–41.

Pickard, S. (2013) A new political anatomy of the older body? An examination of approaches to illness in old age in primary care, *Ageing and Society*, 33(6): 964–87.

Pickett, K. and Wilkinson, R. (2014) A 25-year gap between the life expectancy of rich and poor Londoners is a further indictment of our unequal society, *The Independent*, 15 January.

Pilcher, R. (1995) *Age and Generation in Modern Britain*, Oxford: Oxford University Press.

Pipher, M. (1994) *Reviving Ophelia: saving the selves of adolescent girls*, New York: G.P. Putnam and Sons.

Plummer, K. (2004) Male sexualities. In Kimmel, M., Hearn, J.R. and Connell, R.W. (eds) *Handbook of Studies on Men and Masculinities*, London: Sage, pp. 178–95.

Pollock, G. (2003) *Vision and Difference: femininity, feminism and art*, London: Routledge Classics.

Poovey, M. (1984) *The Proper Lady and the Woman Writer: ideology as style in the works of Mary Wollstonecraft, Mary Shelley and Jane Austen*, Chicago: University of Chicago Press.

Porter, L. (2013) Oxford University Crewdates: a hotbed of booze, 'banter' and some casual sexism, *Daily Telegraph*, 2 April.

Postman, N. (1984) *The Disappearance of Childhood*, New York: Dell Publishing.

Potts, A., Gavey, N., Grace, V.M. and Vares, T. (2003) The downside of Viagra: women's experience and concerns, *Sociology of Health and Illness*, 25(7): 697–719.

Potts, A., Grace, V., Gavey, N. and Vaes, T. (2004) 'Viagra stories': challenging 'erectile dysfunction', *Social Science and Medicine*, 59: 489–99.

Prendergast, S. (2000) 'To become dizzy in our turning': girls, body-maps and gender as childhood ends. In Prout, A. (ed.) *The Body, Childhood and Society*, London: Macmillan, pp. 101–24.

Prendergast, S. and Forrest, S. (1997) Shorties, low-lifers, hardnuts and kings: boys, emotions and embodiment in school. In Bendelow, G. and Williams, S.J. (eds) *Emotions in Social Life: critical themes and contemporary issues*, London: Routledge, pp. 155–72.

Preston, A. (2015) The war against humanities at Britain's universities, *The Observer*, 29 March.

Prime (2014) *The Missing Million: illuminating the employment challenges of the over-50s*, London: Business in the Community.

Prout, A. (2005) *The Future of Childhood: towards the interdisciplinary study of children*, London: Routledge.

Public Health Service's Office in Women's Health (2000) *Eating Disorders Information Sheet*, see http://womenshealth.gov/about-us/.

Pullman, P. (2011) *His Dark Materials*, London: Everyman.

Pyke, K.D. (1996) Class-based masculinities: the interdependence of gender, class and interpersonal power, *Gender and Society* 10(5): 527–49.

Radl, J. (2012) Too old to work or too young to retire? The pervasiveness of age norms in Western Europe, *Work, Employment and Society*, 26(5): 755–71.

Rampell, C. (2015) The great recession's lost generation? Older millennials, *Washington Post*, 2 February.

Reay, D. (2002) Class, authenticity and the transition to higher education for mature students, *Sociological Review*, 50(3): 398–418.

Renold, E. and Allan, A. (2006) Bright and beautiful: high-achieving girls, ambivalent femininities and the feminization of success, *Discourse: Studies in the Cultural Politics of Education*, 27(4): 457–73.

Riach, K. and Cutcher, L. (2014) Built to last: ageing, class and the masculine body in a UK hedge fund, *Work, Employment and Society*, 28(5): 771–87.

Riach, K. and Kelly, S. (2013) The need for fresh blood: understanding organizational age inequality through a vampiric lens, *Organization*, doi:10.1177/1350508413508999

Rich, E. (2005) Young women, feminist identities and neoliberalism, *Women's Studies International Forum*, 28: 495–508.

Richardson, D. (2004) Locating sexualities: from here to normality, *Sexualities*, 7(4): 391–411.

Richardson, D. (2010) Youth masculinities: compelling male heterosexuality, *British Journal of Sociology*, 61(4): 737–56.

Ridge, T. (2002) *Childhood Poverty and Social Exclusion: from a child's perspective*, Bristol: Policy Press.

Ringrose, J. (2007) Successful girls? Complicating post-feminist, neo-liberal discourses of educational achievement and gender equality, *Gender and Education*, 19(4): 471–89.

Riviere, J. (1929) [1986] Womanliness as masquerade. In Burgin, V. and Donald, J. (eds) *Formations of Fantasy*, London: Methuen, pp. 35–44.

Roberts, K. (2009) Opportunity structures: then and now, *Journal of Education and Work*, 22(5): 355–68.

Roberts, K. (2011) *Class in Contemporary Britain* (second edition), Basingstoke: Palgrave Macmillan.

Rockwood, K. (2005) What would make a definition of frailty successful? *Age and Ageing*, 34(5): 432–4.

Rockwood, K., Stadnyk, K., MacKnight, C., McDowell, I., Hebert, R. and Hogan, D. (1999) A brief clinical instrument to classify frailty in elderly people, *The Lancet*, 353: 205–6.

Rockwood, K., Song, X., MacKnight, C., Bergman, H., Hogan, D.B., McDowell, I. and Mitnitski, A. (2005) A global clinical measure of fitness and frailty in elderly people, *Canadian Medical Association Journal*, 173(5): 483–95.

Roebuck, J. (1979) When does 'old age' begin? The evolution of the English definition, *Journal of Social History*, 12(3): 416–28.

Rolfson, D.B., Wilcock, G., Mitnitski, A., King, E., de Jager, C.A., Rockwood, K., Fallah, N. and Searle, S.D. (2013) An assessment of neurocognitive speed in relation to frailty, *Age and Ageing*, 42(2): 191–6.

Rose, G. (2012) *Visual Methodologies: an introduction to researching with visual methods* (third edition), London: Sage.

Rose, N. (1989) *Governing the Soul: the shaping of the private self*, London: Routledge.

Rose, N. (1998) *Inventing Our Selves: psychology, power and personhood*, Cambridge: Cambridge University Press.

Rose, N. (1999) *Powers of Freedom: reframing political thought*, Cambridge: Cambridge University Press.

Rosin, H. (2010) The end of men, *The Atlantic*, July/Aug.

Rowbotham, S. (1973) *Woman's Consciousness, Man's World*, London: Pelican.

Rowe, J.W. and Kahn, R.L. (1987) Human ageing: usual and successful, *Science*, 237: 143–9.

Rowe, J.W. and Kahn, R.L. (1997) Successful ageing, *The Gerontologist*, 37(4): 433–40.

Sacker, A., Kelly, Y., Iacovou, M., Cable, N. and Bartley, M. (2012) Breastfeeding and intergenerational social mobility: what are the mechanisms? *Archives of Disease in Childhood*, downloaded 19.11.2014 doi:10.1136/ archdis-child-2012-303199

Sandel, M. (2012) *What Money Can't Buy: the moral limits of markets*, London: Allan Lane.

Savage, M., Ward, A. and Devine, F. (2005) Capitals, assets, and resources: some critical issues, *British Journal of Sociology*, 56(1): 31–47.

Savage, M., Devine, F., Cunningham, N., Taylor, M., Li, Y., Hjellbrekke, J., Le Roux, B., Friedman, S. and Miles, A. (2013) A new model of social class? Findings from the BBC's Great British Class Survey Experiment, *Sociology*, 47(2): 219–50.

Scott, J., Crompton, R. and Lyonette, C. (2010) Introduction: what's new about gender inequalities in the twenty-first century? In Scott, J., Crompton, R. and Lyonette, C. (eds) *Gender Inequalities in the Twenty-First Century: new barriers and continuing constraints*, Cheltenham: Edward Elgar, pp. 1–16.

Seabrook, J. (2013) *Pauperland: poverty and the poor in Britain*, London: Hurst and Co.

Segal, L. (1994) *Straight Sex: rethinking the politics of pleasure*, Berkeley: University of California Press.

Segal, L. (2007) *Slow Motion: changing masculinities, changing men*, (third edition), London: Palgrave Macmillan.

Segal, L. (2013) *Out of Time: the pleasures and perils of ageing*, London: Verso.

Sennett, R. (1999) *The Corrosion of Character*, New York and London: Norton.

Sharma, A. and Cockerill, H. (2014) *Mary Sheridan's From Birth to Five Years: children's developmental progress* (fourth edition), London: Routledge.

Shilling, C. (2012) *The Body and Social Theory* (third edition), London: Sage.

Shisslak, C.M., Crago, M. and Estes, L.S. (1995) The spectrum of eating disturbances, *International Journal of Eating Disorders*, 18(3): 209–19.

Showalter, E. (1997) *Hystories*, New York: Columbia University Press.

Sidell, M. (1995) *Health in Old Age: myth, mystery and management*, Oxford: Oxford University Press.

Singh, I. (2005) Will the 'real boy' please behave: dosing dilemmas for parents of boys with ADHD, *American Journal of Bioethics*, 5(3): 34–47.

Skeggs, B. (1997) *Formations of Class and Gender: becoming respectable*, London: Sage.

Skeggs, B. (2004) *Class, Self, Culture*, London: Routledge.

Slee, P.T and Shute, R.H (2003) *Child Development – thinking about the theories*, London: Arnold.

Slevin, K.F. (2010) 'If I had lots of money... I'd have a body makeover': managing the aging body, *Social Forces*, 88(3): 1003–20.

Smart, C. (1996) 'Deconstructing motherhood'. In Bortoloia Silva, E. (ed.) *Good Enough Mothering: feminist perspectives on lone motherhood*, London: Routledge, pp. 37–57.

Smith, D. (1987) *The Everyday World as Problematic: a feminist sociology*, Toronto: University of Toronto Press.

Smith, S. (2014) The year reality bites, *Sunday Times*, 14 December.

Sontag, S. (1972) The double standard of ageing, *Saturday Review*, 23 September: 29–38.

Spar, D.L. (2013) *Wonder Women: sex, power, and the quest for perfection*, New York: Sarah Crichton Books.

Spijker, J. and MacInnes, J. (2013) Population ageing: the timebomb that isn't?, *British Medical Journal*, 347: f6598, doi: 10.1136/bmj.f6598

Stafford, Z. (2015) We millennials lack a roadmap to adulthood, *The Guardian*, 30 March.

Stainton Rogers, W. (2003) What is a child? In Woodward, M. and Montgomery, H. (eds) *Understanding Childhood: an interdisciplinary approach*, Milton Keynes: Open University, pp. 1–43.

Stallybrass, P. and White, A. (1986) *The Politics and Poetics of Transgression*, Ithaca, NY: Cornell University Press.

Stein, A., Malmberg, L.E., Leach, P., Barnes, J., Sylva, K. and the FCCC Team (2012) The influence of different forms of early childcare on children's emotional and behavioural development at school entry, *Child: Care, Health and Development*, 39(5): 676–87.

Stoller, R. (1968) *Sex and Gender*, London: Hogarth Press.

Stoltenberg, J. (1984) Refusing to be a Man, *Women's Studies International Forum*, 7(1): 25–7.

Strawbridge, W.J., Wallhagen, M.I. and Cohen, R.D. (2002) Successful ageing and well-being: self-rated compared with Rowe and Kahn, *Gerontologist*, 42: 727–33.

Strenger, C. and Ruttenberg, A. (2008) The existential necessity of midlife change, *Harvard Business Review*, February: 1–9.

Sugarman, L. (2001) *Life-Span Development: frameworks, accounts and strategies* (second edition), Hove: Psychology Press.

Szanton, S.L., Seplaki, C.L., Thorpe, R.J., Jr, Allen, J.K. and Freid, L.P. (2010) Socioeconomic status is associated with frailty: the Women's Health and Ageing Studies, *Journal of Epidemiology and Community Health*, 64(1): 63–7.

Tanner, J.L. and Arnett, J.J. (2009) The emergence of 'emerging adulthood'. In Furlong, A. (ed.) *Handbook of Youth and Young Adulthood*, London: Routledge, pp. 39–45.

Taylor, C. (1985) *Sources of the Self*, Cambridge: Cambridge University Press.

Taylor, C. (1992) *The Ethics of Authenticity*, Cambridge, MA: Harvard University Press.

Terkel, S. (1974) *Working: people talk about what they do all day and how they feel about what they do*, New York: Pantheon.

Thane, P. (2000) *Old Age in English History*, Oxford: Oxford University Press.

Thane, P. (2006) The 'scandal' of women's pensions in Britain: how did it come about? Available at http://www.historyandpolicy.org/policy-papers/papers/the-scandal-of-womens-pensions-in-britain-how-did-it-come-about

Thompson, P., Itzin, C. and Abendstern, M. (1991) *I Don't Feel Old: understanding the experience of later life*, Oxford: Oxford University Press.

Thorne, B. (1993) *Gender Play*, Milton Keynes: Open University Press.

Thuren, B.M. (1994) Opening doors and getting rid of shame: experiences of first menstruation in Valencia, *Women's Studies International Forum* 17(2/3): 217–28.

Toledano, P. (2015) *Maybe*, Stockport: Dewi Lewis.

Tolson, A. (1977) *The Limits of Masculinity*, London: Tavistock.

Tornstam, L. (2003) Gerotranscendence from young old age to old old age, Online publication retrieved from the Social Gerontology Group, Uppsala (Sweden), available at http://www.soc.uu.se/publications/fulltext/gransoldold.pdf

Tornstam, L. (2011) Maturing into gerotranscendence, *Journal of Transpersonal Psychology*, 43(2): 166–79.

Townsend, P. (1981) The structured dependency of the elderly: the creation of social policy in the twentieth century, *Ageing and Society*, 1(1): 5–28.

Tran, M. (2014) Apple and Facebook offer to freeze eggs for female employees, *The Guardian*, 15 October.

Trethewey, A. (2001) Reproducing and resisting the master narrative of decline: midlife professional women's experience of ageing, *Management Communication Quarterly*, 15(2): 183–226.

Tronto, J.C. (1993) *Moral Boundaries: a political argument for an ethic of care*, New York: Routledge.

TUC (2014) Gender pay gap highlights part-time pay penalty. Accessible at: https://www.tuc.org.uk/economic-issues/labour-market-and-economic-reports/equality-issues/gender-equality/gender-pay-gap

Twigg, J. (2000) *Bathing – the Body and Community Care*, London: Routledge.

Twigg, J. (2007) Clothing, age and the body: a critical review, *Ageing and Society*, 27(2): 285–305.

Twigg, J. (2013) *Fashion and Age: the body and later life*, London: Bloomsbury.

Tyler, I. (2008) Chav mum chav scum, *Feminist Media Studies*, 8(1): 17–34.

Utz, R. (2011) Like mother, (not) like daughter: the social construction of menopause and aging, *Journal of Aging Studies*, 25(2): 143–54.

Van Gennep, A. (1975) *The Rites of Passage*, Chicago: University of Chicago Press.

Vares, T., Potts, A., Gavey, N. and Grace, V.M. (2007) Reconceptualizing cultural narratives of mature women's sexuality in the Viagra era, *Journal of Ageing Studies*, 21: 153–64.

Vickerstaff, S. (2010) Older workers: the 'unavoidable obligation' of extending our working lives? *Sociology Compass*, 4(10): 869–79.

Vickerstaff, S. and Cox, J. (2005) Retirement and risk: the individualization of retirement experiences? *Sociological Review*, 53(1): 77–95.

Wainwright, S.P. and Turner, B.S. (2006) Just crumbling to bits? An exploration of the body, ageing, injury and career in classical ballet dancers, *Sociology*, 40(2): 237–55.

Walby, S. (1990) *Theorizing Patriarchy*, Oxford: Blackwell.

Walby, S. (1999) Introduction. In Walby S. (ed.) *New Agendas for Women*, London: Palgrave Macmillan, pp. 1–16.

Walker, A. (1980) The social creation of poverty and dependency in old age, *Journal of Social Policy*, 9(1): 45–75.

Walkerdine, V. (2005) Safety and danger: childhood, sexuality and space at the end of the millennium. In Jenks, C. (ed.) *Childhood: critical concepts in sociology*, London: Routledge, pp. 145–63.

Walkerdine, V. and Lucey, H. (1989) *Democracy in the Kitchen: regulating mothers and socializing daughters*, London: Virago.

Walkerdine, V., Lucey, H. and Melody, J. (2001) *Growing Up Girl: psychosocial explorations of gender and class*, London: Palgrave.

Walter, N. (2015) *Living Dolls: the return of sexism* (second edition), London: Virago.

Ward, A. (2015) Boat Grace, *Sunday Times*, 5 April.

Ward, C., Dale, A. and Joshi, H. (1996) Combining employment with childcare: an escape from dependence? *Journal of Social Policy*, 25(2): 223–47.

Wearing, S. (2007) Subjects of rejuvenation: aging in postfeminist culture. In Tasker, Y. and Negra, D. (eds) *Interrogating Postfeminism: gender and the politics of popular culture (console-ing passions)*, Durham, NC: Duke University Press, pp. 277–310.

Weber, M. (1978) *Economy and Society: an outline of interpretive sociology*, edited by G. Roth and C. Wittich, Berkeley: University of California Press.

Wedge, M. (2015) The ADHD fallacy: it's time to stop treating childhood as a disease, *Time*, 23 April.

Weeks, J., Holland, J. and Waites, M. (eds) (2003) *Sexualities and Society: a reader*, Cambridge: Polity.

Weinstein, S. (2013) Is the 'older generation' a new lost generation? *Psychology Today*, October.

Whelehan, I. (2013) Ageing appropriately: postfeminist discourses of ageing in contemporary Hollywood. In Gwynne, J. and Muller, N. (eds) *Postfeminism and Contemporary Hollywood Cinema*, Basingstoke: Palgrave Macmillan, pp. 78–95.

Willetts, D. (2010) *The Pinch: how the baby boomers took their children's future – and why they should give it back*, London: Atlantic Books.

Williams, G.H. (1984) The genesis of chronic illness: narrative reconstruction, *Sociology of Health and Illness*, 6(2): 175–98.

Williams, R. (1977) *Marxism and Literature*, Oxford: Oxford University Press.

Williams, Z. (2015) Let's ditch the nostalgia that's invaded our TV and seeped into our politics, *The Guardian*, 30 April.

Willis, P. (1977) *Learning to Labour*, Farnborough: Saxon House.

Willis, S.L. and Schail, K.W. (2005) Cognitive trajectories in midlife and cognitive functioning in old age. In Williams, S.L. and Martin, M. (eds) *Middle Adulthood: a lifespan perspective*, Thousand Oaks, CA: Sage, pp. 243–76.

Winch, A. (2013) *Girlfriends and Postfeminist Sisterhood*, London: Palgrave Macmillan.

Wolf, N. (1990) *The Beauty Myth*, London: Vintage.

Woodhead, M. and Montgomery, H. (2003) (eds) *Understanding Childhood: an interdisciplinary approach*, Milton Keynes: Open University.

Woodward, K. (1978) Master songs of meditation: the late poems of Eliot, Pound, Stevens, and Williams. In Spicker, S.F., Woodward, K.M. and van Tassel, D.D. (eds) (1978) *Ageing and the Elderly*, Atlantic Highlands, NJ: Humanities Press, pp. 181–202.

Woodward, K. (1988) Simone de Beauvoir: aging and its discontents. In Benstock, S. (ed.) *The Private Self: theory and practice in women's autobiographical writings*, Chapel Hill: University of North Carolina Press, pp. 90–113.

Woodward, K. (1991) *Aging and its Discontents: Freud and other fictions*, Bloomington: Indiana University Press.

Woodward, K. (1999) Inventing generational models: psychoanalysis, feminism, literature. In Woodward, K. (ed.) *Figuring Age: women, bodies, generations*. Bloomington: Indiana University Press, pp. 3–19.

Woodward, K. (2002) Against wisdom: the social politics of anger and ageing, *Cultural Critique*, 51: 186–218.

Woodward, K. (2006) Performing age, performing gender, *NWSA Journal*, 18(1): 162–89.

World Health Organization (2015) Global health observatory data repository, available at www.http://apps.who.int/gho/data/node.main688

Wurtzel, E. (2009) Failure to launch, *Elle*, June.

Yalom, I.D. (1980) *Existential Psychotherapy*, New York: Basic Books.

Young, I.M. (2005) *'Throwing like a girl' And other essays*, Oxford: Oxford University Press.

Zaretsky, E. (2004) *Secrets of the Soul: a social and cultural history of psychoanalysis*, New York: Vintage.

INDEX